THE FUTURE OF LEARNING AND TEACHING IN NEXT GENERATION LEARNING SPACES

INTERNATIONAL PERSPECTIVES ON HIGHER EDUCATION RESEARCH

Series Editor: Malcolm Tight

Recent Volumes:

Volume 1:   Academic Work and Life: What it is to be an Academic, and How This is Changing – Edited by Malcolm Tight

Volume 2:   Access and Exclusion – Edited by Malcolm Tight

Volume 3:   International Relations – Edited by Malcolm Tight

Volume 4:   Autonomy in Social Science Research: The View from United Kingdom and Australian Universities – Edited by Carole Kayrooz, Gerlese S. Åkerlind and Malcolm Tight

Volume 5:   Interdisciplinary Higher Education: Perspectives and Practicalities – Edited by Martin Davies, Marcia Devlin and Malcolm Tight

Volume 6:   Institutional Transformation to Engage a Diverse Student Body – Edited by Liz Thomas and Malcolm Tight

Volume 7:   Hard Labour? Academic Work and the Changing Landscape of Higher Education – Edited by Tanya Fitzgerald, Julie White and Helen M. Gunter

Volume 8:   Social Justice Issues and Racism in the College Classroom: Perspectives from Different Voices – Edited by Dannielle Joy Davis and Patricia G. Boyer

Volume 9:   Theory and Method in Higher Education Research – Edited by Jeroen Huisman and Malcolm Tight

Volume 10:   Theory and Method in Higher Education Research II – Edited by Jeroen Huisman and Malcolm Tight

Volume 11:   Academic Mobility – Edited by Nina Maadad and Malcolm Tight

INTERNATIONAL PERSPECTIVES ON HIGHER
EDUCATION RESEARCH   VOLUME 12

THE FUTURE OF LEARNING AND TEACHING IN NEXT GENERATION LEARNING SPACES

EDITED BY

KYM FRASER

Victoria University, Melbourne, Australia

Emerald

United Kingdom – North America – Japan
India – Malaysia – China

Emerald Group Publishing Limited
Howard House, Wagon Lane, Bingley BD16 1WA, UK

First edition 2014

Copyright © 2014 Emerald Group Publishing Limited

British Library Cataloguing in Publication Data
A catalogue record for this book is available from the British Library

ISBN: 978-1-78350-986-7
ISSN: 1479-3628 (Series)

This book is dedicated to Susan Webley.

ACKNOWLEDGEMENTS

Editing a book can be a time consuming and difficult process. My work was made easier by the many people who assisted me in bringing the book to publication.

I would like to thank the chapter authors for their support, good humour and timely responses in the writing of this book.

Special thanks to the chapter reviewers who provided comprehensive, thoughtful and constructive reviews of drafts: Dr Trish Andrews, University of Queensland; Dr M. Aaron Bond, VirginiaTech; Dr Jos Boys, Northumbria University; Matt Brett, LaTrobe University; Dr Ken Fisher, University of Melbourne; Dr Ruth Greenaway, University of the Sunshine Coast; Associate Professor Gordon Joughin, University of Queensland; Dr Romana Martin, Curtin University; Professor Matthew Riddle, LaTrobe University; Professor Yoni Ryan, Queensland University of Technology; Dr Caroline Steel, University of Queensland; Dr Lynn Taylor, University of Calgary; Associate Professor Karen Whelan, Queensland University; and Dr Pamela Woolner, Newcastle University.

I am grateful to Malcolm Tight, the editor of 'International Perspectives on Higher Education Research', and Sharon Parkinson, Publisher, Emerald Group Publishing Ltd., for their support in bringing this book to publication.

I would like to acknowledge Associate Professor Nicolette Lee and the Australian Office for Learning and Teaching for permission to use Figure 1 from 'A comprehensive learning space evaluation model. Final report' in Chapter 16. I would also like to acknowledge Godsell Architects, Ramesh Ayyar, Lyons Architecture, and Kevin Francké for permission to use images in Chapter 12. Thank you to Emina Mesinovic who gave permission for the image used in Chapter 14. Thank you to Noel Studio for Academic Creativity, Eastern Kentucky University for the photo used in Chapter 15.

Finally I would like to thank Susan Webley, for your kindness, endless patience and unfailing support.

Kym Fraser
Victoria University, Australia

CONTENTS

LIST OF CONTRIBUTORS   *xiii*

THE FUTURE OF LEARNING AND TEACHING IN NEXT
GENERATION LEARNING SPACES
Kym Fraser   *xv*

SECTION I: THE FUTURE OF NEXT GENERATION
LEARNING SPACES IN UNIVERSITIES

CHAPTER 1   PERSONALISED LEARNING
STRATEGIES FOR HIGHER EDUCATION
Mike Keppell   *3*

CHAPTER 2   DIVERSE PICTURES OF LEARNING:
THE HIDDEN WORK OF SHAPING NEXT
GENERATION LEARNING SPACES
Barbara White, Greg Williams and Rebecca England   *23*

CHAPTER 3   KEEPING PACE WITH THE RAPID
EVOLUTION OF LEARNING SPACES
Anastasia Morrone and Sue B. Workman   *47*

SECTION II: THE FUTURE OF LEARNING AND
TEACHING IN NEXT GENERATION LEARNING SPACES

CHAPTER 4   PEDAGOGIES FOR NEXT
GENERATION LEARNING SPACES: THEORY,
CONTEXT, ACTION
Peter Ling and Kym Fraser   *65*

CHAPTER 5   ASSESSMENT IN NEXT GENERATION
LEARNING SPACES
    Geoffrey T. Crisp   *85*

CHAPTER 6   SPACES FOR ENGAGING,
EXPERIENTIAL, COLLABORATIVE LEARNING IN
HIGHER EDUCATION
    Roger Hadgraft and Jo Dane   *101*

CHAPTER 7   WHAT DOES IT TAKE TO LEARN IN
NEXT GENERATION LEARNING SPACES?
    Rhona Sharpe   *123*

CHAPTER 8   INCLUSIVE PRACTICES IN ACADEMIA
AND BEYOND
    Helen Larkin, Claire Nihill and Marcia Devlin   *147*

SECTION III: THE FUTURE OF SUPPORT FOR TEACHING
IN NEXT GENERATION LEARNING SPACES

CHAPTER 9   FACTORS THAT SHAPE PEDAGOGICAL
PRACTICES IN NEXT GENERATION LEARNING
SPACES
    Nicola Carr and Kym Fraser   *175*

CHAPTER 10   TRANSITION TO NEXT GENERATION
LEARNING SPACES
    Cathy Hall-van den Elsen and Tom Palaskas   *199*

CHAPTER 11   A NEW APPROACH TO
PROFESSIONAL LEARNING FOR ACADEMICS
TEACHING IN NEXT GENERATION LEARNING
SPACES
    Barbara de la Harpe and Thembi Mason   *219*

SECTION IV: THE FUTURE OF DESIGN IN NEXT GENERATION LEARNING SPACES

CHAPTER 12   DEVELOPING THE BRIEFING FOR THE DESIGNING OF THE LEARNING LANDSCAPE: REFLECTIONS ON RMIT (ROYAL MELBOURNE INSTITUTE OF TECHNOLOGY) UNIVERSITY OF TECHNOLOGY & DESIGN'S APPROACH TO NEXT GENERATION LEARNING SPACES
Leon van Schaik   243

CHAPTER 13   LEARNING SPACE EVALUATIONS – TIMING, TEAM, TECHNIQUES
Lisa Germany   267

CHAPTER 14   MOVING FROM CAMPUS TO COMMUNITY
Amanda Achterberg   289

CHAPTER 15   TRANSFORMING THE STUDENT EXPERIENCE THROUGH LEARNING SPACE DESIGN
Jennifer Sparrow and Susan Whitmer   299

SECTION V: THE FUTURE OF RESEARCH IN NEXT GENERATION LEARNING SPACES

CHAPTER 16   THE FUTURE OF RESEARCH IN NEXT GENERATION LEARNING SPACES
Kym Fraser   319

ABOUT THE AUTHORS   341

INDEX   351

LIST OF CONTRIBUTORS

Amanda Achterberg	Victoria University, Melbourne, Australia
Nicola Carr	School of Education, RMIT University, Australia
Geoffrey T. Crisp	RMIT University, Melbourne, Australia
Jo Dane	Woods Bagot, Melbourne, Australia
Barbara de la Harpe	University of Southern Queensland, Queensland, Australia
Marcia Devlin	Federation University, Churchill, Australia
Rebecca England	School of Engineering and Information Technology, Charles Darwin University, Darwin, Australia
Kym Fraser	Centre for Collaborative Learning and Teaching, Victoria University, Melbourne, Australia
Lisa Germany	Victoria University, Melbourne, Australia
Roger Hadgraft	CQ University, Melbourne, Australia
Cathy Hall-van den Elsen	RMIT University, Melbourne, Australia
Mike Keppell	Australian Digital Futures Institute, Research and Innovation Division, University of Southern Queensland, Toowoomba, Queensland, Australia
Helen Larkin	Deakin University, Geelong, Australia
Peter Ling	Centre for Collaborative Learning and Teaching, Victoria University, Melbourne, Australia

Thembi Mason	RMIT University, Melbourne, Australia
Anastasia Morrone	IU School of Education, Indiana University, Indianapolis, IN, USA
Claire Nihill	La Trobe University, Melbourne, Australia
Tom Palaskas	RMIT University, Melbourne, Australia
Leon van Schaik	School of Architecture & Design, RMIT University, Melbourne, Australia
Rhona Sharpe	Oxford Brookes University, Oxford, UK
Jennifer Sparrow	InnovationSpace, Virginia Tech, Blacksburg, VA, USA
Barbara White	School of Engineering and Information Technology, Charles Darwin University, Darwin, Australia
Susan Whitmer	Herman Miller, Inc., FL, USA
Greg Williams	School of Indigenous Knowledges and Public Policy, Charles Darwin University, Darwin, Australia
Sue B. Workman	Indiana University, Bloomington, IN, USA

THE FUTURE OF LEARNING AND TEACHING IN NEXT GENERATION LEARNING SPACES

INTRODUCTION

The genesis of this book came about from a literature review that I did in 2012 on the topic of next generation learning spaces. The vast majority of the literature focused on the design and evaluation of these spaces while very little research literature discussed the impact of these spaces on pedagogic practice and student learning outcomes. Through this book and with a group of like-minded colleagues from Australia, the United Kingdom and the United States of America, I have sought to begin to redress the imbalance in this literature. With a focus on next generation learning spaces, chapter authors discuss student-related topics such as personalised learning strategies, diverse pictures of learning and learner attributes, and teaching related topics, such as pedagogic frameworks, assessment strategies, inclusive teaching practices and implications for curricula.

The learning spaces that are being built in the tertiary sector across the globe are variously called 'Next Generation Learning Spaces', 'New Generation Learning Spaces', 'Emerging Learning Spaces' and 'Net Generation Learning Spaces'. It is quite a challenge to determine when each of the terms was first coined and who used the terms. It's also a challenge to determine how each of the terms are defined and how they differ from each other.

In considering learning and teaching in these spaces, the chapter authors have chosen to use the term 'next generation learning spaces' as the book chapters focus on the future of the spaces as well as learning and teaching, design, support for learning and teaching, and research in these spaces. The actual term 'next generation learning space' seems to have originated in Australia when the University of Queensland hosted in 2007 the 'Next Generation Learning Spaces 2007 Colloquium'. The term has subsequently been used in many different countries.

Although the term next generation learning space doesn't seem to appear in the literature until later in the first decade of this century, reference to the concept of changing learning spaces is apparent in the literature from the turn of the century (Dori et al., 2003; Heppell, Chapman, Millwood, Constable, & Furness, 2004; Van Note Chism, 2002). Van Note Chism (2002) was one of the first researchers to link learning principles with learning space design. Using the American Association of Higher Education 'Learning Principles and Collaborative Action' (1998), she argued that to facilitate connected, active learning in a social context, we need to develop a range of spaces:

• where small groups could meet to work on projects;
• for whole-class dialogue;
• where technology can be accessed easily;
• for displaying ideas and working documents;
• that can accommodate movement and noise; and
• include spill over spaces in corridors and lobbies (Van Note Chism, 2002).

In the absence of a definition of next generation learning spaces, the authors of this book engaged in a very lively email discussion about the definition of the term/concept. Some authors considered the spaces to be physical spaces only (but not necessarily rooms), while others include electronic spaces. Some authors believed that furniture that could be configured and changed easily and quickly was an essential element of the spaces, while others argued that furniture wasn't a defining element. Almost all authors agreed that next generation learning spaces are intentionally designed to facilitate collaborative and interactive learning. However some authors believed that we needed to move beyond collaborative learning to emphasise that these spaces need to enable new pedagogies to be explored and trialled. Even the element of 'technology rich' was debated, as authors pointed out that in some spaces, the technology is limited to Wi-Fi enablement and the devices that students bring with them.

The discussion highlighted that it is difficult to define the concept of next generation learning spaces. Authors of each chapter in this book have slightly different conceptions of next generation learning spaces. Therefore, while next generation learning spaces may vary, typically they:

• enable new pedagogies, including technology enabled pedagogies, to be explored and trialled (Boys, 2011; Carr & Fraser, 2014);
• are intentionally designed to facilitate collaborative, connected and active learning (Heppell et al., 2004; JISC, 2006; Mitchell et al., 2010;

Oblinger, 2005; Radcliffe, Wilson, Powell, & Tibbetts, 2008; Souter, Riddle, Sellers, & Keppell, 2011; Van Note Chism, 2002);

- are technology enabled and allow for students to use their own devices (Morrone & Workman, 2014; White, Williams, & England, 2014);
- include formal and informal spaces, physical and electronic spaces (van Schaik, 2014); and
- have comfortable furniture that is configured easily and quickly by academics and students to suit different pedagogies (Morrone & Workman, 2014; Sparrow & Whitmer, 2014).

As discussed later in this introduction, the book addresses many of the compelling questions that face institutions as they spend considerable sums of money on the development of next generation learning spaces and endeavour to demonstrate the impact of these spaces on teaching practice and student outcomes. The book covers topics which will be of interest to a wide range of professions, including tertiary teaching staff, academic/ education/faculty developers, learning designers, education technologists, students, administrators, audio visual technicians, furniture designers, information technology providers, creative city designers, researchers, Associate Deans (Learning and Teaching), Pro-Vice Chancellors (Learning and Teaching), education architectur specialists, property services/facilities managers, and information technology managers.

SECTIONS OF THE BOOK

The book comprises five sections and takes a futuristic perspective on the unfulfilled promises of next generation learning spaces, bringing to the fore the key elements of the spaces themselves, learning and teaching in the spaces, support for learning and teaching in the spaces, design of the spaces and learning and teaching research and evaluation in the spaces. The book addresses the compelling questions of the decade in an effort to help senior university managers think beyond the pedagogies of yesterday in order to maximise the use and design of next generation learning spaces for the future.

Section I: The Future of Next Generation Learning Spaces in Universities

This first section of the book explores the future of learning spaces in the tertiary sector. The chapters address compelling questions such as: What technologies will support student learning into the future? What is the role of the university in developing next generation learning spaces? and What learning models are appropriate for future students? As the chapters delve into the changing attitudes and practices of both teachers and students, the use of mobile technologies to change teaching practices and the notion of flipping the university, they necessarily overlap with the focus of chapters in Section II, 'The Future of Learning and Teaching in Next Generation Learning Spaces'.

In Chapter 1, 'Personalised Learning Strategies for Higher Education', Keppell introduces the notion of the 'personalised learner', exploring next generation learning spaces where learners traverse physical and virtual spaces using personalised learning strategies in their learning journey. The chapter argues that students need to develop learning space literacies so that they can identify and effectively utilise appropriate learning spaces that optimise engagement. Keppell discusses six broad concepts of personalised learning that teachers can use to assist their students to design their own personalised learning spaces.

White, Williams and England, in Chapter 2, 'Diverse Pictures of Learning: The Hidden Work of Shaping Next Generation Learning Spaces', argue that technology provision and next generation learning spaces should be pedagogically 'agnostic', so privileging multiple 'pictures of learning'. The chapter explores the power of new mobile digital technologies to facilitate the privileging of these multiple pictures of learning. They propose a model to make explicit what they refer to as the hidden work of technology implementation.

Morrone and Workman, in Chapter 3, 'Keeping Pace with the Rapid Evolution of Learning Spaces', focus on learning space design for student's technology-rich lifestyles, with particular reference to the evolution and future of learning spaces in the United States. They explore how selected USA universities have responded to this challenge, highlighting the driving forces behind two strategies for keeping pace with the learning needs of digital natives: the building of flexible, tech-rich spaces that support students' work and study habits and student access to virtualized software in next generation learning spaces.

Section II: The Future of Learning and Teaching in Next Generation Learning Spaces

This section develops models of pedagogic practices, curriculum and learning for next generation spaces. The chapters explore questions such as: What pedagogies are appropriate in next generation learning spaces? What assessment tools are required? What attributes do students need to be successful? and What roles will students and staff play in these new spaces?

Ling and Fraser in Chapter 4, 'Pedagogies for Next Generation Learning Spaces: Theory, Context, Action', develop a framework to guide teaching practice in next generation learning spaces. The framework is informed by both learning and teaching theory and the current context of the sector. The framework provides guidance to those who teach in next generation learning spaces and is illustrated with examples of effective pedagogic practices that use the affordances of next generation learning spaces while avoiding the limiting connotations of some designs.

In Chapter 5, 'Assessment in Next Generation Learning Spaces', Crisp explores assessment opportunities for spaces where we have the potential to merge physical and virtual activities. He argues that assessment needs to incorporate authentic, meaningful tasks that engage students in using the full range of their capabilities and available resources, both physical and virtual. Crisp believes that teachers need to incorporate in their assessment practices diagnostic, formative and summative assessment components within a more holistic educational environment. The chapter discusses assessment through gamification, MOOCs and the semantic web (Web 3.0).

Dane and Hadgraft in Chapter 6, 'Spaces for Engaging, Experiential, Collaborative Learning in Higher Education', explore both the disruptors that make change in learning space design imperative and the opportunities available in both pedagogy and design to create new learning activities and spaces. The authors argue that curricula needs to be dominated by collaborative investigation and problem solving in spaces that encourage and afford such activity.

In Chapter 7, 'What Does It Take to Learn in Next Generation Learning Spaces?', Sharpe does a meta-analysis of the learner experience research, identifying six attributes that learners need in order to learn effectively in new technology rich educational environments. She also identifies potential learner experience research that could be done in the future.

Larkin, Nihill and Devlin in Chapter 8, 'Inclusive Practices in Academia and Beyond', argue that the tertiary sector needs to move from seeing student diversity as problematic and deficit-based, to welcoming, celebrating and recognising diversity for the contributions diversity makes to enhancing the experience and learning outcomes for all students. In their chapter they use the Universal Design for Learning (CAST, 2011) as a framework to ensure that the learning needs of all students are addressed in next generation learning spaces. They argue that when the design of physical and virtual environments does not incorporate universal design principles, the

result is that some students can be locked out of participating in campus or
university life or, for some, the energy required to participate can be
substantial.

Section III: The Future of Support for Teaching in Next Generation Learning Spaces

The chapters in Section III explore the ways in which institutions can support the significant changes in pedagogic practices and learning discussed
in Section II. In Chapter 9, Carr and Fraser identify factors that influence
teaching practice in next generation learning spaces and argue that institutions have a role to play in fostering those factors that support pedagogic
improvements. Chapters 10 and 11 discuss specific case studies of professional development programmes/approaches that can be used to support
staff as they begin to teach in next generation learning spaces. The three
chapters address compelling questions such as: How can institutions
enhance staff teaching capability in next generation learning spaces? Will
teaching staff engage in continual professional learning for teaching in
next generation learning spaces? and How might academic developers support staff to change traditional pedagogical practices?

   Carr and Fraser in Chapter 9, 'Factors That Shape Pedagogical Practice
in Next Generation Learning Spaces', argue that in order to fully realise
significant improvements in student outcomes through the sector's investment in next generation learning spaces, universities need to provide holistic and systematic support across three domains − the external, the
organisational and the personal domains. To maximise the potential of
next generation learning spaces, they propose a model to support universities to change policies, systems, procedures and localised practices to better
facilitate changes in teaching practices.

   In Chapter 10, 'Transition to Next Generation Learning Spaces',
Hall-van den Elsen and Palaskas discuss the professional development programme that prepared 700 faculty to re-imagine their teaching practice as
the College of Business moved to the newly constructed and purpose-built
environment of RMIT University's Swanston Academic Building. The
study identifies the challenges and change management issues faced by the
project team, faculty and other stakeholders. The design and implementation of the programme and transition plan took into account the needs and
perceptions of staff from each discipline area, the affordances of the new
learning spaces and their associated technologies.

de la Harpe and Mason in Chapter 11, 'A New Approach to Professional Learning for Academics Teaching in Next Generation Learning Spaces', explore why and how the design of professional learning for academics teaching in such spaces can and should be transformed. In their chapter they describe a new way to engage academics in their own professional learning, drawing on the fields of organisational psychology, cognitive theory and behavioural economics.

Section IV: The Future of Design in Next Generation Learning Spaces

This section considers the opportunities for designing next generation learning spaces into the future. The chapters discuss the briefing of architects, the involvement of stakeholders, the future proofing of spaces and the development of spaces beyond the campus borders. The chapters address questions such as: What is the role of the university in the design of next generation learning spaces into the future? What are the benefits of moving from campus to community based next generation learning spaces? How do universities ensure a return on expenditure for learning and teaching; and How can learning theories impact the design of spaces?

In Chapter 12, 'Developing the Briefing for the Designing of the Learning Landscape' van Schaik argues that traditional ways of briefing designers are less and less proficient and that designing learning environments is increasingly about mediating between the interactions in real and virtual space of largely self-organising learning communities. The author discusses the development of significant built forms at RMIT University, arguing that there is an emerging trend for the built form and virtual platforms to be developed in tandem in the tertiary sector.

Germany, in Chapter 13, 'Learning Space Evaluations – Timing, Team, Techniques', argues that there is often a concern that next generation learning space design is not informed by input from appropriate stakeholders. The author draws on the literature to provide practical ideas and advice on designing robust, whole-of-lifecycle evaluations for learning space projects. Germany argues that by incorporating pre- and post-occupancy stages, involving a wide array of stakeholders and looking beyond surveys and focus groups as evaluation techniques, universities can ensure that future designs take into consideration the experiences and context of staff and students at the institution as well as lessons-learned from previous projects.

In Chapter 14, 'Moving from Campus to Community', Achterberg reports on the joint partnership between local councils and Victoria

University, Australia, in the development of collaborative, Council based, learning hubs. The hubs, while built in the council locations, provide links back to the university's campus locations. Achterberg argues that the part-nerships engage/re-engage local community members in the art of learning so increasing tertiary participation and completions in areas of the city where residents traditionally do not engage in tertiary education.

Sparrow and Whitmer in Chapter 15, 'Transforming the Student Experience through Learning Space Design', focus on the challenges and the possibilities that exist for College and University leadership, academic planners, instructional technologists, campus planners, architects and others involved in building effective formal and informal learning spaces. They argue that the new spaces of the twenty-first century have disrupted conventional models for academic and campus planning and that the dis-ruptions have led to opportunities to pilot new modalities for curriculum development that blend both online and on ground learning. The authors propose that spaces ideally need to be designed for the unknown and they discuss different types of spaces that support student learning.

Section V: The Future of Research in Next Generation Learning Spaces

In the final chapter of the book, Fraser identifies the research gaps in the learning spaces learning and teaching literature. She argues that as the tertiary sector endeavours to fulfil the promise of next generation learning spaces we know very little about the efficacy of these spaces in relation to pedagogic practice, curriculum design and student outcomes. Fraser argues that there are many opportunities for researchers to provide much needed evidence to institutions on the interrelationships between next generation learning spaces design, teaching practices, curriculum design and learning outcomes.

Kym Fraser
Editor

REFERENCES

American Association for Higher Education, American College Personnel Association, and National Association of Student Personnel Administrators. (1998). Learning principles and collaborative action. Excerpted from *Powerful partnerships: A shared responsibility for learning*. Retrieved from http://spacesforlearning.udayton.edu
Boys, J. (2011). *Towards creative learning spaces*. London: Routledge.

Carr, N., & Fraser, K. (2014). Factors that shape pedagogical practices in next generation learning spaces. In K. Fraser (Ed.), *The future of learning and teaching in next generation learning spaces* (Vol. 12). International Perspectives on Higher Education Research. Bingley, UK: Emerald.

CAST. (2011). *Universal Design for Learning (UDL) guidelines: Full text representation. Version 2.0.* Wakefield, MA: Center for Applied Special Technology.

Dori, Y., Belcher, J., Besette, M., Danziger, M., McKinney, A., & Hult, E. (2003). Technology for active learning. *Materials Today, 6,* 44–49.

Heppell, S., Chapman, C., Millwood, R., Constable, M., & Furness, J. (2004). Building learning futures. A research project at Ultralab within the CABE/RIBA "Building Futures" programme. Retrieved from http://pasaporte.urosario.edu.co/urosario_files/3a/3ab3bd 4d-2bf4-4e5a-94c9-2b6da193db8f.pdf

JISC. (2006). *Designing spaces for effective learning.* London: JISC. Retrieved from http://www.jisc.ac.uk/whatwedo/programmes/elearninginnovation/learningspaces.aspx

Mitchell, G., White, B., Pospisil, R., Kiley, S., Liu, C., & Matthews, G. (2010). *Retrofitting University learning spaces. Final report.* Sydney: The Australian Learning and Teaching Council Ltd. Retrieved from http://learnline.cdu.edu.au/retrofittingunispaces/index.html

Morrone, A., & Workman, S. (2014). Keeping pace with the rapid evolution of learning spaces. In K. Fraser (Ed.), *The future of learning and teaching in next generation learning spaces* (Vol. 12). International Perspectives on Higher Education Research. Bingley, UK: Emerald.

Oblinger, D. (2005). Leading the transition from classrooms to learning spaces. *EDUCAUSE.* Review online. Retrieved from http://www.educause.edu/ero/article/leading-transition-classrooms-learning-spaces

Radcliffe, D., Wilson, H., Powell, D., & Tibbetts, B. (2008). *Designing next generation places of learning: Collaboration at the pedagogy-space-technology nexus.* Sydney: The Australian Learning and Teaching Council Ltd. Retrieved from http://www.olt.gov.au/resource-designing-next-generation-places-of-learning-uq-2008

Souter, K., Riddle, M., Sellers, W., & Keppell, M. (2011). The spaces for knowledge generation. Final report. Sydney: The Australian Learning and Teaching Council Ltd.

Sparrow, J., & Whitmer, S. (2014). Transforming the student experience through learning space design. In K. Fraser (Ed.), *The future of learning and teaching in next generation learning spaces* (Vol. 12). International Perspectives on Higher Education Research. Bingley, UK: Emerald. Retrieved from http://www.olt.gov.au/resource-spaces-knowledge-generation-framework-designing-student-learning-environments-future-2011

University of Queensland. (2007). The Next Generation Learning Spaces 2007 Colloquium. Retrieved from http://www.uq.edu.au/nextgenerationlearningspace/

Van Note Chism, N. (2002). A tale of two classrooms. *New Directions for Teaching and Learning, 95,* 5–12.

van Schaik, L. (2014). Developing the briefing for the designing of the learning landscape: Reflections on RMIT (Royal Melbourne Institute of Technology) University of Technology and Design's approach to next generation learning spaces. In K. Fraser (Ed.), *The future of learning and teaching in next generation learning spaces* (Vol. 12). International Perspectives on Higher Education Research. Bingley, UK: Emerald.

White, B., Williams, G., & England, R. (2014). Diverse pictures of learning: The hidden work of shaping next generation learning spaces. In K. Fraser (Ed.), *The future of learning and teaching in next generation learning spaces* (Vol. 12). International Perspectives on Higher Education Research. Bingley, UK: Emerald.

SECTION I
THE FUTURE OF NEXT
GENERATION LEARNING
SPACES IN UNIVERSITIES

CHAPTER 1

PERSONALISED LEARNING STRATEGIES FOR HIGHER EDUCATION

Mike Keppell

ABSTRACT

This chapter will explore how the places of learning might look in next generation learning spaces where learners traverse physical and virtual spaces using personalised learning strategies. It will examine how learning spaces may represent ubiquitous spaces in which the learner undertakes some form of study or learning. Although there has been extensive examination of the design of spaces for knowledge generation (Keppell & Riddle, 2012, 2013; Souter, Riddle, Sellers, & Keppell, 2011) there has been little attention given to how learners customise and personalise their own physical and virtual learning spaces as they traverse their learning journey. Seven principles of learning space design will be adapted for use by the personalised learner. Personalised learning strategies encompass a range of knowledge, skills and attitudes that empower the learner to take charge of their learning within next generation learning spaces. Personalised learning consists of six broad concepts: digital citizenship, seamless learning, learner engagement, learning-oriented assessment, lifelong and life-wide

The Future of Learning and Teaching in Next Generation Learning Spaces
International Perspectives on Higher Education Research, Volume 12, 3–21
Copyright © 2014 by Emerald Group Publishing Limited
ISSN: 1479-3628/doi:10.1108/S1479-362820140000012001

learning and desire paths. Teachers will need to assist learners to design their own personalised learning spaces throughout formal education to encourage learners to be autonomous learners throughout their lifetime. In order to assist learners in developing personalised learning strategies we need to teach them about learning space literacies. We can't assume learners have the knowledge, skills and attitudes to be able to identify and effectively utilise appropriate learning spaces that optimises engagement.

Keywords: Personalised learning; digital citizenship; seamless learning; learning space literacies

LEARNING IN UBIQUITOUS SPACES

Introduction

Learning spaces represent all spaces in which the learner undertakes some form of study or learning. Also known as distributed learning spaces, these may include: physical/virtual, formal/informal, blended, mobile, outdoor, academic staff spaces, personal and practice-based spaces (Keppell & Riddle, 2012). Higher education learning is no longer typified by a singular place of learning but a range of places and spaces that we seamlessly move through (Keppell & Riddle, 2012). A student may move through a variety of learning spaces on any given day. This may include working at home, reading journal articles on the train, working within a learning management system, or attending formal classes at their University. Learning in higher education takes place in a range of distributed learning spaces. The chapter will explore the rich tapestry of distributed learning spaces and the way learners customise them through personalised learning. It will also focus on learning in the future in a variety of physical, blended and virtual learning spaces connected seamlessly by the learner. Future learners will transition between spaces without difficulty due to their ability to adapt and utilise the affordances of the spaces for learning with their mobile technology. The trend towards personalising learning will have implications for the place and space of learning and will require digital citizens to have sophisticated literacies to embrace ubiquitous learning spaces. There will be an increasing need to educate university teachers and learners in how to best use the diversity of spaces for learning.

Defining Learning Spaces

A broad definition of learning spaces includes all spaces where the learner undertakes some form of study or learning. These may be formal university spaces such as lecture halls/classrooms, as well as informal spaces such as home, train, cafes, and other spaces inhabited or customised by the learner. Learning spaces can be defined as:

- physical, blended or virtual learning environments that enhance learning;
- physical, blended or virtual 'areas' that motivate a learner to learn;
- spaces where both teachers and learners optimise the perceived and actual affordances of the space; and
- spaces that promote authentic learning interactions (Keppell & Riddle, 2012).

Physical, Blended or Virtual Learning Environments that Enhance Learning
Blended learning is 'a design approach whereby both face-to-face and online learning are made better by the presence of each other' (Garrison & Vaughan, 2008, p. 52). Learners optimise the affordances of this enhanced learning environment by interacting in physical and virtual learning spaces. Physical learning spaces are often designed with a singular learning function in mind, for example one-to-many lecture. Lecture rooms, tutorial rooms, and laboratories represent typical examples of physical learning spaces within the traditional University context. These spaces are enhanced through the addition of Wi-Fi, accessible power points for charging computers, tablets and phones, and teachers who accept the connected nature of learners. Motivated learners will enrich their interactions in the physical space by accessing 'knowledge in the network' (Siemens, 2006) as well as virtual spaces within the learning management system or informal virtual spaces such as Twitter related to the topic. By engaging in a rich range of virtual and physical spaces the learner should strengthen their understanding of the traditional lecture content as they are engaged in a blended learning space. These blended learning strategies provide a rich learning environment for both teachers and learners.

Physical, Blended or Virtual 'Areas' That Motivate a Learner to Learn
Within physical spaces the chairs, tables, access to Wi-Fi and power points need to be considered to allow adaptability of the learning environment for the learner. Informal physical learning spaces may include libraries and learning commons that have been explicitly designed to encourage

learners to engage in both independent and peer-learning. Ideal informal spaces provide sufficient flexibility so that learners can re-configure the informal space to suit their own learning needs. Motivated learners will seek spaces that assist their learning engagement. A diverse range of virtual spaces in learning management systems and social media provide an enhanced range of areas that provide spaces for learning as well as assessment.

Spaces Where Both Teachers and Learners Optimise the Perceived and Actual Affordances of the Space

Teachers and learners need to perceive the 'action possibilities' of learning spaces by recognising the types of interactions that are possible within the space (Souter, Riddle, Sellers, & Keppell, 2011). The learning design or pedagogical approach needs to utilise: interactive learning (learner-to-content), networked learning (learner-to-learner, learner-to-teacher), learner-generated content (learners-as-designers), connected learner approaches (knowledge-is-in-the-network) and assessment-as-learning (Keppell, 2010). For example, virtual learning spaces have unique affordances that allow learning interactions that are not possible in the physical learning space. These affordances or 'action possibilities' allow a richer range of learning interactions and may include online discussion forums, blogs, wikis, podcasts and diverse media-rich environments (Norman, 1988). The asynchronous online spaces have unique affordances for learning and teaching.

Spaces That Promote Authentic Learning Interactions

Authentic learning experiences focus on real-world activities that value the application of knowledge to solve real-world problems. Authentic learning has its foundations in situated learning or situated cognition (Lave, 1988; Lave & Wenger, 1991). Learning spaces should promote authentic learning and the transfer of learning to professional settings to enable learners to transition into professional practice. Authentic learning provides a means of engaging learners through all aspects of curricula, units of study (e.g. subject, module, etc.), activities and assessment (Keppell, Suddaby, & Hard, 2011). Although, as stated in Herrington, Oliver, and Reeves (2003), 'it is impossible to design truly authentic learning experiences' (p. 60), committed educators will always strive to provide the best learning experience for their learners' by focussing on real-world problems and by focussing on transfer of knowledge to professional practice.

PERSONALISED LEARNING STRATEGIES

Personalised learning strategies are based on personal learning environments (PLEs) that 'support self-organised, informal, lifelong learning and network learning and translates the principles of constructivism and connectivism into actual practice' (Chatti, Jarke, & Specht, 2010, p. 79). In the PLE model, learners are 'responsible for creating and maintaining their very own learning environments, self-adapted to their individual needs' (Chatti et al., 2010, p. 79). Attwell (2007) suggests that PLEs are a means for organising learning in multiple contexts. Dabbagh and Kitsantas (2012) define personal learning environments as 'a potentially promising pedagogical approach for both integrating formal and informal learning using social media and supporting student self-regulated learning in higher education contexts' (p. 3). They further suggest that self-regulated learning is a cornerstone of PLEs and not all students possess these skills to manage their own PLEs. Within this chapter personalised learning strategies will encompass a range of knowledge, skills and attitudes that empower the learner to take charge of their learning within next generation learning spaces. This section will examine the characteristics of next generation learners and then focus on six personalised learning strategies: digital citizenship, seamless learning, learner engagement, learning-oriented assessment, lifelong and life-wide learning and desire paths.

Next Generation Learners

Next generation tertiary education learners are characterised by having a rapport or relationship with technology. Next generation tertiary education learners interact in a digital age. They adapt and customise their learning and personalise their interactions to suit their needs. Having a rapport with technology suggests that the learner has an affinity with technology; however multiple literacies are required to understand the nuances of the technology for learning and teaching needs. Within the higher education environment there is a need to scaffold and coach learners in the affordances of the technology to meet learning outcomes. Next generation learners also have an inherent need to express themselves through multiple avenues which utilise user-generated content. This content includes artefacts created by the student that are uploaded to the Internet for sharing with other people in the learners network. Common examples include photos, video and blog posts but also include the prolific range of Facebook, Twitter, Instagram and Pinterest posts. There has been a fundamental shift towards creating content, which has been enabled by the low cost hardware and software. The increasing range of networks that learners inhabit through social media enable wide and connected interactions, sometimes with people they have never met. Connectivism (Siemens, 2006) suggests that 'knowledge is in the network'. Knowledge development is now a product of networks and ecologies. Thus, knowledge now requires literacies in networking. Learners connect via virtual and physical networks and regularly adapt and personalise spaces around them for their needs. In addition, learning is increasingly mobile as we move through a wider range of spaces. Learners now expect to be able to work, learn, and study whenever and wherever they want (Johnson, Adams, Cummins, & Estrada, 2012).

Digital Citizenship

All learners in the digital age require a range of knowledge, skills and attitudes related to digital citizenship. Martin (2005) defines digital literacy as the 'awareness, attitude and ability of individuals to appropriately use digital tools and facilities to identify, access, manage, integrate, evaluate, analyze and synthesize digital resources, construct new knowledge, create media expressions, and communicate with others, in the context of specific life situations, in order to enable constructive social action; and to reflect upon this process' (p. 135). Beetham (2010) defines being digitally literate as possessing 'the functional access, skills and practices necessary to become a confident, agile adopter of a range of technologies for personal, academic and professional use'. Digital citizenship encompasses digital literacies as well as safe engagement via networks, appropriate and responsible technology usage and digital wellness. For example a learner needs to use tablet devices in an ergonomically safe way. Digital literacies are a necessity for life in the digital age and a core aspect of digital citizenship. They encompass the knowledge, skills and attitudes that will enable individuals to learn, work, live, play and interact more effectively in a digital age (Johnson et al., 2012). An increasingly wide range of information, media, business services, and entertainment require digital literacies. These new forms of literacies may involve technical, cognitive and social-emotional dimensions (Ng, 2012) as well as mindfulness and the critical appraisal of ubiquitous Internet information (Rheingold, 2012). Other similarly used terms include eLiteracy, electronic literacy, media literacy, information literacy, visual literacy, ICT Literacy, technological literacy and technoliteracy. With the interconnectedness of digital technologies, technology and communication come together to form another literacy commonly referred to as technoliteracy (Walker, Huddlestone, & Pullen, 2010 in Pullen, Gitsaki, & Baguley, 2010). This diversity of definition and plural nature of such literacies elucidates the multiliterate and complex nature of the concept (McLoughlin, 2011; Pullen et al., 2010).

Being digitally literate involves learners and teachers developing their digital identities in an age where our online presence could be as important as our physical presence in social and work environments. Digital identity is focused on how we portray ourselves and represent ourselves online. It includes the etiquette and ethics of communicating and doing business online, leading to safer and more engaged digital citizenship. For example, one does not hesitate calling a friend on the telephone without first announcing the intention with a text message. On the other hand when calling a friend on Skype it is usual practice to first text a message via Skype before calling. According to social constructivists, (Vygotsky, 1978) social interaction is fundamental to the pursuit of high-quality thinking and learning outcomes. Social software promotes such exchanges through the development of online communities with a multitude of communication channels. These interactions can take several forms, including one-to-one (instant messaging or email), one-to-many (blogs or web pages) and many-to-many (wikis). Anderson (2005) suggested that social software are 'networked tools that support and encourage individuals to learn together while retaining individual control over their time, space, presence, activity, identity and relationship' (Anderson, 2005, p. 4).

A major part of digital identity is our digital footprint or digital history that we create as we use the Internet. Digital footprint refers to the audit trail that digital users create as they navigate and click on links throughout the Internet. It can be compared to the 'history' function on web browsers that track each and every website that we personally visit. Betcher (2009) who coined the term digital footprint suggested that: 'I can see a day in the not too distant future (if it's not already here) where your "digital footprint" will carry far more weight than anything you might include in a resume or CV' (Betcher, 2009).

Digital literacies are an essential aspect of personalised learning. All aspects of the learner experience need to examine digital literacies and it will become increasingly important to survive in a digital society. Digital literacies will also become an essential criteria for employment at all levels of society and therefore crucial for success in future employment.

Digital literacies will empower the mobile and nomadic learner as they move seamlessly through a range of diverse learning spaces.

Seamless Learning

Kuh (1996) coined the term seamless learning and suggested that 'the word *seamless* suggests that what was once believed to be separate, distinct parts (e.g. in-class and out-of-class, academic and non-academic, curricular and co-curricular, or on-campus and off-campus experiences) are now of one piece, bound together so as to appear whole or continuous' (p. 136). He further suggested six guiding principles for creating seamless learning environments for university education:

- Generate enthusiasm for institutional renewal.
- Create a common vision of learning.
- Develop a common language.
- Foster collaboration and cross-functional dialogue.
- Examine the influence of student culture on student learning.
- Focus on systemic change (Kuh, 1996).

In particular we need to understand the influence of student culture on student learning particularly in relation to how next generation learners utilise social media, smartphones and tablet devices.

Seamless learning is about 'connecting learning across settings, technologies and activities' (Sharples et al., 2012). Seamless learning has key aspects of continuity and fluidity across the settings or spaces whether these are physical, virtual or blended spaces (Keppell & Riddle, 2012; Sharples et al., 2012). It can also be associated with transitions through school from primary to secondary to university and to the workplace. 'Seams' disappear between formal and informal learning spaces, times, and physical and virtual places. Fluidity is recognised through this lens. The personalised learner will require diverse skills to traverse informal and formal next generation learning spaces. However the flip side of interacting in a supposed seamless environment also needs to be considered. 'Alongside the challenge of creating seamless learning is the related challenge of creating seams in the flow of learning experience, spaces to stop and reflect, spot the gaps in our understanding, take into account the perspectives of others, and gain genuinely new experience' (Sharples et al., 2013, p. 18). Personalised learners will need to develop strategies for stopping and reflecting, listening to peers and genuinely being aware of how a new learning space might influence their learner engagement. Kinshuk (2012) suggested that his 'personal view for the future of personalised learning research is the seamless integration of learning into every aspect of life, which implies immersive, always-on learning that happens so naturally and in such small chunks that no conscious effort is needed to be actively learning while engaged in everyday life' (p. 561).

The following three narratives describe examples of seamless learning. The first narrative describes the journey of a student studying at a distance education university while living in a regional residential college. The second journey describes a journey across the National University of Singapore in an environment of ubiquitous Wi-Fi. The third narrative describes a project in which the leadership team reside in three different countries and describes the learning journey of the three leaders reflecting on this new work space.

The Charles Sturt Journey − Student Journey from Residential to
Formal Class
John awoke from his single bed, single room residential college room on the Thurgoona campus. He set his alarm early so that he could secure the best seat in the lounge room with access to wireless networking. He competes with nine other learners for this prime wireless spot. John is not interested in accessing his formal study sites in the Learning Management System but wants to send an email to his girlfriend living 200 km away. He sends the email, accesses Facebook, and is satisfied with his before-breakfast networking. Other members of the residence stumble to the lounge. Some have been out late socializing, others had assignments to complete and yet others just want to be part of the breakfast social gathering. John is studying Education and needs to walk across the campus to his lecture. It's a traditional lecture room that seats 30 learners, a five-minute walk from the student residences. He then plans to hang out at the 24/7 learning commons in the library discussing an assignment with three other classmates. His classmates helped in clarifying his approach as they spoke about their progress on the assignment. He was reassured by the discussion but still overwhelmed by the amount of work he needed to complete. He retired to a quiet corner in the learning commons to complete some individual work on the assignment. He then packed up his laptop and walked to the Gums café just outside the commons to meet his two friends for lunch. It was always the most relaxing part of the day, joking and laughing, disguising their nervousness at the impending final exams. John walked back to the learning commons, looked for some relevant books in the library,

Googled some websites, interacted in an online discussion forum for one of his subjects and then focused for another two hours on his assignment. He packed his bag with his laptop and called his girlfriend on his iPhone as he walked back to his residence. He was going out tonight to the local pub as it was a Friday. John enjoyed Friday drinks.

This narrative illustrates how this student moves seamlessly through physical and virtual spaces as they complete their learning journey. The narrative represents a student who is comfortable with the transitions and has the digital literacy skills to interact in the wide variety of environments. John also recognises the different affordances of the various physical and virtual spaces.

The National University of Singapore — Ubiquitous Wi-Fi
Whenever I travel overseas the first thing that I search for at my destination is 'how do I connect my mobile devices'. My attempt to purchase a nano SIM card for my iPad was met with difficulty at the airport as most visitors request a phone SIM card. Although disappointed, once I reached my destination I realized that it was unnecessary. Visiting the National University of Singapore (NUS) as a visiting educator I was immediately struck by the size of the campus. It was too large to walk around as it was hilly and the humidity curbed my usual enthusiasm for walking. NUS is the largest university in Singapore with some 35,000 learners. As always I was also struck by the heat outside in contrast to the coolness of the public transport. I was also impressed by the connectivity of the campus. There are some 1,000 base stations around the campus, which means that there is ubiquitous Wi-Fi. No matter where you go on the campus you are able to connect your mobile device. Even the buses are connected as learners stand, headphones in place watching a video as they journey around the hilly terrain of the campus to their classes or lunch. They stand fixated on the movie, semi-aware of their destination. They switch to music as they walk the short distance to lunch.

I have included this narrative to illustrate how the author practices seamless learning when travelling as an academic in another country. It illustrates the importance of connectivity and how important Wi-Fi can be for communicating and continuing work whilst travelling abroad.

Leading a Project across Three Countries and Three Timescapes
The Network of Australasian Tertiary Associations (NATA) is a 2-year ALTC-funded legacy project. The overarching vision for NATA is to facilitate a sustainable collaborative network between established higher

education associations with the intent of fostering best practice in networks to engage members more strongly with Australasian higher education learning and teaching. NATA is a challenging project that traverses the major tertiary education professional associations across Australasia. It is also led by three people across three countries (Australia, New Zealand and Mexico). For the leadership team it is irrelevant that we reside in three different countries, what is important is that we can engage in the same virtual and dialogue spaces to manage and lead the project. We meet each Friday for a regular Skype meeting at 9:00 a.m. Toowoomba time, Australia; 12:00 p.m. Nelson time New Zealand and 9 p.m. Guadalajara, Mexico time. We engage in the project as if there are no timescapes (different time zones) and utilise Google Docs to set the agenda. The project manager documents the actions for each item in real time, which appear on-screen for the three attendees. The agenda refers to various documents in Dropbox, which we all have access to and we read and engage for the meeting. We conclude the meeting 45 minutes later with our action items. After the meeting we edit documents which we send to the NATA team members. The management of the project works because we are engaged in the virtual space and are engaged in the focus of the project.

This narrative describes how a project has been managed across a diverse range of physical and virtual spaces as well as timescapes across the globe. It illustrates the range of skills and attitudes that three project leaders needed to successfully manage a complex network leadership project.

The three narratives demonstrate how seamless learning, distributed learning spaces, technology and people intersect to shape the interactions and the engagement. At the core of the three narratives is personalised learning. Learning wherever we are is referred to as seamless learning and is particularly related to moving through different spaces over a period of time. Learner engagement is an essential characteristic of the personalised learner.

Learner Engagement

Learner engagement has been defined as 'active and collaborative learning, participation in challenging academic activities, formative communication with academic staff, involvement in enriching educational experiences, and feeling legitimated and supported by university learning communities' (Coates, 2007, p. 122). Aligning pedagogical, technical and administrative issues is also a necessary condition of success for creating an engaging learning environment. Coates (2007) also stated that engagement is a multi-dimensional phenomenon. He suggested that student engagement measures intrinsic involvement, assesses student engagement, measures educational outcomes, measures learners involvement in learning, considers the quality of university education on student learning, examines learners interactions with their universities and student. Krause (2005) suggested that student 'engagement refers to the time, energy and resources learners devote to activities designed to enhance learning at university. These activities typically range from a simple measure of time spent on campus or studying, to in- and out-of-class learning experiences that connect learners to their peers in educationally purposeful and meaningful ways' (p. 3). Learners need to be supported and empowered to make engagement meaningful. The introduction of strategies to assist learners to actively engage and manage difficult circumstances in engagement with higher education also needs to be considered. Being aware of how a learning space influences engagement will be an essential skill for personalised learners. Within next generation learning spaces assessment will also need to be personalised and contextualised to the learning journey of the student. Learning-oriented assessment holds promise in achieving this goal.

Learning-Oriented Assessment

'One of the reasons why new models of learning are rare in institutional educational settings is that traditional assessments are inadequate for measuring the outcomes related to self-regulated and collaborative learning. As the assessment practices have a strong guiding influence on education, the most powerful way of changing educational practices is to change the assessment' (Häkkinen & Hämäläinen, 2012, p. 235). Learning-oriented assessment is one approach that has potential as an alternative to an emphasis on assessment-of-learning approaches. Learning-oriented assessment has three core aspects: *Assessment tasks as learning tasks; Student involvement in the assessment processes; and Forward-looking feedback* (Carless, Joughin, Liu, & Associates, 2006). Assessment tasks as learning tasks focus on creating assessment that encompasses the learning outcomes for the course. By involving students in the assessment process the student becomes aware of the characteristics and features of assessment. By providing feedback that can be acted on by the student we are providing forward-looking feedback. Because all assessment leads to some form of learning it is important to thoughtfully design assessment in order to encourage the types of learning outcomes that we value and desire (Boud, 1995, 2010; Carless, 2007; Keppell & Carless, 2006). In addition, because assessment often determines student effort it is essential that we design assessment for learners that are engaging, authentic and relevant. By doing so, learners' efforts are focused on learning while at the same time fulfilling the measurement requirement of the subject or curriculum. Too often assessment focuses on assessment *OF* learning as opposed to assessment *AS* learning. The latter is a central characteristic of learning-oriented assessment. There are a number of important reasons why learners need to be actively involved in the assessment process. Active learning helps learners to learn about assessment and to begin to understand its importance in their own learning. Active learners can determine the quality of their own work through self-evaluation, reflection and self-regulation. Sadler (1989) suggested that by understanding the quality of their work learners are then able to monitor their own progress in relation to this quality standard. An assessment task should require sustained effort over a period of time in order to promote deep as opposed to superficial learning. Feedback as feed-forward suggests that learners receive feedback that can be acted on to improve learning and assessment outcomes. This is one of the most important concepts in learning, being able to act on feedback to improve subsequent performance (Keppell & Carless, 2006). Personalised Learners also need to develop an attitude that learning is a continuous facet of life.

Lifelong and Life-Wide Learning

Personalised learning requires a certain attitude and motivation. A lifelong learner is someone who has embraced change and who has a level of motivation that instils in them continuous learning for life. Lifelong and life-wide learning encompass both formal and informal learning and self-motivated learning (Watson, 2003). In addition to continuous learning for life the concept of life-wide learning focuses on learning experiences across different spaces, places and contexts. Life-wide learning 'recognises that an individual's life contains many parallel and interconnected journeys and experiences' (Jackson, 2010, p. 492). At its core is the self-motivation to continue learning throughout our life. Personalised learners also need to develop their own learning pathways that suit their life circumstances. Desire paths represent a metaphor for this journey.

Desire Paths

Desire paths are the shortest or most easily navigated route between an origin and destination and are often seen as walking or cycling paths that are short-cuts that diverge away from the prescribed path pre-determined by the grounds staff or council staff who design and build walking paths and cycle tracks throughout open spaces in an outdoor environment. Learners often desire the shortest quickest path to achieve their certification or qualification. They also want to tailor the learning experience to best fit their circumstances, needs and work aspirations. Personalised learners will need to continually refine their learning journey by considering their desire paths at different stages of their learning journey. I suggest that personalised learning will require a range of learning space literacies. The following section will explore the concept of learning space literacies for navigating distributed learning spaces.

LEARNING SPACE LITERACIES

There is widespread acceptance of the importance of digital literacies as a 21st century capability for learners and teachers in the digital age (Beetham, 2010; Ng, 2012; Pullen et al., 2010; Rheingold, 2012; Wheeler, 2010). However the concept of literacy is a contested concept. It is a 'plural and dynamic concept' (p. 9) and there is no single notion of literacy as a skill that people possess (Moeller, Joseph, Lau, & Carbo, 2010). Next generation learners will need to adapt space to their own needs and will require a range of learning space literacies as a personalised learner.

I define learning space literacies as the knowledge, skills and attitudes that are required to recognise, utilise and adapt distributed learning spaces so that they allow the personalised learner to engage with their learning.

The learning space literacies discussed below have been adapted from the Spaces for Knowledge Generation (SKG) Project design principles (Souter et al., 2011). The SKG project 'was based on the philosophy that constructivist approaches to learning, as well as to research and study, should make use of technologies and approaches that learners favour, and that learning spaces should therefore be organised to accommodate learner-generated aspects of learning. Spaces for Knowledge Generation provides a model for designing student learning environments that is future-focused and sustainable for the medium term' (Souter et al., 2011). Souter et al.

Table 1.   Learning Space Literacies and Questions for Personalised
Learners.

SKG Learning Space Design Principles	Questions for Personalised Learners
Comfort: a space which creates a physical and mental sense of ease and well-being.	Are the chairs, tables and furniture conducive to learning in this space? You might want to test them out before committing to this learning space. How comfortable do you think this space will be for learning? Is the space noisy or quiet?
Aesthetics: pleasure which includes the recognition of symmetry, harmony, simplicity and fitness for purpose.	What features of the learning space might assist your learning?
Flow: the state of mind felt by the learner when totally involved in the learning experience.	What features of this space promote your learning engagement? Do you feel you can engage with your work in the learning space? Are you looking for a quiet or noisy space?
Equity: consideration of the needs of cultural and physical differences.	Do you think the learning space is inclusive for you and any team members with whom you might be working?
Blending: a mixture of technological and face-to-face pedagogical resources.	Can you utilise your computer, tablet or mobile device in the learning space? How easy is it for you to connect to the network?
Affordances: the 'action possibilities' the learning environment provides the users.	What does this learning space allow you to do that you cannot do in another space? What action possibilities are you looking for in this learning space?
Repurposing: the potential for multiple usage of a space (Souter et al., 2011).	Can you rearrange tables and chairs to create your own learning area?

(2011) suggested seven principles of learning space design which support a constructivist approach to learning and support a learning environment that is student-centred, collaborative, and experiential. The development of these principles explicitly embraced the student voice. The Spaces for Knowledge Generation design principles comprise:

1. *Comfort*: a space which creates a physical and mental sense of ease and well-being.
2. *Aesthetics*: pleasure which includes the recognition of symmetry, harmony, simplicity and fitness for purpose.
3. *Flow*: the state of mind felt by the learner when totally involved in the learning experience.

4. *Equity*: consideration of the needs arising from cultural and physical differences.
5. *Blending*: a mixture of technological and face-to-face pedagogical resources.
6. *Affordances*: the 'action possibilities' the learning environment provides the users
7. *Repurposing*: the potential for multiple usage of a space (Souter et al., 2011).

These seven learning space design principles have also been adapted for the evaluation of learning spaces through a series of evaluation questions (Keppell & Riddle, 2013). In the context of personalised learning these principles will be adapted for assisting the learner to recognise, utilise and adapt distributed learning spaces. Table 1 outlines the types of questions personalised learners need to ask before they engage in a learning space.

CONCLUSION

This chapter has explored how learning might look in next generation learning spaces where learners move through ubiquitous learning spaces using personalised learning strategies. Personalised learning was conceptua-lised as encompassing: digital citizenship, seamless learning, learner engage-ment, learning-oriented assessment, lifelong and life-wide learning and desire paths. It was also suggested that learning space literacies will be essential for next generation learners who traverse distributed learning spaces to undertake their study and learning. Being able to recognise appropriate learning spaces will require a knowledge of the affordances or 'action possibilities' of the space as well as the learning goal to be achieved. Being conversant with how to best utilise the learning space will also be an essential skill to optimise learner engagement. In addition, knowing how to adapt a learning space to suit the learning task will be an essential literacy for mobile and connected learners. Discussion about learning space affor-dances needs to be an ongoing discussion throughout formal education (kindergarten, primary, secondary, university, etc.). Personalised learning strategies encompass a range of knowledge, skills and attitudes that empower the learner to take charge of their learning within next generation learning spaces. Teachers will need to assist learners to design their own personalised learning spaces to encourage lifelong, engaged and autono-mous learners.

REFERENCES

Anderson, T. (2005). Distance learning – Social software's killer app? *Proceedings of the Open & Distance Learning Association (ODLAA) of Australia*, ODLAA, Adelaide.

Attwell, G. (2007). The personal learning environment: The future of elearning? *Elearning Papers*, 2(1), 1–7.

Beetham, H. (2010). *Digital literacy*. Lecture at Greenwich University. Retrieved from http://www.jiscinfonet.ac.uk/infokits/collaborative-tools/digital-literacy. Accessed on August 23, 2011.

Betcher, C. (2009). *Digital footprints*. Retrieved from http://chrisbetcher.com/tag/digitalfootprint/. Accessed on May 14.

Boud, D. (1995). *Enhancing learning through self-assessment*. London: Kogan Page.

Boud, D., & Associates. (2010). *Assessment 2020: Seven propositions for assessment reform in higher education*. Australian Learning and Teaching Council, Sydney. Retrieved from http://www.altc.edu.au/system/files/resources/Assessment%202020_final.pdf. Accessed on December 20, 2011.

Carless, D. (2007). Learning-oriented assessment: Conceptual basis and practical implications. *Innovations in Education and Teaching International*, 44(1), 57–66.

Carless, D., Joughin, G., Liu, N. F., & Associates. (2006). *How assessment supports learning: Learning-oriented assessment in action*. Hong Kong: Hong Kong University Press.

Chatti, M. A., Jarke, M., & Specht, M. (2010). The 3P learning model. *Educational Technology & Society*, 13(4), 74–85.

Coates, H. (2007). A model of online and general campus-based student engagement. *Assessment & Evaluation in Higher Education*, 32(2), 121–141.

Dabbagh, N., & Kitsantas, A. (2012). Personal learning environments, social media, and self-regulated learning: A natural formula for connecting formal and informal learning. *Internet and Higher Education*, 15, 3–8.

Garrison, R., & Vaughan, H. (2008). *Blended learning in higher education: Framework, principles and guidelines*. San Francisco, CA: Jossey-Bass.

Häkkinen, P., & Hämäläinen, R. (2012). Shared and personal learning spaces: Challenges for pedagogical design. *Internet and Higher Education*, 15(4), 231–236.

Herrington, J., Oliver, R., & Reeves, T. C. (2003), Patterns of engagement in authentic online learning environments. *Australian Journal of Educational Technology*, 19(1), 59–71. Retrieved from http://www.ascilite.org.au/ajet/ajet19/herrington.html. Accessed on August 22, 2011.

Jackson, N. J. (2010). From a curriculum that integrates work to a curriculum that integrates life: Changing a university's conceptions of curriculum. *Higher Education Research & Development*, 29(5), 491–505. doi:10.1080/07294360.2010.502218

Johnson, L., Adams, S., Cummins, M., & Estrada, V. (2012). *Technology outlook for STEM + education 2012–2017: An NMC horizon report sector analysis*. Austin, TX: The New Media Consortium.

Keppell, M., & Carless, D. (2006). Learning-oriented assessment: A technology-based case study. *Assessment in Education*, 13(2), 153–165.

Keppell, M., & Riddle, M. (2012). Distributed learning places: Physical, blended and virtual learning spaces in higher education. In M. Keppell, K. Souter, & M. Riddle (Eds.), *Physical and virtual learning spaces in higher education: Concepts for the modern learning environment* (pp. 1–20). Hershey: Information Science Publishing.

Keppell, M., & Riddle, M. (2013). Principles for design and evaluation of learning spaces. In R. Luckin, S. Puntambekar, P. Goodyear, B. Grabowski, J. Underwood, & N. Winters (Eds.), *Handbook of design in educational technology* (pp. 20–32). New York, NY: Routledge.

Keppell, M., Suddaby, G., & Hard, N. (2011). *Good practice report: Technology-enhanced learning and teaching*. Australian Learning and Teaching Council (ALTC). Retrieved from http://www.olt.gov.au/system/files/resources/GPR_Technology_Enhanced_Keppel.pdf

Keppell, M. J. (2010). *Blended and flexible learning standards*. Charles Sturt University. Unpublished report.

Kinshuk. (2012). Guest editorial: Personalized learning education. *Technical Research and Development, 60*, 561–562.

Krause, K. L. (2005). Enhancing student engagement in the first year: 10 strategies for success. In *Good practice guide on enhancing documenting evidence of good teaching practice*. Griffith Institute for Higher Education. Retrieved from http://www.griffith.edu.au/gihe/pdf/gihe_tipsheet_web_ese.pdf. Accessed on August 22, 2011.

Kuh, G. D. (1996). Guiding principles for creating seamless learning environments for undergraduates. *Journal of College Student Development, 37*(2), 135–148.

Lave, J. (1988). *Cognition in practice: Mind, mathematics and culture in everyday life.* Cambridge: Cambridge University Press.

Lave, J., & Wenger, E. (1991). *Situated learning: Legitimate peripheral participation.* Cambridge: Cambridge University Press. ISBN 978-0-521-42374-8.

Martin, A. (2005). DigEuLit – A European framework for digital literacy: A progress report. *Journal of eLiteracy, 2*(2), 130–136.

McLoughlin, C. (2011). What ICT-related skills and capabilities should be considered central to the definition of digital literacy? In T. Bastiaens & M. Ebner (Eds.), *Proceedings of the World Conference on Educational Multi-Media, Hypermedia and Telecommunications* (pp. 471–475). Chesapeake, VA: AACE.

Moeller, S., Joseph, A., Lau, J., & Carbo, T. (2010). *Towards media and information literacy indicators.* UNESCO, 2011. Retrieved from http://www.unesco.org/new/fileadmin/MULTIMEDIA/HQ/CI/CI/pdf/unesco_mil_indicators_background_document_2011_final_en.pdf

Ng, W. (2012). *Empowering scientific literacy through digital literacy and multiliteracies.* New York, NY: Nova Science Publishers.

Norman, D. (1988). *The psychology of everyday things.* New York, NY: Basic Books.

Pullen, D., Gitsaki, C., & Baguley, M. (2010). *Technoliteracy, discourse and social practice: Frameworks and applications in the digital age.* Hershey: Information Science Publishing.

Rheingold, H. (2012). *Net smart: How to thrive online.* Cambridge, MA: MIT Press.

Sadler, R. (1989). Formative assessment and design of instructional systems. *Instructional Science, 18*, 119–144.

Sharples, M., McAndrew, P., Weller, M., Ferguson, R., FitzGerald, E., Hirst, T., & Gaved, M. (2013). *Innovating pedagogy 2013: Open University Innovation Report 2.* Milton Keynes: The Open University.

Sharples, M., McAndrew, P., Weller, M., Ferguson, R., FitzGerald, E., Hirst, T., … Whitelock, D. (2012). *Innovating pedagogy 2012: Open University Innovation Report 1.* Milton Keynes: The Open University.

Siemens, G. (2006). *Knowing knowledge. Creative commons.* Retrieved from http://www.elearn space.org/KnowingKnowledge_LowRes.pdf

Souter, K., Riddle, M., Sellers, W., & Keppell, M. (2011). *Final report: Spaces for knowledge generation.* The Australian Learning and Teaching Council (ALTC). Retrieved from http://documents.skgproject.com/skg-final-report.pdf

Vygotsky, L. S. (1978). In M. Cole, V. John-Steiner, S. Scribner, & E. Souberman (Eds.). *Mind in society: The development of higher psychological processes.* Cambridge, MA: Harvard University Press.

Walker, A., Huddlestone, B., & Pullen, D. (2010). An overview of technology in society: An introduction to technoliteracy. In D. L. Pullen, C. Gitsaki, & M. Baguley (Eds.), *Technoliteracy, discourse, and social practice: Frameworks and applications in the digital age.* Hershey, PA: Information Science Reference.

Watson, L. (2003). *Lifelong learning in Australia (3/13).* Canberra, Australia: Commonwealth of Australia.

Wheeler, S. (2010). *Digital literacies.* Retrieved from http://steve-wheeler.blogspot.com.au/2010/11/what-digital-literacies.html?q=digital+literacies

CHAPTER 2

DIVERSE PICTURES OF LEARNING: THE HIDDEN WORK OF SHAPING NEXT GENERATION LEARNING SPACES

Barbara White, Greg Williams and Rebecca England

ABSTRACT

Technology provision and Next Generation Learning Spaces (NGLS) should respond to the active learning needs of twenty-first century learners and privilege multiple 'pictures of learning' and associated knowledge work. In this sense it is important for NGLS to be pedagogically agnostic – agile enough to cater for a range of pedagogical approaches within the one physical space. In this chapter, the democratising and potentially disruptive power of new digital technologies to facilitate the privileging of these multiple pictures of learning is explored, recognising the significant rise in student ownership and academic use of mobile technologies. With their escalating ubiquity and their facilitation of active knowledge work, research around considerations for the implementation of mobile digital technologies is canvassed, highlighting a range of issues to be considered. This is part of the 'hidden work' of technology implementation. Without this hidden work, the potential of NGLS in

The Future of Learning and Teaching in Next Generation Learning Spaces
International Perspectives on Higher Education Research, Volume 12, 23–46
ISSN: 1479-3628/doi:10.1108/S1479-362820140000012005

facilitating and privileging active learning and multiple pictures of learning is diminished and the potential for reinforcing already powerful and potentially exclusionary modes of knowledge work increases. Finally to assist in articulating the hidden work of digitally enabled NGLS, a model is proposed to help understand how ease of use and confidence impacts on student and academic knowledge work.

Keywords: 'Pictures of learning'; agility; mobile technologies; learning spaces; hidden work; knowledge work

INTRODUCTION

Digital technologies are a powerful democratising and potentially disruptive force in knowledge making. In much the same way that the technologies of pencil, paper and the printing press revolutionised learning in previous ages, digital technologies are now radically transforming the processes of knowledge making in the twenty-first century (McLoughlin & Lee, 2008a, 2008b) as academics employ technological innovation to reconceptualise how teaching and learning can occur. These technologies make information and the wide array of tools for knowledge work accessible to a broader population and have the potential to fundamentally reshape tertiary learning and challenge the dominant and more traditional teaching and learning paradigms. Whilst digital technologies are already present and in use in learning spaces, there can be no assumptions made about the sorts of learning and teaching ends to which digital technologies become the means. Digital technologies assist in the delivery of a wide range of 'pictures of learning', each with educational value in the appropriate context. There is, therefore, a need to critically examine the context of their application and the assumptions implicit in their use. Decisions regarding the provision of digital technology and its use in tertiary education learning spaces can have a considerable impact on the ways learning spaces are used and the 'pictures of learning' that are supported. Uncritical application has the potential to reinforce dominant, transmissive teaching paradigms, at the expense of pedagogies that promote active, student-centred learning (Ling & Fraser, 2014, this volume). Next Generation Learning Spaces (NGLS) by definition, seek to do the reverse, by opening up the interaction between technology and space and facilitating a multiplicity of 'pictures of learning'.

This chapter contends that there is significant 'hidden work' in the application of digital technologies in NGLS and tertiary learning spaces in general. Critical examination of the intent, motives and power relations implicit in the application of different teaching and learning styles has the potential to reveal important work that needs to be addressed to ensure that there is a match between the learning we think is occurring and that which does occur. This work becomes all the more necessary as mobile digital technologies become more comprehensively present in tertiary learning environments. We need to dig deep to explore the fundamental interactions between technologies, people and the material aspects of learning spaces using constructs of usability, learnability and 'keeping up'. These constructs reveal the important 'hidden work' of mobile digital implementation in learning spaces.

Whilst there is an assumption here that learning needs to be 'active' and 'student-based', we contend that it is important not to be pedagogically prescriptive and that general purpose NGLS need to be hybrid spaces (Boys, 2011). They need to be spaces capable of responding to a diversity of knowledge work conceived from a range of pedagogical approaches and now made possible by the presence and uptake of digital technologies. NGLS are necessarily agile (easily reconfigured) and pedagogically agnostic. A framework is presented here which illustrates how various 'pictures of learning' incorporate diverse knowledge work and a variety of ways of employing technology. The framework thus conceptualises the intersections between digital technologies and space using ideas from Scott-Webber (2004) and Boys (2011) and, most importantly, provides a tool for critically analysing the implicit assumptions in any NGLS technology deployment. Acknowledging the existence of, and the need for this hidden work to be carried out, is an important platform from which to examine what constitutes good learning and teaching. Recommendations for use of mobile digital technologies in ways that facilitate and privilege pedagogies are offered as a way to make a start on understanding what this hidden work might be: strategies that promote active, student-centred learning in NGLS, but not to the exclusion of other 'pictures of learning'.

PICTURES OF LEARNING: CONCEPTUALISING INTERSECTIONS OF TECHNOLOGIES AND SPACE

Boys (2011) argues that the learning space is 'one of the (many) mechanisms through which contested ideas about what learning is or should be, are articulated' (p. 121). Traditional learning spaces including lecture theatres, tutorial and laboratory spaces are examples of physical manifestations of our historical understandings of learning in tertiary education. They provide a specific 'picture of learning' and evoke specific teaching repertoires (i.e. passive students; active academic). The concept of 'pictures of learning' is used here to convey an understanding of a more holistic and encompassing vision of how learning in all its complexity is envisioned before it is operationalised into strategies, activities and assessments. The term evokes a visual image of how an academic might see learning occurring in her 'mind's eye'. The choice and use of technologies within these traditional spaces tends to define specific and often exclusive pedagogical roles and the preferred repertoires of particular communities of practice (Boys, 2011; Le Couteur & Delfabbro, 2001) that valorise the knowledge delivery (or transmissive) role of the academic. The technologies and their mode of deployment/employment reflect and reinforce the pictures of learning expected in the learning space, usually at the expense of others. This doesn't mean the value of transmissive pictures of learning that reify knowledge as object should be dismissed unilaterally. Rather, reconceptualising learning space designs and examining the agency of digital technologies, offers alternative and additional 'pictures' of more engaging and democratic models for teaching and learning. NGLS 'make concrete' alternative and differently preferred repertoires of particular communities of practice (Boys, 2011) and in so doing privilege some pedagogical repertoires and practices, but not at the expense of others. This is the work encapsulated in the concept of NGLS, and digital technology choice and deployment within these learning spaces will by necessity contribute to, reinforce or challenge these 'pictures' and the learning encounters they make possible.

Agile reconfiguration is a key characteristic of NGLS (Heppel, Chapman, Millwood, Constable, & Furness, 2004; Mitchell et al., 2010). Agile spaces are configured easily and quickly by academics or students in response to a multiplicity of pictures of learning and teaching, while privileging and fostering knowledge work that is active and student-centred. Boys (2011) describes these spaces as transitional and hybrid spaces: spaces that focus on a range of learning encounters associated with knowledge production and the crucial interaction between the material and the virtual. They allow for alternative pictures of learning without ruling out those that are historically valued. In a recent learning space study (Mitchell et al., 2010) this desire for spaces to be flexible enough to support a range of different learning and teaching activities was a common theme. NGLS are designed in such a way that enables knowledge delivery (sociofugal) repertoires as well as more active (sociopetal) knowledge work (Hall, 1966).

Using Scott-Webber's (2004) analysis of knowledge work in learning spaces, learning and teaching activities may include a variety of these pictures (Scott-Webber, 2004, see Table 1). While Scott-Webber identifies these knowledge processes as often requiring different spaces, we argue that much of this knowledge work needs to be integrated for active learning to

Table 1.   Scott-Webber's Knowledge Work Analysis of Learning Spaces.

	Delivering Knowledge	Applying Knowledge	Creating Knowledge	Communicating Knowledge	Decision Making
Behaviours	• Bring information before the public • Instructor led • Knowledge in one source • Space is arranged so that people can maintain some privacy from others (sociofugal)	• Learner-centred • An apprentice model • Space is patterned so that people can see and interact with others (sociopetal)	• Innovation or knowledge moved from abstract to a product • Space is patterned so that people can see and interact with others (sociopetal)	• Share information • Provide quick exchange • Space is patterned so that people can see and interact with others (sociopetal)	• Make decisions • Space is patterned so that people can see and interact with others and also maintain some privacy from each other (sociofugal/ sociopetal)
Attributes	• A formal presentation • Instructor controls presentation • Focus is on presentation • Passive learning	• Controlled observation • One-to-one learning • Master and apprentice alternate control • Informal • Active learning	• Multiple disciplines work together, or levels of knowledge • Leaderless • Egalitarian • Distributed attention • Privacy • Casual • Active learning	• Knowledge is dispersed • Impromptu delivery • Casual • Active learning	• Knowledge is dispersed • Information is shared • Leader sets final direction • Situation is protected • Semi-formal to formal • Passive and active learning

Source: Adapted from Scott-Webber (2004, p. 44).

occur. Active learning involves academics and students delivering knowledge, and students (and arguably academics) applying, creating and communicating knowledge in a range of different forms and it is often necessary for these to occur within one, agile physical space that may be quickly and easily adapted as needed.

To conceptualise how diverse pictures of learning are possible using digital communication technologies in NGLS, a matrix is proposed that marries Scott-Webber's (2004) different knowledge activities with digital technology components: computing (hardware, software), audiovisual and the required underlying infrastructure supports. Table 2 illustrates how this matrix can be used to identify valuable technology provision for an agile space that responds to a variety of possible learning and teaching repertoires. If spaces are to respond to and facilitate multiple pictures of learning, a variety of technology configurations and users must be considered.

Digital technology provision for NGLS is complex because it is important to consider how these technologies interact with other materialities in the learning space (furniture and fittings, for example). Successful uses of digital technologies in NGLS require careful design and deployment to ensure that all combined technologies (digital and non-digital) work towards the potential for multiple pictures of learning with an agile approach to space usage. This matrix outlined above can be used to critically appraise NGLS plans for development or to systematically analyse what possibilities current teaching spaces provide.

DIGITAL TECHNOLOGIES, PEDAGOGIES AND LEARNING SPACES: A DEMOCRATISING AND POTENTIALLY DISRUPTIVE FORCE

Boys (2011, p. 121) argues that while architectural space is not central to the social and spatial practices of everyday life, it does have a significant role in either dampening or amplifying aspects of those practices. Digital technologies deployed in university learning and teaching spaces contribute in a similar way. Perhaps most importantly, the interface between technology and pedagogical processes provides the opportunity for disruption and innovation. Recent literature reinforces the role of education as a disruptive force (see Christensen, Horn, & Johnston, 2008; Hedberg, 2011; Verran, 1998). Disruption or disconcertment is central to teaching at every level and the creation of affective and cognitively dissonant spaces forms an

Table 2. Technology Considerations for Diverse Knowledge Work.

Technologies	Knowledge Activities			
	Delivering knowledge	Applying knowledge	Creating knowledge	Communicating knowledge
What pictures of learning and teaching?	Knowledge transmission	Knowledge application	Knowledge construction	Knowledge co-construction
Who's involved	Active academics and passive students	Active students and academics	Active students and academics	Active students and active or passive academics
What sorts of interactions/practices?	• Lectures • Online Presentations • Speeches • Texts	• Practice • Problem solving • Simulations • Working with ideas and materials together and individually • Informal conversations between students and academics	• Creating, innovating, experimenting • Collaborative problem solving/investigation • Working with ideas and/or materials together and individually	• Student Presentations using a range of communication media: F to F; blogging; videos; journals; more formal texts
What technology is used?	• Single computer/terminal • Learning management systems • Standard communication packages: word processing; presentation • Browsing software • Video conferencing software • Microphones' speakers	• Mobile • Bring your own device (BYOD) or supplied • Standard communication packages: word processing; presentation • Browsing software • Discipline specialist software	• Mobile • Bring your own device (BYOD) or supplied • Access to internet, e-texts, databases • Web 2 tool/or LMS applications • Discipline specialist software • Large display/shared monitors (touch screens)	• Mobile • Bring your own device (BYOD) or Supplied • Web 2 applications • Social networking tools • Large display/shared monitors (touch screens) • Interactive whiteboards • Camera/video recorder • Audio recorder

embodied disconnect in the learner that needs to be resolved and forms a central tenet of many pedagogical frameworks (e.g. Piaget's, 1977 concept of disequilibrium). The role of context (space and technologies) in the process of engaging the learner by disrupting their current ontic state and to challenging them to rethink, re-evaluate and reform cannot be underestimated.

Digital communication technologies provide tools for creating and reinterpreting knowledge and connecting people with a far wider and diverse range of ideas, knowledge and knowledge-making strategies. Transfer of the control of the technology from the academic to academic *and* learners provides the possibility for the more active knowledge-making processes of application, creation and communication. The academic becomes teacher/ facilitator *and* learner; and the students become learners *and* teachers/ facilitators. Engagement in active learning processes optimises the potential for the learner to invest more significantly in the process and therefore have much more to gain and to lose. This is the democratising and potentially disruptive role of digital technologies. The pictures of learning created by students having access to digital communication devices creates very different possibilities for learning and teaching repertoires than does one where the academic has exclusive control of the technology. Access to digital communication technology democratises both knowledge making and the learning space by opening up access to technology use and shifting the locus of control. Immediate and easy access to both knowledge and tools for its creation and representation potentially empowers the learner to assist in contributing to, shaping and reshaping the learning experience. It has the potential to disrupt the power relations between different people in the learning space. This disruption means that whole new dynamics of learning (and of course, *not* learning) materialise out of the agency of the technology within the space and the reconfigured agencies of now both the academic and the student.

Introducing technology and its democratising ability forces the need to rethink the role of academic/teacher and how 'teaching' is done, alluding to the 'hidden work' that is necessary in reconceptualising roles within a space. This in turn forces a rethink of the space itself and how the space (and what you include in it) responds to the technology and the possibilities for learning that it opens up and constrains. For example, the mere presence of and access to networked technology provides the opportunity for immediate feedback of all kinds within the learning space. Engaged learners can enhance the conversation by following up leads, tracking academic conversations and creating new knowledge all in real time.

Disengaged learners can switch to Facebook, write emails, tweet and doodle in a drawing application and the observant lecturer can read the signals that inform the need for a change of pedagogical approach. The academic then becomes the learner and the power relations in the space are subtly changed.

Equipping students and academics to use digital technologies in learning spaces in ways that allow them to have some control, provides a way of ensuring that the processes of active co-construction of knowledge are foregrounded and have the potential to be enacted. The practice presumes an active role for the student and the teacher (McLoughlin & Lee, 2007; Mejias, 2005). So, to enable this to occur formally in the classroom and informally elsewhere, attention needs to be focused on what technologies will be provided for students and how this will occur. Increasingly, mobile digital technologies are able to bridge the gap between formal and informal learning (Project Tomorrow, 2011); between the classroom and everywhere else, and in doing so more effectively facilitate democratic, active knowledge work. The challenges and opportunities afforded by the use of digital mobile technologies to extend the pictures of learning and repertoires for learning and teaching in NGLS therefore needs analysis.

CHALLENGES AND OPPORTUNITIES PROVIDED BY DIGITAL MOBILE TECHNOLOGY IMPLEMENTATION

Traditionally, student access to classroom-based technology has occurred in spaces designed for single purpose knowledge work (e.g. collaborative teaching and learning spaces at University of Queensland, Australia [see Andrews & Powell, 2009] or computer labs). Mobile digital devices transcend the notion of digital technology for single purpose knowledge work. They have a range of affordances which allow them to be employed across a spectrum of tasks and in a variety of contexts. In this discussion, mobile devices are small, gesture based devices (e.g. iPads, Windows Surface tablets and smartphones) that have similar portability to laptops but can be used while the user is in motion; i.e. while the device itself is mobile (Barton et al., 2012). Recent research has found that student ownership and use of these smart technologies has increased significantly (Dahlstrom, 2012; Dahlstrom, Walker, & Dziuban, 2013; Mackay, 2012). Penetration of mobile devices within the general Australian context has been profound, with smartphone ownership projected to be 93% by 2014 (Mackay, 2013).

Responses by the academy to this uptake are varied. In some situations, mobile devices are discouraged or banned from tertiary classrooms (Dahlstrom et al., 2013). Some students are expected to 'bring your own device' (BYOD) to supplement their learning, whilst in some institutions, often for equity issues, a variety of devices are provided in some way. These varied responses require varied strategies to find ways to capitalise upon the affordances the technology provides and facilitate multiple pictures of learning. Wherever they appear in the classroom and in whatever form, the challenges and opportunities provided by the implementation of digital (mobile) technologies in NGLS need to considered carefully from the perspective of students, academics and the institution.

Challenges and Opportunities for Students

Whilst pedagogically attractive, the fundamental economic cost of accessing digital technologies for learning and the associated equity issues for students must be important considerations in their deployment. Both institutional provision of technology and the adoption of a 'bring your own device' (BYOD) approach will have significant implications for some students being able to fully access learning opportunities. Initially, the questions to be considered would include: Is there a need to provide devices for all students? In what situations is device provision relevant and appropriate and if so, what considerations should be made regarding the affordances and nature of these devices. Additionally, mobile technology has a tendency to be more personal in its use and configuration, so what are student preferences in this area? Do they prefer their own devices to those provided by the university? Given the cost of provision and the maintenance and upkeep of devices, an understanding of local demographics and preferences is necessary before committing to a strategy.

When considering a BYOD strategy, the diverse nature of student laptop and mobile device ownership needs to be considered. While laptop choice is limited primarily to Windows or Mac operating systems, there is a plethora of choice in mobile devices, with students favouring divergence, individuality and constant innovation in their selection (Smith, 2013; Traxler, 2010). Such variance among devices can present difficulties when seeking to integrate them into a class curriculum. Integration is easier if the institution owns and controls the devices and this advantage is lost if students bring their own devices to the learning experience and use them. If integration of personal devices into learning is the goal, inevitably the highly diverse nature of mobile devices needs to be accepted and accommodated.

Encouraging students to use their own devices may be more beneficial to their learning: mobile devices enable a personalisation far beyond that of the standard institutional student computer account. Personal mobile devices thus have the capacity to be central in processes of active co-construction of knowledge because they can be used to both source and communicate information in a personalised environment. If the breadth of educational knowledge work in learning spaces is to include more than just knowledge delivery, it is imperative to think about what computing devices would facilitate more active knowledge making rather than the outcome being left to chance.

One of the opportunities that mobile learning approaches provide is that knowledge co-construction can be seamless across learning contexts. Work started in the classroom can be continued at home and ideas that occur on the move can be shared with colleagues online and then followed up in person (Sharples et al., 2013). In response to this potential: drawing on the advantages and popularity of these devices, their availability and the lower cost of new technologies, many universities have developed institution wide mobile learning initiatives (Duncan–Howell & Lee, 2007; Fuhrman, 2013). It is important to examine the challenges and opportunities of employing an institutional BYOD strategy and it is to this examination we now turn.

Challenges and Opportunities at the Institutional Level

Bonig (2011) writes that the successful integration of mobile devices into learning environments is associated with the deployment of appropriate university-wide policies. A policy informed approach to mobile integration provides the research and infrastructure necessary to ensure a smooth and genuinely useful assimilation of mobile technologies into learning, ensuring long-term maintainability. However Dahlstrom (2012) notes that 'most institutions have no discernible mobile deployment strategy' (p. 21) and Dahlstrom et al. (2013) recommend that institutions 'create (or update) a strategy for incorporating mobile device use into the classroom' (p. 41).

Using three years of implementation data from a university-wide mobile deployment, Bonig (2011) argued that successful adoption of administrative and learning resources required institutional level information technology services. Malisch and Montes (2011) recommend a web-based approach to software resources, using customisation techniques for devices with enhanced capabilities. These authors recommend that once institutional software services, applications and websites have been implemented (or adapted) for mobile provision, it is also important that student's mobile device experiences are monitored. Current research (Dahlstrom et al., 2013; Fuhrman, 2013) reports that students have identified mobile friendly institution software and services as an issue. The amount of support and the general approach that an institution takes towards student and staff use of technologies in general, and mobile technologies in particular, have a far-reaching impact on successful integration.

Therefore, institutional planning and deployment of the digital infrastructure in deployment in NGLS necessitates careful thinking to ensure future proofing. This requires consideration of the diversity of pictures of learning that are possible (and desirable) and understanding the potential costs of enabling and managing these possibilities now and into the future. Investment in both digital technologies and physical infrastructural changes can involve significant financial outlays, so it is important to make sure that current investment:

- is in equipment that will allow the different pictures of learning to be enacted in spaces that are retrofitted or created;
- minimises the need for further investment and financial outlay into the future;
- adapts to ongoing and rapid technological change and to a growth in use of student BYOD devices;
- is monitored for uptake and use; and
- attracts but minimises the need for ongoing institutional support.

Thorough consultation processes should seek to capture current usage as well as both legitimate projected usage and blue sky possibilities.

Institutional future proofing also requires consideration of the interactions between physical space and digital learning technologies. The shape and amenity of the room (including furniture and fittings) all have agency in the way that technology is used, and its use optimised. Different space configurations suggest different pictures of learning and will privilege different uses of technology. If technology is understood to be democratising and is used as a disruptive force, then it makes sense that configurations of space and furniture that privilege collaborative, co-construction of knowledge will enhance (and be enhanced by) the use of digital technology. Institutional future proofing involves ensuring that the investment in elements of NGLS: the infrastructure, the fittings and the technology, will facilitate active learning both now and into the future. Even seemingly simple issues like the location and availability of power outlets in a building (i.e. easy access to power) will enable or constrain the use of digital technologies and therefore the functionality of the space. Future proofing needs to include a provision for BYOD technologies; as an increasing reliance on mobile technologies will also challenge the affordances of physical spaces. In a mobile world, where are the informal places for people to meet, talk and work? The agency of power outlets and the agency of the technology itself will determine where these spaces may appear and what activities may occur and in so doing shape the potential of physical spaces for active learning.

Challenges and Opportunities for Academics

The engagement of academics is critical to the success of creating alternative, democratic pictures of learning in NGLS. Institutional support for academic staff trialing mobile learning initiatives is essential if changes are to move beyond those who are the early adopters (Bonig, 2011; Dahlstrom et al., 2013). Mobile initiatives should begin with a focus on pedagogical need and local successes, then be shared more broadly among staff. The academic community will likely need to be educated regarding the ways in which students can use their smartphones as in-class learning tools, sourcing information, engaging in spontaneous collaboration and capturing ideas as images or audio files.

Just as future proofing is needed for pragmatic considerations of physical facilities and computer hardware and software deployments, it is also an important consideration for the academic users of the spaces. Work is required for teachers and learners to adapt/reshape their personal teaching and learning practices. If the pictures of learning facilitated by NGLS privilege active learning then some pedagogical transformation is unavoidable. The very nature of devices that enable access to the powerful and empowering resources on the web, and tools for creation/recreation of knowledge will necessitate attention to innovation, change and reform. To future-proof is to encourage and sustain the hidden work that is necessary to enable staff and students to engage meaningfully with digital technology and the spaces in which they are used for learning.

With the inevitable move towards the use of mobile devices in learning spaces (either provided or BYOD), the challenge is to examine the possibilities of technology provision in light of their pedagogical advantages, issues of equity and access, engagement of academics, the ability to maintain a

viable support network and the financial outlay required. All these issues
need to be explored to ensure that technology is affordable, pedagogically
functional and accessible, and able to be used into the future. If their use is
to be capitalised upon, then there is a great deal of work that needs to be
done to ensure that they become tools and not distractions in an active
knowledge work environment. This is the hidden work of new technologies;
work that is required to ensure that digital technologies are embedded
within the knowledge work of the spaces and that the processes of interacting with the physical spaces and the infrastructure that sits behind these
spaces is seamless.

HIDDEN WORK OF NEW TECHNOLOGIES FOR ACADEMICS AND STUDENTS

NGLS can be daunting for some. The extensive array of information technology and audiovisual solutions (see Table 2) available in these spaces can
be overwhelming. The usability and affordances of these systems require
careful ongoing consideration before, during and after spaces are built or
retrofitted to ensure technologies are enabling (not disabling) and not privileging some pictures of learning to the exclusion of others. The hidden
work for the academic includes addressing their fears of technology, lack of
technology reliability and cognitive overload. Hidden work for students
often lies in adapting their existing use of digital technologies to the processes of active learning. There is also the hidden work associated with
'keeping up' for both groups. Rapid change in computer software, hardware, audiovisual display and capture technologies used to facilitate and
enable various knowledge activities requires a significant commitment of
time to find, review, learn and evaluate.

The cognitive load of attending to and using these new complex technologies while also facilitating learning is very challenging especially for academics pursuing active learning teaching repertoires in NGLS. Recently
Jaschik and Lederman (2013) found that academics tended to use tools and
processes which were easiest to learn and accommodated their current practices of delivering knowledge while more complex tools and practices were
used by only small numbers of respondents. Similarly in some institutions,
where there are expectations that academics will use synchronous video
conferencing software (e.g. *Go to Meeting* or *Blackboard Collaborate*) while
also conducting face to face lecture presentations and/or discussions the

hidden work is often underestimated. Combining two very different modes of knowledge making in this manner can produce high levels of anxiety and reduce the effectiveness of both tasks. McGrath (2013) recommends that when implementing complex software systems (like video conferencing software) as part of an instructional session, it is helpful to have assistance in 'driving' the technology so that the academic can focus on the knowledge work. Allowing the academic to concentrate on knowledge work provides the possibility of other forms of knowledge making to emerge as anxieties and cognitive load diminish.

Keeping up is another aspect of the hidden work of NGLS. For academics to remain current in their use of technologies they are required to keep up with relevant trends and innovations in the field, especially given the speed with which new devices and software applications and systems change. The academic plays a crucial role in the success of technology integration into any learning environment, so work is necessary for those seeking to integrate new technology tools into a class, to learn about the potential and shortcomings of the software and/or hardware. In separate studies, Laurillard (2010) and Lefoe, Olney, Wright, and Herrington (2009) found that technology integration is most successful when an educator is confident in applying it to student learning. Lefoe et al. (2009) recommend that an academic should 'own' the technology first, and then use it in both personal and professional contexts, in order to develop the skills that students must have in order to use the device in learning. Laurillard (2010) argues that where academics are unfamiliar with the technology, control remains with technical support staff who may or may not understand the pedagogical considerations.

BYOD approaches also include challenging hidden work when academics are expected (or try) to use student technologies as part of their learning and teaching repertoires. Firstly students bring to class highly diverse smart mobile technologies that include a variety of personalised tools. The hidden work of using these technologies in classrooms includes: designing learning activities that cater for the range of devices available; and keeping up, evaluating and trialing potential mobile apps that could be used as part of learning activities and troubleshooting technologies when things go wrong. The cognitive load in developing and deploying activities and the work required to continually keep up with developments is significant.

There is also hidden technology work in NGLS for students. Oblinger (2012) notes that students value the convenience and communication aspects of digital technology with virtually all students using email (99%) text messaging (93%), Facebook (90%), and instant messaging (81%).

Dahlstrom (2012) however found that students indicated that further training and skills were needed to use technologies to learn. While the majority of students felt prepared to use technology at the beginning of their tertiary studies, most indicated that more training was necessary as they progressed through their studies. So students using digital technologies to apply and create knowledge require different types of skills and this necessitates work to develop them.

The 'hidden work' of digital technologies in learning spaces can begin to be understood through an examination of the relationship between digital objects and people. Mitchell et al. (2010) developed a people oriented framework E3C (see Fig. 1) that uses product design characteristics of engagement, empowerment, ease of use and confidence, (Kreitzberg, 2008) to extend a Pedagogy, Space and Technology (PST) model (Radcliffe, Wilson, Powell, & Tibbetts, 2008) developed to explain design and development aspects of NGLS. Including the 'People' dimension considers what students and academics can successfully do in learning spaces to create and work within diverse pictures of learning. Usability and usefulness concepts that are part of this framework are beneficial to analyse aspects of the hidden work in NGLS.

Fig. 2 adapts Mitchell et al.'s (2010) E3C diagram to model how a series of interaction flows between technology, people and space occurs in the

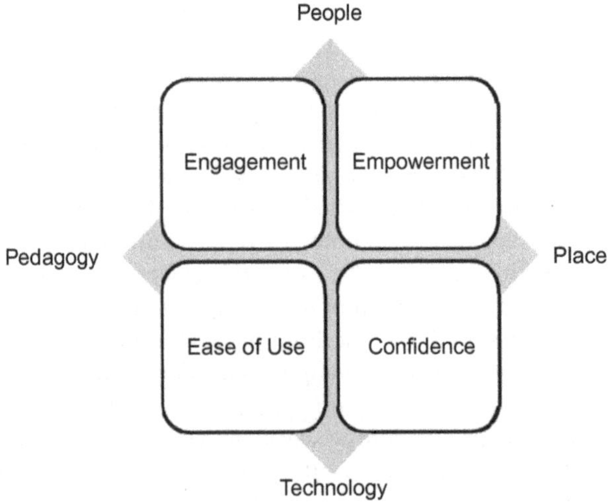

Fig. 1.   E3C Learning Space Design Principles (Mitchell et al., 2010).

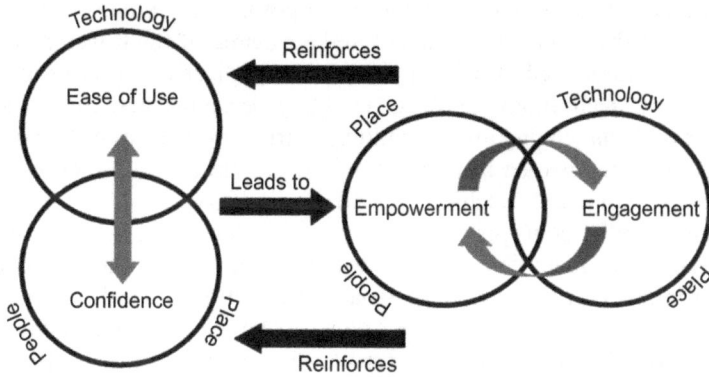

Fig. 2.   Interaction Flows between Technology People and Space for Successful Knowledge.

process of conducting knowledge work. This can be used to understand aspects of the hidden work faced by academics and students when confronted with the host of technologies that are often deployed in NGLS. In this process, *ease of use* relates to design simplicity: the intended use of a space, furniture or technology in a space should either be self-evident to users or require minimal specialist training to utilise. Thus academic users of the space should be able to integrate various forms of knowledge work depending on discipline and student learning needs without too much hidden work like technology training or room configuration issues. Digital objects should accommodate a wide range of literacy levels in users (i.e. it should be easy for a novice user to learn and for an experienced user to utilise its advanced functionality). Interfaces used should have some familiarity for the intended users reducing the hidden work associated with learning new ways of doing familiar processes.

Digital objects that are easy to use build *confidence*. Those that are reliable, robust and fit for purpose, ones that work first time and every time when integrated into various pictures of learning, facilitate the learning and teaching repertoire development of academics and students and reduce hidden work. This leads to empowerment for the academic users of the space/ technology intersections. The concept of *empowerment* in Fig. 2 echoes the research outcomes of Lefoe et al. (2009) and Laurillard (2010) that relate to the way in which ease of use and confidence contribute to overcoming anxiety levels associated with technology use. Lefoe et al. (2009) and Laurillard (2010) argue that appropriate design, placement and support are crucial for reducing anxiety and fear and building empowerment. Finally, *engagement* is a result of the empowered student and academic. If the learning environment is structured well, it will support diversity: diverse learner groups with diverse user technology choices, enabling learning activities that are dynamic and challenging and providing a variety of pictures of learning. An engaged and empowered learner will reinforce confidence in their own ability to work with people, technology and physical spaces.

These usability concepts of ease of use, confidence resulting in empowerment and engagement can be aided at the design level by the consideration of affordances that the technology-space intersections provide for the users. While pictures of learning can be argued to be a perception of the space-technology-pedagogy triad at a macro-level, a consideration of affordances acknowledges the need for an understanding of human perceptions at a micro-level. Affordance (Gibson, 1979; Hartson, 2003; Hartson & Pyla, 2012; Norman, 1988) is a useful concept for helping to analyse the possible hidden work of digital technologies at the level of interfaces (controls) provided for academic and student use. Affordances in terms of digital technologies are described as 'characteristics that help or aid a user to do something', i.e. perform tasks (Hartson & Pyla, 2012, p. 649). Gaver (1991) notes that when affordances suggest actions different from the way something is designed, errors are common and signs are necessary. 'How to' signs especially those created by the space users are an indication that the hidden work associated with the interfaces provided requires more attention!

The affordances of digital technologies within learning spaces are central to how much hidden work is necessary for their intended users. Hartson (2003) suggests thinking about affordances in four categories: cognitive, physical, sensory and functional, helps to analyse where usability issues or hidden work may be identified for users of digital technologies. The following set of questions (Hartson, 2003; Norman, 1988) may be used to identify hidden work in the before and after stages of digital technology interface design and deployment in learning spaces:

- How does a user know what to do?
- How well does the technology design support the user in determining what to do with the system to achieve work domain goals?
- How well does the design support the user in determining how to do what was planned?
- How well does the design support the user in doing the actions? and
- How well does the design show users that their actions have been successful or not?

The affordances suggested by the design, placement and interface controls of technology systems in NGLS will need to support and accommodate a wide range of potential users. NGLS that have sophisticated arrangements of software display and delivery technologies are likely to contribute to feelings of discomfort and or anxiety for some staff and thus increase the amount of hidden work necessary. Drawing on the work of affordances, and applying the concept to NGLS technologies, the intended uses of the technology should be self-evident to users and require minimal specialist training. To reduce the hidden work of new technologies in learning spaces, using familiar look-and-feel approaches to room design, common standards for information technology and audiovisual systems, and simple, clear signage that indicates the role and purpose of any additional classroom element enables technology tools to be used safely and with confidence. Support services need to exist that can respond rapidly to problems in learning spaces and avoid major interruption to any learning activity.

CONCLUSION

We argue in this chapter that it is important to critically examine the context of digital technology application and the assumptions implicit in their use. If twenty-first century learning spaces are going to respond to the active learning needs of learners, digital technology provision should privilege multiple 'pictures of learning' and diverse knowledge work. The democratising and potentially disruptive power of mobile digital technologies has the ability to facilitate the privileging of these multiple pictures of learning and with the significant rise in student ownership and academic use of mobile technologies, it is almost inevitable that they will play a major role in educative processes. Universities need to understand how to leverage and support the use of these technologies to facilitate multiple pictures of learning that enable students to access, apply, create and communicate knowledge in an active learning process.

The growth and penetration of mobile technologies in the university sector is inevitable. Robust institutional policies are required to support the continuing uptake of mobile technologies for pedagogical use. These policies must include explicit strategies that provide technical support in an encouraging climate for staff and students using these technologies for learning. Robust, reliable and well considered infrastructure is a key physical requirement for successful mobile technology implementation reducing the hidden work associated with the use of new technologies for academics.

The 'hidden' work of using digital technologies in NGLS needs to be made explicit and supported. Understanding and evaluating the affordances offered for various pictures of learning shaped by the integration of technologies and space will create spaces that are useful and reliable. The usability and learnability of the interface controls that integrate technologies within learning spaces is of central importance if the hidden work of technology use is to be minimised. Ensuring ease of use is central to ensure pedagogy, space and technology will help empower, engage and build confidence for people in the integration of technologies into the learning space. In so doing, the resulting NGLS space/technology integration enables the enactment of pictures of learning that utilise the democratising nature of digital technologies in the learning practices of academics and learners.

Building in course development support will enable academics to understand not only how to adapt and use various technological tools but also consider possibilities for extending their learning and teaching repertoires to include different pictures of learning. This support can take a number of forms: making people aware of new software 'apps' or hardware that could be appropriate in their teaching; helping people apply these; and driving the technology or being a technology support person in initial trials of the software/hardware. Essentially course development support needs to consider aspects of ease of use; confidence, keeping up, learnability and thus extending repertoires of learning and teaching. Reports such as those prepared by the New Media Consortium (Johnson et al., 2013a, 2013b) and The Grattan Institute (Norton, Sonnerman, & Cherastidtham, 2013) may provide some understanding of the trends in technology and pedagogies in the educational setting, but it is crucial to work out how trending technologies are likely to operate in the local context.

Future proofing the investment in the use of digital technology in tertiary education is multifaceted. It involves the need to attend to the more obvious, common and rationalist issues related to budgets, square metreage of space, room for cabling and quantities and styles of furniture, but it also involves the need to consider managing the very personal interface between digital technologies, space and the different 'pictures of learning' they make possible for the people that use them. Future proofing NGLS classrooms of the twenty-first century will require academics and learners to be 'on the lookout' for the ways in which the fast paced changes in technology will assist and augment the potential for pictures of learning that are engaging and student-active, but not exclusive.

The aim of explicitly examining the detailed interplay between NGLS and use of technology in spaces lets us see how best to use it and how this interplay can be projected into the future. As prospective learners imagine and articulate different ways to implement technology into their own personal learning, the hidden work for tertiary educators will be looking for ways to capitalise on the affordances that digital technologies provide to create the best kind of learning spaces. These will be spaces that deliver the possibility of different types of knowledge work, spaces that permit and privilege active and engaged learning without excluding the possibility of other pictures of learning.

REFERENCES

Andrews, T., & Powell, D. (2009). Collaborative teaching & learning centres at the University of Queensland. In D. Radcliffe, H. Wilson, D. Powell, & B. Tibbetts (Eds.), *Proceedings of the next generation learning spaces 2008 colloquium on learning spaces in higher education: Positive outcomes by design*, University of Queensland, Brisbane, Australia.

Barton, H., Biro, M., Boland, R., Costello, F., Dye, A., & Fagerberg, T. (2012). *Mobile learning: A practical guide. Practical help with integration.* Stockholm, Sweden: Telefonaktiebolaget LM Ericsson.

Bonig, R. (2011). *Best practices for mobile device learning initiatives in higher education.* Stamford, CT: Gartner Inc.

Boys, J. (2011). *Towards creative learning spaces.* London, UK: Routledge.

Christensen, C. M., Horn, M. B., & Johnson, C. W. (2008). *Disrupting class: How disruptive innovation will change the way the world learns* (Vol. 98). New York, NY: McGraw-Hill.

Dahlstrom, E. (2012). *ECAR study of undergraduate students and information technology, 2012 (research report).* Louisville, CO: EDUCAUSE Center for Analysis and Research. Retrieved from http://www.educause.edu/ecar. Accessed on September 18, 2013.

Dahlstrom, E., Walker, J. D., & Dziuban, C. (2013). *ECAR study of undergraduate students and information technology, 2013 (research report).* Louisville, CO: EDUCAUSE Center for Analysis and Research. Retrieved from http://www.educause.edu/ecar. Accessed on August 24.

Duncan-Howell, J., & Lee, K. T. (2007). M-learning: Finding a place for mobile technologies within tertiary educational settings. In R. J. Atkinson, C. McBeath, S. K. A. Soong, & C. Cheers, (Eds.), *Proceedings of the 24th annual conference of ASCILITE 2007 on ICT: Providing choices for learners and learning*, Melbourne, Australia. Retrieved from http://www.ascilite.org.au/conferences/singapore07/procs/duncan-howell.pdf. Accessed on September 23, 2013.

Fuhrman, T. (2013). Go mobile or kiss future students goodbye. *Campus Technology.* Retrieved from http://campustechnology.com/Articles/2013/09/12/Without-Mobile-First-Strategy-Kiss-Students-Goodbye.aspx?=CTMOB&p=1. Accessed on September 14.

Gaver, W. (1991). Technology affordances. In S. P. Robertson, G. M. Olson, & J. S. Olson (Eds.), *Proceedings of the ACM CHI 91 human factors in computing systems conference April 28–June 5, 1991*, Interaction Design Foundation, New Orleans, LA.

Gibson, J. J. (1979). *The ecological approach to visual perception.* Boston, MA: Houghton Mifflin Co.

Hall, E. T. (1966). *The hidden dimension.* New York, NY: Doubleday.

Hartson, H. R. (2003). Cognitive, physical, sensory, and functional afflordances in interaction design. *Behavior and Information Technology, 22*(5), 315–338.

Hartson, R., & Pyla, P. (2012). *The UX Book: Process and guidelines for ensuring a quality user experience.* Waltham, MD: Morgan Kaufmann/Elsevier.

Hedberg, J. G. (2011). Towards a disruptive pedagogy: Changing classroom practice with technologies and digital content. *Educational Media International, 48*(1), 1–16.

Heppel, S., Chapman, C., Millwood, R., Constable, M., & Furness, J. (2004). *Building learning futures. A research project at Ultralab within the CABE/RIBA "Building Futures" programme.* Retrieved from http://rubble.heppell.net/cabe/fflnal report.pdf. Accessed on September 24, 2008.

Jaschick, S. & Lederman, D. (2013). *The 2013 inside higher Ed survey of faculty attitudes on technology.* Washington, DC: Inside Higher Ed.

Johnson, L., Adams Becker, S., Cummins, M., Estrada, V., Freeman, A., & Ludgate, H. (2013a). *NMC Horizon Report: 2013 Higher Education Edition.* Austin, TX: The New Media Consortium.

Johnson, L., Adams Becker, S., Cummins, M., Freeman, A., Ifenthaler, D., & Vardaxis, N. (2013b). *Technology outlook for Australian tertiary education 2013–2018: An NMC horizon project regional analysis.* Austin, TX: The New Media Consortium.

Kreitzberg, C. (2008). *The LUCID framework: An introduction.* Princeton Junction, NJ: Cognetics Corporation.

Laurillard, D. (2010). Effective use of technology in teaching and learning. In P. Peterson, E. Baker, & B. McGaw (Eds.), *International encyclopedia of education* (3rd ed.). Oxford: Elsevier.

Le Couteur, A., & Delfabbro, P. (2001). Repertoires of teaching and learning: A comparison of university teachers and students using Q methodology. *Higher Education, 42*, 205–235.

Lefoe, G., Olney, I., Wright, R., & Herrington, A. (2009). Faculty development for new technologies: Putting mobile learning in the hands of the teachers. In J. Herrignton, J. Mantei, I. Olney, & B. Ferry (Eds.), *New technologies, new pedagogies: Mobile learning in higher education.* Wollongong, Australia: University of Wollongong.

Ling, P., & Fraser, K. (2014). Pedagogies for next generation learning spaces: Theory, context, action. In K. Fraser (Ed.), *The future of learning and teaching in next generation learning spaces* (Vol. 12). International Perspectives on Higher Education Research. Bingley, UK: Emerald Group Publishing Limited.

Mackay, M. (2012). *The Australian mobile phone lifestyle index: September 2012.* Sydney: Australian Interactive Media Industry Association (AIMIA), Mobile Industry Group. Retrieved from http://www.aimia.com.au/enews/AMPLI/AMPLI%202012%20Report_FINAL_upd_ Oct.pdf. Accessed on September 14, 2013.

Mackay, M. (2013). *The Australian mobile phone lifestyle index: October 2013.* Sydney: Australian Interactive Media Industry Association (AIMIA), Mobile Industry Group. Retrieved from http://www.aimia.com.au/enews/2013/Events/AMPLI%202013/Ampli%202013% 20Report_Final_October%2024.pdf. Accessed on November 4, 2013.

Malisch, S., & Montes, B. A. (2011). Loyola University Chicago: There's an App for That. *EDUCAUSE Review Online, 34*(1). Retrieved from http://www.educause.edu/ero/article/loyola-university-chicago-theres-app. Accessed on September 24, 2013

McGrath, D. M. (2013). *Can a virtual classroom become a virtual Swiss army knife?* In *Blackboard Teaching and Learning Conference*. Melbourne, Australia: Blackboard Inc.

McLoughlin, C., & Lee, M. J. W. (2007). Social software and participatory learning: Extending pedagogical choices with technology affordances in the Web 2.0 era. In R. J. Atkinson, C. McBeath, S. K. A. Soong, & C. Cheers, (Eds.), *Proceedings of the 24th annual conference of ASCILITE 2007 on ICT: Providing choices for learners and learning*, Melbourne, Australia. Retrieved from http://www.ascilite.org.au/conferences/singapore07/procs/mcloughlin.pdf. Accessed on September 23, 2013.

McLoughlin, C., & Lee, M. J. W. (2008a). The 3 P's of pedagogy for the networked society: Personalization, participation, and productivity. *International Journal of Teaching and Learning in Higher Education, 20*(1), 10–27. Retrieved from http://www.isetl.org/ijtlhe/articleView.cfm?id=395. Accessed on September 22, 2013.

McLoughlin, C., & Lee, M. J. W. (2008b). Mapping the digital terrain: New media and social software as catalysts for pedagogical change. In R. Atkinson & C. McBeath (Eds.), *Proceedings of the 25th annual conference of ASCILITE 2008 on Hello! Where are you in the landscape of educational technology?*, Melbourne, Australia. Retrieved from http://www.ascilite.org.au/conferences/melbourne08/procs/mcloughlin.html. Accessed on September 23, 2013.

Mejias, U. (2005). *A nomad's guide to learning and social software. The knowledge tree: An e-journal of learning innovation*. Retrieved from http://knowledgetree.flexible learning.net.au/edition07/download/la_mejias.pdf. Accessed on September 18, 2013.

Mitchell, G., White, B., Pospisil, R., Kiley, S., Liu, C., & Matthews, G. (2010). *Retrofitting University Learning Spaces*. Final Report. Support for the original work was provided by the Australian Learning and Teaching Council Ltd. Australian Learning and Teaching Council, Darwin, Northern Territory. Retrieved from http://learnline.cdu.edu.au/retrofittingunispaces/index.html. Accessed on September 14, 2013.

Norman, D. (1988). *The psychology of everyday things*. New York, NY: Basic Books.

Norton, A., Sonnemann, J., & Cherastidtham, I. (2013). *Taking university teaching seriously*. Carelton, Victoria: Grattan Institute.

Oblinger, D. G. (2012). IT as a game changer. In D. G. Oblinger (Ed.), *Game changers: Education and information technologies*. Louisville, CO: EDUCAUSE.

Piaget, J. (1977). *The development of thought: Equilibrium of cognitive structures*. New York, NY: Viking Press.

Project Tomorrow. (2011). *Evaluation report of the impact of project K-Nect on teaching and learning*. Los Angeles, CA: Author. Retrieved from http://www.tomorrow.org/docs/ProjectKNect_Evaluation Report_Mar2011.pdf. Accessed on October 25, 2013.

Radcliffe, D., Wilson, H., Powell, D., & Tibbetts, B. (Eds.). (2008). Learning spaces in higher education: Positive outcomes by design. *Proceedings of the next generation learning spaces 2008 colloquium*, University of Queensland, Brisbane, Queensland.

Scott-Webber, L. (2004). *In sync: Environmental behavior research and the design of learning spaces*. Ann Arbor, MI: The Society for College and University Planning.

Sharples, M., McAndrew, P., Weller, M., Ferguson, R., FitzGerald, E., Hirst, T., & Gaved, M. (2013). *Innovating pedagogy 2013*. Open University innovation report 2. Milton Keynes, UK: The Open University.

Smith, A. (2013). *Smartphone ownership, 2013 update*. Washington, DC: Pew Research Centre.

Traxler, J. (2010). Students and mobile devices. *Research in Learning Technology, 18*(2), 149–160.

Verran, H. (1998). Staying true to the laughter in Nigerian classrooms. *The Sociological Review, 46*(S), 136–155.

CHAPTER 3

KEEPING PACE WITH THE RAPID EVOLUTION OF LEARNING SPACES

Anastasia Morrone and Sue B. Workman

ABSTRACT

This chapter focuses on learning space design for students' technology-rich lifestyles, in particular the evolution and future of learning spaces in the United States. JISC design principles — bold, supportive, future proof, creative, and enterprising — frame discussion in the chapter's first section, "Planning for the learning spaces of tomorrow." The section begins with pioneering work in the field and follows with recent learning spaces (both classrooms and informal learning environments) that seek new and innovative ways for students to collaborate. Examples clearly point to students' need for continual access to flexible, tech-rich spaces that support their work and study habits.

The chapter's second section, "The future of learning spaces: On-demand apps and Bring Your Own Technology (BYOT)," is a case study focused on software virtualization's influence on learning space design at Indiana University. The section brings in examples from the University of South Florida and the University of Iowa, asserting that physical and virtual learning spaces must be designed to come together seamlessly,

The Future of Learning and Teaching in Next Generation Learning Spaces
International Perspectives on Higher Education Research, Volume 12, 47−62
ISSN: 1479-3628/doi:10.1108/S1479-362820140000012006

echoing students' on-the-go lifestyles and constant connectedness. Ultimately, the section makes a bold contention about the evolution of learning spaces: Any space can become a tech-rich learning environment, if students have access to virtualized software.

Throughout, the chapter touches on compelling questions about meeting the learning needs of digital natives: How do we challenge traditional educational paradigms? Can we flip the classroom to further the potential of all learners? What is the role of collaboration in learning? Which models will energize and inspire learners and instructors of the future?

Keywords: Learning classrooms; collaboration spaces; labs; cloud

Many universities are investing in learning environments that encourage and enable students to work together in comfortable settings (Learning Spaces Collaboratory, 2013; Oblinger, 2006). At the same time, in the context of tightening IT budgets and the rise of mobile devices, an important question is how classrooms and learning spaces should evolve to meet the needs of today's mobile learners. Within this book, there are several chapters that speak specifically to the pedagogical practices needed to use next generation learning spaces to improve learning outcomes. Our focus in this chapter is learning space design for student's technology-rich lifestyles, in particular the evolution and future of learning spaces in the United States.

In this chapter, we assert that new collaborative spaces — both classrooms and informal learning environments — are needed more than ever before to empower students in their learning. We will explore this need in more detail, providing examples that demonstrate how select US universities have responded to this challenge (see also Learning Spaces Collaboratory, 2013; Mitchell et al., 2010). In turn, we will touch on the driving forces behind two strategies for keeping pace with the learning needs of digital natives (Oblinger & Oblinger, 2005): (1) build flexible, tech-rich spaces that support students' work and study habits and (2) recognize that any space can become a tech-rich learning environment, as long as students have access to virtualized software.

PLANNING FOR THE LEARNING SPACES OF TOMORROW

We must continue to advocate for change in the way that all spaces are developed and planned, ensuring that innovation to support student learning remains a focus. Ideally, transformed spaces will have the following characteristics (JISC, 2006):

- bold – looking beyond tried and tested technologies and pedagogies;
- supportive – developing the potential of all learners;
- flexible – accommodating both current and evolving pedagogies;
- future-proofed – enabling space to be reallocated and reconfigured;
- creative – energizing and inspiring learners and tutors; and
- enterprising – making each space capable of supporting different purposes.

In the next section, we use the JISC principles as headings to frame our discussion and to demonstrate examples that illustrate larger design goals. Each of the examples clearly point to the need for learning spaces that ensure students have continual access to technology, along with increased access to spaces that encourage and enable collaborative work. We highlight examples, beginning with pioneering work in the field and following with examples of recent learning spaces that seek to provide new and innovative ways for students to collaborate in a technology-rich environment.

Bold – Looking Beyond Tried and Tested Technologies and Pedagogies

SCALE-UP (North Carolina State University)

The impact of Robert Beichner's work with SCALE-UP (Student-Centered Active Learning Environment with Upside-down Pedagogies) has been truly transformative (see Gaffney, Richards, Kustusch, Ding, & Beichner, 2008). This bold pedagogical approach of "upside-down pedagogies" was first introduced more than 14 years ago and is similar to what is now commonly referred to as the "flipped classroom" model, in which most class time is spent with students working together both in and across teams. Course content is read outside of class, and learning experiences are structured using a backward design approach (Wiggins & McTighe, 2005). In SCALE-UP classrooms, students work in teams on "hands-on activities, interesting questions and problems, or simulations exploring a challenging activity or problem." The role of the instructor is that of a facilitator who moves freely around the room, asking questions and encouraging one team to help another team solve a problem. There are three teams seated at each table, with three students in each team (for a total of nine students seated at each table). At their tables, students have access to whiteboards and laptops. More than 150 institutions have adopted or adapted the SCALE-UP approach (for details, see http://scaleup.ncsu.edu).

The University of Minnesota's Active Learning Classrooms
A particularly exciting example of a university's commitment to active learning is the new Science Teaching & Student Services Building at the University of Minnesota, which uses a modified SCALE-UP design (Walker, Brooks, & Baepler, 2011). Their 14 Active Learning Classrooms have round tables that accommodate nine students with the teaching station located in the center of the room. From this central location, instructors can easily display selected information on multiple flat-panel displays on the walls around room. Students typically bring their own laptops and connect to the wireless network. A unique feature of these rooms is the use of a 360-degree glass-surface marker board. For more about the University of Minnesota Active Learning Classrooms, see http://www.classroom.umn. edu/projects/ALCOverview.html

Indiana University's Collaborative Learning Studio
Indiana University's newest Collaborative Learning Studio draws on the lessons learned by pioneers in the field — SCALE-UP (North Carolina State University), Active Learning Classrooms (University of Minnesota), and Transform, Interact, Learn, Engage (TILE, University of Iowa). This project involved a major renovation of a large space that began as a swimming pool and was later converted to a map library. The goal of this project was to create a large, technology-rich classroom designed to promote collaborative learning.

The room includes 16 collaborative student tables — each with flat-panel displays, a 20-foot video wall (16 flat panels), and multiple control locations to allow the instructor to move freely around the classroom. The video wall is designed to allow the instructor to feature all 16 student table displays (called the "gallery view"), with one table image per video panel. Because of the size of the room, the gallery view is intended to let a professor quickly scan what students are working on while moving through the space. In addition to the gallery view, students benefit from the ability to see their work and the work of their peers displayed as four images ("quad view") or two images as part of class discussion. This flexibility allows for highlighting and comparing student work on the video wall as part of class discussion (Fig. 1).

Preliminary research on this classroom (Morrone & Siering, 2014) suggests that faculty who redesigned their courses with a focus on instructional strategies that promote collaborative learning found the classroom to support their pedagogical approach, but faculty who prefer to teach using

Fig. 1. Collaborative Learning Studio at Indiana University Bloomington.

more traditional methods (such as lecture) did not find that the classroom was a good fit for them. Beginning in spring 2014, the new classroom will be assigned only to faculty members who request it.

Supportive – Developing the Potential of All Learners

MIT's Technology Enabled Active Learning (TEAL) Project
The Massachusetts Institute of Technology (MIT) TEAL classrooms were modeled after Rensselaer Polytechnic University's physics studio and Beichner's SCALE-UP with the goal to fundamentally change the way freshman physics was taught at MIT (Dori et al., 2003). This change involved moving from a traditional lecture format to an active learning model that combined innovative technology with a SCALE-UP classroom design to provide a supportive environment for students. Because the TEAL classroom was specifically designed for physics teaching, MIT also added visualizations of electricity and magnetism to meet the requirements of the subsequent introductory physics course in electromagnetism. Dori and Belcher (2005), in a study of the effects of the TEAL environment on students' conceptual understanding of electromagnetism, found that TEAL students showed greater gains in their understanding of electromagnetism

than students in the control group (for more information on TEAL, see
http://web.mit.edu/edtech/casestudies/teal.html).

Flexible — Accommodating Both Current and Evolving Pedagogies

The University of Iowa's TILE program
The TILE (Transform, Interact, Learn, Engage) program, which began in
2010, is designed to create new learning spaces that address a range of
teaching and learning needs (Van Horne, Murniati, Gaffney, & Jesse,
2012). At the heart of the TILE program is a commitment to transform
teaching practices, enhance learning, and increase faculty/student engagement. TILE instructors use student-centered, instructional strategies such
as collaborative, problem-based, and team-based learning in classroom
spaces that have been intentionally designed to facilitate collaborative and
engaged active learning. As in SCALE-UP classrooms, the teaching station
is in the center of the room. Students are seated at circular tables that have
laptops, flat screen displays, multiple projectors, and whiteboards. A key to
the success of the TILE program is comprehensive faculty support that
includes one-on-one consulting, workshops, and online learning opportunities. For more about the TILE program, see http://tile.uiowa.edu/
content/about-tile.

St. Louis University's Learning Studio
Another classroom studio project with video wall technology and support
for mobile learners is the Learning Studio at St. Louis University. This
classroom is a flexible learning environment that includes bar seating
and moveable furniture, a large multi-input video wall, wireless projection
capabilities for iPads and tablet PCs, a high definition video camera
for video conferencing, lecture capture, and ample whiteboard space. The
room was designed for a maximum of 25 students, which enables freedom
of movement in the technology-rich space. For more about SLU's Learning
Studio, see http://www.slu.edu/cttl/teaching-innovations/learning-studio.

Informal Learning Spaces: Future Proof, Creative, Enterprising

Informal learning spaces — those outside the classroom — present particularly intri-
guing opportunities for pioneering and cultivating new teaching and learning practices.

These spaces, while informal, are key areas for student academic work. Students spend far more time in these spaces than they do in formal classrooms. Research, web browsing, writing, statistical analysis, and compiling lab reports all take place in the library, study hall, media center, dorm room, and learning commons. Because of their enthusiasm for IT and their experiential, hands-on approach to learning tasks, Net Gen students will easily "tune into" the virtual aspects of informal spaces. Well-designed and integrated physical layouts and IT "tool sets" will find a ready audience with Net Gen students. (Brown, 2005)

This quote from Malcolm Brown in the recent Learning Spaces Collaboratory (2013) report underscores the need for informal learning spaces that support and enrich the educational experiences of today's students. To that end, we now turn to a few examples of innovative spaces that are very different from traditional library and computer lab spaces of the past. These spaces, in our view, represent excellent examples of three of the design goals:

- future-proofed – enabling space to be reallocated and reconfigured;
- creative – energizing and inspiring learners and tutors; and
- enterprising – making each space capable of supporting different purposes.

North Carolina State University's Hunt Library
The Hunt Library at North Carolina State University, from our perspective, represents one of the most innovative library spaces in the United States for students and faculty. The open floor plan provides an environment that has multiple spaces designed to meet the needs of today's students. The building is full of natural light and provides a highly functional and comfortable setting. Interesting furniture arrangements with rich colors make the library a particularly inviting place for students and faculty. There is an Apple Technology Showcase (named after donors Lawrence and Ella Apple) that is surrounded by glass walls. This showcase area provides a very visible space for students to explore the latest devices available and to check out these devices from the library. The library also includes a next generation learning commons that includes an innovative gaming lab and provides students with access to interactive computing, gaming, and new technologies. The library also features numerous technology-rich group study spaces and ample white boards, all designed to fully support collaborative learning. For more on the Hunt Library, see http://www.lib.ncsu.edu/huntlibrary/vision.

University of Denver's Academic Commons
Nancy Allen, dean of the Penrose Library at the University of Denver, articulated the vision for the new Academic Commons as a space that "will be a dynamic center that will support social learning, interactive technologies, student-centered programs, and, of course, individual study and reflection." Like the Hunt Library, the new Academic Commons at the University of Denver was designed as an inviting space with plentiful natural light and ample room for students to work collaboratively with their peers and professors in a technology-rich environment. What is particularly attractive about the new space is that it honors the tradition of a university library with collections of books and journals, while also realizing the vision for a new "people-focused" space. Consistent with a learning commons approach, the Academic Commons also provides students with one-stop academic support services through the Writing Center, the Research Center, the Math Center, and the Technology Help Desk (for more, see http://www.du.edu/ascend/AC-message-allen.html).

Penn State University's Knowledge Commons
Another innovative library space is the Knowledge Commons at Penn State University. This library space is home to a Tech Tutor program, a multimedia Mac classroom, and a robust media authoring program that includes support for multimedia production. The Knowledge Commons includes spaces for students to work individually or in groups, in a contemporary, technology-rich environment. For more about the PSU Knowledge Commons, see http://www.libraries.psu.edu/psul/kc.html.

The above examples of classroom, library, and computing spaces underscore that meeting the needs of today's mobile learners requires advocating for change in the planning and development of learning spaces – in other words, ensuring that innovation to support student learning remains a focus in room design, technology infrastructure, and furnishings. The overarching goal is to empower students – giving them the flexibility to choose however they want to work, using whichever technology they prefer. In the next section, we take a focused look at how Indiana University (IU) and other US universities are moving into roles focused on being more of a technology enabler than a technology provider. Ultimately, this means physical and virtual learning spaces need to be designed to come together seamlessly, echoing students' on-the-go lifestyles and constant connectedness, all in support of their learning. In IU's experience, virtualized software is key to maintaining those connections.

THE FUTURE OF LEARNING SPACES: ON-DEMAND APPS AND BRING YOUR OWN TECHNOLOGY (BYOT)

Planning learning spaces becomes more complex every day. Whereas once this process amounted to providing mainly places for quiet, individual concentration, today it means creating more places that accommodate a wide range of activities, technologies, and participants – both in person and connected virtually. In these spaces, people need to be able to create, retrieve, combine, display, and share information, then do it all over again, all in a space that they can easily reconfigure and is well supported by staff that meet and anticipate their needs. (NCSU Libraries, brightspot strategy, & AECOM Strategy Plus, 2012)

Discussions of next generation learning spaces inevitably lead to a much-debated question: In today's BYOT environment (when most mobile devices have built-in input, output, and networking), do we still need computer classrooms and labs? IU's response is clearly yes – students will always need spaces to study, work, collaborate, and explore. However, if most students have two or three devices, then why are we providing redundant, expensive computing equipment? Students need access to software and peripherals like printers, monitors, and collaboration technologies that are not readily accessible, as well as power. Many also need WiFi and network access, but that is changing with the availability of cellular plans. What happens if we deliver the software they need almost anywhere on almost any device, and make sure peripherals and power are available in WiFi-rich learning spaces?

On its eight campuses, IU maintains over 6,000 computers within classroom and lab spaces that serve 110,000+ students. These computers host access to 300+ software applications, some location dependent. Over a couple of decades, IT staff has honed processes to build and maintain these computers efficiently. User satisfaction for hardware, software, and consulting has averaged in the high 90th percentile over the past five years. The labs are full much of the time, logging over 8 million seat hours a year (the total amount of time per year that students use the lab computers). All told, what's the problem? IU is spending money to buy, maintain, and life-cycle 6,000 computers when most students have a device sitting next to them or in their pocket. We can definitely use this funding in a more value-added way to buy more software or tools – or redirect it to other initiatives (such as redesigning learning spaces), rather than redundantly buying computers.

The Linchpin: On-Demand Cloud Software

IU now provides a local, cloud-based virtual application delivery service to IU students, faculty, and staff. IU has named this virtual application deployment IUanyWare. In turn, the service provides access to cloud and server storage, mobile printing, and even accessible software tools on almost any device (desktop, laptop, tablet, or smartphone) in almost any place. Students no longer have to go to a particular location and wait to access software. They get access anytime from their dorm room, favorite hangout, or place of work — without the need to travel to a computing lab to look for an open seat. Those taking online courses benefit even more from virtual apps.

Licensed software packages are securely accessible on any device supported by the virtual client — meaning most modern devices, such as desktops, notebooks, tablets, smartphones, and thin clients (thin clients have limited local processing, and little or no storage, and serve applications virtually from configured servers in the data center). For access to files from these apps, students use a university-developed cloud storage configurator that connects any app to a choice of storage — a local file server, SharePoint, Microsoft MySite, DropBox, Google Drive, or an IU enterprise Box account with 50 GB of storage space. The upshot: From a tablet or smartphone (or computer), students can access any of the 300+ software packages, formerly in labs, on demand. Software such as SPSS, Adobe Creative Suite, GIS, Microsoft Office, or a specialized departmental app is at their fingertips, along with instant file access.

This is quite valuable for commuters. Students can study from their living room with their smartphone connected to a TV, or from a bus while commuting to campus, or from any other preferred workspace. This model allows education to thrive for all by removing barriers of cost, timing, and location. One IU student, via a user survey, said that this access has boosted her ability to take certain classes toward earning her degree. She has on-demand access to software that she previously had to go to a lab to use. She is a working mother and cannot take her three-year-old child to a lab at 9 p.m. to complete assignments, and cannot otherwise afford to buy the software herself. This allows her to do her work at home, with her child in bed, continuing progress toward her degree.

All of this is part of IU's strategic plan for information technology, which calls for more efficient and effective use of technology resources. Virtualized software responds to several of the plan's calls to action:

- maintain and refresh IT infrastructure by consolidating enterprise-scale (multi-campus) services, while also enabling innovative departmental-scale technology;

- explore technologies such as desktop virtualization to help reduce the costs and extend the lifecycles of personal computing devices;
- continue to pioneer and provision effective means of user support through advanced tools for self-service and connection to university IT experts; and
- expand formal and informal engagements with the IU community to ensure continuous, timely dialogue, and flow of information to adapt IT services to user needs.

Today's students expect to be able to download and use apps on-demand from any location on any device. IU cloud software can be accessed from $250 thin clients rather than $600+ computers − or even from a <$100 stick PC, a new device that looks much like a USB flash drive, but has storage, Bluetooth, and wireless, and runs on Android or Windows operating systems. This provides freedom, while ensuring secure apps and secure access to storage and printing resources. Software apps are no longer dependent on individuals updating systems regularly, and the initiative improves operational efficiencies without insisting on a uniform IT environment. Furthermore, the service targets a BYOT model defined by the user community itself instead of university technology staff.

IU Student and Instructor Outcomes

Virtual software will also have a positive impact on visually disabled students, who use campus computer labs to browse the web, research, and study. In the past, IT staff had to load software such as comprehensive screen-reading software programs for low vision and blind users on each computer, monitoring the effects of operating system patches. Licensing did not allow for every lab computer to host this software, so visually impaired students had to go to certain labs and vie for certain computers. Just traveling to these places late at night or in inclement weather can be dangerous for these students. Now they have the ability to access this crucial software anytime, anywhere, on their own devices, and with ease.

The virtual software restores valuable class time by giving instructors and students on-demand access to applications. In courses requiring specialty software, professors often spend the first hours, or even days of class walking students through installation and working through installation issues. Moreover, the cloud storage service ensures that the class has access to the files they need, when and where they need them. Overall, the software/storage package boosts flexibility. Faculty can teach from an iPhone or Android device using a projection screen, access the service via a thin client, and run multiple versions of the same software even after upgrades. For instance, the service lets users choose between both Windows 7 and 8 environments, and Office 2010 and Office 2013 — meeting student desires for the latest and greatest, while eliminating disruptive changes for faculty.

Here are some examples of other faculty and student benefits:

- The Kelley School of Business has lifted technology restrictions for K201 ("The Computer in Business"), a required course that enrolls nearly 2,000 students each semester. The course is ongoing and uses Windows-only statistical software to help students solve complex business problems. Now, students can access this software on almost any device.
- IU's School of Public and Environmental Affairs (SPEA) had a single computer lab with 12 computers loaded with discipline-specific software (unavailable for fee-free download). SPEA's 650 graduate students frequently endured long waits to use these 12 machines. Now they can access the resources they need anywhere, anytime, and at no additional cost.
- Mac users (with OSX and iOS devices) are now able to use IU's virtual application delivery, IUanyWare, to gain real-time access to Windows applications — using their preferred technologies, rather than seeking out PCs in various labs to run course software.
- Online courses are no longer plagued by cumbersome network setups or local software installations. Troubleshooting was time-consuming and sometimes required a student to mail their computer to tech support, meaning they could not use the computer for their studies.

Keeping Pace with Students

Traditional computer labs look much like those shown in Fig. 2, but increasingly, IU user surveys show that students do not want to travel to a lab that has rows and rows of computers facing forward and sitting 36 inches apart.

Students want collaboration spaces designed for working on a team project, collaboratively editing an assignment, or videoconferencing with students or faculty in another location. Software virtualization has tremendous implications for next generation learning spaces — like the bold, supportive, flexible, future-proofed, creative, and enterprising spaces discussed in the previous section. Students like using their own devices, when access to software apps is easy and power is available for charging.

Fig. 2. Traditional Computer Lab Example.

Like faculty, they don't want to use valuable class time to troubleshoot software installations. Ultimately, labs need to be virtually anywhere. Yes, universities can supply labs — but so can the local coffee shop (with the right setup!).

Admittedly, delivering software virtually presents licensing challenges. Vendors with enterprise agreements typically extend licensing to virtual deployments, but often require amendments to contracts. Other vendors with more limited agreements do not always allow virtual deployments, and not many are willing to count licenses based on concurrency models. Each agreement is separate and must be renegotiated to make sure software licenses are in compliance. However, virtualization gives us the ability to see how much software is really needed, and to secure quantity discounts. Furthermore, authentication ensures that the person using the software is still affiliated with the university, and in an appropriate role to use the software.

Unlike many initiatives of this scope, IU's software virtualization project sought most of its resources through reallocating, restructuring, and retooling existing staff and processes. Project staffing came from existing lab personnel who benefited from professional development ranging from formal training to informal coaching. For example, a senior support advisor developed sufficient skills to serve as the project's principal enterprise systems engineer. As staff members depart, their positions are analyzed in light of fit with the new environment. This is typically not the way a major shift in technology works. As a result, IU has been able to retain – and redesign – necessary labs while shifting to new technologies with close to the same resources.

In addition to IU, several other US universities have pursued software virtualization as a means of using technology resources more efficiently and effectively:

The University of South Florida

Much like IU, the University of South Florida (USF) also decided to virtualize their student technology labs for the following reasons (Woolley & McCallister, 2013):

- students need access to university-owned software;
- students now work 24×7;
- students use multiple technology devices; and
- decreasing physical lab machines means significant cost savings.

In turn, the USF required that the project address the following needs (Woolley & McCallister, 2013):

- leverage existing software licenses;
- provide student experiences similar to working in a physical computer lab; and
- deliver functionality and consistent user experiences on multiple platforms and operating systems (device independence).

The project went live in January 2011, reaching 47,000 students and 13,000 faculty and staff. As a result, USF has been able to reduce the number of student labs from eight to one by 2013, while also reducing the total lab budget from $357,000/year to $72,000/year. USF is now considering extending this model for administrative uses.

The University of Iowa

The University of Iowa has been offering access to virtual applications since 2003, with the goal of providing remote applications. The first offerings provided student and faculty access to the same software provided in university technology labs. As the service developed, Iowa began deploying specialized applications from a virtual environment. Iowa currently delivers approximately 120 applications virtually, and a summer 2013 internal assessment of the Virtual Desktop Service found the primary benefits to be:

- increased security for sensitive data;

- access from non-Windows client platforms;
- availability from off campus;
- access to applications that are needed infrequently;
- ability to run applications (such as statistical software) that require long, complicated installs and often create support issues; and
- ability to make very large applications available without including them in a desktop image.

IU, USF, and Iowa have all been challenged by vendor agreements, however all have worked through the individual licenses to serve software virtually. At Iowa, five of the seven applications that are accessed most often are statistical applications. Users found it useful to not have to install these applications on their devices, and the virtual environment has more power behind it for faster processing. Iowa also finds more usage by graduate students than undergrads, primarily because of the statistical software. Similar to Iowa, USF and IU also have high use of statistical software packages — but they also see significant use of office and productivity tools, as well as larger photo editing packages.

TRANSCENDING PHYSICAL LEARNING SPACES

Until very recently, computer classrooms and student labs were often the only places where students could access software they needed to complete their coursework. The rapid advancement of software virtualization is fundamentally changing the way we think about classrooms and learning spaces. Students can now access the software they need, whenever and wherever they need it. This provides opportunities to re-envision traditional computer classrooms and labs — and to engage students with different learning processes and styles. Combined, next generation learning spaces and cloud-based virtual apps mean that higher education becomes more dynamic, and more capable of evolving along with the community it serves. With on-demand access to software, any space can become a tech-rich learning environment — fitting seamlessly into students' mobile lifestyles.

REFERENCES

Brown, M. (2005). In D. Oblinger & J. L. Oblinger (Eds.), *Educating the net generation*. Retrieved from http://www.educause.edu/ir/library/pdf/pub7101.pdf

Dori, J. Y., Belcher, J., Bessette, M., Danziger, M., McKinney, A., & Hult, E. (2003, December). Technology for active learning. *Materials Today*. Retrieved from http://www.sciencedirect.com/science/article/pii/S1369702103012252

Dori, Y. J., & Belcher, J. W. (2005). How does technology-enabled active learning affect undergraduate students understanding of electromagnetism concepts? *The Journal of Learning Sciences, 14*(2), 243–279.

Gaffney, J. D. H., Richards, E., Kustusch, M. B., Ding, L., & Beichner, R. (2008). Scaling up educational reform. *Journal of College Science Teaching, 37*(5), 48–53.

JISC. (2006). *Designing spaces for effective learning: A guide to 21st century learning spaces.* Retrieved from http://www.jisc.ac.uk/uploaded_documents/JISClearningspaces.pdf

Learning Spaces Collaboratory. (2013). *A guide for planning and assessing 21st century spaces for 21st century learners.* Retrieved from http://www.pkallsc.org/assets/files/LSCGuide-PlanningforAssessing(1).pdf

Mitchell, G., White, B., Pospisil, R., Kiley, S., Liu, C., & Matthews, G. (2010). *Retrofitting University Learning Spaces.* Final Report. Support for the original work was provided by the Australian Learning and Teaching Council Ltd., an initiative of the Australian Government. Retrieved from http://learnline.cdu.edu.au/retrofitting unispaces/index.html

Morrone, A. S., & Siering, G. (February, 2014). *Leveraging collaborative technologies and pedagogies in large active learning classrooms.* Presentation at the annual meeting of the EDUCAUSE Learning Initiative (ELI) conference, New Orleans, LA.

NCSU Libraries, brightspot strategy, & AECOM Strategy Plus. (2012). *Learning Space Toolkit.* Retrieved from http://learningspacetoolkit.org/about/

Oblinger, D. (2006). *Learning spaces.* Retrieved from http://www.educause.edu/research-and-publications/books/learning-spaces

Oblinger, D., & Oblinger, J. L. (2005). *Educating the net generation* (p. 264). Retrieved from http://www.educause.edu/ir/library/pdf/pub7101.pdf

Van Horne, S., Murniati, C., Gaffney, J., & Jesse, M. (2012). Promoting active learning in technology-infused TILE classrooms at the University of Iowa. *Journal of Learning Spaces, 1*(2). Retrieved from http://libjournal.uncg.edu/ojs/index.php/jls/article/view/344/280

Walker, J. D., Brooks, C., & Baepler, P. (2011). Pedagogy and space: Empirical research on new learning environments. *EDUCAUSE Review.* Retrieved from http://www.educause.edu/ero/article/pedagogy-and-space-empirical-research-new-learning. Accessed on December 15.

Wiggins, G., & McTighe, J. (2005). *Understanding by design* (2nd ed.). Upper Saddle River, NJ: Pearson Education.

Woolley, C., & McCallister, M. (May, 2013). *Virtual software applications for students.* Presentation at EDUCAUSE southeast regional conference, Atlanta, GA.

SECTION II
THE FUTURE OF LEARNING AND
TEACHING IN NEXT GENERATION
LEARNING SPACES

CHAPTER 4

PEDAGOGIES FOR NEXT GENERATION LEARNING SPACES: THEORY, CONTEXT, ACTION

Peter Ling and Kym Fraser

ABSTRACT

The purpose of this chapter is to provide a framework to guide learning and teaching practice in next generation learning spaces. The framework is informed by both learning and teaching theory and the current context of the sector. The framework provides guidance to those who teach in next generation learning spaces and is illustrated with examples of effective pedagogic practices that use the affordances of spaces while avoiding their limitations. The chapter discusses the tension between next generation learning space design and use. Design is influenced by drivers ranging from a need to accommodate ever-larger student numbers and responding to digital technologies and other developments in educational media, to providing for new approaches to learning. Use is determined by understandings of the teaching task, which can range from presentation by a teacher through to students working individually or in groups to generate meaningful knowledge, useful skills and professional values. In this chapter we identify drivers underpinning the creation and design of next generation learning spaces in universities today and associated expectations of the ways in which the spaces will be used. We reflect on

The Future of Learning and Teaching in Next Generation Learning Spaces
International Perspectives on Higher Education Research, Volume 12, 65–84
Copyright © 2014 by Emerald Group Publishing Limited
All rights of reproduction in any form reserved
ISSN: 1479-3628/doi:10.1108/S1479-362820140000012008

understandings of sound pedagogic practice and work through to implica-
tions for learning and teaching in NGLS. In some cases advocated peda-
gogic practice asks teaching staff to make the most of spaces designed to
allow students to engage constructively in their learning. In other cases it
involves teaching constructively in spite of the design of the space.

Keywords: Pedagogy; constructivism; connectivism; situated learning;
complexity theory; next generation learning spaces

INTRODUCTION

Every year the international higher education sector spends billions of dollars developing and retrofitting physical, on-campus, state of the art spaces.
While there is a significant literature on the design of learning spaces
(Brown & Lippincott, 2003; JISC, 2006; Johnson & Lomas, 2005; Mitchell
et al., 2010; Oblinger, 2005), there is little research to support the notion
that we are using those spaces most effectively to impact student learning
outcomes (Lee & Tan, 2011).

Some new spaces are designed for lectures. Using them in ways that
facilitate student construction of meaning and effective learning outcomes
provides a challenge. Other new spaces are designed to foster collaborative,
active and technology-enabled learning. When faced with these new spaces,
many teaching staff continue to teach as they have always taught, and as
they had been taught. For many, that means lecturing, in spite of the new
spaces not providing the most appropriate structure for a lecture. Even
when teaching staff endeavour to incorporate more active and collaborative
learning activities for their students, the results may not lead to the
intended student outcomes. To be effective, learning activities in any learning space need to be underpinned by pedagogy.

The authors of this chapter are Australian and the chapter is written
from an Australian perspective. However, our reading of the international
literature suggests that the discussion in this chapter is relevant to other
countries. Universities across the world have invested billions of dollars in
the building of next generation learning spaces. The reasons for this investment are multifaceted and as unique as each university context. We can
infer that in some cases, the investment is prompted by the belief that such
infrastructure will:

- foster the university's reputation as 'cutting edge';

- give the university a competitive edge in attracting students;
- support the university to teach increased student numbers; and
- support the university to cope with tight funding situations.

If next generation learning spaces are to deliver on these expectations, the learning and teaching activities conducted in them need to engage students and be tailored to help them achieve intended learning outcomes.

In devising best practice in the use of these spaces we argue that it is time to revisit some powerful learning theories and consider some more contemporary ones. We take key elements of these learning theories, using the term 'learning theory' generously to refer to circumstances of learning as well as how we learn, and determine their implications for teaching practice, and for what makes for a rich and effective learning environment. We then identify and describe sector drivers and constraints that influence the design of next generation learning spaces in universities and consider the implications for teachers and learners utilising the spaces. From the theories, the drivers and the constraints, we derive a pedagogic framework for use in next generation learning spaces.

SOME PEDAGOGIC UNDERPINNINGS

We start with theories that we see as particularly pertinent to fostering learning and then move on to their application to next generation learning spaces in the current context. The established learning theories of constructivism and situated learning, along with connectivism and complexity theory, are employed in this chapter as the basis of a pedagogic framework that can underpin learning and teaching practices in these spaces. These learning theories, which are well accepted in the sector, have a lot to offer teachers who are teaching in these spaces.

Constructivist Understandings of Learning and Connectivism

Constructivism hypothesises that learners construct knowledge when information is assimilated with existing knowledge developed on the basis of the learner's previous experiences. There are two broad schools of thought: social constructivism and cognitive constructivism. *Social constructivists* hypothesise that knowledge is first constructed in a social context and then assimilated by individuals (Palincsar, 1998; Vygotsky, 1978). Learning is an active, social process, which these days may involve a virtual rather than physical social presence. The *cognitive form of constructivism*, associated with the work of Piaget in the case of children (Piaget, 1968) and Williams in the case of higher education (Perry, 1999), does not necessarily involve social interaction but it too proposes that learning needs to be active. In both cases teaching and learning activities need to be student-centred in the sense of relating to and building on the existing understanding, values and abilities of students; understandings that may vary between students.

Connectivism, 'a learning theory for the digital age' (Siemens, 2005, p. 1) can be seen to share some of the understandings of social constructivism. It postulates that learning occurs through a network of connections between learning communities or nodes. Both the networks and the information available are dynamic. The learner's understanding of a subject and ability to learn about it change over time (Kop & Hill, 2008).

In this context, where learning activities are conducted in next generation learning spaces they need to be active and interactive between student and teacher or student and student and not bounded by the perimeters of the space but allowing connection and input from the outside world. (However solid the walls of these spaces may appear to be, supplied devices and student-owned devices penetrate them.) Collaborative learning activities, co-learning and peer feedback are underpinned by these theories.

These understandings of student learning then require more than exposure to information. Students can readily access more or less pertinent materials from the Internet. To achieve desired learning outcomes in higher education we are looking for more than pertinent information; we are looking for critical reflection, one of the big challenges of the virtual learning environment where information appears limitless. Connectivism looks for more than '... the ability to seek out current information'; it also involves '... the ability to filter secondary and extraneous information' (Kop & Hill, 2008, p. 1). Careful choice of sources and specifying their authority is part of the task. Using sources such as Wikipedia is good for providing informed, reviewed conventional wisdom but quoting slabs from Wikipedia falls short of demonstrating assimilation and learning at a high level. From a constructivist approach we are looking for meaningful connections with the students' existing understanding that add to their understanding or challenge it. Either way we are looking for a personalised appreciation. This might be demonstrated by students re-expressing information in their own words, providing their own interpretation, illustrating from their own experiences, providing their own metaphors, evaluating examples, and the like.

We are also looking for critical engagement, which can mean different things for different disciplines (Dunworth, Drury, Kralik, & Moore, 2013). It can mean following the academic norms, rules and procedures for the particular discipline. In general terms it is to engage in reasonable and reflective thinking in deciding what to believe (Ennis, 1987). It requires questioning – I see what this article says; should I believe it? What are its underlying assumptions and values? What is the evidence or authority for its assertions? From a cognitive constructivist point of view questioning might include – how does this relate to what I knew before I came across this material? and how do its underlying assumptions/values relate to my assumptions/values? This involves something akin to the processes adopted in educating students about avoiding plagiarism; making it their own and relating it to their previous knowledge, skill and values.

The role of the teacher, rather than being the provider of all wisdom, which is an impossibility in the information age, is to facilitate a process of learning in which students are encouraged to be responsible and autonomous, making their own connections to information sources and making new learning their own. 'Flipping the classroom' has become a popular term (Tenneson & McGlasson, 2006); making learners rather than the teacher the centre of attention. With students at the centre there can be multiple sources of learning including online resources and interaction with peers. In this context both peers and teachers can be seen as co-learners, assisting in the construction of meaning. Teacher-student interaction can include 'cognitive apprenticeship' (Brown, Collins, & Duguid, 1989) where a teacher acts as a learning model for students and a source of feedback. Cognitive constructivists theorise that feedback is important to the development of skills and knowledge (Derry, 1996). Feedback can reinforce attainment of desired learning outcomes and assist students to reconstruct misunderstandings or inappropriate responses. Social constructivism, which involves construction of meaning from interaction with others, also points to the value of feedback.

Situated Learning and Complexity Theory

Learning occurs in a physical space, even online learning, not cyber space but earthly space, wherever you are located at the time. Spaces can be more or less conducive to learning and to the students learning preferences (some like silence, some like sound and even video operating as they study). Spaces can be seen as coming with 'locational capital' (Temple, 2009,

p. 209) that can relate to learning. Lecture theatres and classrooms have locational capital related to learning and indeed identified with particular forms of learning. Your home study or the chair and desk in your bedroom can also have locational capital relating to your learning (Kahu, 2013). This role of space and place in learning makes situated learning theory pertinent.

Situated learning theories see learning as situated in the activity and the social and physical context in which it takes place (Lave & Wenger, 1991). While this has been taken to imply that meaningful learning will only take place if it is embedded in the social and physical context within which it will be used, in the age of simulation, situated learning can take place in crafted learning spaces provided it involves authentic learning tasks and the provision of a rich learning environment with appropriate learning resources and opportunities for social interaction. Rich learning environments can involve learning through social interaction but they can also provide for learning through interaction with material elements of the environment such as laboratory and other equipment.

Authentic, rich learning environments can include things such as in-situ work experience, field trips and other environments that involve the complexities and the distractions of real-life situations. In these complex environments some of what is learnt may be tangential to what was intended. Rich learning environments can also be contrived in learning spaces such as studios, laboratories and workshops. They can be provided through activities such as role-plays and interaction with peers, models and/or mentors. Authentic learning tasks involve tasks sustained over time, complex and linked rather than short term, disconnected learning tasks (Herrington & Herrington, 2006). Technology may be used to bring industry/ community/other students into the classroom (e.g. watching live surgeries, working with students from other universities on projects). Learning in a rich learning environment is more readily applied to the world beyond university than is fragmented learning isolated from the complexities of the world.

Lest situated learning be seen as a product of the last century, the idea of using rich learning environments could be seen to have some alignment with 21st century *complexity theory* '… a theory of change, often in the interests of survival' (Morrison, 2006, p. 1). Universities, as Ronald Barnett observes, now operate in a world of 'supercomplexity' of 'intellectual, cognitive and value mayhem' where the challenge for university teaching is to develop '… the capacity to cope, prosper and delight in a world in which there are no universals … instead of knowing the world, being-in-the-world has to take the primary place in the conceptualisations that inform university teaching' (Barnett, 2005, pp. 794–795). It is therefore important to provide learning and teaching environments that would be in empathy with complexity theory and include '... non-linear and holistic approaches, in which relations within interconnected networks are the order of the day' (Morrison, 2006, p. 1). Learning situated in a rich and complex environment fits with this idea. Among approaches to learning and teaching said to be implied by complexity theory are promoting connectivity and creativity among the students and staff, inquiring critically into our own understandings of learning and teaching, and seeking ways of valuing emergent learning and encouraging education '... at the edge of chaos' (Tosey, 2013, p. 1). Again this has something in common with situated learning tenets but pushes the boundaries further and makes the outcomes of the learning encounter less predictable.

Adopting situated learning approaches or those aligned to complexity theory in new learning spaces is challenging where desired learning outcomes are prescribed. The teaching challenges in a rich learning environment include *focusing learning*, selection of resources, encouraging *critical engagement* and providing for the *application* of knowledge and skills. In rich learning environments students may need to be assisted to *selectively engage* with relevant resources from the possibilities available in the learning space and beyond. Ensuring focus involves making clear to students the desired learning outcomes and how they are to be assessed. Part of the teacher's role is to provide scaffolding for student learning, for example by questioning or providing prompts, guides or templates. A marking rubric may assist students to focus.

DRIVERS AND CONSTRAINTS IN THE DEVELOPMENT AND USE OF NEXT GENERATION LEARNING SPACES

In this chapter we are working toward providing a framework to guide pedagogical practice in next generation learning spaces. Before we get to that point we identify pertinent features of the current context of higher education provision, including the design of physical spaces.

What makes some newly constructed learning and teaching accommodation worthy of the tag 'next generation learning spaces' is design based on contemporary understandings of how students learn. Other chapters in this book provide some instances. These chapters describe learning spaces that are designed to foster individual and collaborative learning; learning hubs that facilitate group work around projects; spaces equipped to simulate learning in rich, complex environments; and spaces that facilitate access to global resources and internet communications. So one of the key drivers of next generation learning spaces then is their design for learning.

Below we identify other sector level drivers that may or may not align with contemporary understandings of effective learning and teaching activities. As well as university level interests, sector-wide factors that have both driven and constrained the development, design and use of next generation learning spaces, include: changes in learning mode; technological developments; increased participation rates; and expectations about outcomes, academic standards and graduate employability.

Modes of Learning

In many universities students now have access to fully online programs that allow them to access the learning environment at a time and place of their choosing. Online learning options more recently include Massive Open Online Courses (MOOCs), which may be taken to support study or as an introduction to particular programs. MOOCs have been the centre of speculation since 2012, with some articles suggesting that they would change the nature of education and result in the reduction of universities to a handful in any one country (Marginson, 2012). While there may be a perception that the MOOC approach will cater for increased student numbers, not all students are likely to be able to succeed through MOOCs alone. From a pedagogic perspective, the curriculum design of mass or tailored online learning is critical if they are to be more than an information 'dump' and if they are to assist learners to construct knowledge.

Over the last decade, the sector has moved to providing students with blended learning curricula which offer flexibility in terms of access and participation (just in time, just for me learning environments). Through blended learning, programs offer students the opportunity to study intensively in a face-to-face mode, online from a distance, in work-based and community settings, in overseas environments, and through traditional classroom attendance. Arguably, while some fully online education has a place within universities, a blended learning approach that includes face-to-face learning and teaching opportunities provides the best scope for engaging and retaining students (Kitchenham, 2011; Moskal, Dziuban, & Hartman, 2013).

Online learning options, including blended learning and MOOCs, draw attention to the need to design and use next generation learning spaces for what face-to-face student-student and student-teacher encounters offer, namely interactions and communications enriched by features and dynamics of physical presence which are hard to replicate at a distance. Experiential learning, group work and collaborative learning may be undertaken online but the dynamics are not the same. Indeed the nature of the space occupied in itself is likely to influence teacher and student behaviours (Keppell, 2012; Oblinger, 2005; Savin-Baden, 2008).

Let us turn from technologies employed to provide learning online to those used in learning spaces.

Technology

A key technology driver that influences the design of next generation learning spaces is the continual change in technology. Technology is always in transition and as such, a lesson learnt from the literature is the importance of future-proofing spaces in terms of the technology used in the space. Today's technology is out of date virtually as soon as it is purchased. In part, recent approaches to future-proof these spaces have focused on using technology that students bring to the spaces (currently lap tops, phones, tablets) (Souter, Riddle, Sellers, & Keppell, 2011). The assumptions underpinning this approach are that: (1) all or most students will have the devices, (2) that students are likely to keep their own technology relatively up to date, and (3) that the cost for the technology transfers from the university to the student.

One ironic consequence of some new technology is that its use in next generation learning spaces can lead to a reversion to old teaching methods. New lecture theatres with automated video recording, a fixed podium, microphone, and presentation screen raise the expectation for teachers and students alike of a presentation by an expert. How does this design square with sound learning and teaching practice? Using this approach, we may well design next generation learning spaces around the available 'educational' technologies rather than adopting design influenced by understandings of effective student learning activities in face-to-face settings. The learning theories that we considered before suggest that the design of NGLS needs to be learning-centred and supported by appropriate technologies rather than designed in response to presentation and recording technologies.

Increased Participation in Higher Education

In Australia, as in many countries, there has been a large increase in the number of students participating in higher education over the last decade. Between 2005 and 2010 the number of students in Australian higher education rose by approximately 25 per cent (Australia Bureau of Statistics, 2012, p. 443). In 2012 the Australian government removed limits on enrolment in university undergraduate places aiming for 40 per cent of 25–34 year olds to have a bachelor degree or higher by 2025 (Grattan Institute, 2013). Participation rates for school leavers aged between 17 and 19 years and for people in their twenties doubled between 1982 and 2010. These younger students incidentally often bring with them particular expectations about communication technologies (Duncan-Howell, 2012).

Government initiatives have particularly targeted an increase in participation of students from lower socio-economic groups, who have been under-represented in higher education – the Higher Education Participation and Partnerships Program. To retain and progress an increasingly diverse student cohort requires systematic and purposeful efforts on the part of universities. As a result there has been a corresponding need for the educators, curricula and student support services to engage students and foster retention. In this context next generation learning spaces have a particular role to play in student retention. They can provide an environment that engages students. A review of informal learning spaces for science students at the University of Queensland found that students who used these spaces demonstrated higher levels of engagement compared to those students who did not use these spaces (Matthews, Andrews, & Adams, 2011). Engagement has been shown to be of particular importance to first-year students and to students who are under-prepared for higher education (Carini, Kuh, & Klein, 2006). Providing students with the opportunity to work collaboratively with their peers on authentic and meaningful projects, a possibility afforded in many next generation learning spaces, aligns with social constructivism and situated learning theory and has been shown to be related to the engagement and the retention of students (Krause & Coates, 2008).

There can be a tension between providing spaces that can accommodate increased student numbers and providing spaces that facilitate the most productive learning experiences for students. Building bigger lecture theatres to accommodate the increase in student numbers, even high-tech ones, may not encourage collaboration, active learning, or learning experiences tailored to the individual needs. Such new learning spaces do not ensure engagement and may have the opposite effect. Responses to increasing student numbers, however, have to be pragmatic. While student numbers are rising, funds available to Australian universities have failed to keep pace. Student to staff ratios are rising (Ross, 2013; University of Melbourne, 2011). As we indicate in our discussion of appropriate pedagogies above, creative approaches to design and/or imaginative teaching and learning activities in the spaces provided are needed, if students are to be engaged and attain learning outcomes that go beyond the ability to recall information.

Outcomes Expectations

The higher education sector is expected to develop graduates who can demonstrate higher order knowledge and skills and apply that knowledge and skill set. As indicated below some learning and teaching approaches serve this end better than others. Next generation learning spaces can play a significant role in fostering the development of these valued learning outcomes. In this section, in the next generation learning space context we discuss both the Australian Qualification Framework and graduate attributes and employability skills.

Academic Standards

What is higher about higher education? If we refer back to Bloom's taxonomy of the 1950s (Bloom, Englehart, Furst, Hill, & Krathwohl, 1956) or more recent versions (such as Anderson & Krathwohl, 2001), higher education can be said to be concerned with more than knowledge and comprehension. In the cognitive domain it targets learning outcomes involving application, analysis, synthesis, and evaluation. In the affective domain it might involve organising and characterising, and in the psychomotor domain higher education might involve complex responses, adaptation and origination. This has implications for the design and use of next generation learning spaces if higher education students are to be given the opportunity to *practice* these domains in a learning and teaching environment rather than only learning about them. Expectations that higher education involves higher level learning outcomes have been reinforced by national and international attempts to distinguish levels of educational qualifications. The Bologna Process in Europe provides the most significant international instance (Bologna Secretariat, 2010), while the Australian Qualifications Framework provides an Australian example.

In 1995 the Australian Qualifications Framework (AQF) was introduced to '... underpin the national system of qualifications in Australia encompassing higher education, vocational education and training and schools' (Australian Qualifications Framework Council, 2013, p. 9). The framework is designed to achieve many objectives including supporting the provision of '... contemporary, relevant and nationally consistent qualification outcomes which build confidence in qualifications' (Australian Qualifications Framework Council, 2013, p. 9). In 2011 the AQF was revised to define the '... relative complexity and depth of achievement and the autonomy required of graduates to demonstrate that achievement' at each of the 10 AQF levels (Australian Qualifications Framework Council, 2013, p. 11). At bachelor degree level graduates are expected to be able to:

- analyse and evaluate information and generate and transmit solutions to unpredictable and sometimes complex problems;
- have well-developed cognitive, technical and communication skills to select and apply methods and technologies; and
- demonstrate autonomy, well-developed judgement and responsibility and be able to transmit knowledge, skills and ideas to others.

Higher level awards have higher expectations of student learning outcomes. Next generation learning spaces then need to facilitate learning activities commensurate with these requirements. They also need to accommodate curricula that increase the employability of our graduates.

Employability
For over 20 years, industry and business in Australia, the United Kingdom and the United States of America have regularly commented on the skills deficits of university graduates (Business Council of Australia (BCA), 2011; Business Industry & Higher Education Collaboration Council (BIHECC), 2007). 'In 2011 the Australian Business Higher Education Round Table (BHERT) conducted a series of industry-based round tables where employers repeatedly referred to deficits in teamwork, problem-solving, and communication skills, while acknowledging that these skills are essential for leaders and the knowledge economy' (Fraser & Ryan, 2013, p. 93).

Since 1992, Australian universities have been required to develop and assess generic skills through their programs (Fraser & Thomas, 2013). Australian research shows that academics often lack the expertise and confidence to teach broad, generic skills (Barrie, Hughes, & Smith, 2009; Oliver, 2010). More recent research from the Office of Learning and Teaching (OLT) funded *Assessing and Assuring Graduate Learning*

Outcomes (AAGLO) project reveals that often when academics develop programs, they do not refer routinely to generic skills and ethical understandings in the programs nor do they use assessment tasks that more appropriately assess skills and understandings (Crisp, Barrie, Hughes, & Benneson, 2012).

Barrie et al found in 2009 that '… almost all Australian universities currently have some sort of strategic project underway to support the embedding (or integration) of graduate attributes in curriculum' (Barrie et al., 2009, p. 10). The nature of graduate attributes that universities claim to develop has implications for the learning and teaching activities appropriate to university education; they constitute '… an orienting statement of education outcomes used to inform curriculum design and the provision of learning experiences at a university' (Barrie et al., 2009, p. 4). Amongst the most frequently cited graduate attributes of Australian universities are:

- learn both independently and co-operatively;
- take initiative and lead others;
- work collaboratively and network effectively to achieve common goals and to solve problems;
- find and manage information effectively and efficiently;
- practice intellectual curiosity, creativity and critical thinking;
- use information to construct new concepts or create new understandings;
- appreciate the diversity of communication styles employed by individuals from different national and cultural backgrounds; and
- communicate effectively and confidently orally and in written forms.

To date '… though graduate attributes have been enshrined in educational policy … the sector has produced little convincing evidence of authentic curriculum integration or of impact on student learning' (Barrie et al., 2009, p. 9). If universities are to produce graduates with the attributes they espouse, they need to be reflected in the intended learning outcomes specified in the curriculum. Then, taking up the theory of constructive alignment (Biggs & Tang, 2011), there needs to be alignment between the intended outcomes and learning activities as learning is constructed by the activities in which the students engage. While next generation learning spaces are not a panacea to this complex and difficult problem of skill development through higher education programs, they can be designed to foster and assess teamwork, problem-solving and teamwork skills. Drawing on the learning theories discussed above, learning and teaching activities in these spaces should engage students in such things as working collaboratively as well as independently, in working with a diversity of communication styles employed by individuals from different national and cultural backgrounds, in finding and managing information and using it to construct new concepts or create new understandings. Learning activities of this sort stand in contrast to passive activities such as listening to lectures, reading Powerpoint slides and taking notes.

These then are some of the drivers and constraints that influence the development, design and use of next generation learning spaces. We turn next to developing a guide or framework for good practice in learning and teaching in next generation learning spaces.

IMPLICATIONS OF DRIVERS AND LEARNING THEORIES FOR PEDAGOGY IN NEXT GENERATION LEARNING SPACES

Next generation learning spaces in higher education institutions can be designed to assist students to attain desired, usually specified, learning *outcomes*. Providing the rich learning environments that situated learning theory suggests can assist students to build on their previous experiences and develop knowledge and skills as constructivist learning theories claim but to what end? Learning outcomes from rich learning environments are likely to be diverse and divergent. This contrasts with the convergence of traditional approaches that are designed to focus learning and produce the same, possibly sophisticated but nevertheless the same, learning outcomes in students. Sometimes we are looking for development of knowledge, skills and propensities specific to academic disciplines and/or professional competencies. Sometimes we are looking for originality and/or creativity as a learning outcome but within a specified frame of reference.

Whether convergent or divergent outcomes are the aim of our discussion of understandings of learning can help us to identify pedagogic approaches appropriate to next generation learning spaces. From constructivist and situated learning understandings we can say that learning environments need to foster activities that are *student-centred* in the sense of allowing students to relate information, values and skills to their existing understandings, values and skills, thereby *making meaning* for themselves. Higher education learning spaces need to allow students to be active and interactive, in rich and *challenging* learning environments in a way that is focused, *selective* and *critical*. *Active learning* may involve *application* – applying understandings in practice, reinforcing and potentially extending learning. To promote active learning is not to say that activity equals learning or at least learning related to intended learning outcomes. Achieving intended learning outcomes requires the careful design of and monitoring of activities on the part of the teacher. It involves provision of guidance and *feedback* on the part of the teacher. On the part of the learner it involves reflection and connection. Van Note Chism (2002) argued that to facilitate *connected*, active learning in a *social* context, we need to develop a range of spaces (also identified as a 'desperate' need by Souter et al., 2011):

• where small groups could meet to work on projects;
• for whole-class dialogue;
• where technology can be accessed easily;
• for displaying ideas and working documents;
• that can accommodate movement and noise; and
• include spill over spaces in corridors and lobbies (Van Note Chism, 2002).

In summary, constructivism and connectivism suggest that pedagogic practice needs to be student-centred and encourage individual connections and meaning making through challenging social and active learning opportunities about which timely and targeted feedback is provided.

Situated learning and complexity theory suggests the desirability of rich learning environments with a freedom to explore. The role of the teacher here is to focus learning on desired outcomes, and encourage selective and critical engagement. To promote higher order cognitive functions, students need to be able to apply their learning in new situations. Based on this understanding, we have developed a pedagogic framework for learning and teaching design in next generation learning spaces (Table 1).

Table 1. A Pedagogic Framework for Use in Next Generation Learning Spaces.

Learning Spaces Need to Provide	Learning Activities Need to Be	Learning Activities Need to Involve	Learning Activities Need to Facilitate
Rich learning environments that reflect the real world so are: • Authentic • Complex and use technology appropriately	Student-centred Focused and outcome oriented Connected Challenging and facilitate individual meaning making	Active learning Social interaction Provision of guidance and feedback	Selective engagement Critical engagement Application

USE AND ABUSE OF NEXT GENERATION LEARNING SPACES

Research indicates that there is a relationship between the nature of the space teachers who are assigned to teach in and the teaching activities in which they engage (Keppell, 2012; Oblinger, 2005; Savin-Baden, 2008). Some next generation learning spaces have design elements including break out rooms, or break out areas within the space, and monitors on walls that several students can use simultaneously and that allow students to log into the same document and contribute to its development. These spaces are designed for student–student interaction. Some spaces utilise design elements such as simulations, virtual work places, and one way glass that facilitate role-plays. These spaces are designed as rich learning environments with potential for students to learn from interaction with elements in the space.

Some new learning spaces appear to be designed for presentation, designed around what could be called the iterative theory of learning, that is if the teacher has presented it the students have learnt it. We couldn't find a current educational theorist who supports this understanding of how students learn. With this approach to design, the pedagogic principles discussed earlier in this chapter suggest misusing new learning spaces, that is using them in a way that runs counter to the design. As observed above, some technology-equipped learning spaces are designed for presentation and recording of presentations. They tie the teacher to the podium where controls for slide projection, microphones and lighting are housed. Their layout conveys to both teachers and learners an expectation of delivery via presentation. In ages past where the teacher was the font of all knowledge and means of communication were limited to the spoken word this may have been appropriate. The invention of the printing press provided other avenues to learning. In the current era where information is everywhere, and where lecture notes and PowerPoint slides are available online, where 'declarative knowledge is now supplemented or even supplanted by knowing where knowledge can be found' (Wheeler, 2012, p. 1), face-to-face learning spaces need to be used for what face-to-face situations are good for – interaction and response.

There are possibilities for active learning even in a large lecture theatre. Students can be given a little time to problem solve and to share their solutions with their immediate neighbours. This calls for a pre-arranged cue to end the activity and return to a focus on the teacher. A portable microphone can allow the teacher to engage with selected students in a large class though this becomes a bit problematic where classes are video recorded. Document cameras can be used to display a student contribution. Clickers can allow students to predict solutions, generating expectations that build on their current understandings. The use of clickers can create an interest in the answer. This needs to be followed up with appropriate explanation so that students can construct their understanding and reconstruct their misunderstanding. Clickers can also allow teachers to assess student understanding and misconceptions and target learning needs. Some adaptation of design for large numbers can provide for interaction and response. For instance providing two rows of swivel seats per tier in lecture theatres allows for the temporary formation of groups of four to six to discuss issues, share experiences, solve problems and raise questions.

Of course, as we observed in the introduction to the chapter, some teachers, perhaps scheduled for the space rather than there by choice, will attempt to take a presentational approach in next generation learning spaces that are designed for collaborative, active and technology-enabled learning. The discussion above suggests that teachers should choose teaching activities informed by current learning theories and their own understandings of their students and how their students best learn. For some teachers this is easier said than done and provision of appropriate professional development for teaching staff, as addressed in Chapters 10 and 11 is important here.

CONCLUSION

Our task in this chapter was to develop a framework to guide learning and teaching practice in next generation learning spaces. While this has been our focus, our discussion of uses and appropriate abuses of these spaces carries an implication for their design as well as their use. Some next generation learning spaces are designed simply to accommodate large student numbers. We understand the imperative but our discussion of learning theory suggests it is desirable, even in spaces for large student numbers, to develop a design that allows opportunities for students to reflect and make their own meaning from the information.

We have identified drivers in the design and creation of next generation learning spaces and implications for the use of space arising from contemporary understandings of how students best learn. The drivers include a desire to provide for effective learning activities in a dynamic social environment. In some cases, however, technology takes the reins rather than learning. In other cases the driver is a means of providing for increased student numbers without a commensurate increase in teaching staff. This driver may not involve design informed by understandings of how students best learn. The use of next generation learning spaces is likely to be determined by teachers' understandings of the teaching task, which can range from provision of information by a teacher to an appreciation that students need to build on or challenge their existing understandings through interaction with teachers, students and other elements of their social, physical and virtual environment. This calls for the use of pedagogically designed next generation learning spaces in sympathy with their design and the adaptation of those spaces that are currently focused on presentation, to provide an effective learning environment.

REFERENCES

Anderson, L. W., Krathwohl, D. R., Airasian, P., Cruikshank, K., Mayer, R., Pintrich, P., ... Wittrock, M. (Eds.). (2001). *A taxonomy for learning, teaching, and assessing: A revision of bloom's taxonomy of educational objectives.* Boston, MA: Allyn & Bacon (Pearson Education Group).

Australia Bureau of Statistics. (2012). *Year book Australia* (Vol. 92). Canberra: Commonwealth of Australia.

Australian Qualifications Framework Council. (2013). *Australian qualifications framework.* Retrieved from http://www.aqf.edu.au

Barnett, R. (2005). Recapturing the universal in the university. *Educational Philosophy and Theory, 37*(6), 785–797.

Barrie, S., Hughes, C., & Smith, C. (2009). *The national graduate attributes project: Integration and assessment of graduate attributes in curriculum report.* Sydney: Australian Learning and Teaching Council.

Biggs, J., & Tang, C. (2011). *Teaching for quality learning at university* (4th ed.). Buckingham: Open University Press/McGraw-Hill.

Bloom, B. S., Englehart, M. D., Furst, E. J., Hill, W. H., & Krathwohl, D. R. (1956). *Taxonomy of educational objectives: Handbook 1: Cognitive domain.* New York, NY: David McKay.

Bologna Secretariat, B. (2010). *Towards the European higher education area: Bologna process.* Retrieved from http://www.ond.vlaanderen.be/hogeronderwijs/bologna/

Brown, J. S., Collins, A., & Duguid, P. (1989). Situated cognition and the culture of learning. *Educational Researcher, 18*(1), 32–42.

Brown, M., & Lippincott, J. K. (2003). Learning spaces: More than meets the eye. *EDUCAUSE Quarterly, 26*(1), 14–16.

Business Council of Australia (BCA). (2011). *Lifting the quality of teaching and learning in higher education.* Retrieved from http://www.bca.com.au/Content/101818.aspx

Business Higher Education Round Table (BHERT). (2011). *Business/finance round table 2.* Retrieved from http://www.bhert.com/activities/2011-banking-finance-round-table-2

Business Industry and Higher Education Collaboration Council (BIHECC). (2007). *Graduate employability skills.* Retrieved from http://www.dest.gov.au/NR/rdonlyres/E58EFDBE-BA83-430E-A541-2E91BCB59DF1/20214/GraduateEmployabilitySkillsFINALREPORT1.pdf

Carini, R., Kuh, G., & Klein, S. (2006). Student engagement and student learning: Testing the linkages. *Research in Higher Education, 47*, 1–33.

Crisp, G., Barrie, S., Hughes, C., & Benneson, A. (2012). How can I tell if I'm assessing graduate outcomes appropriately? Paper presented at the Higher Education Research and Development Society of Australasia conference, Hobart.

Derry, S. J. (1996). Cognitive schema theory in the constructivist debate. *Educational Psychology, 31*(3–4), 163–174.

Duncan-Howell, J. (2012). Digital mismatch: Expectations and realities of digital competency amongst pre-service education students. *Australasian Journal of Educational Technology, 28*(5), 827–840.

Dunworth, K., Drury, H., Kralik, C., & Moore, T. (2013). The place of English language development in the higher education curriculum. Paper presented at the Higher Education Research and Development Society of Australasia conference, Auckland.

Ennis, R. H. (1987). A taxonomy of critical thinking dispositions and abilities. In J. B. Baron & R. J. Sternberg (Eds.), *Teaching thinking skills: Theory and practice* (pp. 9–26). New York, NY: Freeman/Times Books/Henry Holt & Co.

Fraser, K., & Ryan, Y. (2013). Could MOOCs answer the problems of teaching AQF-required skills in Australian tertiary programmes? *Australian Universities Review, 55*(2), 93–98.

Fraser, K., & Thomas, T. (2013). Challenges of assuring the development of graduate attributes in a Bachelor of Arts. Higher Education Research and Development. *Higher Education Research and Development, 32*(4), 545–560.

Grattan Institute. (2013). *Mapping Australian higher education* (pp. 1–95). Melbourne. Retrieved from http://grattan.edu.au/static/files/assets/28a92f8b/184_2013_mapping_higher_education.pdf

Herrington, T., & Herrington, J. (2006). *Authentic learning environments in higher education.* Hershey, PA: Information Science Publishing.

Higher Education Participation and Partnerships Programme. Retrieved from http://education.gov.au/higher-education-participation-and-partnerships-programme-heppp

Higher Education Supplement. *The Australian.* Retrieved from http://www.theaustralian.com.au/higher-education/student-staff-ratios-continue-to-slide/story-e6frgcjx-1226597873064#

JISC. (2006). *Designing spaces for effective learning: A guide to 21st century learning space design* (pp. 1–36). Retrieved from http://www.jisc.ac.uk/uploaded_documents/JISClearningspaces.pdf

Johnson, C., & Lomas, C. (2005). Design of the learning space: Learning and design principles. *EDUCAUSE Review*, July/August.

Kahu, E. (2013). Engaging in spaces: How mature distance students fit study into their homes and lives. Paper presented at the Higher Education Research and Development Society of Australasia Conference, Auckland.

Keppell, M. (2012). Distributed learning spaces in higher education learning and teaching. Paper presented at the Australian Society for Computers in Learning in Tertiary Education Conference.

Kitchenham, A. (2011). *Blended learning across disciplines: Models for implementation.* Hershey, PA: Information Science Reference.

Kop, R., & Hill, A. (2008). Connectivism: Learning theory of the future or vestige of the past? *The International Review of Research in Open and Distance Learning, 9*(3). Retrieved from http://www.irrodl.org/index.php/irrodl/article/view/523/1103

Krause, K. L., & Coates, H. (2008). Students' engagement in first-year university. *Assessment & Evaluation in Higher Education, 33*(5), 493–505.

Lave, J., & Wenger, E. (1991). *Situated learning: Legitimate peripheral participation.* London: Cambridge University Press.

Lee, N., & Tan, S. (2011). *A comprehensive learning space evaluation model: Final report.* Retrieved from http://www.swinburne.edu.au/spl/learningspacesproject/

Marginson, S. (2012, 12 August). Yes, MOOC is the global higher education game changer. *University World News*. Retrieved from http://www.universityworldnews.com/article. php?story=2012080915084470

Matthews, K. E., Andrews, V., & Adams, P. (2011). Social learning spaces and student engagement. *Higher Education Research & Development, 30*(2), 105–120.

Mitchell, G., White, B., Pospisil, R., Kiley, S., Liu, C., & Matthews, G. (2010). Retrofitting university learning spaces: Final report. Retrieved from http://learnline.cdu.edu.au/ retrofittingunispaces/index.html

Morrison, K. (2006). Complexity theory and education. Paper presented at the Asia-Pacific Education Research Association Conference, Hong Kong. Retrieved from http://edisdat. ied.edu.hk/pubarch/b15907314/full_paper/SYMPO-000004_Keith Morrison.pdf

Moskal, P., Dziuban, C., & Hartman, J. (2013). Blended learning in higher education: Policy and implementation issues. *The Internet and Higher Education, 18*(July), 15–23.

Oblinger, D. (2005). Leading the transition from classrooms to learning spaces. *EDUCAUSE Quarterly, 1*, 14–18.

Oliver, B. (2010). Benchmarking partnerships for graduate employability. ALTC Fellowship report. Retrieved from http://www.olt.gov.au/resource-benchmarking-partnerships-oliver-curtin-2010

Palincsar, A. S. (1998). Social constructivist perspectives on teaching and learning. *Annual Review of Psychology, 49*, 345–375.

Perry, W. G. (1999). *Forms of ethical and intellectual development in the college years*. San Francisco, CA: Jossey-Bass.

Piaget, J. (1968). *Six psychological studies New York*. New York, NY: Vintage Books.

Ross, J. (2013, 16 March). Staff-student ratios continue to slide.

Savin-Baden, M. (2008). *Learning spaces: Creating opportunities for knowledge creation in academic life*. Maidenhead: Open University Press/McGraw-Hill.

Siemens, G. (2005). Connectivism: A learning theory for the digital age. *International Journal of Instructional Technology and Distance Learning, 2*(1). Retrieved from http://www. itdl.org/Journal/Jan_05/article01.htm

Souter, K., Riddle, M., Sellers, W., & Keppell, M. (2011). The spaces for knowledge generation: Final report. Retrieved from http://www.olt.gov.au/resource-spaces-knowledge-generation-framework-designing-student-learning-environments-future-2011

Temple, P. (2009). From space to place: University performance and its built environment. *Higher Education Policy, 22*, 209–223.

Tenneson, M., & McGlasson, R. (2006). The classroom flip [PowerPoint Presentation]. Retrieved from http://www.fontbonne.edu/upload/TheClassroomFlip.ppt

Tosey, P. (2013). *Complexity theory: A perspective on education* (pp. 1–10). Retrieved from http://www.heacademy.ac.uk/assets/documents/resources/database/id53_complexity_theory_a_perspective_on_education.pdf

University of Melbourne. (2011). *Higher education base funding review submission*. Retrieved tpfrom http://www.unimelb.edu.au/publications/docs/uom-base-funding-submission-2011.pdf

Van Note Chism, N. (2002). A tale of two classrooms. *New Directions for Teaching and Learning, 92*, 5–12.

Vygotsky, L. (1978). *Mind in society*. London: Harvard University Press.

Wheeler, S. (2012). *Theories for the digital age: Connectivism*. Retrieved from http://steve-wheeler.blogspot.com.au/2012/10/theories-for-digital-age-connectivism.html

CHAPTER 5

ASSESSMENT IN NEXT GENERATION LEARNING SPACES

Geoffrey T. Crisp

ABSTRACT

This chapter will explore how assessment might look in next generation learning spaces where we have the potential to merge physical and virtual activities. Students now have ready access to a world of resources within their classroom and this fundamentally changes the nature of learning and assessment. The trend toward gamification of learning and assessment will be examined and the issue of assessment in new educational environments such as MOOCs will be explored. The impact of the semantic web (Web 3.0), where web objects and their context are all linked and objects have memory of how an individual student used them on previous occasions, will be discussed.

Next generation learning spaces encapsulate the affordances of both physical and virtual spaces and yet many assessment tasks are still designed as if students occupied only one of these spaces. Teachers will need to design more authentic, meaningful tasks that will engage students in using the full range of their capabilities and available resources, both physical and virtual. Students come together physically to engage in the social construction of their knowledge and can use the virtual spaces to broaden the social dimension of their learning environment.

The Future of Learning and Teaching in Next Generation Learning Spaces
International Perspectives on Higher Education Research, Volume 12, 85–100
Copyright © 2014 by Emerald Group Publishing Limited
All rights of reproduction in any form reserved
ISSN: 1479-3628/doi:10.1108/S1479-362820140000012009

Gamification of learning and assessment will require new approaches to defining tasks as teachers will need to decide how to incorporate diagnostic, formative, and summative assessment components within a more holistic educational environment. Game theory will be blended with learning theory in curriculum design and will result in the redesign of learning and assessment activities that are based on engagement (flow), user needs, and an evidence-centered design approach.

Keywords: Assessment; gamification; semantic web; MOOC

LEARNING, ASSESSMENT AND SPACE

Introduction

Teachers and students now have available a wide variety of new web tools that support global social networking and the ability to undertake personal publishing using mixed media formats; minimal technical knowledge is usually required for students or teachers to use many of these new opportunities. Wikipedia demonstrated that knowledge can be co-constructed, shared freely and openly critiqued, rather than being created by a small group of specialists and subjected to restricted peer review and access. The current Internet is referred to as Web 2.0 and consists of participatory engagement with an underlying philosophy of collaboration and social interaction (Bennett, Bishop, Dalgarno, Waycott, & Kennedy, 2012). Traditional assessment models, based on the student as an isolated individual with limited access to resources, are not appropriate for this new environment that is open, collaborative, cooperative, and distributed with access to almost unlimited resources.

Next generation learning spaces (NGLS) have most often been associated with physical spaces that are augmented with technology so as to enhance the learning opportunities for students (Brooks, 2012). Recent approaches to describing NGLS have also prompted the review of the learning activities that take place within these spaces and whether these activities can effectively deliver on the community expectations for a 21st century higher education (Keppell, Souter, & Riddle, 2012). This review of current educational practices and questioning whether they can deliver an appropriate experience for our students has prompted a rethinking of how we use our current learning spaces and the relationship between those spaces and the teaching and assessment approaches adopted by staff. Changing the physical space can promote changes in approaches to teaching (Woolner, McCarter, Wall, & Higgins, 2012). Rather than lecture halls filled with seats in neat rows being the predominant physical learning space, NGLS promote the mixing of the physical and virtual, with both individual and group learning, and a blended mobile presence that facilitates the personal engagement of each student with the learning process.

Although the relationship between spaces and learning has been seen as increasingly important, the same level of interest has not been shown for the relationship between spaces and assessment. Despite a generally held belief that assessment drives approaches to learning (Biggs, 1999), there has been little attention paid to the need to reimagine assessment in NGLS (Crisp, 2012).

Elliott (2008) proposed the term Assessment 2.0 to describe the characteristics of tasks that use the affordances of the virtual space. These characteristics include:

- authenticity through the use of real-world knowledge and skills;
- personalization through being tailored to the knowledge, skills and interests of each student;
- active student participation through negotiated task setting;
- depth as the tasks are holistic and not just based on content knowledge;
- collaborative as group tasks are often used; and
- reflective as they make use of self- and peer-review.

These characteristics have much in common with a number of the assessment characteristics proposed by Boud and Associates (2010) and the use of NGLSs should facilitate many of the reforms proposed for current assessment practices.

Universities are striving to enhance the student experience and students' educational outcomes. Both these aspirations will be dependent on a multitude of factors, including the alignment of physical and virtual spaces, the design of the curriculum and its effective delivery, and the engagement of the student at both the cognitive and social level. The interplay between these factors is often synergistic with the student remaining as the focus of the activities; how a teacher understands this synergistic relationship between these dimensions will determine their approach to teaching and assessment.

Types of Assessment Tasks

Traditional approaches to learning tended to concentrate on a behaviorist paradigm; this was eventually replaced with a constructivist approach

(Nichols, 1994) and more recently with an analysis of learning from a neuroscience perspective (Kao, Lin, & Hung, 2013). What is expected from students in terms of assessment responses has become more complex (Crisp, 2012). No longer do we privilege the simple recall of factual (declarative) knowledge with its associated assessment analysis being dichotomous − the response being either correct or incorrect. We require our students to construct complex responses based on their learned strategies to problem solving and creativity. Teachers need to construct assessment tasks that are matched to the more sophisticated requirements of tracking and evidencing complex problem solving abilities and an awareness of the consequences of proposed solutions to complex issues.

Appropriately constructed assessment tasks allow teachers to probe functional (discipline specific) or procedural knowledge (how students perform or how they operate in a given context). The way in which a student approaches an assessment task will often be determined by the reward mechanisms that are put in place by the teacher. How can space influence students' approaches to assessment? Standard assessment tasks encourage standard student responses, so the teacher needs to design assessment tasks that encourage and reward nonstandard responses. How do NGLS facilitate non-standard approaches to assessment?

NGLS facilitate active engagement with social media and collaborative activities through the presence of personal learning environments (Dabbagh & Kitsantas, 2012). In order for students to be able to tackle assessment tasks that probe functional or procedural knowledge, they need to undertake activities in class that reflect the core concepts of effective approaches to problem solving, engaging productively with others, and having ready access to resources and information in order to probe their level of understanding.

There are three traditional types of assessments, namely diagnostic, formative, and summative. Alternative terms that are sometimes used for these task types are assessment *for*, and assessment *of* learning, as well as the more recent term, assessment *as* learning (Hickey, Taasoobshirazi, & Cross, 2012). In higher education, it has not been routine practice to incorporate diagnostic assessment into the curriculum; yet diagnostic tasks can inform both students and teachers of the current readiness of students to engage with new learning. Diagnostic assessment can be used to test declarative, procedural, and functional knowledge and provides a mechanism for students to update their prior knowledge or skills so they are better prepared to assimilate new concepts or understandings. NGLS that are designed for collaborative student discussions and the use of personal response systems (Stewart & Stewart, 2013) can facilitate the incorporation of diagnostic assessment as a live class activity.

Formative assessment is used to probe current learning and provide of constructive feedback that directs students to appropriate resources. Both teachers and students can use the feedback processes to initiate targeted learning activities that lead to the improvement of newly developed skills, capabilities or strategies for problem solving. NGLS are particularly suited to formative assessment tasks because they facilitate collaborative engagement between students, peer review and feedback and allow students to have ready access to resources and information via the Internet so that they test and refine their skill and knowledge levels.

Summative assessments are designed primarily to grade or judge student's performance for progression or certification purposes; they are most often taken at a stage when no further learning is required for the course being assessed. Clearly there are some overlaps between the different assessment types and teachers often use low stakes summative tasks for formative purposes; the marks or grades being used as an incentive for students to complete the tasks in order to receive the feedback. NGLS can also be used for summative assessment where students use their own devices to access the assessment. There have been a number of interesting developments in testing secure exam scenarios using students' own devices (Fluck, Pullen, & Harper, 2009; Westin, 2012).

Types of Assessment Responses

When reviewing assessment in NGLS, we need to consider the types of responses that students are expected to make to a particular task. Assessment responses are either of a convergent or divergent type (Torrance & Pryor, 2001). Convergent responses are where every student is expected to provide the same response, whereas for divergent responses students may provide different but equally acceptable responses.

There is clearly a relationship between approaches to teaching and the use of NGLS; if teachers are requiring convergent responses then there is little need to provide multiple formats for course delivery as every student is expected to provide the same response and so learning can be packaged in a standardized format. So NGLS would add little value if teachers only required convergent responses from students to assessment tasks. For teachers who are designing tasks requiring divergent responses, it is more likely that the use of NGLS will provide students with a multitude of experiences and access to resources and collaboration, thus encouraging the production of divergent constructed responses. The new affordances associated with Web 2.0 have provided new opportunities for teachers to redesign their assessment tasks so that students' divergent responses can be constructed using new digital tools. This allows students to be more creative and to provide more convincing evidence of deep and holistic learning.

NEXT GENERATION LEARNING SPACES DEMAND NEW APPROACHES TO ASSESSMENT

We will examine some of the recent developments in the virtual space and see how these can be integrated with assessment activities traditionally based on physical spaces. The dominant mode of teaching delivery is still dependent on physical space and our current assessment practices have been developed on this model of delivery. Blended learning models have been incorporated into many teaching approaches in universities and this mode does begin to integrate the affordances of both virtual and physical spaces. The "flipped classroom" approach of teaching is an example of this integrated blended mode (Herreid & Schiller, 2013).

Massive Open Online Courses (MOOCs)

MOOCs have caught the imagination of the community at large since they seem to promise universal access to free higher education; they offer an illusory goal, that of open access to a serious educational experience with minimal entry requirements. The increased media coverage given to MOOCs as both the harbinger of death for traditional universities and a major disruptor to educational practices as we know them (Moore, 2013; Powell & Yuan, 2013) has prompted more discussions about higher education pedagogy in the general community than most of the existing research literature.

Whatever eventuates from the current scramble to offer or use MOOCs, the very concept of free and open access to higher education content, packaged in a way that makes it accessible and engaging for everyone irrespective of prior educational background, will fundamentally change many of the aspects of higher education delivery.

How is assessment undertaken in MOOCs and how would this relate to NGLS? To reflect on this issue, we need to review the different types of

MOOCs. cMOOCs emphasize that learning is enhanced through human connections and uses the social networking potential of the Internet to facilitate the learning experience and a sense of belonging in participants (Clarà & Barberà, 2013). Thus cMOOCs could be used effectively in NGLS with students engaging with each other physically in a classroom and the technology bringing in other students through the MOOC interface. Diagnostic and formative assessment tasks could be delivered via the cMOOC and completed in the NGLS using students who are physically and virtually co-located. xMOOCs on the other hand are designed for massive participation levels and scalability is the predominant paradigm. The content in xMOOCs is meant to be engaging in its own right and designed to move participants from one activity to the next. Social interaction can take place in xMOOCs but the learning activities are usually designed to be individually completed. Thus xMOOCs are less appropriate for NGLS unless the purpose of the activity is to examine and critique MOOCs.

The invigilation of individual contributions to assessment responses is one of the issues under debate in the use of MOOCs within formal qualifications. Synchronous invigilation through webcam technology is now offered through vendors (Kryterion, 2013), and testing centers have been established were students present physically, are authenticated and are invigilated during the testing process. Work is progressing on statistical methods to detect anomalous response patterns from students through the use of item response theory models; this methodology is possible because of the large numbers participating in many MOOCs (Meyer & Zhu, 2013).

MOOC providers are also incorporating methods for automatically assessing text-based responses into their offerings. EdX is using the Automated Essay Scoring (AES) application to assess written assignments and Coursera has promoted the use of a calibrated peer review process, such as UCLA's Calibrated Peer Review™ product (Balfour, 2013). These alternative approaches may be used concurrently, with AES providing formative feedback to students and some form of calibrated peer review being used for summative tasks. Students could use this formative feedback for discussion activities in NGLS where both physically co-located students and virtually co-located students are able to participate effectively.

Semantic Web

Even as teachers come to understand the educational opportunities afforded by the Web 2.0 environment, researchers are developing the semantic web, referred to as Web 3.0 (Jeremić, Jovanović, & Gašević, 2013). The semantic web has the potential to have a profound impact on the design and delivery of educational programs. Semantic technologies add meaning and context (metadata) to web content so that the relationships between objects can be investigated, interpreted, and used by computer algorithms in a predictive manner. A simple example would be when a web site offers the reader suggestions for new content based on past searches or downloads. Much of the current discussion about the semantic web relates to the design of standardized ontologies and the necessity for learning and assessment objects to be made more public and not embedded in password protected institutional learning management systems. The semantic ontology is a shared set of definitions related to a learning or assessment object and the relationships between those definitions (metadata); these features are in a form that is machine processable so that computer algorithms can readily use the metadata to present different objects or responses to participants depending on the previous actions of the participant.

An interesting application of semantic technologies in education is the generation of feedback to open text responses in online tests (Sánchez-Vera, Fernández-Breis, Castellanos-Nieves, Frutos-Morale, & Prendes-Espinosa, 2012). Feedback is generated through the Ontology eLEarning (OeLE) platform that uses ontologies, semantic annotations, natural language processing and semantic similarity functions. The application of these techniques is still experimental, but is modeling the use of the Web Ontology Language (OWL) to learning and assessment objects. In these examples the teacher can define how prescriptive the interpretation of the ontology needs to be in order to provide particular levels of feedback to the student. There is still a way to go with converting these experimental approaches to using online learning and assessment objects with enhanced metadata features so that discipline teachers are able to use them routinely in assessments. It is likely that semantic technologies will be used initially in large-scale standardized testing where the scale will provide useful evidence for the efficacy of their use.

It is still too early to predict how the semantic web will influence assessment in NGLS. However, it is possible to postulate that coupling a much richer form of metadata with web objects will allow more sophisticated uses of those objects in collaborative student activities, especially around the use of peer review and critique. This type of activity is especially useful in developing skills associated with procedural knowledge discussed previously and could be used for formative tasks in NGLS. The semantic web could direct students to specific resources for improving their learning or skill development based on their diagnostic or formative assessment results and the specified learning outcomes for the course. This feedback could be used in synchronous physical sessions and the teacher could plan self-directed learning and assessment tasks that utilized the semantic feedback generated for students.

Remote Laboratories and Field Trips

Web-based laboratories and field trips can be either simulations that involve the manipulation of virtual data or objects, or remote where students manipulate real objects or engage with real physical sites using a web interface. Both formats can be useful as replacements or complements for the use of expensive laboratory equipment or difficult to reach locations. Students can be given access to remote laboratories or field sites where they can download data to their local computer using a remote sensor; students can then use this authentic data in assessment tasks. This is a particularly useful learning space for science and engineering disciplines since access to much of the equipment or field sites may be impossible because of cost or safety reasons. Formatives tasks can be set in NGLS using remote access to either laboratories or field sites and collaborative tasks can be designed for students so that they develop both declarative and procedural knowledge.

Remote laboratories most often use a keyboard for students to manipulate the equipment at the remote location (Azad, Auer, & Harward, 2012). Recent investigations have focused on a more authentic experience for students through the use of gesture-based technologies that allow students to use the natural actions of the hand to manipulate the remote equipment (Maiti, 2013). This approach uses aspects of augmented reality through the use of web cameras to detect real physical motion and software to relay these movements across the Internet to real objects. Such activities could be readily built into NGLS so that students could collaborate with peers in disparate geographical locations.

Geography and environmental studies disciplines could make effective use of remote field trips (Stokes et al., 2012). NGLS facilitate the incorporation of such remote trips into the classroom activity by providing students with wireless connectivity and large display screens so that they can readily access sites fitted with remote cameras. Teachers can design authentic learning and assessment activities by allowing students to access such sites and building them in to the classroom sessions. Additionally, mobile devices with built in cameras and global positioning systems allow students to broadcast from remote locations to their class and allow teachers to connect students in synchronous activities while they are geographically dispersed. Students can use these informal NGLS to collect live data for assessment purposes.

Virtual Worlds

Second Life and Active Worlds represent examples of multiuser online role-plays where students can take on a persona in the form of an avatar and explore an imaginary world and complete tasks set by the teacher (Duncan, Miller, & Jiang, 2012). Activities in virtual worlds usually highlight student performance rather than the accumulation of content knowledge (de Freitas & Neumann, 2009; Richardson & Molka-Danielsen, 2009). Virtual worlds have the potential to facilitate authentic learning and assessment, but for many discipline teachers the new skills that must be learned in order to construct objects in virtual worlds are significant and will often militate against the general use of virtual worlds in the curriculum.

Although virtual worlds can be used for assessments, it is most common to see the student undertaking an activity in the virtual world and then being assessed outside of the virtual world. Recent examples of assessment tools for use within virtual worlds are quizHUD (Bloomfield & Livingstone, 2009) and WorldofQuestions (Ibáñez, Rueda, Morillo, & Kloos, 2012). These tools integrate common selected response questions so that an avatar can respond at key points or locations within the virtual world. The question types are familiar to the student and the assessment tasks are seen as part of the activities within the virtual world. Teachers could use virtual worlds for formative assessment and by displaying the inworld activities on a screen for all students to see, peer feedback could be incorporated into the activity.

A hybrid approach to purely virtual worlds is the use of augmented reality (AR) whereby participants are immersed in an environment that has elements from the real physical world and the digital world (Dunleavy & Dede, 2014). AR uses a physical device such as a head-mounted display or mobile phone to connect the user with the virtual world. This type of NGLS is relatively new and used most often in disciplines such as medicine and engineering, although the appearance of new devices such as Google Glass (Staner, 2013) will likely expand the number of disciplines that incorporate AR into their everyday activities for students. AR can incorporate digital location data, contextual factual information, and historical data onto a real object that is being observed by the student. AR can influence assessment spaces by allowing students to be mobile when undertaking an assessment and use real objects to analyze during the assessment period. Teachers would be able to track student activity in an AR environment and use information on key decisions students made at designated locations as part of the assessment process.

Role-Plays and Scenario-Based Activities

In online role-plays, the student takes on a persona as defined by the teacher and responds to a scenario as that defined persona. The outcomes from a role-play are not usually predetermined even though the teacher may have prescribed the characteristics of the various personas that students take on and the task that is to be undertaken. Role-plays are examples of assessments requiring divergent, constructed responses where students must reflect on the consequences of their decisions. In common with virtual worlds, role-plays tend to assess a student's performance rather than their acquisition of declarative knowledge; role-plays revolve around complex problems that do not have a prescribed solution. Role-plays make use of virtual NGLS but do not necessarily require specialized software; they can be undertaken using any system that has group features such as discussion boards, wikis, blogs, and e-portfolios.

Whereas in a role-play the student takes on a persona and their actions are based on their perceptions of how that persona might act in a particular context, in scenario-based learning the student would normally respond as themselves and act as they believe they should in the context presented. Scenario-Based Learning Interactive (SBLi) allows for the creation and delivery of scenarios for problem-based learning or enquiry-based learning (Norton et al., 2012). Selected response questions can be incorporated into the scenario as well as questions requiring a text response that is later evaluated by the teacher.

Both role-plays and scenario-based learning activities could be used as components of formative assessment tasks where the purpose of the task was to provide opportunities for peer and teacher feedback. Allowing students in remote locations to be synchronously participating in group assessment tasks would be a possibility in NGLSs.

GAMIFICATION OF LEARNING AND ASSESSMENT

Prensky (2001) advocated the more systematic use of computer games in education and training, particularly games for military training, business education and activities for raising social awareness. The use of games in learning and the gamification of learning are not necessarily the same thing. Clearly a game can be designed around the learning outcomes for a course, and game designers can construct a sequence of activities for students to undertake in order to meet those learning outcomes. The gamification of learning does not necessarily mean a game has to be used for the learning activities; what it does imply is that the design principles used for games, such as flow, and the components of games such as storytelling, achievement, decision making and consequences, can all be incorporated into curriculum design and delivery (Cheong, Cheong, & Filippou, 2013). NGLS allow the design principles of games, such as flow, engagement, and formative assessment with direct and timely feedback, to be readily incorporated into learning and assessment activities.

An interesting example of the use of a game to solve real life problems is that of *FoldIt* in which students use a web-based game to learn about protein folding (Farley, 2013). The game is designed for participants of all ages and experience; a background in biochemistry is not required to play the game as the rules of the game have been articulated in non-specialist terms. This game could be used within NGLS for a series of exercises in chemistry or biochemistry where assessment *as* learning is the underlying methodology used to engage students in understanding the concepts associated with protein folding.

If we consider a game-based approach to learning in which the student spends much of their time within an environment that uses a virtual or a social media environment, then the assessment tasks must also be aligned with this approach, otherwise there is a disconnect in the learning and assessment space. The term stealth assessment has been used to describe assessments that are integrated seamlessly into game-like activities used for learning (Shute & Ke, 2012). Embedding formative and summative assessments into game-like experiences using an evidence-centered design approach (Hendrickson, Ewing, Kaliski, & Huff, 2013) would allow teachers to more effectively monitor a student's level of achievement and competency. Well-designed games encourage participants to be totally immersed in completing tasks and progressing through the levels; students do not necessarily realize they are completing assessment tasks and receiving instant feedback that is influencing their strategies that are used to complete the next task in the game. This approach would allow teachers to scaffold the development of skills and competencies required to achieve the learning outcomes of the course. This approach could also be coupled with adaptive assessment principles (Kuo & Wu, 2013) that could present different pathways to the student, depending on their sequential responses to a complex assessment task.

The use of evidence-centered design (ECD) is a core component of the proposed stealth assessment approach (Shute & Ke, 2012). ECD uses a structured approach to assessment design and would allow the affordances of NGLS to be incorporated more systematically into curricula and would provide more convincing evidence of student achievement of learning outcomes and competencies. ECD would support the embedding of diagnostic, formative and summative assessments in a more holistic way into the student's journey through their course. The main drawback for the more widespread use of ECD in all assessments is the cost of implementing a full-scale ECD framework model. For large-scale standardized assessments, ECD is cost effective, but it becomes increasingly costly to apply at the individual teacher or subject level. An approach that may be appropriate is to adapt the design framework of ECD, rather than a full implementation of whole model. The key elements of the framework are the student models, the task models, and the evidence model which are implemented within the assembly model and the presentation model (Rupp, Gushta, Mislevy, & Shaffer, 2010). Incorporating the basic design principles for these components is possible at the subject level and could be implemented within a reasonable workload model for teachers.

One of the key features of games that could be usefully applied to learning and assessment within NGLS is the concept of not interrupting the flow in participant activity. We constantly interrupt flow in teaching; we allow students to undertake some learning, then we administer an assessment and feedback comes much later and in the meantime new learning has been taking place without the benefit of this feedback. Students' responses are always time and space separated in our traditional learning spaces. By redesigning learning activities and assessment tasks so that the flow of student engagement is not interrupted would allow assessment to be seen more from the perspective of assessment as learning, rather than a time and space separated assessment of learning.

CONCLUSION

Assessment will gradually change as teachers incorporate more diagnostic and formative tasks into NGLS; students cannot continue to be treated as isolated individuals, cut-off from access to resources and other people during their assessment tasks. NGLS offer the opportunity to bring the world of digital resources into the face-to-face sessions and connect students both in the classroom and those engaging with their studies from other locations. Educational institutions will need to expand their conception of assessment spaces to include virtual and collaborative spaces created within the web that allow students to construct their responses with access to whatever resources are required to complete authentic tasks. Students will demand more authentic, meaningful tasks that will engage them in using the full range of capabilities they have developed during the learning process, including the knowledge, strategies, behaviors, and collaborations they have developed.

REFERENCES

Azad, A. K. M., Auer, M. E., & Harward, J. (2012). *Internet accessible remote laboratories: Scalable e-learning tools for engineering and science disciplines.* Hershey, PA: IGI Global.

Balfour, S. P. (2013). Assessing writing in MOOCs: Automated essay scoring and calibrated peer review™. *Research & Practice in Assessment, 8,* 40−48.

Bennett, S., Bishop, A., Dalgarno, B., Waycott, J., & Kennedy, G. (2012). Implementing Web 2.0 technologies in higher education: A collective case study. *Computers & Education, 59,* 524−534.

Biggs, J. (1999). *Teaching for quality learning at university.* Buckingham, UK: SRHE and Open University Press.

Bloomfield, P. R., & Livingstone, D. (2009). Immersive learning and assessment with quizHUD. *Computing and Information Systems Journal, 13*(1), 20−26.

Boud, D., & Associates. (2010). *Assessment 2020, seven propositions for assessment reform in higher education.* Retrieved from http://www.uts.edu.au/sites/default/files/Assessment-2020_propositions_final.pdf

Brooks, D. C. (2012). Space and consequences: The impact of different formal learning spaces on instructor and student behavior. *Journal of Learning Spaces, 1*(2).

Cheong, C., Cheong, F., & Filippou, J. (2013). Using design science research to incorporate gamification into learning activities. In J.-N. Lee, J.-Y. Mao, & J. Thong (Eds.), *Pacific Asia conference on information systems 2013,* USA (June 18−22, pp. 1−14). Retrieved from http://aisel.aisnet.org/pacis2013/156

Clarà, M., & Barberà, E. (2013). Learning online: Massive open online courses (MOOCs), connectivism, and cultural psychology. *Distance Education, 34,* 129−136.

Crisp, G. T. (2012). Assessment in virtual learning spaces. In M. Keppell, K. Souter, & M. Riddle (Eds.), *Physical and virtual learning spaces in higher education: Concepts for the modern learning environment* (pp. 199–218). Hershey, PA: IGI Global.

Dabbagh, N., & Kitsantas, A. (2012). Personal learning environments, social media, and self-regulated learning: A natural formula for connecting formal and informal learning. *The Internet and Higher Education, 15*, 3–8.

de Freitas, S., & Neumann, T. (2009). The use of 'exploratory learning' for supporting immersive learning in virtual environments. *Computers & Education, 52*, 343–352.

Duncan, I., Miller, A., & Jiang, S. (2012). A taxonomy of virtual worlds usage in education. *British Journal of Educational Technology, 43*, 949–964.

Dunleavy, M., & Dede, C. (2014). Augmented reality teaching and learning. In J. M. Spector, M. D. Merrill, J. Elen, & M. J. Bishop (Eds.), *Handbook of research on educational communications and technology* (4th ed., pp. 735–745). New York, NY: Springer.

Elliott, R. J. (2008). Assessment 2.0. *International Journal of Emerging Technologies in Learning (iJET), 3*, 66–70.

Farley, P. C. (2013). Using the computer game "FoldIt" to entice students to explore external representations of protein structure in a Biochemistry course for nonmajors. *Biochemistry and Molecular Biology Education, 41*, 56–57.

Fluck, A., Pullen, D., & Harper, C. (2009). Case study of a computer-based examination system. *Australasian Journal of Educational Technology, 25*, 509–523.

Hendrickson, A., Ewing, M., Kaliski, P., & Huff, K. (2013). Evidence-centered design: Recommendations for implementation and practice. *Journal of Applied Testing Technology, 14*, 1–27.

Herreid, C. F., & Schiller, N. A. (2013). Case studies and the flipped classroom. *Journal of College Science Teaching, 42*, 62–66.

Hickey, D. T., Taasoobshirazi, G., & Cross, D. (2012). Assessment as learning: Enhancing discourse, understanding, and achievement in innovative science curricula. *Journal of Research in Science Teaching, 49*, 1240–1270.

Ibáñez, M. B., Rueda, J. J. C., Morillo, D., & Kloos, C. D. (2012). Creating test questions for 3D collaborative virtual worlds: The WorldOfQuestions authoring environment. *Journal of Universal Computer Science, 18*, 2556–2575.

Jeremić, Z., Jovanović, J., & Gašević, D. (2013). Personal learning environments on the social semantic web. *Semantic Web, 4*, 23–51.

Kao, F.-C., Lin, Y.-K., & Hung, C.-C. (2013). Brainwave analysis during learning. *Advanced Science Letters, 19*, 439–443.

Keppell, M., Souter, K., & Riddle, M. (2012). *Physical and virtual learning spaces in higher education: Concepts for the modern learning environment.* Hershey, PA: IGI Global.

Kryterion. (2013). Retrieved from http://www.kryteriononline.com

Kuo, C.-Y., & Wu, H.-K. (2013). Toward an integrated model for designing assessment systems: An analysis of the current status of computer-based assessments in science. *Computers & Education, 68*, 388–403.

Maiti, A. (2013). Interactive remote laboratories with gesture based interface through Microsoft Kinect. *10th international conference on Remote Engineering and Virtual Instrumentation (REV)* (6–8 February, pp. 1–4), IEEE, Sydney, NSW.

Meyer, J. P., & Zhu, S. (2013). Fair and equitable measurement of student learning in MOOCs: An introduction to item response theory, scale linking, and score equating. *Research & Practice in Assessment, 8*, 26–39.

Moore, M. G. (2013). Independent learning, MOOCs, and the open badges infrastructure. *American Journal of Distance Education, 27*, 75–76.

Nichols, P. D. (1994). A framework for developing cognitively diagnostic assessments. *Review of Educational Research, 64*, 575–603.

Norton, G., Taylor, M., Stewart, T., Blackburn, G., Jinks, A., Razdar, B., ... Marastoni, E. (2012). Designing, developing and implementing a software tool for scenario based learning. *Australasian Journal of Educational Technology, 28*, 1083–1102.

Powell, S., & Yuan, L. (2013). *MOOCs and open education: Implications for higher education.* Bolton: CETIS. Retrieved from http://publications.cetis.ac.uk/wp-content/uploads/2013/03/MOOCs-and-Open-Education.pdf

Prensky, M. (2001). *Digital games-based learning.* New York, NY: McGraw-Hill.

Richardson, D., & Molka-Danielsen, J. (2009). Assessing student performance. In J. Molka-Danielsen & M. Deutschmann (Eds.), *Learning and teaching in the virtual world of second life* (pp. 52–60). Trondheim, Norway: Tapir Academic Press.

Rupp, A. A., Gushta, M., Mislevy, R. J., & Shaffer, D. W. (2010). Evidence-centered design of epistemic games: Measurement principles for complex learning environments. *Journal of Technology, Learning, and Assessment, 8*(4).

Sánchez-Vera, M. del. M., Fernández-Breis, J. T., Castellanos-Nieves, D., Frutos-Morales, F., & Prendes-Espinosa, M. P. (2012). Semantic web technologies for generating feedback in online assessment environment. *Knowledge-Based Systems, 33*, 152–165.

Shute, V. J., & Ke, F. (2012). Games, learning, and assessment. In D. Ifenthaler, D. Eseryel, & X. Ge (Eds.), *Assessment in game-based learning: Foundations, innovations, and perspectives* (pp. 43–58). New York, NY: Springer.

Staner, T. (2013). Project glass: An extension of the self. *IEEE Pervasive Computing, 12*, 14–16.

Stewart, S., & Stewart, W. (2013). Taking clickers to the next level: A contingent teaching mode. *International Journal of Mathematical Education in Science and Technology, 44*(8), 1093–1106.

Stokes, A., Collins, T., Maskall, J., Lea, J., Lunt, P., & Davies, S. (2012). Enabling remote access to fieldwork: Gaining insight into the pedagogic effectiveness of "direct" and "remote" field activities. *Journal of Geography in Higher Education, 36*, 197–222.

Torrance, H., & Pryor, J. (2001). Developing formative assessment in the classroom: Using action research to explore and modify theory. *British Educational Research Journal, 27*, 615–631.

Westin, S. (2012). A sandbox approach to online exam administration. *International Journal of Online Pedagogy and Course Design (IJOPCD), 2*, 49–62.

Woolner, P., McCarter, S., Wall, K., & Higgins, S. (2012). Changed learning through changed space: When can a participatory approach to the learning environment challenge preconceptions and alter practice? *Improving Schools, 15*, 45–60.

CHAPTER 6

SPACES FOR ENGAGING, EXPERIENTIAL, COLLABORATIVE LEARNING IN HIGHER EDUCATION

Roger Hadgraft and Jo Dane

ABSTRACT

A key challenge for higher education institutions around the world is to provide active and engaging learning encounters for a new generation of students to develop their skills for work in a rapidly changing environment. Typically, these students are accustomed to being digitally connected 24/7 and they have real-time access to truly global learning resources. The challenge facing higher education providers is how to create active and engaging learning encounters within an aging stock of infrastructure by a generation of traditional academics, both of which generally foster teacher-led instruction.

In considering this conundrum, this chapter is viewed through two lenses: (1) a teacher practising problem-based learning (PBL) for more than 20 years and (2) an educational planner who designs learning spaces. Together the paper explores the challenges *of* pedagogy *and* design, some *disruptors* that are making change imperative and, specifically, the

The Future of Learning and Teaching in Next Generation Learning Spaces
International Perspectives on Higher Education Research, Volume 12, 101–122
Copyright © 2014 by Emerald Group Publishing Limited
All rights of reproduction in any form reserved
ISSN: 1479-3628/doi:10.1108/S1479-362820140000012010

opportunities *available in both pedagogy and design to create new learning activities and spaces. The paper argues that curricula need to be dominated by collaborative investigation and problem solving in spaces that encourage and afford such activity.*

Keywords: NGLS; learning spaces; MOOC; problem-based learning; student-centred learning; standards

PEDAGOGY CHALLENGES

Focus on Learning Activities

The effectiveness of didactic learning experiences has been challenged over the last 40 years. Bligh (1972), Penner (1984) and Ramsden (1992) are some of the numerous education researchers who have asserted that students learn more effectively when they are active and able to interact with peers. Students develop understanding through discussing, brainstorming, drawing, mapping, problem-solving, debating and collaborating with others, a vastly different scenario to the relative passivity of listening in lectures. As Shuell (1986) states: 'If students are to learn desired outcomes in a reasonably effective manner, then the teacher's fundamental task is to get students to engage in learning activities that are likely to result in their achieving those outcomes .... It is helpful to remember that what the student does is actually more important in determining what is learned than what the teacher does' (p. 429).

A review of the literature on effective teaching and learning has revealed six common characteristics (Table 1). When a teacher is planning classroom encounters for effective teaching and learning they will be carefully considering not only the types of activities that will foster learning, but the types of activities that are possible in the classroom environment.

Growth in Universities

Despite the plethora of literature that supports a more active, student-centred approach to learning, universities continue to timetable large format lectures and supporting tutorials, and to build large-scale auditoria. Ironically, the predominance of lectures is due to the rising number of student enrolments as a result of increasing accessibility of higher education to

Table 1.   The Effective Teaching and Learning Framework.

Effective teaching and learning in formal higher education classrooms:

1. promotes student activity and engagement with content, empowers students with choices and maintains interest through a variety of activities, resources and learning styles (Biggs & Tang, 2007; Chickering & Gamson, 1987; Entwistle, 2009; Hounsell, 1997; Prosser & Trigwell, 1999; Ramsden, 2003; Shuell, 1986; Skinner, 2010)
2. encourages the teacher to view teaching from the student's perspective and build meaningful relationships with students (Entwistle, 2009; Laurillard, 2002; Marton & Booth, 1997; Prosser & Trigwell, 1999; Ramsden, 2003; Rogers, 1969)
3. is a social process whereby knowledge is socially constructed (Dewey, 1897, 1961; Garrison & Archer, 2000; Laurillard, 2002; Lave & Wenger, 1991; Piaget & Inhelder, 1969; Vygotsky, 1978)
4. fosters a deep approach to learning that encourages student independence (Dewey, 1961; Entwistle, 1984; Hounsell, 1997; Marton & Säljö, 1997; Rogers, 1969)
5. is contextualised and relevant; teachers have an awareness of student prior learning (Biggs & Tang, 2007; Entwistle, 2009; Hounsell, 1997; Laurillard, 2002; Prosser & Trigwell, 1999; Ramsden, 2003; Rogers, 1969; Shuell, 1986; Skinner, 2010)
6. involves the teacher providing effective and timely feedback and appropriate methods of assessment (Biggs & Tang, 2007; Chickering & Gamson, 1987; Entwistle, 2009; Hounsell, 1997; Laurillard, 2002; Prosser & Trigwell, 1999; Ramsden, 2003)

Source: Dane (2014).

a higher percentage of the Australian population. Government policy over the past 30 years has fostered significant growth in the tertiary sector. In 1980, there were 19 universities and 330,000 undergraduate students in Australia (Department of Education Training and Youth Affairs (DETYA), 2001), compared with 2012 statistics confirming 39 Universities and over 1.2 million undergraduate students (Department of Industry, I., Climate Change, Science, Research and Tertiary Education, 2013). To cope with the rising demand for programs, universities have had no choice but to increase the quantity and capacity of lectures, reinforcing reliance upon teacher-centred learning, despite the educational literature that promotes active, student-centred modes of learning.

Limitation of Infrastructure to Implement New Pedagogies

Traditional university infrastructure promotes teacher-led instruction and inhibits effective teaching and learning. Lecture theatres and high-density tutorial rooms encourage the teacher to teach from the front of the class and reinforce to students that the teacher is the dominant force (and knowledge source) in the classroom (Dane, 2004; Jamieson, 2004; Jamieson, Fisher, Gilding, Taylor, & Trevitt, 2000). While teacher-led instruction has dominated education for centuries (Majcherek, 2008; Olmert, 2003), it is difficult to change teaching and learning practice without also addressing necessary changes to the environment that foster behavioural change. Table 2 indicates that behaviour associated with teacher-led instruction is influenced by the design of the classroom.

A New Generation of Learners – Digitally Connected

A key issue being experienced in the higher education sector at present is the sharp demise in attendance at lectures (Cardall, Krupat, & Ulrich, 2008; Massingham & Herrington, 2006; Traphagan, Kucsera, & Kishi, 2010). University audits and lecturers regularly observe high attendance in weeks 1 and 2 of semester, with sharp decline thereafter. Students are voting with their feet by not attending face-to-face lectures, opting instead to tune into web-based recordings of the same lecture (Cardall et al., 2008). Even those who do attend lectures physically are often observed to be digitally elsewhere, thanks to the omnipresence of mobile technologies such as laptops, tablets and mobile phones. Universities can embrace these 'digitally elsewhere' practices, restrict their practices or they can engage students in meaningful activity that makes social media distractions a less attractive option.

Table 2. Teacher-Led Behaviours and Environment.

Teacher-Led Behaviour	Teacher-Led Classroom
Teacher is the dominant force in the classroom room.	Teacher is positioned at the front of the room. Students sit in rows and face the teacher.
Teacher does most of the talking, either through lecturing or facilitating discussion with the whole class.	Fixed wall technology (blackboard, whiteboard, or data projector) is located conveniently for the teacher.
The teacher asks questions and answers occasional questions.	Student learning happens outside the classroom through revision of notes, practice problems and exam study.
Students listen to the teacher and take notes.	
Teacher controls the technology.	
Assessment occurs via examinations and individual assignments.	

Wesch (2007) undertook a 'digital ethnography' project with over 200 students in which commentary included statements such as 'I Facebook through most of my classes' and 'I bring my laptop to class, but I'm not working on class stuff'. Mann and Robinson (2009) undertook a research project surveying over 200 students as to why they are bored at university, with results indicating that '59% of students find their lectures boring half the time and 30% find most or all of their lectures to be boring' (p. 243). Tapscott (2009) presents seven tips for educators in the new digital age, stating that 'broadcast learning doesn't work for this generation. Start asking students questions and listen to their answers. Listen to the questions students ask, too. Let them co-create a learning experience with you' (p. 148).

Coughlan (2013) reported the sentiments of Wikipedia founder Jimmy Wales, who argued that 'the traditional university lecture should have been condemned decades ago and replaced with an online video recording that can be stopped and started.' These responses and many more beg the question: if we were to create a higher education system based upon demand and what we know about how students learn, what would it look like? Laurillard (2002), an influential education researcher, posed a similar question:

> If we forget the eight hundred years of university tradition that legitimises [lectures], and imagine starting afresh with the problem of how best to enable a large percentage of the population to understand difficult and complex ideas, I doubt that lectures will immediately spring to mind as the obvious solution. (Laurillard, 2002, p. 93)

DESIGN CHALLENGES

There are numerous challenges to creating classroom environments that support and enable effective teaching and learning practice, such as procurement processes, resistance to change from teachers, facilities managers and administrators, and developments in education technologies.

Procurement Processes

New buildings and infrastructure refurbishment projects are typically managed by the University's Property Campus division and occasionally supported by an education advisor. Architects and designers are commissioned by the Property Campus division rather than the Faculty or School concerned. While there are logical reasons why this is the case, the process leaves open the possibility of a knowledge gap between the architects and the end users (both academics and students).

At the beginning of the 21st Century a new discourse emerged, relating to the conjunction of space and pedagogy (Belcher, 2001; Jamieson et al., 2000; Van Note Chism & Bickford, 2002). Because of their critical role in managing space on campus, facility managers found themselves, unwittingly, at the forefront of promoting pedagogical change through the procurement of new types of learning spaces. Many facility managers sought out academic champions to assist with this process and a new classroom space typology resulted in what has vicariously become known as 'Next Generation Learning Spaces' (NGLS).

The Tertiary Education Facilities Management Association (TEFMA), the organisation that represents university facility managers, has been proactive and engaged in developing NGLS on campus (Fisher, 2005). Initiatives for developing NGLS projects are usually undertaken in collaboration with an academic champion whose objective is to promote active and student-centred learning. The resultant spaces look distinctly different to traditional classrooms (Mitchell et al., 2010). They have:

- furniture arranged for group work;
- mobile furniture and technology that can be reconfigured;
- multiple technologies and active wall surfaces for access by students as well as teachers — large screen monitors, projectors, whiteboards and pinup boards;
- space to move around and perform;
- no obvious front of the room for the teacher.

These features lead to further challenges such as encouraging teachers to familiarise themselves with NGLS and training teachers to use new technology. (Note, students generally do not need training. They typically learn technological systems through trial and error, and from each other.)

Resistance from Teachers

Advances in NGLS have been tempered by teachers resistant to changing their teaching practice. NGLS classrooms, designed to foster active and collaborative learning, encourage academics to adapt their teaching practice by reducing the instructional components and increasing student activity (in line with the earlier quote from Shuell).

Regardless of the academic who champions the change to student-centred teaching practice and the provision of appropriate space to do so, many academics resist change and continue teaching using the same didactic methods they have used for years. The most common claims are that academics have too much research to do or too much content to cover to be able to invest time to adapt their teaching practice. It is much easier to keep teaching the way they have taught for years and, in some cases, decades. Quite simply, the incentive to change teaching practice is often not a high priority for academics. Promotions are, more often, biased towards research excellence rather than teaching excellence (Chalmers, 2010).

Contrasting this perspective is the positive sentiments of students whose learning experiences demonstrate engagement in their learning activities and a sense of collegiality with their peers. An unpublished research study at Monash University (Dane, 2011) included numerous observations of students spending up to three hours of formal class time in a next generation learning space, undertaking a variety of learning activities as facilitated by the teacher. This led the author to conclude that it appeared virtually impossible to disengage from the learning process during class. 'There is a sense that students increase their learning initiative and independence through being empowered to use the technology when, where and how they need to' (*ibid.*).

Therefore, while some teachers resist changing their teaching practice to more student-centred modes, students appear to thoroughly enjoy (and learn from) interactive and collaborative classroom learning experiences.

PEDAGOGY DISRUPTORS

MOOCs

While several aspects of university life have changed very little, exemplified by lectures as the predominant mode of teaching, financial challenges in the sector in the last decade have led to declining teaching hours for face-to-face instruction and increased tuition costs. Students are well within their rights to question why the cost of higher education has continued to rise and, apart from achieving a qualification, what value are they really getting from attending university?

However, when we look outside the university, we see many start-up companies that are attempting to reinvent higher education, as we know it, for example Udacity, Coursera, edX, and Codecademy, to name a few. Udacity is a spin-off of the initiative by Sebastian Thrun and Peter Norvig, who in 2011 ran an online course at Stanford University titled 'An Introduction to Artificial Intelligence' (Martin, 2012). The course attracted more than 100,000 registrations and is recognised as one of the first Massive Open Online Courses, also known as MOOCs.

Although universities have been delivering online courses and distance education for many years, MOOCs are different because they are free, have no restriction on enrolment numbers, no prerequisites to enrol and no certified qualifications. Students can enrol and participate simply for their interest in a topic (Trounson, 2014). The argument in this paper is not that MOOCs offer a better *quality* of learning experience compared to traditional university classes, but they are offering a *form of access* to university expertise that is shaking the foundations of traditional higher education.

On-campus lectures are being recorded so that students can access them online, with students increasingly relying upon the online version, choosing not to attend the face-to-face format. Online learning programs feature lecture content. And now MOOCs and programs such as the Khan Academy are further establishing that instructional content can be placed successfully online.

The time has come to question why the majority of lectures need to be delivered on campus at all? MOOCs have demonstrated that lecture material can be broadcast to student numbers far in excess of the capacity of any on-campus lecture theatre. Therefore, the opportunity exists for universities to expand and adapt their value offering. If students can already access significant online lectures for free, what can the university provide that students will pay for and value? The answer is an interactive, student-centred, collaborative on-campus experience and, of course, an accredited and recognised degree.

The Flipped Classroom

Higher education literature relating to how students learn has systematically ignored the influence of the physical classroom on teaching practice (Biggs, 2003; Marton, Hounsell, & Entwistle, 1997; Prosser & Trigwell, 1999). As the discourse into space and pedagogy developed, so too did the notion that learning is physically situated somewhere, and in particular on university campuses (Dane, 2004; Fisher, 2003; Jamieson et al., 2000).

In the wake of the emergence of NGLS, another new concept has recently been added to the lexicon of teaching and learning: the flipped classroom.

The 'flipped classroom' refers to the process of flipping classroom activities and homework activities (Bergmann & Sams, 2012). Students typically read, watch and listen to instructional content via video or audio files for homework. They may also undertake online assessment that builds basic skills, in the style of the Khan Academy. They come to class to complete more challenging tasks such as project-based learning. While the concept was initially developed for primary and secondary schools, the notion of the 'flipped classroom' appears to have significant traction in higher education.

Theoretically the 'flipped classroom' has many parallels with student-centred learning. The primary objective is to enable students to work through activities and problems in class where they can work at their own pace individually or collaboratively and seek the teacher's assistance when needed. It means that class time and interaction between students is focussed on developing complex, professional skills.

Job-Ready Graduates and Learning Standards

While alternatives to lecturing may currently be emerging in the guise of technology-enabled video clips through MOOCs and websites such as the Khan Academy, this does not necessarily address the issue of *what* is being taught and its relevance to work practice or industry. An overhaul of curricula for various disciplines has been demanded to better prepare graduates for work. For example, the Australian Government has exerted greater control by encouraging the development of *standards* for disciplines and for organisational performance (Gora, 2010). The call for learning and teaching standards is intended to ensure that the quality of graduates is not diminished by increasing student numbers.

Beyond the university, graduates face a challenging world filled with complex problems. For example, climate change is one of the most daunting global challenges for the foreseeable future. Contributing to climate change is the rapid industrialisation of countries such as China, India and Brazil and the aspiration of another 2 billion people to live middle class lives, demanding more resources than the planet may be able to provide.

So, building a sustainable world is a challenge for many professions. What kinds of capabilities do graduates need to face these challenges, such as providing clean water, sanitation, health services and boosting agricultural production to feed the population's expanding expectations, providing learning opportunities in new knowledge-based economies, making solar energy more economical (though this is progressing more rapidly than we ever thought possible) and growing our cities while making them more sustainable (National Academy of Engineering, 2007).

Many international reviews of higher education (Sheppard, Macatangay, Colby, & Sullivan, 2008) have called for a change to active and learning centred pedagogies. It is not enough to teach content from textbooks. Students need the fundamental concepts of their discipline; however, they also need to understand how to apply those fundamental concepts to a range of increasingly complex problems, for example the 'wicked problems' described in Kolko (2012) and Richardson (2006). Learning standards, which define graduate capabilities, reconcile the disciplinary knowledge base, the cross-disciplinary process skills (such as design or investigation) and the universal skills of communication and teamwork.

The process of defining graduate capabilities has proven beneficial to many disciplines such as the Arts and Sciences (e.g. Hay, 2011; Jones & Yates, 2011). Engaging national communities, Deans, Heads of Schools, and key industry leaders has been very effective and enlightening.

Consider the Science Threshold Learning Outcomes (Jones & Yates, 2011) proposed as part of the Australian Learning and Teaching Council's Learning and Teaching Academic Standards project (Box 1).

These look different to any university science curriculum you might like to examine. The focus is on action: analyse and solve scientific problems, communicate them to a diverse audience and work effectively with others. This suggests that rapid redesign of curricula will be necessary to balance the tendency to focus on teaching the disciplinary knowledge (only one of the five outcomes) in favour of the *practice* of science.

Similar trends are observable in other discipline areas, for example History (Hay, 2011) (Box 2).

Again, the emphasis is on action: identify and interpret historical issues, analyse evidence, construct arguments, reflect critically. Both science and history share many of the same capabilities. Students need to be able to investigate problems (issues) in their domain. They need to be able to scope the problem, collect evidence, pose possible solutions or interpretations and argue their case to others. History and science seem underpinned by similar intellectual processes.

The set of discipline standards, developed so far, tend to focus on *process* skills rather than knowledge content as indicated for the Science and

Box 1.   Science Threshold Learning Outcomes (Jones & Yates, 2011).

Understanding science

Demonstrate a coherent understanding of science by articulating the methods of science and explaining why current scientific knowledge is both contestable and testable by further inquiry and explaining the role and relevance of science in society.

Scientific knowledge

Exhibit depth and breadth of scientific knowledge by demonstrating well-developed knowledge in at least one disciplinary area and demonstrating knowledge in at least one other disciplinary area.

Inquiry and problem solving

Critically analyse and solve scientific problems by gathering, synthesising and critically evaluating information from a range of sources and designing and planning an investigation and selecting and applying practical and/or theoretical techniques or tools in order to conduct an investigation and collecting, accurately recording, interpreting and drawing conclusions from scientific data.

Communication

Be effective communicators of science by communicating scientific results, information, or arguments, to a range of audiences, for a range of purposes, and using a variety of modes.

Personal and professional responsibility

Be accountable for their own learning and scientific work by being independent and self-directed learners and working effectively, responsibly and safely in an individual or team context and demonstrating knowledge of the regulatory frameworks relevant to their disciplinary area and personally practising ethical conduct.

Box 2.   History Threshold Learning Outcomes (Hay, 2011).

Upon completion of a bachelor degree with a major in History, graduates will be able to:

Knowledge
1. Demonstrate an understanding of at least one period or culture of the past.
2. Demonstrate an understanding of a variety of conceptual approaches to interpreting the past.
3. Show how History and historians shape the present and the future.

Research
4. Identify and interpret a wide variety of secondary and primary materials.
5. Examine historical issues by undertaking research according to the methodological and ethical conventions of the discipline.

Analysis
6. Analyse historical evidence, scholarship and changing representations of the past.

Communication
7. Construct an evidence-based argument or narrative in audio, digital, oral, visual or written form.

Reflection
8. Identify and reflect critically on the knowledge and skills developed in their study of History.

These Threshold Learning Outcomes may be achieved through a combination of individual and collaborative work.

History examples (Discipline Scholars Network, 2013). Many of the process skills across a wide range of disciplines look something like this:

1. understand the problem or issue to be addressed, in context,
2. use systematic problem-solving processes (which vary between disciplines to some extent),
3. apply disciplinary knowledge and skills,

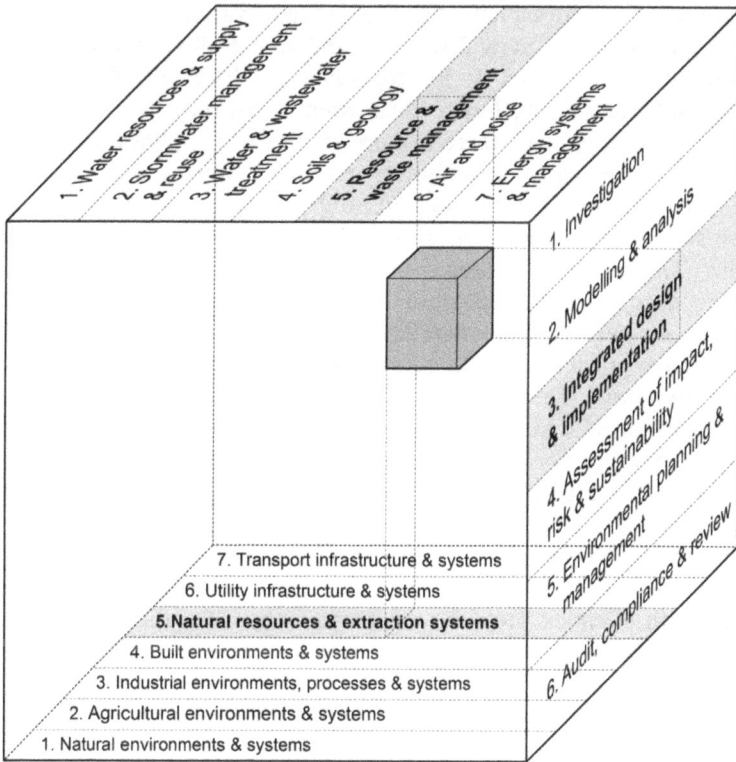

Fig. 1. Environmental Engineering Capability Cube.

4. work with others and communicate effectively,
5. understand, manage and develop oneself.

In an environmental engineering context, these process skills have been elaborated in more detail by Dowling and Hadgraft (2013b) to produce the capability cube (Fig. 1). Subsequent work has demonstrated the applicability of the method to several non-engineering disciplines (Dowling & Hadgraft, 2013a), demonstrating the need for graduate capabilities in process skills (such as investigation, design and modelling), disciplinary knowledge skills (e.g. collect environmental data) and generic skills (such as communication, teamwork and reflective practice).

The insight that problem solving (or investigation) lies at the heart of many disciplines is very significant because it means that many curricula need to be restructured around this skill, merging content knowledge with problem scenarios. It explains the popularity of various forms of problem-based learning across many disciplines and across all year levels from kindergarten to PhD (Boud & Feletti, 1998; Duch, Groh, & Allen, 2001; Evensen & Hmelo, 2000; Jones, Rasmussen, & Moffitt, 1997; Savin-Baden, 2000). It also means that there is more scope for disciplines to be working together in studio-based learning, for example designers with business students with social scientists (Jones et al., 1997). Future economies and, indeed, human survival will depend on the combined capacity of disciplines to work together. This is largely ignored in our universities at the moment, where curricula focus on teaching in-depth disciplinary knowledge, in most cases. Therefore, we need curricula that engage students in real problems. We have and will have greater access to educational technology to provide the disciplinary knowledge. There should be less need to dictate this in lectures.

The work around standards has given us a clearer view of what process skills students need for the future. Learning these process skills is not necessarily easily delivered by technology. For example, effective team skills are likely best learned face-to-face, though they can then be practised and enhanced through online collaborations. These kinds of studio-based learning demand new typologies of learning spaces that will enable students to grapple with complex problems, to prepare them for future collaborative work situations.

DESIGN AND PEDAGOGICAL OPPORTUNITIES

How does campus design support and promote these disruptions? The concept of moving lectures to a primarily online environment presents an opportunity for universities to focus the campus experience on active and student-centred modes of learning. This will demand the increased presence of innovative learning spaces across campuses and the decline of lecture theatres and other traditional classroom typologies.

The majority of students have access to multiple mobile devices (phone, tablet, laptop) and are connected to the Internet 24/7. Universities are encouraging students to use their own devices on campus, enabling access to critical digital infrastructure. This reduces the demand for university-owned computer hardware and specialist computer laboratories (Morrone & Woodman, 2014). Through the mobility of student devices, learning activities can occur anywhere on campus, not just where the infrastructure is located. This has implications for wireless and power infrastructure. It also increases the pressure on classroom technology systems to connect seamlessly to multiple student devices and for students to share content easily.

Students will come to campus if they know they will have access to their teachers, be able to discuss their understanding of a topic, solve problems, make friends and even have fun. This new generation of students, more so than any that has come before it, is social and connected; students constantly blur the boundaries of their digital and physical worlds. It is time that university campuses begin to reflect this new paradigm of hybrid environments, of having an immersive digital, as well as physical presence.

What this means for the design of university campuses is the provision of a range of purposeful learning spaces. There will be more demand for interactive and collaborative classrooms, multimedia lounges where students can access online material, informal learning spaces where students can (collaboratively or individually) study between classes and social spaces where students can access food, wi-fi and recreational amenity. There will be less demand for lecture theatres, traditional tutorial rooms and computer laboratories.

The historical approaches, that have made university campuses recognisable for over a thousand years, are currently being dismantled. The campus of the future will be a vastly different place from the campus of the past. The emergence of NGLS is a major step in the shift towards the establishment of a new paradigm of university campus. Design characteristics that exemplify an NGLS should therefore enable a wide range of learning experiences and behaviours. The teacher and students should share equal and democratic access to the room amenity and, through technology, access global resources and information (Table 3).

Fundamental to this is the spaciousness of the room. While university facility managers actively seek to optimise (reduce) floor areas of teaching spaces, next generation learning environments demand *more* floor space. This is necessary to foster the learning experience as an active, interactive and *effective* process. Beyond that requirement, universities should encourage the next generation classroom to be designed in different ways. This affords a freedom of design not typically presented to designers and architects of education spaces. It encourages architects to design spaces that students (and teachers) can effectively teach and learn in, that do not conform to an institutional template, but rather are designed to elicit curiosity and discovery. The walls, floor, ceiling and furniture that make up a classroom become a canvas for designers to explore colour, texture, ambience, form and, where possible, sound and volume.

Table 3. Next Generation Learning Behaviours and Environment to Support Them.

Next Generation Learning Behaviour Student-centred	Next Generation Classroom Student-centred
All walls are active and shared between teacher and students.	There is no 'front' of the room.
Students work in groups which may include discussing, creating, problem solving, producing, brainstorming, hypothesising, etc.	Students face each other in collaborative settings.
Students access Internet-enabled resources during class.	Multiple digital screens are present, usually one per group setting.
Teacher and students share the technology.	Teacher and students can equitably access technology resources.
Students use their mobile devices to take digital notes, share notes and access resources via the Internet.	Technology needs to be seamless and integrated.
Student learning happens in real time in the classroom, working collaboratively on open-ended problems or scenarios.	Furniture is mobile and the room can be reconfigured to suit each learning encounter.
Students ask questions and explore possible solutions.	The environment needs acoustic treatment to account for additional noise levels of students.
Assessment occurs through a combination of individual and group problem-based learning assignments.	Students can present to each other and assess each other.
Students are engaged.	The place is humming with activity.

Technology

Technologies in next generation classrooms have so far largely been conceptualised as multiple wall-based screens that teachers and students can access one at a time for various activities. This represents a major advance from traditional classroom environments but is really the tip of the iceberg in terms of what will be possible in the future. Large format digital screens that are accessible to each group of students form a vital function that should not be underestimated (Morrone & Woodman, 2014). Large screens that are visible across a classroom environment enable students to scan the room to identify what other groups are doing. This fosters *confidence* (that their own group is on the right track), *concern* ('why are others doing this differently?') and *curiosity* ('I wonder what that group is doing?'). Such reactions encourage students to move around the room to engage with other groups, adding a rich layer of discovery. Concerns and questions can be raised immediately, instilling students with the confidence to progress their ideas in real time. However in the not-so-distant future, technologies will become increasingly synchronous, intuitive and multi-use. Sharing material between students and teachers will be simplified, similar to how Apple TV currently works from a hand-held device to a single digital screen, but recognising multiple hand-held devices and screens.

Wireless capacity is an essential requirement in any NGLS. Many students and staff carry three mobile devices, perhaps not active at any one time. Nevertheless, the quick shift from tablet to phone to laptop must be supported by very responsive wireless capacity. An additional problem is power consumption of all these devices. In the past, laptops had battery life of around 3 hours at best, so regular charging was necessary. Getting power to every group table severely impacts the design and construction of spaces. Fortunately, this may be one problem that will vanish over the next 5 years as laptops appear on the market with 10 + hours of battery life to match tablets and mobile phones. A student will be able to go all day without needing to recharge their devices regularly and rooms will be freed from the cascade of charger cables we frequently see at the moment, often with consequential safety implications.

Emerging Trends

Gaming and gamification has been acknowledged in the Horizon Report (Johnson et al., 2013) as a technology trend that is anticipated to become more important in the next 2–3 years. Therefore we may see gaming consoles in classrooms, fostering digital problem-solving platforms embedded with competency-based assessment targets. Universities are expected to become major developers of applications to support learning processes both inside and outside the classroom, further necessitating in-classroom technologies to support student activation of applications through mobile devices as well as digital screens.

Learning analytics have also been identified in the Horizon Report (Johnson et al., 2013) as a technology trend to emerge in the next 2–3 years. What this means is that teachers will be able to track student progress in real time and respond to common issues that can be addressed immediately. These support systems will lead to increased engagement and learning in the classroom environment, rather than the time lag associated with more time consuming forms of feedback, such as class tests.

Further into the future, students and teachers will be wearing technologies that prompt environmental cues such as automated login, lighting settings and information on the presence of other students studying similar topics. MIT's Sixth Sense project (Mistry, 2010) presents a glimpse into this type of future. Hand gestures and face recognition will activate security, technology, and other aspects of the environment. People will be even more connected than today, and increasingly networks will be more interconnected.

While the higher education sector currently remains cognisant of the continuing potential of online learning, including the emergence of MOOCs, what these future technologies will never replace is the value and effectiveness of face-to-face learning. The sector is at the forefront of reconceptualising the higher education learning experience, to ensure the continued development of a sustainable knowledge economy. This will not be exclusively undertaken online. Universities will realise that their greatest asset is not the online environment, but is actually the campus environment. Students will enrol and pay for higher education because of the value inherent in the face-to-face learning experience, appropriately supported by a complementary online learning experience.

CONCLUSION

The future of higher education lies not in the traditional approaches that have sustained the sector for centuries, but in the ability of universities to prepare students for a rapidly changing world. The modern reality is a new generation of students with distinctly different characteristics compared to previous cohorts, the ability for students to access and filter vast amounts of information, and a plethora of complex world problems that will demand interdisciplinary problem-solving capabilities.

Pedagogical change to an activity-focussed curriculum will be needed to meet these challenges but will demand a hybrid learning environment consisting of a fluid online learning platform, as well as a new generation of on-campus formal and informal learning spaces to support a diverse range of learning activities and experiences.

What will the University of the Future look like? In the years and decades to come, universities are likely to transform from the current teacher-centred and silo-based research centres to a more dynamic, student-centred, social and interdisciplinary research environment that embraces both online and on-campus environments. The accompanying chapters will present many of the issues facing the higher education sector as universities move towards this new reality.

REFERENCES

Belcher, J. W. (2001). *TEAL – Technology enhanced active learning*. Retrieved from http://groups.csail.mit.edu/mac/projects/icampus/projects/teal.html. Accessed on November 23, 2010.

Bergmann, J., & Sams, A. (2012). *Flip your classroom: Reach every student in every class, every day*. Washington, DC: International Society for Technology in Education.

Biggs, J. (2003). *Teaching for quality learning at university* (2nd ed.). Berkshire, UK: Open University Press.

Biggs, J., & Tang, C. (2007). *Teaching for quality learning at university* (3rd ed.). Berkshire, England: Open University Press.

Bligh, D. A. (1972). *What's the use of lectures?* Harmondsworth, Middlesex: Penguin Books Ltd.

Boud, D. J., & Feletti, G. (1998). *The challenge of problem-based learning*. London: Routledge.

Cardall, S., Krupat, E., & Ulrich, M. (2008). Live lecture versus video-recorded lecture: Are students voting with their feet? *Academic Medicine, 83*(12), 1174–1178.

Chalmers, D. (2010). *National teaching quality indicators project: Rewarding and recognising quality teaching in higher education*. Retrieved from http://www.education.uwa.edu.au/__data/assets/pdf_file/0005/1891706/TQI_Final_Report.pdf. Accessed on February 23, 2014.

Chickering, A. W., & Gamson, Z. F. (1987). Seven principles for good practice in undergraduate education. *American Association of Higher Education Bulletin, 39*(7), 3–7.

Coughlan, S. (2013). Jimmy Wales: Boring university lectures 'are doomed'. *Online news article*. Retrieved from http://www.bbc.co.uk/news/business-22160988

Dane, J. (2004). Designing environments that stimulate student-centred learning. Paper presented at the Tertiary Education Facility Managers Association, Hobart, Tasmania, 26–29 September.

Dane, J. (2011). *Educational post occupancy evaluation report: Geoscience G60 laboratory*. Melbourne: Monash University.

Dane, J. (2014). *New generation learning environments in higher education*. PhD Thesis in progress.

Department of Education Training and Youth Affairs (DETYA). (2001). *Higher education students time series table* (No. 6714 HERC01A). Commonwealth of Australia. Retrieved from http://www.deewr.gov.au/HigherEducation/Publications/HEStatistics/Publications/Documents/2000TimeSeries.pdf

Department of Industry, I., Climate Change, Science, Research and Tertiary Education. (2013). *2012 Student full year*. Retrieved from http://innovation.gov.au/higheredu cation/HigherEducationStatistics/StatisticsPublications/Pages/Students12FullYear.aspx

Dewey, J. (1897). My pedagogic creed. *School Journal, 54*(January), 77–80.

Dewey, J. (1961). *Democracy and education: An introduction to the philosophy of education*. New York, NY: Macmillan.

Discipline Scholars Network. (2013). *Discipline Standards in Australia*. Retrieved from http://disciplinestandards.pbworks.com/. Accessed on November 4, 2013.

Dowling, D., & Hadgraft, R. (2013a). *The DYD stakeholder consultation process – A user guide*. Retrieved from http://www.olt.gov.au/resource-DYD-defining-your-discipline. Accessed on November 4, 2013.

Dowling, D., & Hadgraft, R. (2013b). *Graduate capabilities for environmental engineering degree programs – A guide for Australian Universities*. Retrieved from http://www.olt.gov.au/resource-DYD-defining-your-discipline. Accessed on November 4, 2013.

Duch, B. J., Groh, S. E., & Allen, D. E. (2001). *The power of problem-based learning: A practical 'how to' for teaching undergraduate courses in any discipline.* Sterling, VA: Stylus Publishing, LLC.

Entwistle, N. (1984). Contrasting perspectives on learning. In F. Marton, D. Hounsell, & N. Entwistle (Eds.), *The experience of learning* (2nd ed.). Edinburgh: Scottish Academic Press.

Entwistle, N. J. (2009). *Teaching for understanding at university: Deep approaches and distinctive ways of thinking.* Basingstoke: Palgrave Macmillan.

Evensen, D. H., & Hmelo, C. E. (2000). *Problem-based learning: A research perspective on learning interactions.* Mahwah, NJ: Lawrence Erlbaum Associates Publishers.

Fisher, K. (2003, March). Clicks, bricks and spondulicks. Paper presented at the Organisation for Economic Co-operation and Development (OECD) – Program on Educational Building (PEB) Seminar, Brisbane, Australia.

Fisher, K. (Ed.). (2005). *Learning environments in tertiary education* (Draft ed.). Brisbane: Tertiary Education Facility Managers Association.

Garrison, R., & Archer, W. (2000). *A transactional perspective on teaching and learning: A framework for adult and higher education.* Oxford: Elsevier Science Ltd.

Gora, J. (2010). Watch out! Here comes the TEQSA juggernaut. *The Australian Universities' Review, 52*(2), 76–78.

Hay, I. (2011). *History – Learning and teaching academic standards statement.* Retrieved from http://disciplinestandards.pbworks.com/w/file/fetch/52684123/altc_standards_HISTORY_080211_v2.pdf. Accessed on November 4, 2013.

Hounsell, D. (1997). Understanding teaching and teaching for understanding. In F. Marton, D. Hounsell, & N. Entwistle (Eds.), *The experience of learning: Implications for teaching and studying in higher education* (pp. 238–257). Edinburgh: Scottish Academic Press.

Jamieson, P. (2004). Designing more effective on-campus teaching and learning spaces: A role for academic developers. *International Journal for Academic Development, 8*(1&2), 119–133.

Jamieson, P., Fisher, K., Gilding, T., Taylor, P., & Trevitt, C. (2000). Place and space in the design of new learning environments. *Higher Education Research & Development, 19*(2), 221–237.

Johnson, L., Adams Becker, S., Cummins, M., Estrada, V., Freeman, A., & Ludgate, H. (2013). NMC Horizon Report: 2013 Higher Education Edition. The New Media Consortium, Austin, TX.

Jones, B. F., Rasmussen, C. M., & Moffitt, M. C. (1997). *Real-life problem solving: A collaborative approach to interdisciplinary learning.* Washington, DC: American Psychological Association.

Jones, S., & Yates, B. (2011). *Science – Learning and teaching academic standards statement.* Retrieved from http://disciplinestandards.pbworks.com/w/file/52690236/altc_standards_SCIENCE_240811_v3.pdf. Accessed on November 4, 2013.

Kolko, J. (2012). *Wicked problems: Problems worth solving.* Retrieved from http://www.wickedproblems.com/. Accessed on February 4, 2014.

Laurillard, D. (2002). *Rethinking university teaching: A conversational framework for the effective use of learning technologies* (2nd ed.). London: RoutledgeFalmer.

Lave, J., & Wenger, E. (1991). *Situated learning: Legitimate peripheral participation.* Cambridge: Cambridge University Press.

Majcherek, G. (2008). Academic life of late antique Alexandria: A view from the field. In M. El-Abbadi & O. Fathallah (Eds.), *What happened to the ancient library of Alexandria?* Leiden, The Netherlands: Koninklijke Brill NV.

Mann, S., & Robinson, A. (2009). Boredom in the lecture theatre: An investigation into the contributors, moderators and outcomes of boredom amongst university students. *British Educational Research Journal, 35*(2), 243–258.

Martin, F. G. (2012). Will massive open online courses change how we teach? *Communications of the ACM, 55*(8), 26–28.

Marton, F., & Booth, S. (1997). *Learning and awareness.* Mahwah, NJ: Lawrence Erlbaum Associates.

Marton, F., Hounsell, D., & Entwistle, N. (Eds.). (1997). *The experience of learning* (2nd ed.). Edinburgh: Scottish Academic Press Limited.

Marton, F., & Säljö, R. (1997). Approaches to learning. In F. Marton, D. Hounsell, & N. Entwistle (Eds.), *The experience of learning.* Edinburgh: Scottish Academic Press.

Massingham, P., & Herrington, T. (2006). Does attendance matter? An examination of student attitudes, participation, performance and attendance. *Journal of University Teaching & Learning Practice, 3*(2), 3.

Mistry, P. (2010). *Sixth sense: Integrating information with the real world.* Retrieved from http://www.pranavmistry.com/projects/sixthsense/

Mitchell, G., White, B., Pospsil, R., Killey, S., Liu, C., & Matthews, G. (2010). Retrofitting University learning spaces – Final report. Support for the original work was provided by the Australian Learning and Teaching Council Ltd., an initiative of the Australian Government Department of Education, Employment and Workplace Relations. Queensland University of Technology.

Morrone, A., & Woodman, S. (2014). Keeping pace with the rapid evolution of learning spaces. In K. Fraser (Ed.), *The future of learning and teaching in next generation learning spaces* (Vol. 12). International Perspectives on Higher Education Research. Bingley, UK: Emerald Group Publishing Limited.

National Academy of Engineering. (2007). *Grand challenges for engineering.* Retrieved from http://www.engineeringchallenges.org/. Accessed on October 6, 2008.

Olmert, M. (2003). *Smithsonian book of books.* Washington, DC: Smithsonian Institution.

Penner, J. G. (1984). *Why many college teachers cannot teach.* Springfield, IL: Charles C. Thomas Publisher.

Piaget, J., & Inhelder, B. (1969). *The psychology of the child.* New York, NY: Basic Books.

Prosser, M., & Trigwell, K. (1999). *Understanding learning and teaching: The experience in higher education.* Buckingham: SRHE and Open University Press.

Ramsden, P. (1992). *Learning to teach in higher education.* London: Routledge.

Ramsden, P. (2003). *Learning to teach in higher education* (2nd ed.). London: Routledge Falmer.

Richardson, A. (2006). Wicked problems: Today's business problems can be impossible to define, let alone solve. *Design Mind.* Retrieved from http://designmind.frogdesign.com/articles/fall/wicked-problems.html-0. Accessed on February 4, 2014.

Rogers, C. (1969). *Freedom to learn a view of what education might become* (1st ed.). Columbus, OH: Charles E. Merill.

Savin-Baden, M. (2000). *Problem-based learning in higher education: Untold stories.* London: Society for Research into Higher Education.

Sheppard, S. D., Macatangay, K., Colby, A., & Sullivan, W. M. (2008). *Educating engineers: Designing for the future of the field.* San Francisco, CA: Jossey-Bass.

Shuell, T. (1986). Cognitive conceptions of learning. *Review of Educational Research, 56*(4), 411–436.

Skinner, D. (2010). *Effective teaching and learning in practice.* London: Continuum International Publishing Group.

Tapscott, D. (2009). *Grown up digital.* New York, NY: McGraw-Hill.

Traphagan, T., Kucsera, J., & Kishi, K. (2010). Impact of class lecture webcasting on attendance and learning. *Educational Technology Research & Development, 58*(1), 19–37.

Trounson, A. (2014). MOOCs largely for the learned. *The Australian*, 21 February.

Van Note Chism, N., & Bickford, D. J. (Eds.). (2002). *The importance of physical space in creating supportive learning environments* (Winter ed., Vol. 92). San Francisco, CA: Jossey-Bass.

Vygotsky, L.S. (1978). *Mind in society: The development of higher psychological processes.* In M. Cole, V. John-Steiner, S. Scribner, & E. Souberman (Trans., 14th ed.). Cambridge, MA: Harvard University Press.

Wesch, M. (Writer). (2007). *A view of students today.* Retrieved from http://www.youtube.com/watch?v=dGCJ46vyR9o

CHAPTER 7

WHAT DOES IT TAKE TO LEARN IN NEXT GENERATION LEARNING SPACES?

Rhona Sharpe

ABSTRACT

This chapter identifies the attributes that learners need in order to learn effectively in new technology rich educational environments. There are a number of different ways of synthesising the findings from this emerging literature which relies heavily on qualitative research. This chapter reports on a literature review which adopted a deliberately interpretative qualitative meta-analysis, synthesising the findings from 15 key studies. As such, the chapter demonstrates a way of reviewing and compiling current research. The synthesis resulted in the identification of six attributes that learners need to do well in next generation learning spaces. These are engaged, connected, confident, adaptable, intentional and self-aware. Although some of these attributes are applicable to all learning contexts, those of being connected, confident, adaptable, and intentional seem to be particularly important in learning in next generation learning spaces. The challenge is to design learning activities that encourage and reward the development of these attributes. The hope is that through both its

The Future of Learning and Teaching in Next Generation Learning Spaces
International Perspectives on Higher Education Research, Volume 12, 123–145
ISSN: 1479-3628/doi:10.1108/S1479-362820140000012011

findings and its method, this chapter provokes debate on what it now means to be a successful learner in today's technology rich world.

Keywords: Meta-analysis; literature review; learning; attributes; learner experience

INTRODUCTION

The chapters in this section have explored the teaching, learning and assessment activities that will enable us to unleash the potential of next generation physical and online learning spaces. Ling and Fraser (2014) in this volume remind us to focus on the learner in our design, with recommendations informed by theoretical understandings of how students learn through constructivism and situated learning. Similarly Crisp (2014) in this volume encourages assessment approaches informed by evidence of learner needs. Putting the learners at the centre of our design is clearly important when designing for learning in the new spaces that are explored in this book. In order to plan learning activities that will help develop effective learners, we need to have a clear picture of what it is that learners do in such environments, and particularly, what it is that successful learners do.

Three recent models of digital literacy might be a starting point. First, the European Commission's Joint Research Centre consulted with experts and produced a model of Digital Competence defined as 'involving the confident and critical use of Information Society Technology (IST) for work, leisure and communication' (Ala-Mutka, 2011, p. 5). Through its exposition of 'critical and confident use', this model recognises that having IT skills is not sufficient. Despite using the title of 'competence' this report concludes that we need to move our attention from access to technology to understanding how individuals can benefit from their *use* of technology in meaningful ways. Consequently their model encompasses three areas:

1. instrumental knowledge and skills for digital tool and media usage;
2. advanced skills and knowledge for communication and collaboration, information management, learning and problem-solving, and meaningful participation; and
3. attitudes to strategic skills usage in intercultural, critical, creative, responsible and autonomous ways.

The European Commission's model reflects a shift in conceptualising the requirements to learn effectively in a digital age from digital *skills* to

appropriate *use*. Such a shift can also be seen in the iterative development
of the Seven Pillars model developed by the Society of College, National
and University Libraries in UK and Ireland (SCONUL). This was first
published in 1999 as a framework for 'information skills'. It was updated
in 2011 and re-titled 'information literacy', and in 2012 a further framework was added: the seven pillars of information literacy through a digital
literacy lens (SCONUL, 1999, 2012). The 2012 framework includes statements related to digital identity (the need to consider the digital self and
one's online presence), confidence (confidently use the digital media appropriate for presentation) and personalisation (personalise the digital environment according to need).

The third and final model arose from a series of studies funded by the
JISC in the UK under its learner experiences of e-learning programme.[1]
Like the European Commission's report described above, the JISC programme also found that access and skills are necessary but not sufficient to
explain successful learning with technology. In order to explain what had
been discovered about how learners progress towards effective use of technology for learning, a developmental model was created with four layers:
access, skills, strategies and creative appropriation (Sharpe & Beetham,
2010). The model emphasises that the attributes and actions of effective
learners are built upon a set of technology-based practices, which in turn
require appropriate skills and functional access to the relevant technologies.
The description originally given of creative appropriation was

> At this stage [of the model] the learner has 'creatively appropriated' available technolo-
> gies and learning opportunities to meet his/her own goals. At this stage, personal attri-
> butes and styles come to the fore, as do personal motivations for learning, and beliefs
> about both learning and technology. (Sharpe & Beetham, 2010, p. 92)

This model set out what was known about the strategies, beliefs, behaviours and attitudes of learners, but was rather vague about the attributes
that might be important. The model says little about what drives some learners to creatively appropriate the technology they have available to them in
ways that support their study. Indeed it can be quite difficult to elicit these,
despite being aware of their importance. For example, Brown and
Czerniewicz (2007) explored the relationship between access to and use of
technology to support learning in South Africa. Although their findings
show, as expected, that students with poor access to technology make less
use of technology for learning, the reverse is not true. That is, high access
does not guarantee high use. Brown and Czerniewicz used the concept
of agency to explain why some students make more use of their access

than others. We also know from studies based on the technology acceptance model that learners' intentions to use technology influence their patterns of use (Edmunds, Thorpe, & Conole, 2012; Liao & Lu, 2008; Liaw,
2008). Specifically, learners are more likely to use technology if they are
more satisfied with it and if they perceive it to be useful.

Learner experience research offers a way of exploring learner attributes
further.[2] Learner experience research has developed rapidly within the field
of learning technology in the last few years. New ways of eliciting, capturing
and analysing learners' experiences are being tried and researchers are showing a growing confidence in applying these methods. Learner experience
approaches use qualitative, exploratory and often participatory, research
methods to elicit learner experiences and generate rich descriptions which
foreground learners' perspectives, beliefs and behaviours. Reviewing studies
that have utilised such approaches should help us to uncover what it is that
distinguishes successful from less successful learners. Given the dominant
qualitative methods used, such studies should be particularly helpful in
describing the less tangible aspects of digital literacy that have appeared in
recent models of digital literacy such as attitudes and attributes.

A final point before embarking on the review of learner attributes is that
this is not to dismiss the role of context. It is clear that both local contextual factors such as course design (Kirkwood & Price, 2005), and wider
social and contextual factors (Lea & Jones, 2011) shape learners' use of
technology. Indeed, the review which follows might be framed within
Biggs's (1989) 3Ps model, where the presage factors of learner attributes,
instructional attributes, and contextual attributes are all understood to
have an influence on practice. However, here we are only interested in one
of those presage factors — learner attributes.

THE REVIEW

This review of literature is driven by the research question 'What can learner experience research tell us about the attributes of successful online learners?' This review will inform models of digital literacy, which are already
showing signs of moving beyond specification of skills and competencies. It
draws on qualitative research arising from the field of learners' experiences
of e-learning. Although learner experience research has exposed and given
a platform for authentic learners' voices, it has been criticised for relying
on small-scale research, and it has been a challenge to integrate the

results from many studies in ways which produce meaningful advice for practitioners.

Meta-analyses have played an important role in other emerging disciplines (e.g. in cognitive neuroscience see Cabeza & Nyberg, 2000) because they can test the reliability of our findings, by averaging out the results from many studies, each of which may have used slightly different data collection methods or research questions. The influence of idiosyncratic features of individual studies are lessened in a meta-analysis where what is of interest are the findings which are common to all studies. Qualitative meta-analyses allow us to draw stronger inferences from the review then could be concluded from a single study. The methodology for this review is a qualitative systematic review drawing on the interpretative meta-ethnography approach used by Noblit and Hare (1988) and Sharpe and Savin-Baden (2007). This method allows for comparison, analysis and interpretations of previous research to be made in order to integrate the findings from qualitative, small-scale studies.

Paper Search

A number of different search terms were tried initially. The terms that were found to produce the papers which most closely matched the research questions for the review were 'educational technology' AND 'learner experience'. These search terms were applied to the full text of the article, limiting the search to peer reviewed publications and to those published in the last five years. The number of papers returned from keyword searches is given in Table 1.

Table 1. Databases, Search Terms and Number of Hits.

Database	Number of Papers Returned
Academic Search Complete	74
Applied Social Sciences Index and Abstracts	8
Australian Education Index	62
BEI	2
Cumulated Index to Nursing and Allied Health Literature (CINAHL)	0
ERIC	5
Ingenta Connect	0
PsychINFO	1

In addition to searching databases, several other methods were used including scanning bibliographies of articles found, hand searching of contents pages of relevant journals, following up reference lists and consulting with experts in the field. Each paper was read in full and evaluated against the criteria in Table 2. Papers that were excluded at this stage were excluded most often because they did not have a qualitative component to their data collection and/or because they did not discuss learner attributes. A summary of the final set of 15 studies is given in Table 3. It is noted that the final set included studies of technology use in fully online, blended and face-to-face contexts.

Allocating Keywords

Each paper was allocated keywords. Given the open research question to identify learner attributes associated with effective learning in technology

Table 2. Inclusion and Exclusion Criteria.

Criteria	Include Studies	Exclude Studies
1. Context	Technology use in a learning context	Technology use not in a learning context
2. Topic	Attributes of learners, for example intentions, conceptions, beliefs.	Evaluation of a course, for example course design features.
	Practices or strategies of learners that were effective, from which attributes can be inferred.	Examination of learner access, use or skills.
	Studies that identified attributes and/or practices that contributed to effective learning in digital environments.	
3. Location	Worldwide but published in English	
4. Level	Adults (18 +) in tertiary or higher education	Primary (K−12), secondary, adult education, basic skills.
5. Date	Published 2008 or later	Published prior to 2008
6. Design	Primary research	Review paper, opinion piece, anecdotal evidence.
	Qualitative research design, for example case studies	Primary research which collects and analyses only quantitative data.
	Mixed method with qualitative data, for example interviews, focus groups, observation logs/diaries	
7. Quality, robustness	Peer reviewed, journal articles and theses.	Non-peer reviewed publications, conference papers and proceedings.

Table 3. Summary of Papers Included in Final Set.

Paper	Learners and Their Context	Methods	Summary of Learner Attributes
Anagnostopoulou, Parmar and Priego-Hernandez (2009)	First year undergraduates from a UK university. Compared student 'withdrawers' and 'persisters'. Questions focused on personal experience, perceptions of learning and the use of technology in relation to learning.	Telephone interviews (withdrawn students, $n = 42$) and questionnaires (not withdrawn students $n = 130$). Thematic analysis.	Retained group showed awareness of how they learn as individuals. They reported learning most effectively through active participation with their peers and in collaboration with their tutors.
Andrews and Tynan (2012)	Distance learners in Australia, purposively sampled to include those working full and part-time. Questions asked about the experience of technology for teaching and learning.	Phenomenological approach, using the day experience method, charting the week's activities, photos of learning spaces and focus groups ($n = 12$).	Individualness, connectedness, mobility and resourcefulness.
Brown, Hughes, Keppell, Hard, and Smith (2013)	First-time distance learners in Australasia. Compared data from 'support seekers' with 'lone wolves'.	A pre- ($n = 62$) and post- ($n = 57$) semester survey and a video diary phase ($n = 20$).	Seeking contact with lecturers, enjoying the opportunity to make a personal connection with lecturers, a deep approach to learning.
Buckley, Pitt, Norton, and Owens (2010)	First year undergraduate Sport Studies students enrolled on a blended module, which makes use of the VLE email and online submission of assignments.	Approaches and Study Skills Inventory for Students ($n = 144$). Focus group interviews ($n = 19$), with inductive thematic analysis.	Learners saw discussion forums as a place which could help them develop and learn new skills, and where they could share personal experiences and reflect upon themselves as learners.

Table 3. *(Continued)*

Paper	Learners and Their Context	Methods	Summary of Learner Attributes
Dujardin (2009)	Mature postgraduate student on a fully online master's module on research design.	Ethnography. Key informant: multiple interviews with one student over five months.	Key informant described as being 'fluent in her online self-presentation, she valued her interactions with others and contributed to the overall sociability of the VLE'.
Ellis, Bliuc, and Goodyear (2012)	First year foundational pharmacy course in an Australian metropolitan university. The relevant learning activities were a field trip and an online investigative task.	Phenomenographic approach. Survey of conceptions and approaches to learning through enquiry ($n = 124$) and interviews ($n = 22$).	Deep approach to learning. Being active, critically engaged and aware of the intrinsic value of authentic contexts/discovery. Understanding what constitutes engaged enquiry.
Hoekstra (2008)	Use of clickers in lectures in a chemistry course in USA.	Ethnographic – the meanings students assign to clickers. Participant observation, survey and interviews over three years.	Cooperation in class. A desire to be actively engaged. Not being anxious about sharing own ideas.
Holley (2009)	Widening access students. Questions focussed on the personal spaces which learners create for learning.	Interviews using the biographical narrative interpretative method.	A framework with three axes: control over technology used for learning, expectations for education, and preferences for inhabiting social spaces. Students at low risk have a good match between their expectation of education combined with high control over their home environment and use of technology.

Table 3. (*Continued*)

Paper	Learners and Their Context	Methods	Summary of Learner Attributes
Jeffrey et al. (2011)	Four higher education institutions in New Zealand ran 10 workshops for staff and students about the use of digital technology.	Case study design with 42 participants. Researcher observations and notes, focus group interviews, an email forum, reflective journals, pre- and post-surveys.	Seven major themes: collaboration, access, confidence and self-efficacy, time and permission to play, openness and learning from play, changing their approach to learning and personal growth.
Kear, Woodthorpe, Robertson, and Hutchison (2010)	Open university distance learners using a wiki for online tutorials.	Questionnaire to students ($n = 53$) with open response option, and unstructured online feedback from tutors.	Some students commented on the value of a wiki as a tool for creative collaboration, for example producing a shared document.
Lea and Jones (2011)	UK undergraduates from a pre-1992 university, a post-1992 university and a further education college. Questions focussed on students' literacy practices in relation to technology for learning.	Interviews with $n = 34$ students on three to four occasions over a six-month period with observations of students' use of texts and technologies. Also 'shadowing' keeping in contact with short email and text chats.	The social and cultural contexts that shape literacy practices. Embracing social networking to gain support, taking on multiple identities in order to gain support, separating personal and university communications.
Masterman and Shuyska (2012)	Postgraduate students from nine different blended, taught master's courses at Oxford University, UK.	Initial survey ($n = 77$), reflective survey ($n = 65$). Variant of email interviewing with extended conversations over time ('pen-pal' method) ($n = 23$).	Students were adept at accessing and evaluating information and communicating in digital environments. They implemented strategies to resist distractions from social tools.

Table 3. (*Continued*)

Paper	Learners and Their Context	Methods	Summary of Learner Attributes
Seale, Draffan, and Wald (2010)	UK higher education students with a disability. Questions focussed on how disabled learners experience and participate in technology rich learning environments.	Participatory approach. Online survey, interview with artefact, focus group ($n = 31$).	Digital agility: being extremely familiar with technology, using a wide range of strategies, and having high levels of confidence in their own ability to use technology.
Stein, Wanstreet, and Calvin (2009)	Students enrolled in a blended, US graduate-level course on adult education in American society.	Online chat sessions ($n = 15$) and in-depth interviews ($n = 5$).	Reducing the transactional distance space by creating a voice for learning, connecting in a space for learning and creating a time for learning.
Winter, Cotton, Gavin, and Yorke (2010)	University staff taking postgraduate courses in teaching development.	Survey and semi-structured interviews ($n = 10$).	Students who used technology effectively for learning utilised appropriate e-technologies to meet their own learning needs, used networks to access support and were effective e-communicators.

rich environments, keywords arose from the papers themselves. There was no attempt to reinterpret the original data, hence the keywords represent the attributes that had been identified by the authors of the papers, using their original terms. The keywords and their frequency of occurrence are listed in Table 4. It is remarkable that there are 47 keywords arising from just 15 papers, of which most appeared in one paper and none appeared in more than four papers. It is clear that we do not yet share a common terminology for describing the attributes of learners in a digital age.

Table 4. List of Keywords to Describe Characteristics of Effective Learners in Technology Enhanced Learning Environments and Number of Papers Allocated This Keyword.

Keywords	Number of Papers Allocated This Keyword ($n = 18$)
Active learning	2
Adaptability	1
Affiliation	1
Affordances	3
Agility	1
Belief	1
Boundaries	1
Camaraderie	1
Collaboration	2
Communication	2
Conceptions	2
Confidence	3
Connections	2
Contribution	2
Control	1
Cooperation	1
Critical engagement	1
Deep approach	4
Distraction	3
E-communication skills	1
E-research skills	1
Engagement	1
Expectations	1
Experimentation	1
Fluency	1
Gender	1
Help-seeking	2
Identity	1
Incidental learning	1
Information literacy	3
Initiating	1
Inquisitive	1
Intentionality	1
Meta-cognition	2
Networks and networking	2
Openness	2
Participation	1
Personalisation	2
Playfulness	1
Prior experience	2
Prioritisation	1
Reflection	2

Table 4.   (*Continued*)

Keywords	Number of Papers Allocated This Keyword ($n=18$)
Resourcefulness	1
Sharing	3
Sociability	1
Space	1
Voice	1

It is worth noting that the keywords arose in the findings and discussion sections. That is, few of the studies set out to identify the attributes of successful learners. Rather they tended to observe that not all learners responded in similar ways to the environments they were presented with and went on to explore the duality they found between 'some' or 'many' learners. It also seems that successful learners in these environments are still not the norm. Some of the included studies commented that generally students were less IT competent than expected (Masterman & Shuyska, 2012), not very experienced using e-learning (Winter et al., 2010) or were naïve about the role of technology in learning (Anagnostopoulou et al., 2009; Katic, 2008). Indeed, a number of studies that I expected to include were excluded from the final set because they did not find any attributes or practices that were contributing to effective learning in digital environments. This included Katic's (2008) study of conceptions of technology in trainee teachers, where neither of the participants recognised the potentially transformative impact of technology for education, and Ferguson's (2010) evaluation, which uncovered only negative experiences of using online forums in a distance learning setting.

Developing Themes for Analysis

Finally the findings sections of each of the 15 papers were coded against the keywords, and themes were allowed to emerge. This allowed for expansion of the themes and iterative levels of interpretation. The keywords enabled searching of the endnote database for the relevant literature on each learner attribute. Table 5 gives how themes emerged over the iterative interpretations of the findings in response to multiple readings, using memos, annotations and sketches. The second-order interpretations largely draw on the concepts identified by the original authors. The challenge between the second and subsequent order interpretations was to move

Table 5.   Developing Levels of Interpretation.

Overarching Concepts	Second-Order Interpretations	Third-Order Interpretations	Fourth-Order Interpretations
Learning approach	Deep Collaborative Reflective Networked Active Cooperative Engagement Experimental	Understanding and making use of the potential of new technology for: • Activity • Openness • Sharing • Collaboration • Customisation • Personalisation	Learner attributes well suited to next generation learning environments. I am: − Engaged − Connected − Confident − Adaptable − Intentional − Self-aware
Technology	Access Affordances Personalisation Familiarity Prior experience		
Identity	Affiliation Camaraderie Gender Voice	Intentionally adopting an approach that is well suited to networked learning environments: • Contributing • Engaging • Participating • Networking • Initiating • Generating	
Personal approach	Agility Adaptability Confidence Playfulness Fluency Inquisitiveness Resourcefulness		
Conceptions	Beliefs Expectations Meta-cognition Choices Control	Understanding my own role in making use of new technology: • Manage boundaries and distractions • Network • Communicate with others • Present myself • Personalise my tech • Use a wide range of strategies	

Table 5. (*Continued*)

Overarching Concepts	Second-Order Interpretations	Third-Order Interpretations	Fourth-Order Interpretations
Skills	E-research E-communication Information literacy Personalisation Networking Help-seeking Prioritisation Space Boundaries Distraction		

beyond simple categorisation of keywords to reveal a subtext which cuts across the initial overarching concepts. The fourth-order interpretations return to the core issue of attributes well suited to next generation learning environments.

FINDINGS AND DISCUSSION

The analysis resulted in six attributes that describe students who thrive in next generation learning environments. The discussion that follows explores the evidence for these attributes and what they each mean within the context of next generation learning environments. Returning to the original studies allows these attributes to be expanded and illustrated with examples, with an emphasis on those expressed in the words of learners themselves.

Engaged

What does it mean to be an engaged learner within next generation learning environments? Being engaged was variously described as being active (Anagnostopoulou et al., 2009), actively engaged (Hoekstra, 2008) or critically engaged (Ellis et al., 2012). Some studies also referred to the need for learners to contribute or participate (Anagnostopoulou et al., 2009;

Brown & Czerniewicz, 2007; Dujardin, 2009). In addition Brown et al. (2013), Buckley et al. (2010) and Masterman and Shuyska (2012) noted that many of the students they worked with exhibited characteristics of a deep approach to learning.

Ellis et al. (2012) offered the most systematic investigation of engagement in their phenomenographic analysis of interviews with students who had experienced various kinds of enquiry-based learning. They found that what distinguished students was their understanding of what constitutes engaged enquiry, specifically learning through enquiry by being 'active, critically engaged and aware of the value of authentic contexts/discovery processes' (p. 617). Here engagement is not just for its own sake, rather learners with this conception 'engaged sufficiently with the experience to discover what the real knowledge is in order to participate effectively' (p. 618). Although Ellis et al. specifically related engagement to enquiry-based tasks, there are clear parallels here with other types of learning activities. For example, Hoekstra (2008) found that some students talked about their desire to be actively engaged when using clickers in lectures.

Connected

What does it mean to be a connected learner within next generation learning environments? Around half of the studies mentioned being adept at communicating in digital environments as important to their learners (Andrews & Tynan, 2012; Brown et al., 2013; Dujardin, 2009; Lea & Jones, 2011; Masterman & Shuyska, 2012; Stein et al., 2009; Winter et al., 2010). It is not just that students must be skilled at e-communications, they must also be well connected and value these interactions. Being skilled includes issues of voice, identity and awareness of self-presentation. Making use of networks for informal support is also a significant feature of this attribute.

Dujardin (2009) described her single fluent e-learner as 'fluent in her online presentation, she valued her interactions with others and contributed to the overall sociability of the VLE'. For Stein et al. (2009) creating 'a voice for learning' was a significant part of reducing transactional distance for novice online learners.

Winter et al. (2010) also identified being a good e-communicator as important, where these skills were used to sustain relationships with colleagues, facilitate learning through academic networks and gain support through formal and informal channels, as in this example:

> I hassle people [through email] for help with the things I am stuck on. There are also a lot of mailing lists that you can get information from. (Winter et al., p. 76)

Andrews and Tynan (2012) reported that being able to participate in informal networks was highly valued by students, particularly for accessing help on technical issues. Indeed, connectedness was a key theme in their study, defined as 'students' ability to interact with each other, their lecturers and the institution' (p. 571). Andrews and Tynan noted that students made use of both institutionally supported and personal technologies to do this. This example was of students working together informally to prepare for an individually assessed task:

> Log into Facebook and Skype to see what others are doing − we have a quiz for one of the units that we decide that we'll try and do together this afternoon. (Andrews & Tynan, p. 574)

The use of informal networks was explored in more detail by Lea and Jones (2011) who found students embraced social networking in order to gain support. Here students took on multiple identities in order to gain support and worked in ways which protected each other and the connections they had built.

Making use of support was a key theme for Brown et al. (2013). Here students who sought support did so not only from peers, they also expressed a desire to have contact with lecturers for the purpose of discussion, reassurance and feedback.

Confident

Even if students adopt an engaged approach to their learning, and value and use the connections they have with others, it seems they need something else in order to take the extra step and make use of the technology, networks and learning tasks available to them. This was described by some studies as confidence to use technology (Jeffrey et al., 2011; Masterman & Shuyska, 2012; Seale et al., 2010), and by others as a willingness to initiate interaction (Brown et al., 2013) or a willingness to share (Hoekstra, 2008; Jeffrey et al., 2011; Kear et al., 2010).

For Seale et al. (2010) confidence in one's own ability to use technology was an important element of their notion of digital agility. For Jeffrey et al. (2011) confidence with technology use also included digital identity and privacy. However, it is recognised that confidence in using technology is the most problematic of the attributes explored in this chapter. Students frequently overestimate their own confidence and self-reported confidence does not relate well with appropriate technology use. This was illustrated well by Masterman and Shuyska (2012) in their discussion of confidence:

> Educ81 initially confessed 'I generally don't not have much confidence in my technology abilities', but was adopting a wide range of technologies in her dissertation fieldwork. (Masterman & Shuyska, 2012, p. 348)

A willingness to share with others was expressed in a number of studies including not being anxious about sharing own ideas when cooperating with classmates in lectures that used clickers (Hoekstra, 2008). Jeffrey et al. (2011) expressed such willingness to share as 'The collaborative process revealed the importance of a particular disposition underpinning digital and information literacy, namely sharing' (p. 397).

Adaptable

Being adaptable can be described as having a wide range of strategies on which to draw (Anagnostopoulou et al., 2009; Seale et al., 2010), a resourcefulness to overcome challenges and prioritise competing demands (Andrews & Tynan, 2012; Holley, 2009), and/or a tendency to experiment with technology (Jeffrey et al., 2011; Masterman & Shuyska, 2012; Seale et al., 2010). Interestingly, being adaptable seemed to enable students to develop the strategies they needed in order to use technology in ways that met their own individual learning needs.

Anagnostopoulou et al. (2009) found that learners who persisted were aware of how they learnt in a wide range of situations and had strategies to draw on. Seale et al. (2010) in their study of disabled learners listed the wide range of strategies that each individual learner had developed. Here learners described how they used experimentation or trial and error in order to learn how to use a new tool:

> I'd just use it — trial and error. I'd possibly ask my peers, but as I'm quite good with computers, I can just get stuck in. Most of the time I would probably just have a play. (Seale et al., 2010, p. 453)

Such experimentation was also highlighted by Jeffrey et al. (2011). This learning from experimentation was related to the time given to play, but also to an attitude to being open to learn new things in a new way:

> I just click here and oops that isn't what I wanted, so I do a lot of that and I find it quite helpful. You learn something every time you go around and around the menus. (Jeffrey et al., 2011, p. 403)

For both Andrews and Tynan (2012) and Holley (2009), being resourceful meant being able to combine and prioritise the competing demands of education, work and family life. Indeed, part of the reason students need to be adaptable is to find solutions for their own individual learning needs (Andrews & Tynan, 2012; Seale et al., 2010; Winter et al., 2010).

Intentional

The attribute of intentionality arose from an inspection of the examples of strategies that were given in the papers and the degree of choice that learners exerted. It seems to be important that learners are aware of their own agency in the learning process and that they know that they need to take action. While there were many examples of effective strategies it was the intent with which they are adopted which is of interest here. For example Winter et al. concluded that students who used technology effectively for learning recognised and utilised technologies to meet their own learning needs.

Another good example is the support seekers in Brown et al.'s study, who demonstrated early engagement with the online learning environment and regular contribution to online discussion forums. In order to achieve the desired levels of engagement they intentionally introduced strategies to help, such as creating mobile phone alerts whenever new posting were made. Similarly, a participant in the Jeffrey et al. study described how she tried to keep up with everyone else's blogs once a week. Andrews and Tynan (2012) reported that several students 'made a deliberate decision' to purchase mobile technologies to support their desire to access learning materials on the move.

Intentional strategies might go against the advice or expectations of lecturers and institutional guidance. Lea and Jones (2011) discussed in some detail students' preferences for instant messaging and personal email, even when they had been explicitly asked to use the institutional virtual learning environment. Student choices even extend to not using technology when it suited them better not to (Masterman & Shuyska, 2012; Winter et al., 2010). Winter et al. explored this specifically in relation to managing boundaries and distractions, where one student explained:

> No, of course I do not have my computer on when I am trying to learn because some-times it distracts me because I have the Messenger on or I will read the newspapers and I don't like that if I am trying to learn. (Winter et al., 2010, p. 78)

Self-aware

An awareness of one's own learning is important whether the context is technological or not. Anagnostopoulou et al. (2009) illustrated this, finding that students who persisted at university demonstrated an awareness of how they learn as individuals. In Ellis et al.'s study it was seen to be important that learners were aware of the 'intrinsic value' of learning contexts. This meta-cognition was well expressed by one of their interviewees:

> I find it easier to understand things if you do things hands-on, rather than just copying it out from a text book or learning things by rote learning, that sort of thing. (Ellis et al., 2012, p. 617)

In technological contexts, such an awareness of one's own learning needs to be complemented by an understanding of the affordances of the technology. Seale et al. (2010) report that the most frequently given reason for a particular technology use was whether students perceived it to support their learning or socialising.

Four of the studies referred to students' conceptions of discussion forums (Buckley et al., 2010; Dujardin, 2009; Stein et al., 2009; Winter et al., 2010). Winter et al. found that students with previous experience of online asynchronous discussions recognised the 'opportunities for reflection, expressing opinion and sharing ideas' (p. 77). Buckley et al. (2010) reported that students understood that discussion forums were a place where 'drawing on the experiences of others could help them to develop and learn new skills', and a place where they could share personal experiences and reflect upon themselves as learners. Dujardin's single 'fluent' e-learner said:

> It is very good to post the task to a forum where students can discuss each other's thoughts and point out issues that other students might miss otherwise.

Similarly Stein et al. (2009) explained how, as the course progressed, the fictional single learner 'Pat' came to understand the role of the discussions in knowledge creation:

> In this particular class, the dialogue caused us, I think, to really think through an issue because you weren't just making one-way communication, doing research and throwing it back out there. You were being challenged daily by your classmates to try and put something positive together and by the people [in] the other [groups]. (Stein et al., 2009, p. 308)

Effective learning also requires a self-awareness of the need to create times and spaces for learning. Holley (2009) recognised that learners do much to create their own spaces, finding that it is important that learners have high control over their home environment and use of technology. Stein et al. (2009) saw creating a time for learning as a key theme. For them, this meant prioritising and organising home life and study to accommodate online tasks.

CONCLUSIONS

Although models of digital literacy have recently started to make reference to learner attributes alongside skills and practices, few studies have set out to study the attributes of learners who are effective in next generation learning environments. Learner experience research, which uses qualitative methods to generate rich descriptions of learners' perspectives, has already shown the value of learning from learners themselves. Learning experience research can make a valuable contribution to our search for attributes that might characterise effective learners. Therefore this chapter used a meta-analysis technique to interpret the findings from existing learner experience research studies. The initial reading and allocation of keywords showed that researchers do not yet share a common terminology for describing the attributes of learners in a digital age. There is a need for more sharing and collaboration of the kind that takes place between researchers who are members of the ELESIG community.[3] It would be worthwhile now to use the methods developed by learner experience researchers to explore learner attributes in order to expand our models of digital literacy.

This review was deliberately interpretative in nature, developing iterative levels of interpretation to reduce the initial 47 keywords to six key attributes. Although it is unlikely to be the only way of representing the findings from these 15 studies, the review conceptualises those students who learn well as those who are engaged, connected, confident, adaptable, intentional and self-aware. I would suggest that being engaged and self-aware are applicable in all learning contexts. However, this review also hints that technology may be changing what it means to be a successful learner. While it might be argued that being confident, adaptable and intentional are also characteristics of good learners, it would be worthwhile to investigate in more detail how these attributes differ between traditional and next generation learning contexts. The attribute that might be especially worthy of further interrogation is 'connected'. For example, what does it mean to be connected as a learner and how does it differ from being social in more traditional learning spaces?

Finally, it was noted at the outset that context is enormously important in determining how students behave. This chapter sets a challenge for teachers, learning technologists, librarians and instructional designers to work to design learning activities which encourage and reward the development of these attributes.

NOTES

1. For details on the JISC Learner Experience Programme, see http://www.jisc.ac.uk/whatwedo/programmes/elearningpedagogy/learnerexperience.aspx
2. Here 'attributes' are taken to mean the qualities or characteristics of the learner.
3. ELESIG is an international community of educational researchers and practitioners who are involved in investigations of learners' experiences and uses of technology in learning. See http://www.elesig.net

ACKNOWLEDGEMENTS

Thanks to the anonymous reviewer and to my colleague Helen Beetham, who both provided valuable feedback on an earlier draft of this chapter.

REFERENCES

Ala-Mutka, K. (2011). *Mapping digital competence: Towards a conceptual understanding.* Seville: JRC-IPTS.

Anagnostopoulou, K., Parmar, D., & Priego-Hernandez, J. (2009). An exploration of the perceptions of learning and e-learning. *Brookes eJournal of learning and teaching, 2*(4). Retrieved from http://bejlt.brookes.ac.uk/. Accessed on April 12, 2013.

Andrews, T., & Tynan, B. (2012). Distance learner: Connected, mobile and resourceful individuals. *Australian Journal of Educational Technology, 28*(4), 565–579.

Biggs, J. B. (1989). Approaches to the enhancement of tertiary teaching. *Higher Education Research and Development, 8*, 7–25.

Brown, C., & Czerniewicz, L. (2007). If we build it will they come? Investigating the relationship between students' access to and use of ICTs for learning. *South African Journal of Higher Education, 21*(6), 732–747.

Brown, M., Hughes, H., Keppell, M., Hard, N., & Smith, L. (2013). Exploring the disconnections: Student interaction with support services upon commencement of distance education. *FYHE International Journal, 4*(2), 63–74.

Buckley, C. A., Pitt, E., Norton, B., & Owens, T. (2010). Students' approaches to study, conceptions of learning and judgements about the value of networked technologies. *Active Learning in Higher Education, 11*(1), 55–65.

Cabeza, R., & Nyberg, L. (2000). Imaging cognition II: An empirical review of 275 PET and fMRI studies. *Journal of Cognitive Neuroscience, 12*, 1–47.

Crisp, G. (2014). Assessment in next generation learning spaces. In K. Fraser (Ed.), *The future of learning and teaching in next generation learning spaces* (Vol. 12). International Perspectives on Higher Education Research. Bingley, UK: Emerald Group Publishing Limited.

Dujardin, A.-F. (2009). Conversations with an e-learner. *Brookes eJournal of Learning and Teaching, 2*(4). Retrieved from http://bejlt.brookes.ac.uk/. Accessed on April 12, 2013.

Edmunds, R., Thorpe, M., & Conole, G. (2012). Student attitudes towards and use of ICT in course study, work and social activity: A technology acceptance model approach. *British Journal of Educational Technology, 43*(1), 71–84.

Ellis, R. A., Bliuc, A. M., & Goodyear, P. (2012). Student experiences of engaged enquiry in pharmacy education: Digital natives or something else? *Higher Education, 64*(5), 609–626.

Ferguson, R. (2010). Peer interaction: The experience of distance students at university level. *Journal of Computer Assisted Learning, 26*(6), 574–584.

Hoekstra, A. (2008). Vibrant student voices: Exploring effects of the use of clickers in large college courses. *Learning, Media and Technology, 33*(4), 329–341.

Holley, D. L. (2009). *Spaces and places: Negotiated learning in the context of new technology.* Doctor of philosophy, Institute of Education, London.

Jeffrey, L., Bronwyn, H., Oriel, K., Merrolee, P., Coburn, D., & McDonald, J. (2011). Developing digital information literacy in higher education: Obstacles and supports. *Journal of Information Technology Education, 10*, 383–413.

Katic, E. K. (2008). Preservice teachers' conceptions about computers: An ongoing search for transformative appropriations of modern technologies. *Teachers & Teaching, 14*(2), 157–179.

Kear, K., Woodthorpe, J., Robertson, S., & Hutchison, M. (2010). From forums to wikis: Perspectives on tools for collaboration. *Internet & Higher Education, 13*(4), 218–225.

Kirkwood, A., & Price, L. (2005). Learners and learning in the 21st century: What do we know about students' attitudes and experiences of ICT that will help us design courses? *Studies in Higher Education, 30*(3), 257–274.

Lea, M. R., & Jones, S. (2011). Digital literacies in higher education. Exploring textual and technological practice. *Studies in Higher Education, 36*(3), 377–393.

Liao, H.-L., & Lu, H.-P. (2008). The role of experience and innovation characteristics in the adoption and continued use of e-learning websites. *Computers & Education, 51*(4), 1405–1416.

Liaw, S.-S. (2008). Investigating students' perceived satisfaction, behavioral intention, and effectiveness of e-learning: A case study of the blackboard system. *Computers & Education, 51*(2), 864–873.

Ling, P., & Fraser, K. (2014). Pedagogies for next generation learning spaces: Context, theory, action. In K. Fraser (Ed.), *The future of learning and teaching in next generation learning spaces* (Vol. 12). International Perspectives on Higher Education Research. Bingley, UK: Emerald Group Publishing Limited.

Masterman, E., & Shuyska, J. A. (2012). Digitally mastered? Technology and transition in the experience of taught postgraduate students. *Learning, Media & Technology, 37*(4), 335–354.

Noblit, G. W., & Hare, R. D. (1988). *Meta-ethnography: Synthesizing qualitative studies.* Newbury Park, CA: Sage.

SCONUL. (1999). Seven Pillars of Information Literacy. Retrieved from http://www.sconul.ac.uk/groups/information_literacy/seven_pillars.html. Accessed on April 30, 2009.

SCONUL. (2012). Seven Pillars of Information Literacy through a digital literacy lens. Retrieved from http://www.sconul.ac.uk/tags/digital-literacy. Accessed on April 12, 2013.

Seale, J., Draffan, E. A., & Wald, M. (2010). Digital agility and digital decision-making: Conceptualising digital inclusion in the context of disabled learners in higher education. *Studies in Higher Education, 35*(4), 445–461.

Sharpe, R., & Beetham, H. (2010). Understanding students' uses of technology for learning: Towards creative appropriation. In R. Sharpe, H. Beetham, & S. De Freitas (Eds.), *Rethinking learning for a digital age: How learners are shaping their own experiences* (pp. 85–99). London: Routledge.

Sharpe, R., & Savin-Baden, M. (2007). Learning to learn through supported enquiry. A literature review conducted for the L2L through supported enquiry FDTL5 project. Retrieved from http://www.som.surrey.ac.uk/learningtolearn/Resources.asp. Accessed on May 14, 2014.

Stein, D. S., Wanstreet, C. E., & Calvin, J. (2009). How a novice online adult learner experiences transactional distance. *Quarterly Review of Distance Education, 10*(3), 305–311.

Winter, J., Cotton, D., Gavin, J., & Yorke, J. (2010). Effective e-learning? Multi-tasking, distractions and boundary management by graduate students in an online environment. *ALT-J: Research in Learning Technology, 18*(1), 71–83.

CHAPTER 8

INCLUSIVE PRACTICES IN ACADEMIA AND BEYOND

Helen Larkin, Claire Nihill and Marcia Devlin

ABSTRACT

This chapter explores a set of principles that underpin ensuring that the learning needs of all students are addressed in next generation learning spaces. With increasingly diverse higher education environments and populations, higher education needs to move from seeing student diversity as problematic and deficit-based, to welcoming, celebrating and recognising diversity for the contributions it makes to enhancing the experience and learning outcomes for all students. The principles of Universal Design for Learning (CAST, 2011) provide a framework for high-quality university teaching and learning, as well as guidance on the multiple methods and means by which all students can be engaged and learn in ways that best suit their individual styles and needs. An inclusive approach is important pedagogically and applies to both the physical and virtual environments and spaces inhabited by students. When the design of physical environments does not incorporate universal design principles, the result is that some students can be locked out of participating in campus or university life or, for some, the energy required to participate can be substantial. With the digital education frontier expanding at an exponential rate, there is also a need to ensure that online and virtual

The Future of Learning and Teaching in Next Generation Learning Spaces
International Perspectives on Higher Education Research, Volume 12, 147–171
ISSN: 1479-3628/doi:10.1108/S1479-362820140000012012

*environments are accessible for all. This chapter draws on the relevant
research and the combined experience of the authors to explore an
approach to inclusive practices in higher education next generation learning spaces and beyond.*

Keywords: Universal design; inclusive design; higher education;
teaching and learning; diversity

INTRODUCTION

The final report of the Bradley review of Australian higher education in
2008 stated:

> The nation will need more well-qualified people if it is to anticipate and meet
> the demands of a rapidly moving global economy. Work by Access Economics predicts
> that from 2010 the supply of people with undergraduate qualifications will not keep
> up with demand. To increase the numbers participating we must also look to members
> of groups currently under-represented within the system, that is, those disadvan-
> taged by the circumstances of their birth: Indigenous people, people with low socio-
> economic status, and those from regional and remote areas. (Commonwealth of
> Australia, 2008, p. xi)

The review recommended a demand-driven system and national and
institutional targets for the participation and performance of students
from low socio-economic status backgrounds, as well as increased funding
for these students and these recommendations were accepted and actioned
by the Australian government. In the context of the Australian government's response to the Bradley review, the sector is now on a trajectory
predicted by Trow (1972) who wrote of higher education expansion and
transformation from elite, through mass, to universal access. This chapter
is underpinned by the assumption that as the sector moves forward from
the beginning of massification brought about by the Dawkins reforms of
the late 1980s and into the Bradley reforms toward universality, '… it is
appropriate to work toward successful experiences for all students who
study within these changing frameworks, including the greater number,
and proportion, of non-traditional students who will increasingly study
alongside traditional students' (Devlin, 2010, p. 1). This necessitates a
focus not only on access but also on achievement for all students. As the
International Association of Universities (2008) puts it, 'The goal of
access policies should be successful *participation* in higher education, as

access without a reasonable chance of success is an empty phrase' (p. 1, emphasis added).

Today's massified higher education environment, argue Devlin and Larkin (2013) '... has opened [university] up to a larger number and wider range of students' (p. 145) than in the past. The 'typical' university student no longer exists and Devlin and Larkin argue that assumptions can no longer be made about the skills and abilities of those attending university. Given these increasing participation rates, Thomas and May (2010) suggest adopting a more sophisticated understanding of diversity than historical, deficit-based understandings. In the past, universities have provided support services that target specific student groups including students with disabilities and students who have English as an additional language. These services have typically adopted an approach, whereby difference and diversity were seen as problematic and as requiring some sort of remedial attention to promote assimilation into the dominant culture (Dunworth & Briguglio, 2011).

An inclusive approach to student learning in higher education is highly applicable in the technology-enabled and collaborative spaces now favoured in next generation learning spaces, as well as in many other formal and informal spaces inhabited by students. With so many new technologies emerging almost daily, it can be difficult for teaching staff to critically analyse the benefits of new technologies, particularly given the perceived pressure to embrace these innovations. By taking an inclusive approach, it is possible to identify where such technologies may either facilitate or inhibit student learning and to ask how the needs of all students in next generation learning spaces can be met.

At the heart of inclusive teaching and learning is collaboration. 'Nothing about us without us' is a catchphrase that has often been used in the past within a number of so-called minority groups, particularly people who live with disability. However, this concept is equally relevant to the diverse group of students who attend university. To enable participation and success, we need to be inclusive. But what does this mean in higher education and what does this mean in an education environment that is becoming increasingly complex and challenging? Bringing together collaborative approaches and inclusivity in the design and use of next generation learning spaces is a necessary element to addressing this complexity.

This chapter examines the traditional deficit-based model historically applied to accommodating the needs of students who do not fit the 'typical student' profile. A more sophisticated definition of diversity is offered and through this lens, it is argued that student diversity enhances the educational experience for all. The chapter then explores the principles of Universal Design (Connell et al., 1997) in relation to built environments and how these have led to the principles of Universal Design for Learning (CAST, 2011). A model for embedding these principles into the design of next generation learning spaces is proposed and the argument is made that all learning spaces and places whether they be traditional or newer and emerging can disadvantage some students some of the time. It is proposed therefore that when considering the impact and use of next generation learning spaces, teachers continue to ask themselves questions about who is being disadvantaged at any point in time by their teaching choices within these learning spaces. It is proposed that one approach to contextualising these pedagogical reflections is the use of the principles of Universal Design for Learning. The authors also explore the challenges of embracing such diversity in work integrated learning programs that are increasingly becoming part of many students' new learning places and spaces.

THE POTENTIAL BENEFITS AND CHALLENGES OF NEXT GENERATION LEARNING SPACES

With increasing numbers of non-traditional students entering higher education, questions about how to teach diverse student cohorts effectively, inevitably arise (Northedge, 2002). One approach that the literature indicates is a critically important way to improve the overall quality of teaching and learning with diverse student cohorts, is the use of technology, often used in next generation learning spaces (Bullen & James, 2007; Milliken & Barnes, 2002; O'Flaherty, Scutter, & Albrecht, 2010). Such spaces are typically considered to be more student-centred and to be purpose-built to promote small group, and formal and informal collaborative learning through the capacity for flexible furniture configurations where multiple activities can occur (Dane, 2010). Thus the design of the physical environment, including seating, tables and general ambience, in combination with digital technologies designed to be accessible to both students and teachers (Wilson & Randall, 2012), aims to optimise student engagement (Oliver & Nikoletatos, 2009).

According to the literature, the use of technology in next generation learning spaces can make classes more engaging, raise student commitment and performance and in terms of social inclusion, allow for greater access for all students (Kuh & Vesper, 2001; Milliken & Barnes, 2002; Nelson

Laird & Kuh, 2005). Milliken and Barnes argue that '... new technologies offer novel opportunities for learning that take account of individual aptitude and interest' (p. 226). However, there is also evidence that next generation learning spaces can disadvantage some students. Issues include students feeling pressured to work within groups when this may not be their preferred learning style (Dane, 2010) and the positioning of equipment and screens that makes it difficult for teachers and students to have eye contact (Wilson & Randall, 2012). Not only may this be potentially disengaging and isolating for students and teachers, it can also seriously impact on learning for students who have a hearing impairment and are dependent to greater or lesser extent on being able to see the face of the person talking. The physical design of these spaces can also lead to obstructions of circulation space for students and staff with mobility impairments and assumptions made about the accessibility and use of the located digital technologies may not always be correct.

In planning and implementing appropriate learning activities and assessment tasks, teaching staff are encouraged to question and consider who is being disadvantaged at any point in time by the chosen approach within next generation learning spaces. All assessment tasks and teaching activities will disadvantage some students some of the time. The emergence of next generation learning spaces does not change this fact and we need to continue to question our assumptions and approaches and consider whether we are continuing to disadvantage some students in new ways.

STUDENT DIVERSITY AND AN INCLUSIVE APPROACH

Thomas and May (2010) argue that diversity needs to be considered from a number of dimensions. Their central ideas are outlined in Table 1. Using these dimensions, diversity extends far beyond the groups traditionally defined as diverse and is inclusive of a broad range of students. Furthermore, the dimensions reinforce the notion that students' individual circumstances cannot be confined to specific minority categories or reduced to one or two single dimensions (Tange & Kastberg, 2013). It is more likely that '... multiple identities and personal circumstances will influence learning' (Carey, 2012, p. 742). Within a massified system, the likelihood of students from a wide diversity of backgrounds is significantly magnified and the need for inclusivity is highlighted.

Table 1.   Dimensions of Diversity.

Student Diversity	
Diversity dimensions	Examples
Educational diversity	Level/type of entry qualifications; skills; ability; knowledge; educational experience; life and work experience; learning approaches.
Dispositional diversity	Identity; self-esteem; confidence; motivation; aspirations; expectations; preferences; attitudes; assumptions; beliefs; emotional intelligence; maturity; learning styles; perspectives; interests; self-awareness; gender; sexuality.
Circumstantial diversity	Age; disability; paid/voluntary employment; caring responsibilities; geographical location; access to IT and transport services; flexibility; time available; entitlements; financial background and means; marital status.
Cultural diversity	Language; values; cultural capital; religion and belief; country or origin/residence; ethnicity/race; social background.

Source: Adapted from Thomas and May (2010, p. 5).

Rather than students needing to self-identify and disclose their requirements for specific and individualised supports to enable participation in all aspects of higher education, May and Bridger (2010) argue that this more sophisticated understanding of diversity in all its dimensions:

> … necessitates a shift away from supporting specific student groups through a discrete set of policies or time-bound interventions, towards equity considerations being embedded within all functions of the institution and treated as an ongoing process of quality enhancement. Making a shift of such magnitude requires cultural and systemic change at both the policy and practice levels. (p. 2)

This approach to diversity celebrates and embraces difference not as something to be marginalised and considered as 'other' or 'special', but as '… including everyone regardless of who or what they are so inclusive for one means inclusive for all' (Thomas & May, 2010, p. 20).

WHY IS AN INCLUSIVE APPROACH IMPORTANT?

As discussed earlier in this chapter, next generation learning spaces embrace collaborative approaches to teaching and learning and the use of new and always emerging technologies. However, unless the fundamental principles of an inclusive approach are central to the design of the teaching and learning spaces and the activities that occur within these spaces, students may continue to be marginalised in ways that have always existed or in new ways not previously experienced.

Dunworth and Briguglio (2011) argue that '... in a globalised world, intercultural and international interactions are increasingly becoming the norm rather than the exception' (p. 2). It makes sense, then, that higher education teaching and learning spaces and places reflect that same diversity but also benefit from it. Inclusive practices have the potential to enhance and enrich the curriculum and academic achievement of all students.

The presence of international students in higher education provides an illustration of these benefits. In relation to international students, Milem (2003) states there is evidence that the '... educational experiences and outcomes of individual students are enhanced by the presence of diversity on campus' (p. 129). In an inclusive and collaborative classroom, whether it be traditional, next generation, physical or virtual, Tange and Kastberg (2013) believe that rather than seeing cultural and language diversity as a problem to be fixed, an international curriculum acknowledges and builds on other ways of knowing and different knowledge systems. Rather than the conventional interpretation of international students in particular as being the '... net receivers of Euro-American wisdom' (p. 1), an inclusive environment and teaching draws on this diversity and brings a range of insights and perspectives into the classroom that would otherwise be unavailable. They stress the importance of not privileging Western perspectives and ways of knowing at the expense of alternative approaches.

Effective teaching ensures the alignment of teaching activities with learning outcomes and assessment tasks as a way of making the curriculum more explicit and scaffolded for all students (Biggs & Tang, 2007). All areas of study, regardless of discipline, have a language and discourse of their own that needs to be made explicit to students as part of the curriculum. At times this is viewed to be problematic only for students whose native language is not English, however, '... most students, no matter what their language background, are likely to benefit from explicit induction into the vocabulary, the different types of text and the communicative style of their chosen discipline' (Dunworth & Briguglio, 2011, p. 4).

The need for effective educators to ensure that graduates have a high level of critical thinking and reflection is well recognised in the literature (Larkin & Pépin, 2013) and in the graduate learning outcomes embraced by many universities worldwide. Commitment to such practice underpins and is entirely consistent with incorporating inclusive pedagogical practices. Nolan and Sim (2011) define reflective practice as the ability to:

> Identify one's own values, beliefs and assumptions, consider other perspectives or alternative ways of viewing the world: being able to identify what perspectives are missing from one's account; identify how one's own views can have a particular bias that privileges one view over another; perceive contradictions and inconsistencies in one's own account of events; and, imagine other possibilities. (p. 123)

Effective educators value such an approach, specifically teach it and are committed to inclusive pedagogy so that perspectives and ways of knowing alternative to the dominant ones are included as part of the curriculum and experience for students. This needs to occur regardless of whether the teaching occurs in traditional or next generation learning spaces. One aspect of effective teaching is adopting a learner-centred approach for cooperative and collaborative learning and enabling the participation of as broad a range of students as possible. It ensures that all students are able to access and engage with course materials and curriculum and that assessment processes allow students to demonstrate their strengths and learning (Equality Challenge Unit, 2013).

PREPARING WORK READY GRADUATES

Encouraged by the government, universities are increasingly emphasising the importance of graduates developing a range of generic skills and competencies that prepare them for the workforce. In Australia, these often include concepts related to global citizenship, emphasising the need for an appreciation and understanding of international perspectives and the ability to apply these skills and competencies within diverse communities. Dunworth and Briguglio (2011) argue that a globalised world '... requires skills and knowledge that will enable graduates to function effectively: a world in which they will need to negotiate cultural, linguistic and professional differences' (p. 2). It is important, therefore, that multiple standpoints are critically examined within the curriculum and that teaching ensures that students are well prepared for current and future workforce demands. Thus an understanding and embracing of diversity is becoming highly valued.

In the context of next generation learning spaces and preparing work ready graduates, there is a tendency to think only of technology-enabled teaching spaces. However, in a higher education sector that values and increasingly seeks work integrated learning opportunities for students (Patrick et al., 2008), it can be argued that workplace learning spaces and workplaces are 'next generation' for those universities that continue to seek workplace experiences not only in traditional discipline areas but also in study programs where they have previously not existed.

THE PRINCIPLES OF UNIVERSAL DESIGN FOR LEARNING

In considering the design of next generation learning spaces, it is useful to consider the concept of universal design, which aims to ensure that products and physical environments are '... usable by all people, to the greatest extent possible, without the need for adaptation or specialised design' (Connell et al., 1997, para. 1). With '... an increasing emphasis on diversity, equity and access in the social and political agendas globally' (Larkin, Hitch, Watchorn, Ang, & Stagnitti, 2013, p. 414), these principles are being seen as a foundation for community change. Connell et al. (1997) outlined seven principles of Universal Design and these are summarised in Table 2.

Table 2. The Principles of Universal Design.

Principle	Descriptor
(1) Equitable use	The design is useful and marketable to people with diverse abilities.
(2) Flexibility in use	The design accommodates a wide range of individual preferences and abilities.
(3) Simple and intuitive use	Use of the design is easy to understand, regardless of the user's experience, knowledge, language skills or current concentration level.
(4) Perceptible information	The design communicates necessary information effectively to the user, regardless of ambient conditions or the user's sensory abilities.
(5) Tolerance for error	The design minimises hazards and the adverse consequences of accidental or unintended actions.
(6) Low physical effort	The design can be used efficiently and comfortably and with a minimum of fatigue.
(7) Size and space for approach and use	Appropriate size and space is provided for approach, reach, manipulation and use regardless of user's body size, posture or mobility.

Source: Connell et al. (1997); Copyright© 1997 NC State University, The Center for Universal Design.

As a result of the work done on the seven principles of Universal Design by North Carolina State University to guide the design of built environments and products, the Center for Applied Special Technology (CAST) were inspired to build on these principles and investigate how they might translate to the educational context. They developed the principles of Universal Design for Learning (CAST, 2011) that focus on ensuring access by students to all aspects of the curriculum and learning in general to help '... address learner variability by suggesting flexible goals, methods, materials and assessments that empower educators to meet these varied needs' (CAST, p. 4).

The principles of Universal Design for Learning are:

- Principle 1: provide multiple means of representation (the 'what' of learning);
- Principle 2: provide multiple means of action and expression (the 'how' of learning); and
- Principle 3: provide multiple means of engagement (the 'why' of learning) (CAST, 2011, p. 5).

McGuire, Scott, and Shaw (2006) emphasise that these principles should not be used as a panacea for solving the perceived problem of accommodating the learning and personal needs of diverse student cohorts. These authors have also warned against '... quick solutions ...' (p. 172) that might be assumed to result from the application of these principles. The intent is that the application of Universal Design for Learning principles '... reduces barriers in instruction, provides appropriate accommodations, supports and challenges, and maintains high achievement expectations for all students' (CAST, 2011, p. 6). CAST argue that the principles need to be at the heart of the design of all teaching and learning-related activities '... from the outset to meet the needs of all learners, making costly, time-consuming, and after-the-fact changes unnecessary' (p. 4). As outlined earlier, the focus is not on the dumbing down of curriculum but instead on providing 'high support/high challenge' academic environments (Larkin & Richardson, 2013) where all students have the opportunity to participate and flourish while adhering to appropriate academic standards.

These principles are core to ensuring that technology-enabled and collaborative next generation learning spaces promote high-quality student learning experiences. Much of the technology that is now available facilitates multiple means of representation, action, expression and engagement. However, teaching technologies need to be critiqued against the principles to ensure that their use adds value and/or choice. It should also be noted that the adoption of such technology to the exclusion of other teaching modes that may be considered more traditional runs the risk of excluding some students. All teaching strategies and methods will disadvantage some students some of the time. The application of principles of Universal Design for Learning minimises such disadvantage.

TOWARDS BEING INCLUSIVE IN ACADEMIA AND BEYOND

While the application of Universal Design for Learning principles in universities has historically been situated within architectural and/or disability domains (McGuire et al., 2006), to ensure a truly inclusive approach across institutions, a shift is necessary to the design and practice of every learning opportunity, subject and course or programme.

Ideally, university subjects are designed with learning outcomes aligned to assessment tasks and activities as outlined by Biggs and Tang (2007). Combining this constructive alignment approach with the Universal Design for Learning principles, along with new digital technologies where relevant, provides a framework for scaffolding effective learning for the broadest range of students possible. Hall and Stahl (2006) argue that this facilitates experiences for students that are not only more equitable but more effective.

Fig. 1 illustrates a model for embedding Universal Design for Learning in the development and implementation of effective and inclusive teaching. It goes beyond accessibility, by applying a constructivist paradigm to pedagogy and practice to promote engagement, motivation and a personal connection for students in their learning. Aspects of such an approach include:

- *learning outcomes* that are designed with clarity and flexibility for all students;
- *learning activities* that make space for a diversity of learners;
- *assessment* tasks that enable all students to demonstrate to their full potential;
- *course-specific knowledge* that focuses on mastery of learning outcomes; and
- *graduate learning outcomes* that are embedded.

This model takes into account Biggs and Tangs' (2007) constructive alignment theory, the inclusive approaches to curriculum change from the

University of Wolverhampton (2011) and the CAST (2011) principles of Universal Design for Learning.

APPLYING UNIVERSAL DESIGN FOR LEARNING PRINCIPLES TO PRACTICE

The infusion model of inclusive pedagogy as shown in Fig. 1 embraces the principles of Universal Design for Learning, that is, multiple models of representation, expression and engagement (CAST, 2011), and emphasises their application to the whole curriculum in terms of intended learning outcomes, learning activities and materials, assessment tasks, course-specific skills and graduate learning outcomes. The model also provides

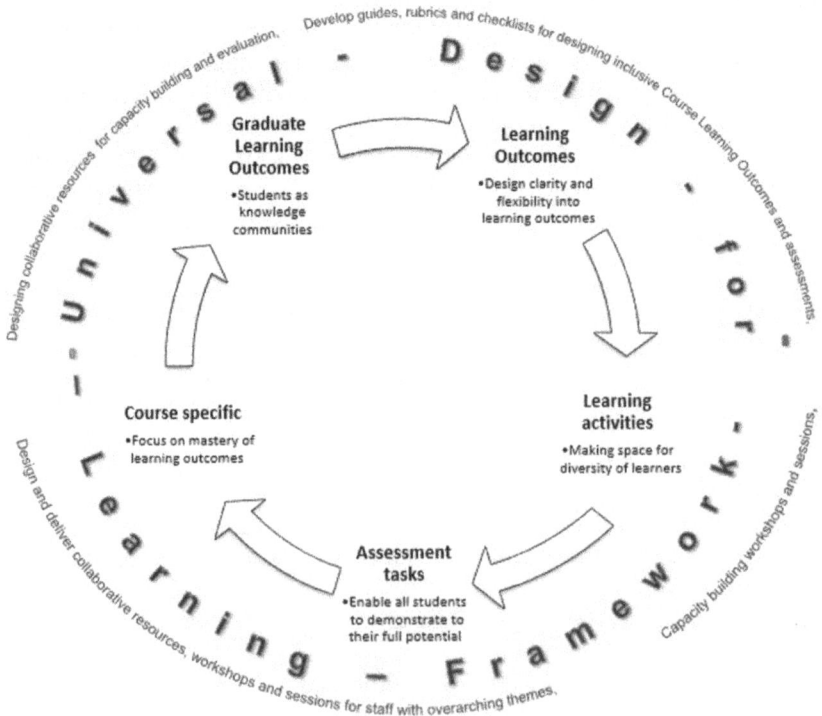

Fig. 1.   Infusion Model of Inclusive Pedagogy.

practical suggestions for academic staff and others for developing inclusive curriculum and resources. Each of these curriculum areas is now considered in turn.

Learning Outcomes

Learning outcomes provide students with details about the features and requirements necessary for completing subjects and courses successfully. They are essential to students' understanding of what they can expect to learn.

Intended learning outcomes that are clear statements with explicit language and unambiguous vocabulary set the background for learning to take place. Universal Design for Learning provides a reminder that learning outcomes need to be clear to all students and should not make assumptions about their background knowledge, skills and abilities. For example, academics often assume that all students understand what they mean when they ask them to 'reflect' or 'evaluate' or 'critique'. However, such terms are not necessarily uniformly understood even within discipline-specific programs of study. Therefore, academics need to think about creating learning objectives in ways to ensure they are explicit for the broadest group of students.

Language is not simply a conduit for the communication of ideas but shapes and interprets those ideas (Dunworth & Briguglio, 2011). There are benefits to all students in unpacking terminology, avoiding jargon and slang and de-mystifying highly technical language through the use of glossaries and other means. In this way academics can assist all students, regardless of language, academic literacy and preparedness for university, to '... identify and understand terms as they are being used in context' (DeFazio & Nihill, n.d., p. 6).

Learning Activities and Materials

Universal Design for Learning is not only about making materials more accessible. It is also about providing multiple means of expression, representation and engagement so that all students have the opportunity to learn. In adopting this aspect of the principles, different ways of doing this that are authentic and meaningful can be considered. In the past, universities have been dominated by lectures and books. However, there are multiple ways of representing materials and activities to suit the needs of all users. It is important that the potential of both traditional and newer technologies is realised to suit the needs of as many students as possible. While some academics have begun to move away from hard copy readers and course materials, instead choosing to put these materials online, this can disadvantage those students who prefer hard copy materials, particularly those who are financially disadvantaged and have to bear the costs of printing out documents. It is possible to lose sight of such issues when the focus is on state-of-the-art technology-driven next generation learning spaces.

The lead author of this chapter has applied the principles of Universal Design for Learning to the teaching of anatomy to health students. The teaching includes traditional lecture content, practical surface anatomy tutorials and textbook material. In addition, an online multimedia resource has been developed with a series of mini tutorials, and students also have an interactive online resource available to be accessed via the library catalogue. In-class teaching also employs the Essential Anatomy 3D™ app for tablets. Students are, therefore, provided with multiple means of representation and engagement with the learning materials and are able to choose the methods that best meet their personal learning styles and circumstances.

Course and teaching materials can include or exclude students. Using non-discriminatory and non-stigmatising language for case studies is essential for inclusion. For example, words such as 'parents' as opposed to 'mothers and fathers' offers legitimate knowledge to students, without excluding people from same sex relationships or alternative parenting arrangements. Case study and other materials need to reflect the same level of diversity as experienced in communities without the reproduction and reinforcement of stereotypes, thus acknowledging different ways of being and knowing.

With multimedia resources being increasingly used in teaching, combined with new digital technologies, it would be dangerous to assume that these somehow necessarily lead to more effective or engaging student learning. For example, some students can be disadvantaged by videos that do not have captioning. While closed captioning in traditional deficit-based models of accommodating student diversity can assist students with a hearing impairment (Brett, 2010), applying the more sophisticated understanding of diversity by Thomas and May (2010) indicates that the benefits of captioning are much broader. Not only does it benefit students and others (including staff) with a hearing impairment, it also benefits students for whom English is an additional language, students without the most up-to-date computer hardware and those who do not have access to headsets and may not have the opportunity to study in isolation. Some students' learning styles will preference written content over auditory presentation and they, too, will find captioning helpful. With the increasing use of videos in higher education and the cost of captioning becoming more affordable, consideration should be given to increased use of captioning for videos.

Assessment Tasks

Assessment in higher education has traditionally focused on examining students' performance, typically through exams and assignments. Assessment is a tool of and for learning, and is a key driver of learning; embedding feedback into the process is essential. Regular feedback into assessment tasks using peer and self-assessment can encourage and support self-management and self-reflection in individual students. Traditionally, when it has been given, feedback has often been staged and separated from summative assessment. However, an inclusive approach using the principles of Universal Design for Learning highlights the need for using a range of assessment modes within summative and formative assessment to determine to what extent learning outcomes have been met.

In a study of assessment and inclusivity, Gravestock and Grace (2008) proposed a set of particular considerations for designing fair and consistent assessment using Universal Design for Learning strategies. They suggested that academics ask themselves whether they were clear that:

- my learning outcomes use verbs that express the varying levels of sophistication of what I wish the students to learn;
- the outcomes are addressing different learning domains appropriately;
- the types of assessment available are as inclusive as possible — do I need/ is it possible to offer more flexibility; and
- the assessment methods are varied for different approaches and preferences — as far as is fair and practical (Gravestock & Grace, pp. 184–185).

Adopting a variety of assessment types across a course of study provides more opportunity for a greater range of expression of knowledge for a diverse student body. To scaffold the learning of all students, and to make the learning explicit, the assessment tasks chosen need to be authentic to the relevant intended learning outcomes. How best to assess various aspects of learning and ensure that the link between learning and assessment is clear for all students, needs careful consideration and planning.

Students' ability to critically reflect is enhanced through receiving feedback and using it effectively to become better learners. Strategies that require students to: self-assess against the assessment criteria; reflect on their learning as part of the assessment criteria in specific assignments; and, reflect on how they incorporated feedback from a previous assignment into the next assignment, will assist students to construct their own meaning in any given subject. The embedding of reflective practice into teaching activities and assessment tasks is an important way that students are able to individualise their own learning experiences, taking on board their personal needs, aspirations and skills.

Course-Specific and Graduate Learning Outcomes

From an inclusive perspective, the more information students are given that is course specific, the better. Information can include the purpose of the course, and the competencies, skills and knowledge that students can expect to demonstrate at the end of the course. A focus on the course enables mastery of the learning outcomes as a whole. Teaching staff need to be knowledgeable about the overall course curriculum so that they can make explicit for students, the cross-subject connections where appropriate. Academic literacies, reflective practice and other generic skills and attributes can be gradually scaffolded horizontally and vertically across the curriculum when a course approach is taken, although this is even more challenging for courses that are not structured for professional or other accreditation and those that offer many electives and pathways for students.

That said, Universal Design for Learning can provide a blueprint for embedding ways to acquire certain graduate outcomes, in the ways students express and communicate what they know. For example, a student with a refugee background who is studying nursing can be introduced to the community of nursing practice through certain topics or concepts around engaging ethically with diverse communities and cultures. By using these clear signposts, students with certain sets of knowledge and different educational experiences can tap into their own personal response, evaluation and self-reflection to content and activities.

INCLUSIVE PHYSICAL AND VIRTUAL ENVIRONMENTS

Students' ability to participate and flourish in higher education needs to be considered in the context of both physical and virtual environments. Wilson and Randall (2010) emphasise the importance of the design of the physical space in next generation learning spaces, while Van Note Chism (2002) outlines the disadvantages to student engagement and collaboration by poorly designed teaching spaces. As we understand the benefits of next generation learning spaces to be about enhanced collaboration, it is important that all students are therefore afforded these opportunities.

While good physical design of the classroom is essential for all to learn, regardless of educational, dispositional, circumstantial or cultural diversity (Thomas & May, 2010), it is essential also to realise the impact of the whole of the university campus and related services. With increased connectivity and the availability of collaborative learning spaces not only in classrooms but in libraries, cafes and other informal communal spaces where students come together, the design of these environments is crucial. As Oblinger (2005) put it, the entire university campus can now be considered as an interactive learning device.

While there are Australian standards related to accessibility, a minimalist application of these building standards whilst conforming to the relevant legislation will not lead to an inclusively designed campus or learning spaces, next generation or otherwise. For example, universities generally accept the need for classrooms to be physically accessible, but often tiered teaching spaces only allow students with mobility impairments to access the seated areas, and then only in a small targeted area. Staff with mobility impairments, however, may not get the same consideration and may not be able to perform their job due to inaccessible teaching spaces. Next generation learning spaces, without sufficient flexibility in relation to furniture design and use, may equally contribute to stigmatisation and also provide barriers to student collaboration and learning. The application of the principles outlined in this chapter and careful thought and planning, however, can maximise student collaboration and learning.

As a signatory to the United Nations Convention on the Rights of Persons with Disabilities, Australia recognises its responsibility to ensure that people with disability can access and participate equally in all aspects of their life, including education (Bialocerkowski, Johnson, Allan, & Phillips, 2013). The Disability Discrimination Act (1992) and its related legislation and the Disability Standards for Education (2005) mandate the need for all education providers to operate within the requirements of the Commonwealth discrimination legislation to ensure that students with a disability are not subject to discrimination and that all reasonable adjustments have been made to accommodate their needs and ensure course progression (Bialocerkowski et al.). In 2005, changes to the Disability Discrimination Act further strengthened the obligations of education providers to make 'unlawful the development or approval of curriculum that excludes people with disability from participation' (Brett, 2010, p. 5).

Beyond the legislative requirements, the principles of universal design provide a framework for considering the design of teaching spaces and their accessibility and equity for all users. Of course many universities are housed in old buildings where the cost of retro-fitting and meeting accessibility requirements is not only expensive but rarely leads to good design outcomes (Hitch, Larkin, Watchorn, & Ang, 2012). Large university campuses may also cause difficulties for students, staff and visitors navigating from one part of the campus to another. New buildings and facilities need to be designed within the parameters of inclusive and universal design to ensure that everyone is able to use all facilities and that their use is not based on ill-conceived assumptions about who does what in which space. However, although research into the design of next generation learning spaces is only evolving, there is evidence that universities can continue to make the same mistakes (Wilson & Randall, 2010) or that next generation learning spaces can provide great opportunities to get it right (Tom, Voss, & Scheetz, 2008).

In technology-rich next generation learning spaces (Wilson & Randall, 2010), it is important that the design of online and other web-based environments conform to the international guidelines for the accessibility for web content (W3C®, 2008). Such guidelines ensure that all students and staff can access the materials with minimal need for additional modification or support.

Many subjects require students to undertake collaborative group activities and assessments in the online environment without ever having physically met. In some cultures, this can be very uncomfortable for students who may feel unable to connect with a group to perform a common task unless they have previously had the chance to make a face-to-face connection. Skilled online moderation and/or the provision of opportunities to meet in person can be included in learning design to ensure students are not inadvertently excluded.

It is now common practice for more formal face-to-face teaching to be podcast for the use of off-campus students or those who either were not able to attend, prefer not to attend or those who wish to use lecture recordings to review their learning (Larkin, 2010). A simple yet effective way to ensure that those using the podcasts are not disadvantaged is to give page numbers for the PowerPoint™ slides so that those students who are learning asynchronously can follow the podcast and thereby feel included in the learning experience. Academics can also repeat student questions for the benefit of those using the recordings so they can follow the discussion more easily and understand the summing up at relevant points. These simple techniques can benefit all students, regardless of their physical or virtual presence.

INCLUSIVE WORK INTEGRATED LEARNING

Any higher education environment that seeks to support and promote the broadest possible learning of its students needs to proactively promote inclusion so as to '... respond to the needs of existing students but also to anticipate the needs of prospective students' (Matthews, 2009, p. 233), otherwise universities are dependent on students disclosing their specific circumstances and needs. While students from equity groups are encouraged to seek assistance, many choose not to do so. While the reasons for this are not always clear, Matthews suggests that, '... it is unlikely that it will ever be possible to encourage all students with additional learning needs to disclose' (p. 233). Universities are therefore becoming more aware of the need for teaching and learning environments and services that embrace and welcome diverse student cohorts.

Such an approach, however, can become more complex in professionally accredited courses designed to enable entry to a specific profession (for example, nursing and teaching) where increasing student diversity can lead to '... concern over implications regarding fitness for practice and public safety' (Carey, 2012, p. 741). This is despite the fact that it is increasingly recognised that student diversity mirrors the diversity of communities that students will ultimately need to serve. Carey (2012) and Bialocerkowski et al. (2013) argue that the notion of aspiring to an inclusive curriculum and practices at university may be in conflict to ensuring that students are safe for practice and that they are able to meet the entry level standards required by accrediting authorities.

This tension, and at times, contradiction, between two opposing sets of ideals poses an ongoing challenge for educators, professional accrediting authorities and practice partners to ensure that '... universities and their ... [industry] partners continue to expect and make explicit, a high standard of professional practice for students but that this sits within a student or learner-centred approach' (Larkin & Watchorn, 2012, p. 465). One area where this tension is commonly evident is when students for whom English is an additional language, participate in work integrated learning programmes. At university, these students can feel well supported and be afforded flexibility in demonstrating their learning through various means. However, the experience of the lead author is that while on a fieldwork practicum, these students may struggle because the same accommodations or supports are not available, nor necessarily appropriate. They are often required to read vast amounts of written information, interview people and write reports, all within relatively short turnaround times. There can also be a disconnect between the attitudes, values and approaches that universities adopt towards inclusivity, and those of universities' work integrated learning partners. As a result, students can experience stigmatisation and isolation in workplace settings (Carey, 2012). With increasingly diverse student groups entering university, consideration about how their diversity can be accommodated in work experiences is essential while at the same time ensuring that graduates are 'fit to practice' (Bialocerkowski et al., 2013, p. 3). Thus the tensions that exist between promoting the participation and engagement of a broad cohort of students as opposed to the standards required by accrediting authorities (Carey) can be difficult for those academics who are responsible for discipline-specific programs of study. While many accommodations can be made in the university environment, employers and those offering workplace learning do not always have the same willingness or capacity to offer similar flexibility and inclusive practices. Universities can often find themselves out of step with employers, or is it vice versa?

As Costa (2008) and Carey (2012) highlight, some professions have historically not been particularly diverse. As such, the professionals who are responsible for supervising students in workplace-based learning can be challenged by the current student diversity. In addition, practice educators often without any formal teaching background may be inclined to supervise students in ways that they were supervised many years earlier or in the ways in which they personally prefer to learn. Workplace educators may be unaware of the changes that have occurred in universities and in the students who attend (Larkin & Watchorn, 2012) and so may be underprepared for the students they manage. They are providing workplace learning for students who are generationally different, are from diverse cultural, socio-economic, circumstantial and language backgrounds, who may not have the same social and/or cultural capital or who have not yet developed their professional identity. Students are often being judged and assessed by practice educators who are members of a profession or workplace that may not be diverse. Whilst maintaining professional standards is essential for all professions, it is equally important to ensure that universities prepare graduates who are best able to serve the needs (existing and emerging) of the diverse communities in which they will work.

Carey (2012) argues that to establish a robust inclusive curriculum in an accredited course, '… a coordinated and consistent response from the higher education establishment, professional bodies, practitioners and policy-makers is necessary' (p. 741). However, he contends that the reality is that this is difficult to achieve due to a lack of clear direction or a coordinated, committed approach from the higher education institution. As a result, the implementation of inclusive teaching within such programs and subjects is often left to the interests and values of individual academic staff. The successful implementation of inclusive teaching and learning on such a broad scale, particularly in relation to work integrated learning, requires genuine commitment and support at the senior management and executive level of universities (Hockings, Brett, & Terentjevs, 2012).

CONCLUSION

It is not necessary to be expert on the needs or backgrounds of all students to provide an inclusive higher education experience in next generation learning spaces. Inclusive approaches encourage collaboration between staff and students, the adoption of critical reflection in teaching and greater flexibility to 'engage in discussion and make appropriate changes' (DeFazio & Nihill, n.d., p. 2). As teaching practices are expanded and improved, the need for individualised support for some students may still be necessary. This is partly because, to date, the application of universal design for learning and inclusive teaching to facilitate and add value to the learning of all students has been an aspirational goal and is likely to continue to be so for some time. The principles of universal design for learning have been used in this chapter to provide a framework that promotes continuous reflection on, and questioning of teaching practices related to next generation learning spaces, be they physical, virtual, formal, informal or workplace-based.

ACKNOWLEDGEMENT

We would like to thank the reviewers for their helpful comments on earlier versions of this chapter.

REFERENCES

Bialocerkowski, A., Johnson, A., Allan, T., & Phillips, K. (2013). Development of physiotherapy inherent requirement statements – An Australian experience. *BMC Medical Education, 13*, 54. Retrieved from http://www.biomedcentral.com/content/pdf/1472-6920-13-54.pdf

Biggs, J., & Tang, C. (2007). *Teaching for quality learning at university.* Berkshire, England: Open University Press.

Brett, M. (2010). Challenges in managing disability in higher education, illustrated by support strategies for deaf and hard of hearing students. *The Open Rehabilitation Journal, 3*, 4–8. Retrieved from http://www.benthamscience.com/open/torehj/articles/V003/SI0001TOREHJ/4TOREHJ.pdf

Bullen, M., & James, D. P. (Eds.). (2007). *Making the transition to e-learning: Strategies and issues.* Philadelphia, PA: Information Science Publishers.

Carey, P. (2012). Exploring variation in nurse educators' perceptions of the inclusive curriculum. *International Journal of Inclusive Education, 16*(7), 741–755.

CAST. (2011). *Universal Design for Learning (UDL) guidelines: Full text representation. Version 2.0.* Wakefield, MA: Center for Applied Special Technology.

Commonwealth of Australia. (1992). *Disability Discrimination Act 1992.* Canberra: Commonwealth of Australia.

Commonwealth of Australia. (2008). *Review of Australian higher education.* Final report. Department of Education, Employment and Workplace Relations, Canberra. Retrieved from www.deewr.gov.au/he_review_finalreport

Commonwealth of Australia. (2010). *The Disability Standards for Education 2005.* Canberra: Commonwealth of Australia.

Connell, B., Jones, M., Mace, R., Mueller, J., Mullick, A., Ostroff, E., … Vanderheiden, G. (1997). *The principles of universal design. Version 2.0.* North Carolina State University, NC: The Center for Universal Design. Retrieved from http://www.ncsu.edu/www/ncsu/design/sod5/cud/about_ud/udprinciplestext.htm

Costa, D. M. (2008). Fieldwork issues: A vision for fieldwork. *OT Practice, 13*(12), 20–22.

Dane, J. (2010). Teaching in student-centred learning environments. In M. Devlin, J. Nagy, & A. Lichtenberg (Eds.), *Research and development in higher education: Reshaping higher education* (Vol. 33, pp. 191–202). Melbourne: Higher Education Research and Development Society of Australasia. Retrieved from http://www.herdsa.org.au/wp-content/uploads/conference/2010/papers/HERDSA2010_Dane_J.pdf. Accessed on July 6–9, 2010.

DeFazio, T., & Nihill, C. (n.d.). *Inclusive teaching practices.* Deakin University. Retrieved from http://www.deakin.edu.au/learning/capacity-building/learning-2013-resources/teaching-practice-guides/inclusive-teaching-practices. Accessed on September 17, 2013.

Devlin, M. (2010). Non-traditional student achievement: Theory, policy and practice in Australian higher education. *Refereed proceedings of the First Year in Higher Education (FYHE) international conference*, 27–30 June, Adelaide. Retrieved from http://www.fyhe.com.au/past_papers/papers10/content/pdf/Marcia_Devlin_keynote_4.pdf. Accessed on January 29, 2014.

Devlin, M., & Larkin, H. (2013). The student experience. In S. Loftus, T. Gerzina, J. Higgs, M. Smith & E. Duffy (Eds.), *Educating health professionals: Becoming a university teacher* (pp. 145–158). Rotterdam: Sense Publishers.

Dunworth, K., & Briguglio, C. (2011). *Teaching students who have English as an additional language: A handbook for academic staff in higher education.* Milperra, NSW: Higher Education Research and Development Society of Australasia.

Equality Challenge Unit. (2013). *Equality and diversity for academics: Inclusive practice.* UK: Equality Challenge Unit. Retrieved from www.ecu.ac.uk/publications/e-and-d-for-academics-factsheets. Accessed on August 5.

Gravestock, P., & Grace, S. (2008). Assessment time: How do we attempt to ensure fairness for all? In P. Gravestock & S. Grace (Eds.), *Inclusion and diversity: Meeting the needs of all students* (pp. 176–207). Hoboken, NJ: Taylor and Francis.

Hall, T., & Stahl, S., (2006). Using Universal design for learning to expand access to higher education. In M. Adams & S. Brown (Eds.), *Towards inclusive learning in higher education* (pp. 67–78). London: Routledge, Taylor and Francis Group.

Hitch, D., Larkin, H., Watchorn, V., & Ang, S. (2012). Community mobility in the context of universal design: Inter-professional collaboration and education. *Australian Occupational Therapy Journal, 59*, 375–383.

Hockings, C., Brett, P., & Terentjevs, M. (2012). Making a difference: Inclusive learning and teaching in higher education through open educational resources. *Distance Education, 33*(2), 237–252.

International Association of Universities. (2008). Equitable access, success and quality in higher education: A policy statement by the International Association of Universities. Adopted by IAU 13th general conference, July, Utrecht. Retrieved from http://www.iau-aiu.net/access_he/access_statement.html. Accessed on May 25, 2010.

Kuh, G. D., & Vesper, N. (2001). Do computers enhance or detract from student learning? *Research in Higher Education, 42*, 87–102.

Larkin, H. (2010). 'But they won't come to lectures …' The impact of audio recorded lectures on student experience and attendance. *Australasian Journal of Educational Technology, 26*(2), 238–249.

Larkin, H., Hitch, D., Watchorn, V., Ang, S., & Stagnitti, K. (2013). Readiness for interprofessional learning: A cross-faculty comparison between architecture and occupational therapy students. *Journal of Interprofessional Care, 27*(5), 413–419.

Larkin, H., & Pépin, G. (2013). The reflective practitioner. In K. Stagnitti, A. Schoo, & D. Welch (Eds.), *Clinical and fieldwork placement in the health professions* (2nd ed., pp. 31–42). Melbourne: Oxford University Press.

Larkin, H., & Richardson, B. (2013). Creating high challenge/high support academic environments through constructive alignment: Student outcomes. *Teaching in Higher Education, 18*(2), 192–204.

Larkin, H., & Watchorn, V. (2012). Changes and challenges in higher education: What is the impact on fieldwork education? *Australian Occupational Therapy Journal, 59*(6), 463–466.

Matthews, N. (2009). Teaching the 'invisible' disabled students in the classroom: Disclosure, inclusion and the social model of disability. *Teaching in Higher Education, 14*(3), 229–239.

May, H., & Bridger, K. (2010). *Developing and embedding inclusive policy and practice in higher education.* New York, NY: The Higher Education Academy. Retrieved from http://www.heacademy.ac.uk/assets/documents/inclusion/DevelopingEmbeddingInclusivePP_Report.pdf. Accessed on August 23, 2013.

McGuire, J. M., Scott, S. S. & Shaw, S. F. (2006). Universal design and its applications in educational environments. *Remedial and Special Education, 27*(3), 166–175.

Milem, J. F. (2003). The educational benefits of diversity: Evidence from multiple sectors. In W. D. Chang, M. J. Jones, & K. Hakuta (Eds.), *Compelling interest: Examining the evidence on racial dynamics in colleges and universities* (pp. 126–166). Stanford, CA: Stanford University Press.

Milliken, J., & Barnes, L. P. (2002). Teaching and technology in higher education: Student perceptions and personal reflections. *Computers and Education, 39*, 223–235.

Nelson Laird, F. N., & Kuh, G. D. (2005). Student experiences with information technology and their relationship to other aspects of student engagement. *Research in Higher Education, 46*(2), 211–233.

Nolan, A., & Sim, J. (2011). Exploring and evaluating levels of reflection in pre-service early childhood teachers. *Australasian Journal of Early Childhood, 36*(3), 122–130.

Northedge, A. (2002). Organizing excursions into specialist discourse communities: A sociocultural account of university teaching. In G. Wells & G. Claxton (Eds.), *Learning for life in the 21st century: Sociocultural perspectives on the future of education* (pp. 252–264). Oxford: Blackwell Publishers.

Oblinger, D. (2005). Leading the transition from classrooms to learning spaces. *EDUCAUSE Quarterly, 1*, 4–8.

O'Flaherty, J., Scutter, S., & Albrecht, T. (2010). How podcasts of lectures are used by diverse groups of students. *Higher Education Research and Development Society of Australasia (HERDSA) conference*, 6–9 July, Melbourne.

Oliver, B., & Nikoletatos, P. (2009). Building engaging physical and virtual learning spaces: A case study of a collaborative approach. In *Proceedings of the ascilite Auckland 2009 on same places, different spaces.* Retrieved from http://www.ascilite.org.au/conferences/auckland09/procs/oliver.pdf

Patrick, C-j., Peach, D., Pocknee, C., Webb, F., Fletcher, M., & Pretto, G. (2008). The WIL [Work Integrated Learning] report: A national scoping study [Australian Learning Teaching Council (ALTC) Final Report]. Queensland University of Technology, Brisbane. Retrieved from http://www.acen.edu.au/resources/docs/WIL-Report-grants-project-jan09.pdf

Tange, H., & Kastberg, P. (2013). Coming to terms with 'double knowing': An inclusive approach to international education. *International Journal of Inclusive Education, 17*(1), 1–14.

Thomas, L., & May, H. (2010). *Inclusive teaching in higher education.* New York, NY: The Higher Education Academy. Retrieved from http://www.heacademy.ac.uk/assets/documents/inclusion/InclusiveLearningandTeaching_FinalReport.pdf

Tom, J. S. C., Voss, K., & Scheetz, C. (2008). The space is the message: First assessment of a learning studio. *EDUCAUSE Quarterly, 2,* 42–48.

Trow, M. (1972). *The expansion and transformation of higher education.* New York, NY: General Learning Press.

University of Wolverhampton. (2011). Learning to teach inclusively – A multi media Open access module for HE staff. Online Educational Resources. Higher Education Academy/JISC Open Educational Resources programme. Retrieved from http://lab-space.open.ac.uk/course/view.php?id=6224

Van Note Chism, N. (2002). A tale of two classrooms. *New Directions for Teaching and Learning, 92,* 5–12.

W3C®. (2008). Web content accessibility guidelines (WCAG) 2.0. Retrieved from http://www.w3.org/TR/WCAG20/#intro

Wilson, G., & Randall, M. (2010). Implementing and evaluating a 'next generation learning space': A pilot study. In C. Steel, M. Keppell, P. Gerbic, & S. Housego (Eds.), *Ascilite 2010 Sydney. Curriculum, technology & transformation for an unknown future* (pp. 1096–1100). Brisbane: University of Queensland. Retrieved from http://www.ascilite.org.au/conferences/sydney10/procs/Wilson-concise.pdf

Wilson, G., & Randall, M. (2012). The implementation and evaluation of a new learning space: A pilot study. *Research in Learning Technology, 20,* 14431. doi:10.3402/rlt.v20i0.14431

SECTION III
THE FUTURE OF SUPPORT FOR TEACHING IN NEXT GENERATION LEARNING SPACES

CHAPTER 9

FACTORS THAT SHAPE PEDAGOGICAL PRACTICES IN NEXT GENERATION LEARNING SPACES

Nicola Carr and Kym Fraser

ABSTRACT

International figures on university expenditure on the development of next generation learning spaces (NGLS) are not readily available but anecdote suggests that simply retrofitting an existing classroom as an NGLS conservatively costs $AUD200,000, while developing new buildings often cost in the region of 100 million dollars and over the last five years, many universities in Australia, Europe and North America have developed new buildings. Despite this considerable investment, it appears that the full potential of these spaces is not being realised.

While researchers argue that a more student centred learning approach to teaching has inspired the design of next generation learning spaces (Tom, Voss, & Scheetz, 2008) and that changed spaces change practice (Joint Information Systems Committee, 2009) when 'confronted' with a next generation learning spaces for the first time, anecdotes suggest that many academics resort to teaching as they have always taught and as

The Future of Learning and Teaching in Next Generation Learning Spaces
International Perspectives on Higher Education Research, Volume 12, 175–198
ISSN: 1479-3628/doi:10.1108/S1479-362820140000012013

they were taught. This chapter highlights factors that influence teaching practices, showing that they are to be found in the external, organisational and personal domains.

We argue that in order to fully realise significant improvements in student outcomes through the sector's investment in next generation learning spaces, universities need to provide holistic and systematic support across three domains — the external, the organisational and the personal domains, by changing policies, systems, procedures and localised practices to better facilitate changes in teaching practices that maximise the potential of next generation learning spaces.

Keywords: Pedagogical practices; next generation learning spaces; higher education; communities of practice; technology; signature pedagogies

INTRODUCTION

Since the 1990s, the higher education sector has been enamoured with the potential of technology to transform education, in terms of student learning, the pedagogical practices of teachers, and the finances of institutions. In more recent times, technology is being combined with innovative learning spaces to support more participative approaches in face to face learning in higher education institutions. In this chapter we focus on teacher pedagogical practices in next generation learning spaces (NGLS) and the factors that shape the pedagogical choices academics make and that influence their capacity to change those practices.

The Integration of Participatory Pedagogical Practices into NGLS

Recent research suggests that best practice pedagogy in next generation learning spaces demonstrates the transformative use of technology and space, and incorporates socio-constructivist approaches to learning and teaching (Oblinger, 2005). Ways of teaching that reflect socio-constructivist epistemologies of learning have been developed since the early part of the 20th century through the social constructivism theories of Lev Vygotsky (1934), John Dewey's (1956) views on learning through solving problems that involve exploration and experiences, and ideas around collaborative and cooperative learning espoused by Johnson (1975) to name but a few. Such approaches to learning and teaching that have participation rather than teacher exposition and student information 'acquisition' as the pedagogical basis were largely developed in a non-technological era but have been appropriated by proponents of next generation learning spaces as those most likely to be effective partners in technology enriched NGLS.

In essence, next generation learning spaces provide opportunities for transformation of practices, that is, significant modification and redefinition of practices, rather than merely augmenting existing teaching practices (Fluck, 2010). Arguably existing practices tend to be dominated by teacher exposition, information transmission and reliance on textbooks or 'broadcast pedagogies' (Rowan & Bigum, 2008). Instead, transformative pedagogies in next generation learning spaces may be characterised by students working collaboratively on complex, real world problems; including people and resources from beyond the physical classroom; requiring students to take more responsibility for what and how they learn; and by academics providing greater differentiation of tasks and approaches to suit the individual learners' needs (Fluck, 2010). Such pedagogies can be exemplified by the 'flipped classroom' in which lectures are provided as digital recordings and the lecture time used for students to actively collaborate with peers to explore challenging aspects of the topic of study (Khan, 2011).

However, for many academics such pedagogical practices represent a significant shift from current practice (Georgina & Olsen, 2008). Modification and redefinition of practices requires extensive scholarly support as well as a consideration of the contextual factors that act to shape the choices academics make regarding their teaching, and it is to these factors that we now turn.

DOMAINS OF INFLUENCE

A study of the education literature (higher/vocational/secondary education) suggests that the following three intertwined domains influence the pedagogical choices of academics:

- The *external* domain — where academics and universities operate within a broader, societal context that shapes how they perform teaching practices.

- The *organisational* domain — where academics are part of a collective, negotiating their identity as a community/discipline member and part of the material practices of an organisation.
- The individual, *personal* domain — where academics endeavour to reconcile their beliefs, knowledge and skills about learning, teaching and technology garnered from formal and informal education with ways of enacting teaching in practice.

In this chapter we argue that these domains act in concert and at times in messy ways to influence the pedagogical practices that academics adopt when teaching in next generation learning spaces. We discuss the influences on academic pedagogical practices that emerge from the wider societal and policy context. The chapter also discusses the tendency for higher education pedagogical practices to be reproduced rather than transformed, as more experienced academics from within the discipline resist developing new pedagogical practices. Further, we discuss the effects generated by the materiality of higher education — the physical spaces, artefacts and organisational structures and localised policies and the interplay of these elements

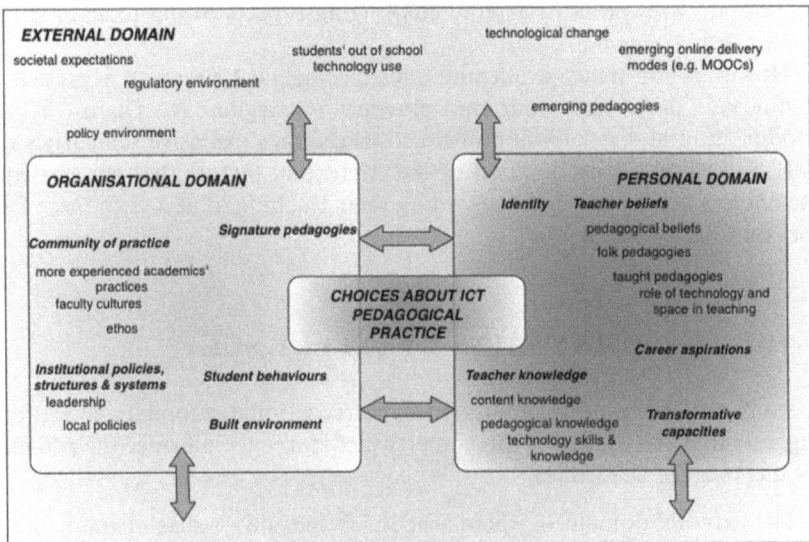

Fig. 1. Interrelated Factors That Influence Pedagogical Practices in Next Generation Learning Spaces.

that shape the ways and the extent to which academics change their pedagogical practices in next generation learning spaces.

In Fig. 1 we outline a model illustrating the factors that we believe shape pedagogical practices in next generation learning spaces. The model highlights the messiness of teaching practices as they are performed and how a broader range of factors intersect and interact to generate powerful effects that act on the dispositions and capacities of academics to integrate technology, student collaboration, peer learning and other socio-constructivist approaches into the pedagogical practices they adopt within next generation learning spaces.

The External Domain

All practices, those of individual academics as well as those of higher education institutions, take place within a broad, external environment where factors not immediately part of that practice still have an impact on that practice. Higher education is subject to a range of factors that operate in the external environment and ultimately impact to varying extents on teaching practice in both positive and negative ways. They collectively provide the broad, underlying platform upon which pedagogical practices are enacted. In the current climate, this platform is characterised by far-reaching change and fundamental transformation.

In this section we discuss the following elements that form the external environment in which universities operate, and identify their impact on teaching practice in next generation learning spaces:

- societal and student expectations of higher education with respect to technology;
- policy environment and the potential impact this has on teaching practices; and
- technological change and new pedagogies that emerge as a result.

Societal and Student Expectations

Very few areas of society are immune to the influence and impact of technology in the 21st century. Technology is perceived by many to be an instrument of better quality education, despite little hard evidence to support this magic bullet claim (Nnazor, 2009). Such is the belief in the potential of technology that society and those who employ university graduates

expect universities to use the latest available technology and teaching practices, in the belief that graduates will receive a better quality education and
will be conversant in the ways that industry makes use of technology.

Students also expect higher education institutions to offer technologically enriched learning experiences and access to appropriate technology
and spaces that will enable them to develop the necessary skills and know-
how to enable them to function effectively and productively in a technologically dominated world. Increasingly young people expect to be able to
use technology to support their studies (Rasmussen, Davidson-Shivers, &
Savenye, 2011). Young people tend to be relatively high users of technology, both in terms of the range of technologies they use and the kinds of
technological activities with which they engage (Eynon & Malmberg,
2011). Students also bring technology with them into higher education.
Anecdotally, many academics acknowledge the need to embrace technology
in their own practices if for no other reason than the significant role that
technology plays in the lives of their students.

Some researchers argue that current students are digital natives for
whom technology is just a part of the fabric of life, there to make life easier
and better, or in most cases, just there, just how things are now done
(Bennett, Maton, & Kervin, 2008; Prensky, 2012). To people like Prensky,
members of this next generation of learners have different learning characteristics to other generations, they learn at 'twitch speed', crave interactivity
and prefer visual modes of learning (Prensky, 2012).

However, arguments about digital natives are predicated on the assumption that young people have comparatively universal and uniform digital
upbringings (Kennedy, Judd, Churchward, & Krause, 2008). On the contrary, there is evidence of diversity in access, ability and predispositions
among young people towards using technology (Kennedy, Krause, Judd,
Churchward, & Gray, 2006) and there is evidence that students' competencies are superficial and hide ineffectiveness and shallow uses of technology
(Lei, 2009).

Within this societal context of student technology use, is our modern
day reality of constantly changing technology.

Technological Change and Subsequent Emerging Pedagogies

New devices and software applications bombard us on a daily basis. This
environment of rapid technological change impacts universities and academics and their ability to keep pace with technology, let alone develop
and implement new pedagogies that integrate technology.

Next generation learning spaces bring with them opportunities to do things in classrooms that were previously inconceivable, or to do the same things in fundamentally different ways. The combination of technologies and new approaches to designing learning spaces brings opportunities for new pedagogical practices. These emerging pedagogies represent new ways of teaching but may be ill-defined or not fully developed as teachers at the leading edge of teaching in next generation learning spaces explore new practices. Emerging pedagogies that capitalise on the affordances of next generation learning spaces might challenge (some) academics' conventional pedagogical practices. At the very least they sit in the background as a potential threat to conventional pedagogical practices or provide opportunities for teachers to take a new approach to pedagogy in their classrooms.

Universities once held the role as the originators and keepers of knowledge, but in a connected 21st century world, with information increasingly freely available online, people have the opportunity to construct knowledge without the benefit of educators. The democratisation of information and the trend to more online delivery of content through informal and formal mechanisms such as massive open online courses (MOOCs) pose challenges to more traditional bricks and mortar delivery of higher education. The development of next generation learning spaces as a way of delivering rich, on-campus experiences is one response to the threats from online delivery of courses from other higher education institutions and online providers (Ernst & Young, 2013).

Within the broad societal context of changing technology and student use of technology, universities operate in a national regulatory and policy environment.

Policy Environment

Government policy directly or indirectly impacts strategic initiatives in higher education including the development of next generation learning spaces and the associated integration of technology, often determining the parameters of such initiatives through laws, regulations and the allocation of funds (Nnazor, 2009). Shifts in policies that shape the delivery of higher education can impact on practices, in both positive and negative ways.

The particular Australian policies that can be seen to influence the use of technology and change in pedagogical practices in next generation learning spaces are:

• Higher education funding;
• The National Broadband Network;

- policies relating to increased participation and access to higher education; and
- accountability requirements.

Recent changes to Higher Education funding policies in Australia have resulted in far greater competition for prospective students amongst universities that is unlikely to be reversed (Ernst & Young, 2013). In response, universities are seeking ways to differentiate their offerings to prospective students. Being seen to be at the forefront of technological advances is one strategy being adopted by some universities, through the promotion of next generation learning spaces and technology integration.

On top of the competition for students, budgetary constraints in universities resulting from Government funding cuts and, in Australia, reduced demand for fee paying places by offshore international students (Lane, 2012) are pressures to increase efficiency and productivity, translating into larger class sizes (Rasmussen et al., 2011). Next generation learning spaces are seen to offer greater flexibility in accommodating larger class sizes without compromising the quality of student learning.

Further, policy shifts have recently emphasised the need for universities to accommodate a more diverse student population, with a particular emphasis on including more students from disadvantaged backgrounds. At the same time, the student profile has shifted − universities are teaching an increasingly diverse student population: students from Non English speaking backgrounds, students with a disability, students from multiple generations, first in family students, international and indigenous students. A more diverse student population brings the need for additional supports to be provided by universities, placing more pressure on academic staff to accommodate more diverse learning needs (Rasmussen et al., 2011) and an increased focus on retention strategies. Such pressures may reduce the time academic staff have to explore and develop new pedagogical practices in next generation learning spaces. Alternatively, next generation learning spaces may offer pedagogical possibilities that are more suited to the diverse student population.

The higher education sector in Australia is increasingly subjected to increased surveillance and accountability (Webb, 2009). The language of universities has shifted from the mission of universities as places of a learned community focused on teaching, research, knowledge building and service, to that of efficiency, productivity and accountability (Rasmussen et al., 2011). Teaching quality and student experiences are used to measure the efficacy and viability of higher education programs, as well as the performance of individual academics. The increased compliance burden of reporting and evidence requirements associated with performance evaluation and career advancement may reduce the time academics have available to explore new pedagogical practices in NGLS. Alternatively, the increased prominence of accountability measures may act as an incentive for academics to develop new pedagogical practices and NGLS as ways of responding to student feedback and to improve student retention.

In addition to factors that operate from outside higher education institutions, are those factors that are particular to the organisation itself.

The Organisational Domain

So far our discussion of factors that shape the pedagogical practices and use of technology by academics teaching in next generation learning spaces has focused on the external domain, a set of factors that operate beyond higher education but that nonetheless form the broader context in which academics teach. However, in any discussion of pedagogical practices that best make use of NGLS, it is important to consider not just the broad environment in which academics operate, but also the organisational and material context − the strategies, policies, structures, systems, resources, leadership, discipline groupings and communities of practice − that mediate pedagogical practices in the institution's physical spaces (Somekh, 2010). A university can be seen as an assemblage of diverse elements of texts, bodies, spaces and things (Fenwick & Edwards, 2010). All of the elements that make up the assemblage play a role in shaping how other elements within the assemblage perform.

In this section we discuss the following institutional elements and their impact on changing teaching practices in next generation learning spaces:

- institutional policies, structures and systems
- built environment
- communities of practice
- signature pedagogies

Institutional Strategies, Policies, Structures and Systems
Societal expectations in education, outlined in the previous section, are reflected in broad national and state education policies as well as in institutional policies. National policies regarding the uncapping of undergraduate student places have resulted in some universities strategically targeting

significant increases in student numbers in particular programs. Arguably, the increase in student numbers has had an impact on staff-student ratios (Larkins, 2011) resourcing and possibly even pedagogical practices. Obvious teaching practices that often change when academics teach increasing numbers of students are those of assessment and of 'mode of delivery'. Academics often resort to exams and multiple-choice tests when faced with large numbers of students and very tight grading timelines. They also employ the large lecture format to cope with increasing numbers of students. In both cases, these practices appear to be antithetical to collaborative learning environments in which student skills as well as knowledge are developed and assessed.

Internal policies within many universities, place an emphasis on the transformative potential of technology enriched next generation learning spaces. As indicated in this volume by Ling and Fraser (2014), senior university leaders feel the pressure to be seen to be keeping pace with innovations in learning spaces and technologies. The development of next generation learning spaces is seen in some institutions to foster a 'cutting edge' reputation and provide the institution with a competitive advantage in attracting students. However, providing the buildings does not necessarily lead to transformative pedagogic practices. While senior leaders may well set the direction of the institution, academics enjoy relative autonomy within their own classrooms. Consideration needs to be given to the culture in which academics teach, including their incentives and support for changing their practices.

At a different institutional level, systems such as timetabling processes that determine which teachers are allocated to next generation learning spaces also shape the extent to which these spaces are used to provide collaborative, technology enriched learning opportunities. It would seem logical that those teachers with a higher predisposition to teaching in these ways might be timetabled into those spaces. However, this is not always a consideration in the timetabling process. Anecdotally academics who would dearly love to teach in new spaces aren't timetabled into them, while staff who are timetabled into them have been known to express their concern that the spaces don't support how they teach (i.e. didactically).

Built Environment

Many if not most classrooms in a typical university comprise rows of tables facing the front of the room where the teacher's table is positioned at the head of a room in front of a whiteboard and projection screen. Such a built environment conveys strong constraining messages about the type of teaching that takes place in the space (Oblinger, 2005). These spaces reify traditional pedagogical practices where the academic, who is the focal point of the classroom, transfers information and instructions either by writing notes on whiteboards or via PowerPoint presentations to the relatively passive students (Chism, 2006). Instruction is undifferentiated teacher exposition. These spaces passively discourage the use of more social constructivist participatory pedagogical practices and the integration of technology.

Such practices are not consistent with best practice pedagogy that make the most of the opportunities offered by technology, which emphasise a more active role by the student in creating personalised learning rather than passively consuming information (refer to Keppell's chapter in this volume, 2014).

In the last decade, many universities have invested significantly in the building of next generation learning spaces that are technologically enabled and designed to promote active, collaborative and peer-based approaches to learning (Brown, 2005; Joint Information Systems Committee, 2009; Oblinger, 2005; Steel & Andrews, 2012). While authors argue that a more student centred learning approach to teaching has inspired the design of next generation learning spaces (Tom, Voss, & Scheetz, 2008) and that changed spaces change practice (Joint Information Systems Committee, 2009), Lee and Tan (2011) note that there is little evidence that changes in spaces effect long-term change in practice saying that in the literature to date (2011), '... there are no details regarding the interaction of space and teaching practice, curriculum and students' (*ibid.*, p. 12). They go on to say that the sector needs to engage in long-term evaluations to determine if a changed space changes teaching practices, perspectives and activities.

While academics may not teach in the ways that next generation learning spaces foster, as universities retrofit old spaces and build new spaces, academics at least have the opportunity to take advantage of the space to provide collaborative, active, technology-enabled learning opportunities. To do so, academics need the barriers described in this chapter to be removed and they need professional learning support, as discussed in the chapters in this volume by Hall and Palaskas (2014) and de la Harpe and Mason (2014).

Having discussed the built environment and its potential impact on pedagogy, we turn now to consider the impact of the community of practice in which academics work and learn.

The Disciplinary Community of Practice and Signature Pedagogies

When someone learns a practice he is initiated into the traditions of a community of practitioners and the practice world they inhabit. He learns their conventions, constraints, languages ... their repertoire of exemplars, systematic knowledge and patterns of knowing-in-action. (Schon, 1987, pp. 36–37)

Communities of Practice and Senior Leadership. Organisations, via their leadership, can play a significant role in aligning national goals, organisational goals and community of practice goals. Institutional leaders play an important role in interpreting and translating national policy or making sense of the policy at the level of the institution, that is positioning new policies within an organisational narrative or vision about how the institution works and what it does (Ball, Maguire, & Braun, 2012).

Good leaders are those who can displace cherished misconceptions and 'mistaken beliefs' (Dede, 1993, p. 24) through creating and communicating a compelling alternative to current paradigms and practices. Leaders therefore have the potential to indirectly shape practices by developing and negotiating goals that are common to the organisation and to the communities of practice that exist within the organisation.

Change, such as the transformative pedagogical practices in next generation learning spaces that this chapter discusses, requires its champions and advocates in the face of competing institutional expectations and counter discourses that may emanate from dominant communities of practice.

Champions need to be well regarded by members of the community of practice in order to have influence over the community's practices. They need to be 'charismatic individuals' who can overcome resistance that the new innovation can provoke within an organisation (Rogers, 2003).

In communities of practice theory, groups of people who share a common set of problems or passions, such as academics, also share a repertoire of actions, styles, artefacts, discourses and stories and ultimately share a common sense of identity. Learning a practice involves taking on the conventions and 'rules' of that practice. According to Lave and Wenger (1991), newcomers to a community of practice learn that practice at the metaphoric feet of the more established and experienced members of that practice (Lave & Wenger, 1991), gradually taking on the approaches of their more experienced peers. Learning a practice is seen as inseparable from the doing of the practice. Learning how to perform the practice of teaching takes place within the context of a community of more experienced teachers. Within a university, learning to teach inevitably occurs within one's disciplinary context.

If senior members of the discipline, including programme directors who lead teaching teams and programme curriculum design and renewal, teach in didactic and teacher centred ways, it is arguably more difficult for newer academics within those teams to adopt participatory pedagogical practices.

We can imagine that discussions in staff rooms and staff meetings may not engender the embracing of transformative pedagogical practices. Resistance by senior discipline academics and counter politics generate powerful effects, as colleagues, particularly new entrants to the profession, are influenced by the proponents of the counter discourses.

Senior academics and discipline leaders have the opportunity to develop a discipline culture that encourages the adoption of scholarly teaching practices. Scholarly teaching refers to the ongoing learning of academics and occurs when they reflect on their teaching practices, engage with the pedagogic literature on teaching and learning relevant to their discipline, and use this as a basis for making improvements to their own teaching (Lueddeke, 2003; Richlin, 2001). The application of new knowledge about teaching and learning by the teacher is one of the end products of scholarly teaching. The purpose of engaging *in* scholarly teaching is to continually improve the activity of teaching and associated student learning. On the other hand, engaging in the scholarship *of* teaching '... results in a formal, peer-reviewed communication in [an] appropriate media or venue, which then becomes part of the knowledge base of teaching and learning in higher education' (Richlin, 2001, p. 58).

In a discipline culture that supports scholarly teaching practices, we can imagine the collaborative development of a shared vision around the types of participatory pedagogical practices that best support learning and teaching in NGLS that might occur, providing a compelling alternative to traditional, teacher centred practices.

Signature Pedagogies. Signature pedagogies (Shulman, 2005) refer to the 'types of teaching that organise the fundamental ways in which future practitioners are educated for their new professions' (p. 52). Signature pedagogies are the 'modes of teaching and learning that are ... replicated in nearly all the institutions that educate in those domains' (p. 54), that is the approaches to teaching and learning in particular disciplines that we immediately identify with and intuitively come to expect. Signature pedagogies implicitly define what counts as knowledge in a field and how things become known. Such pedagogies are not always explicit, rather they incorporate the tacit conventions and rules of thumb that have taken hold within the discipline. For example, the quasi-Socratic interactions between teacher and students in a law faculty; the bedside teaching involving the triad of patient, clinician and students in medicine; the blackboard full of mathematical representations of physical processes typical in engineering; and so forth (Shulman, 2005).

As newcomers to a profession adjust to their professional roles they engage in 'role prototyping' (Ibarra, 1999), observing role models and learning the tacit rules and ways of being in the profession are part of the process of socialisation. They experiment with and adopt provisional identities based on the role models around them as part of the process of becoming an accepted member of that community (Scanlon, 2011).

We contend that, if the dominant teaching practice in a discipline reflects a strong focus on information transmission and teacher as expert, new academics will be socialised into existing, entrenched teaching practices, the traditional signature pedagogies. A key characteristic of signature pedagogies is that they routinise significant components of pedagogy (Shulman, 2005). Teaching is complex and challenging and at times overwhelming, especially for new entrants to the profession and for those for whom teaching is not their primary discipline. Adopting signature pedagogies simplifies the challenge of teaching since once they are learned and internalised, they require little thought; rather they become habitual, tacit practices.

However, as Shulman (2005) points out 'habits are both marvellous scaffolds for complex behaviours as well as dangerous sources of rigidity and preservation' (p. 56). Conformity can bring about an emphasis on reproduction of practice rather than any transformation of that practice. As Britzman (2003) argues:

> Conformity is more than uniformity of thought and standardisation of activity. Conformity diminishes prospects of becoming something other than what has previously been established. In this sense, the forces of conformity are repressive ... Conformity privileges routinised behaviour over critical action. Its centripetal force pulls toward reproducing the status quo as it mediates our subjective capacity to intervene in the world. (p. 46)

In a sense, the pedagogical practices of academics can be extremely durable, or even sedimented (Youdell, 2010). Attempts to introduce new ideas can be strongly resisted by senior academics. It is therefore essential for discipline leadership to overcome defensiveness and a culture of conformity about pedagogical practices, in order to develop a culture of continuous critical reflection, or scholarly teaching, by academics.

Our discussion of what shapes the pedagogical practices of academics teaching in next generation learning spaces has so far focused on those factors that stem from what we refer to as the external and organisational domains. We argue that there is a third domain, the personal domain, which focuses particularly on the role of the individual academic in changing their teaching practices.

Personal Domain

A range of factors that operate at the individual level is thought to significantly influence the extent to which, and the ways in which, academics are prepared to adopt new teaching practices in next generation learning spaces that emphasise technology integration. In this section we discuss the following personal elements and their impact on changing teaching practice when teaching in next generation learning spaces:

- teacher beliefs about pedagogy and about next generation learning spaces;
- teacher knowledge;
- teacher capacity; and
- career aspirations and identity.

Teacher Beliefs

There is a body of literature that argues that beliefs about a practice are a more important determinant of what people actually do in a practice than knowledge about that practice. Beliefs about a practice inform attitudes to that practice (Belland, 2009). Pajares (1992) posits that beliefs are formed early and tend to self-perpetuate, and the earlier a belief is formed the more difficult it is to alter. Beliefs help individuals define and understand the world and themselves.

Beliefs and knowledge are inextricably linked but beliefs have a stronger affective component, which makes them a lens through which new experiences and information are filtered. This filtering system screens, redefines, distorts or reshapes subsequent thought processes. Beliefs about pedagogy are therefore necessary to consider.

Beliefs and Knowledge about Pedagogy. Some studies suggest that, rather than change their practices to take advantage of the affordances of next generation learning spaces, academics will use a next generation learning spaces, in ways that fit with and sustain their existing pedagogical practices (Howell, 2007). Bain and McNaught argue that there is a distinct contrast in the literature between academics who think of learning as reproducing established knowledge and those who think of learning as the outcome of an understanding process (2006). For example, those who believe that students learn best through teacher-delivered lectures will lean towards using technology and NGLS to facilitate this type of learning, whereas those who believe in exploratory and collaborative learning will use technology and spaces quite differently to support more participative learning experiences. However, Bain and McNaughs' own study suggests that such a binary does hot reflect the complexity of decision making about how academics integrate technology, or the variation in beliefs about learning and teaching held by academics (2006).

A significant proportion of people who teach in higher education do not come from an education or teaching background. They are experts in their field, highly knowledgeable about their particular discipline; they are often researchers, adept at investigating the world around them, and many have neither a background in teaching nor formal teacher education (Kane, Sandretto, & Heath, 2002). However, all academics have first-hand experiences in being taught, based on their own experiences as school students and as higher education students. Bruner (1996) termed the beliefs about learning and teaching that develop as a result of our personal experiences of education 'folk pedagogies'. Bruner argues that teachers act on these folk pedagogies rather than any professed beliefs about learning and teaching; such is the strength of influence of personal experiences as students. Our own experiences as learners provide a road map for our experiences as teachers. The folk pedagogies of the majority of academic staff in higher education are likely to have been characterised by a strong focus on the lecturer as the fountain of knowledge, with information transmission the order of the day. That is, the majority of academic staff would have experienced very traditional pedagogies in their own higher education experience. It therefore follows that, in the absence of alternative models of teaching that are more suited to the affordances of next generation learning spaces, academics may revert to the sort of pedagogical practices that dominated their own experiences as higher education students.

However, whilst potentially an important influence, folk pedagogies are not necessarily a determinant of practice. They may influence the pedagogical practices of an academic but they do not necessarily determine such practices and the degree to which practices are influenced by folk pedagogies may vary. Other factors may act as countervailing influences.

The folk pedagogies developed by academics can be influenced by further experiences of next generation learning spaces and technology through exposure to propositional knowledge about innovative or transformative pedagogical practices through formal or informal professional learning programs undertaken by academics. In other words, folk pedagogies are potentially replaced with or modified by taught pedagogies, that is, the beliefs about pedagogies that teachers develop as a result of professional learning activities and their further experiences.

Changes in beliefs tend to follow changes in behaviour, rather than pre-cede them (Gusky, 2002; Pajares, 1992). That is, academics do not believe it until they see/do it. Changes in belief are influenced most strongly by personal success in the relevant domain, through prolonged and deeply engaging experiences, as well as by vicarious experiences, that is, seeing success occur for others that allows for comparison with our own experiences (Pajares, 1992). Thus, it could be expected that observation or first-hand experience of teaching in NGLS could also provide opportunities for experiences that might influence or shift beliefs about the role of spaces in pedagogies. However, academics have traditionally had limited opportunity to observe other academics' practices, suggesting that opportunities for supporting and celebrating experimentation with new approaches to teaching in NGLS are important in helping to shape academics' beliefs and self-efficacy in relation to technology-enabled teaching spaces (Ertmer & Ottenbreit-Leftwich, 2010).

Beliefs and Confidence about Using Next Generation Learning Spaces. Another important set of beliefs that influence or shape an academic's teaching practice in next generation learning spaces is their belief in their own ability to use the affordances of these spaces effectively. Bandura (2000) argues that belief of personal efficacy is the foundation of human agency, that is, unless people believe that they can produce desired effects by their actions, they have little incentive to act. Self-efficacy is based on beliefs about what a person can accomplish with the skills and knowledge they already possess (Preston, Cox, & Cox, 2000).

Technology forms an integral part of next generation learning spaces, either in the form of technology that is integrated into these spaces or in the form of technology devices that students increasingly bring with them into these spaces. Technology thus forms part of the landscape of learning and teaching in next generation learning spaces and offers opportunities for new approaches to teaching practices. However, when academics are unfamiliar with technology, or lack confidence in their ability to make effective use of the technology within an next generation learning space, then practices are unlikely to change. Academics who are confident in their ability to adapt their pedagogical practices and to use the technology that is an integral part of new generation learning spaces, will have more positive attitudes towards teaching in such spaces than those who are less confident or resistant to changing practices (Ertmer & Ottenbreit-Leftwich, 2010).

Teacher Knowledge

Attitudes about the role technology and space can have on learning and teaching are also influenced by teacher knowledge. Literature related to the integration of technology into teaching in the schools sector has been dominated in recent years by the TPACK model, a theoretical framework for conceptualising the relationship between technology and teaching (Mishra & Koehler, 2006). More recently, the TPACK model is being applied to those who teach in the higher education sector (Rienties, Brouwer, & Lygo-Baker, 2013). TPACK focuses on the synergies and dynamic interconnections between technological, pedagogical and content knowledge. That is, teachers need to know the content that they teach (CK), have a generic understanding of the processes and practices of teaching (PK), have understanding and mastery of specific technologies (TK), and have understanding the challenges students are likely to experience as they learn the content (PCK). Importantly the TPACK model identifies the importance of knowing how teaching and learning might change with the use of particular technologies (TPK) (Koehler & Mishra, 2008). Effective teaching therefore occurs at the intersection of these knowledge domains, suggesting that improvements in teaching will result if academics' knowledge about pedagogy and technology in particular is improved in relation to the content they teach.

Capacities, Not Just Knowledge

However, a conceptualisation of what it takes for teachers to teach effectively in next generation learning spaces needs to go beyond a focus on teacher knowledge, in whatever form (Law, 2008). Academics need to move beyond using these spaces and their associated technologies to sustain or strengthen current pedagogical practices, to teach in next generation learning spaces in ways that disrupt or subvert current pedagogical practices, and create new pedagogical practices. To leverage these spaces for innovative pedagogical practices and to use them in ways that are transformative, academics need additional capacities not discussed in the TPACK model. Making use of the affordances of new tools and spaces depends upon the development of a vision of what might be possible. To foster a more participatory, collaborative, non-hierarchical pedagogy requires not only cognitive but social-metacognitive capacities on the part of the academic to work in more reflective and connected ways with colleagues in what is increasingly knowledge building in a community (Scardamalia, 2002). Finally, to leverage next generation learning spaces in innovative and transformative ways, academics need courage and motivation, a social-emotional capacity, to teach in ways that are unfamiliar. That is, to use these spaces in ways that are transformative, subversive or disruptive that result in new practices, academics need more than knowledge. They need a range of capacities, personal and organisational, that support their risk taking.

Career Aspirations and Identity

The age groups of tenured and continuing academics in higher education are skewed towards the older end of the spectrum (Bexley, James, & Arkoudis, 2011) with a significant proportion of academics approaching retirement age in the near future. Anecdotally the majority of late career academics appear much less comfortable with the role of technology in their teaching than their younger counterparts, are concerned about changing expectations of students, and feel that the higher education sector is not moving in a direction with which they identify (Bexley et al., 2011). There is little incentive for these academics to make the sorts of changes to their teaching practices that are afforded by next generation learning spaces.

Further, the emphasis on research outputs in higher education generates a belief that teaching is not sufficiently valued (Bexley et al., 2011). When institutional priorities are placed on research activity, academics may be less likely to devote the time and energies needed to make substantial changes to their teaching practices, instead preferring to build their research capacity. The perception among academics is that career rewards are more likely to flow from discipline research activities rather than from teaching practices.

Further, higher education institutions in Australia employ a high proportion of teaching staff in casual or sessional capacities (May, Strachan, Broadbent, & Peetz, 2011). Casual and sessional academics generally have limited access to the support and professional development opportunities around next generation learning spaces and technologies that are afforded to ongoing academics. Thus there may be a 'lost generation' of academics who miss the boat of training and development of new pedagogical practices associated with next generation learning spaces.

CONCLUSION

The factors that influence the pedagogical practices that we use in next generation learning spaces. are complex and many (Fig. 1). As we have seen from the preceding sections of the chapter, building the spaces does not ensure that academics will use pedagogical practices that the spaces were intended to support. Universities that wish to support academics to teach in pedagogically sound ways in these spaces need to do so holistically and systematically, across a number of areas including:

- providing the support and incentives for schools, departments and faculties to develop scholarly teaching cultures and evaluating and improving those cultures;
- identifying, fostering and rewarding champions of pedagogical change;
- aligning institutional policies, structures, systems and resources to maximise the affordances of next generation learning spaces;
- requiring evidence of improved pedagogical practices and improved student learning outcomes for promotion and in recruitment, probation, and annual performance management next generation learning spaces;
- ensuring that next generation learning spaces are used by staff who want to teach in them;
- developing course and unit guide templates and systems to foster collaborative learning outcomes; and
- providing and expecting academics who teach to engage in continuing professional learning opportunities.

If the goals of improving the learning experience of students through transformed teaching practices in NGLS are to be realised, then universities need to pay attention to the complex range of factors, both large and small, across the external, organisational and personal domains.

REFERENCES

Bain, J. D., & McNaught, C. (2006). How academics use technology in teaching and learning: Understanding the relationship between beliefs and practice. *Journal of Computer Assisted Learning, 22*(2), 99–113.
Ball, S. J., Maguire, M., & Braun, A. (2012). *How schools do policy: Policy enactments in secondary schools.* Abingdon, Oxon: Routledge.

Bandura, A. (2000). Exercise of human agency through collective efficacy. *Current Directions in Psychological Science, 9*(3), 75–78.

Belland, B. R. (2009). Using the theory of habitus to move beyond the study of barriers to technology integration. *Computers & Education, 52*, 353–364. doi:10.1016/j.compued. 2008.09.004

Bennett, S., Maton, K., & Kervin, L. (2008). The 'digital natives' debate: A critical review of the evidence. *British Journal of Educational Technology, 39*(5), 775–786.

Bexley, E., James, R., & Arkoudis, J. (2011). *The Australian academic profession in transition: Addressing the challenge of reconceptualising academic work and regenerating the academic workforce.* Melbourne: Centre for the Study of Higher Education.

Britzman, D. P. (2003). *Practice makes practice: A critical study of learning to teach.* Albany, NY: State University of New York Press.

Brown, M. (2005). Learning spaces. In D. Oblinger & J. Oblinger (Eds.), *Educating the net generation* (pp. 12.11–12.22). EDUCAUSE. Retrieved from http://net.educause.edu/ir/ library/pdf/pub7101.pdf

Bruner, J. (1996). *The culture of education.* Cambridge, MA: Harvard University Press.

Chism, N. V. N. (2006). Challenging traditional assumptions and rethinking learning spaces. In D. Oblinger (Ed.), *Learning spaces* (pp. 2.1–2.12). EDUCAUSE. Retrieved from http://www.educause.edu/research-and-publications/books/learning-spaces

Dede, C. (1993). Leadership without followers. In G. Kearsley & W. Lynch (Eds.), *Educational technology: Leadership perspectives* (pp. 19–28). Englewood Cliffs, NJ: Educational Technology Publications.

de la Harpe, B., & Mason, T. (2014). A new approach to professional learning for academics teaching in next generation learning spaces. In K. Fraser (Ed.), *The future of learning and teaching in next generation learning spaces.* International Perspectives on Higher Education Research (Vol. 12, pp. 219–240). Bingley, UK: Emerald Group Publishing Limited.

Dewey, J. (1956). *The child and the curriculum, and the school and society.* Chicago, IL: University of Chicago Press.

Ernst & Young. (2013). *University of the future: A thousand year old industry on the cusp of profound change.* Australia: Ernst & Young.

Ertmer, P. A., & Ottenbreit-Leftwich, A. T. (2010). Teacher technology change: How knowledge, confidence, beliefs and culture intersect. *Journal of Research on Technology in Education, 42*(3), 255–284.

Eynon, R., & Malmberg, L.-E. (2011). A typology of young people's Internet use: Implications for education. *Computers & Education, 56*(3), 585–595.

Fenwick, T., & Edwards, R. (2010). *Actor network theory in education.* London: Routledge.

Fluck, A. (2010). From integration to transformation. In A. McDougall, J. Murnane, A. Jones, & N. Reynolds (Eds.), *Researching IT in education: Theory, practice and future directions.* Abingdon, Oxon: Routledge.

Georgina, D. A., & Olsen, M. R. (2008). Integration of technology in higher education: A review of faculty self-perceptions. *Internet and Higher Education, 11*(1), 1–8.

Gusky, T. R. (2002). Professional development and teacher change. *Teachers and Teaching: Theory and Practice, 8*(3/4), 381–391.

Hall, C., & Palaskas, T. (2014). Transition to next generation learning spaces. In K. Fraser (Ed.), *The future of learning and teaching in next generation learning spaces.* International Perspectives on Higher Education Research (Vol. 12, pp. 199–218). Bingley, UK: Emerald Group Publishing Limited.

Howell, G. (2007). *The experience of University academic staff in their use of ICT.* Unpublished doctoral dissertation, Australian Catholic University, Fitzroy, Australia.

Ibarra, H. (1999). Provisional selves: Experimenting with image and identity in professional adaptation. *Administrative Science Quarterly, 44*(4), 764–789.

Johnson, D. W. (1975). *Learning together alone: Cooperation, competition and individualisation.* Englewood Cliffs, NJ: Prentice Hall.

Joint Information Systems Committee. (2009). *Designing spaces for effective learning. A guide to 21st century learning space design.* Bristol, UK: Joint Information Systems Committee.

Kane, R., Sandretto, S., & Heath, C. (2002). Telling half the story: A critical review of research on the teaching beliefs of university academics. *Review of Educational Research, 72*(2), 177–228.

Kennedy, G., Judd, T., Churchward, A., & Krause, K.-L. (2008). First year students' experiences with technology: Are they really digital natives? *Australasian Journal of Educational Technology,* 24(1), 108–122.

Kennedy, G., Krause, K.-L., Judd, T., Churchward, A., & Gray, K. (2006). *First year students' experiences with technology: Are they really digital natives? Preliminary report of findings* (p. 27). Melbourne: University of Melbourne.

Keppell, M. (2014). Personalised learning strategies for higher education. In K. Fraser (Ed.), *The future of learning and teaching in next generation learning spaces.* International Perspectives on Higher Education Research (Vol. 12, pp. 3–22). Bingley, UK: Emerald Group Publishing Limited.

Khan, S. (2011). *Let's use video to reinvent education.* TED.

Koehler, M., & Mishra, P. (2008). Introducing TPCK. In AACTE Committee on Innovation and Technology (Ed.), *Handbook of technological pedagogical content knowledge (TPCK) for educators.* New York, NY: Routledge/Taylor & Francis Group.

Lane, B. (2012). Overseas students are expected to return. *The Australian Higher Education Supplement.* Retrieved from http://www.theaustralian.com.au/higher-education/overseas-students-are-expected-to-return/story-e6frgcjx-1226372973632-mm-premium

Larkins, F. (2011). *Academic staff trends: At what cost to teaching & learning excellence.* Retrieved from http://www.themartininstitute.edu.au/nsights-blog/2011/10/65-academic-staffing-trends-at-what-cost-to-teaching-and-learning-excellence. Accessed on August 30, 2012.

Lave, J., & Wenger, E. (1991). *Situated learning: Legitimate peripheral participation.* Cambridge: Cambridge University Press.

Law, N. (2008). Teacher learning beyond knowledge for pedagogical innovations with ICT. In J. Voogt & G. Knezek (Eds.), *International handbook of information technology in primary and secondary education.* New York, NY: Springer.

Lee, N., & Tan, S. (2011). *A comprehensive learning space evaluation model.* Final Report. Australian Learning and Teaching Council, Sydney.

Lei, J. (2009). Digital natives as pre-service teachers: What technology preparation is needed? *Journal of Computing in Teacher Education, 25*(3), 87–97.

Ling, P., & Fraser, K. (2014). Pedagogies for next generation learning spaces: Theory, context, action. In K. Fraser (Ed.), *The future of learning and teaching in next generation learning spaces* (Vol. 12). International Perspectives on Higher Education Research. Bingley, UK: Emerald Group Publishing Limited.

Lueddeke, G. R. (2003). Professionalising teaching practice in higher education: A study of disciplinary variation and 'teaching-scholarship'. *Studies in Higher Education, 28*(2), 213–228. doi:10.1080/0307507032000058082

May, R., Strachan, G., Broadbent, K., & Peetz, D. (2011). The casual approach to university teaching: Time for a re-think? In K.-L. Krause, M. Buckridge, C. Grimmer, & S. Purbrick-Illek (Eds.), *Research and development in higher education: Re-shaping higher education* (Vol. 34, pp. 188–197). Gold Coast, Australia: Higher Education Research and Development Society of Australasia (HERDSA).

Mishra, P., & Koehler, M. J. (2006). Technological pedagogical content knowledge: A framework for teacher knowledge. *Teachers College Record, 108*(6), 1017–1054.

Nnazor, R. (2009). A conceptual framework for understanding use of information and communication technology in teaching in universities. *International Journal of Instructional Technology and Distance Learning, 6*(1). Retrieved from http://www.itdl.org/journal/jan_09/article05.htm

Oblinger, D. (2005). Leading the transition from classrooms to learning spaces. *EDUCAUSE Quarterly, 28*(1), 14–18.

Pajares, M. F. (1992). Teachers' beliefs and educational research: Cleaning up a messy construct. *Review of Educational Research, 62*(3), 307–332.

Prensky, M. (2012). *From digital natives to digital wisdom: Hopeful essays for 21st century education.* Thousand Oaks, CA: Corwin.

Preston, C., Cox, M., & Cox, K. (2000). *Teachers as innovators: An evaluation of the motivation of teachers to use ICT.* London: MirandaNet.

Rasmussen, K. L., Davidson-Shivers, G. V., & Savenye, W. C. (2011). The near future of technology in higher education. In D. W. Surry, R. M. Gray Jr., & J. R. Stefurak (Eds.), *Technology integration in higher education: Social and organizational aspects* (pp. 326–342). Hershey, PA: IGI Global.

Richlin. (2001). Scholarly teaching and the scholarship of teaching. *New Directions for Teaching and Learning, 86*, 58–68.

Rienties, B., Brouwer, N., & Lygo-Baker, S. (2013). The effects of online professional development and teachers' beliefs and intentions towards learning facilitation and technology. *Teaching and Teacher Education, 29*, 122–131.

Rogers, E. M. (2003). *Diffusion of innovation* (5th ed.). New York, NY: Free Press.

Rowan, L., & Bigum, C. (2008). Landscaping on shifting ground: Teacher education in a digitally transforming world. *Asia-Pacific Journal of Teacher Education, 36*(3), 245–255.

Scanlon, L. (2011). 'Becoming' a professional. In L. Scanlon (Ed.), *"Becoming" a professional* (pp. 13–32). Dordrecht: Springer Science.

Scardamalia, M. (2002). Collective cognitive responsibility for the advancement of knowledge. In B. Smith (Ed.), *Liberal education in a knowledge society.* Chicago, IL: Open Court.

Schon, D. (1987). *Educating the reflective practitioner.* San Francisco, CA: Jossey-Bass.

Shulman, L. (2005). Signature pedagogies in the professions. *Daedalus, 134*(3), 52–59.

Somekh, B. (2010). The practical power of theoretically informed research into innovation. In A. McDougall, J. Murnane, A. Jones, & N. Reynolds (Eds.), *Researching IT in education: Theory, practice and future directions* (pp. 129–141). London: Routledge.

Steel, C., & Andrews, T. (2012). Re-imagining teaching for technology-enriched learning spaces: An academic development model. In M. Keppell, K. Souter, & M. Riddle (Eds.), *Physical and virtual learning spaces in higher education.* Hershey, PA: Information Science Reference.

Tom, J., Voss, K., & Scheetz, C. (2008). The space is the message: First assessment of a learn-
ing studio. *EDUCAUSE Quarterly, 31*(2), 14.
Vygotsky, L. (1934). In A. Kouzlin (Trans.), *Thought and language*. Cambridge, MA: Harvard
University Press.
Webb, P. T. (2009). *Teacher assemblage*. Rotterdam: Sense.
Youdell, D. (2010). *School trouble: Identity, power and politics in education*. London: Routledge.

CHAPTER 10

TRANSITION TO NEXT GENERATION LEARNING SPACES

Cathy Hall-van den Elsen and Tom Palaskas

ABSTRACT

This chapter takes an implementation case study approach to inform project planners, senior academics, and academic developers about the design and implementation of a professional development (PD) program that prepared 700 faculty in an Australian university to reimagine their teaching practice. The catalyst for this transformation was the move from traditional classrooms to next generation learning spaces (NGLS) in the newly constructed and purpose-built environment of RMIT University's Swanston Academic Building (SAB). The study identifies the challenges and change management issues faced by the project team, faculty, and other stakeholders.

Default teaching styles for many tertiary teachers can replicate the "best" and "worst" practices from their own student experience. As actors in their own classrooms tertiary teachers autonomously create learning environments that they consider appropriate to communicate the content, context, and culture of their particular discipline. The design and implementation of the PD and transition plan took into account the needs and perceptions of staff from each discipline area, the affordances of the new learning spaces, and their associated technologies.

The Future of Learning and Teaching in Next Generation Learning Spaces
International Perspectives on Higher Education Research, Volume 12, 199–218
Copyright © 2014 by Emerald Group Publishing Limited
All rights of reproduction in any form reserved
ISSN: 1479-3628/doi:10.1108/S1479-362820140000012014

This chapter contributes to a growing body of knowledge about the experience of academic and teaching staff during transition from traditional to NGLS, providing a description of the process undertaken in one university, the outcomes achieved, and the lessons learnt.

Keywords: Teacher transition; teaching practice in next generation learning spaces; drivers of pedagogical change

INTRODUCTION

This chapter describes a project in an Australian university to develop a professional development (PD) program to support a physical and transformational transition in teaching practice initiated by a move to next generation learning spaces (NGLS). The background to the project, pedagogical underpinnings of the associated PD program, and the change management challenges encountered are discussed.

The methodology employed is that of an implementation case study as described by the Commonwealth Association for Public Administration and Management (CAPAM). The implementation case study methodology focuses on four aspects of a case: identifying the significance of the challenge; explaining the context in which the challenge occurs; describing the chosen strategy; and discussing the results achieved and the lessons learned. CAPAM advocates this type of case study in which scrutiny is placed on the stages of the process rather than the long-term outcome, to "… identify techniques that can be replicated elsewhere …" (CAPAM, April, 2010, p. 3). Each of these phases, illustrated in Fig. 1, is discussed in this chapter.

THE BACKGROUND

In 2012 RMIT University's College of Business moved from a former office building, repurposed for teaching some twenty years earlier, to NGLS in a purpose-built, urban campus called the Swanston Academic Building (SAB), in the heart of Melbourne's central business district.

The SAB teaching and learning environment contains a variety of different types of learning spaces. These comprise lecture theaters seating up to

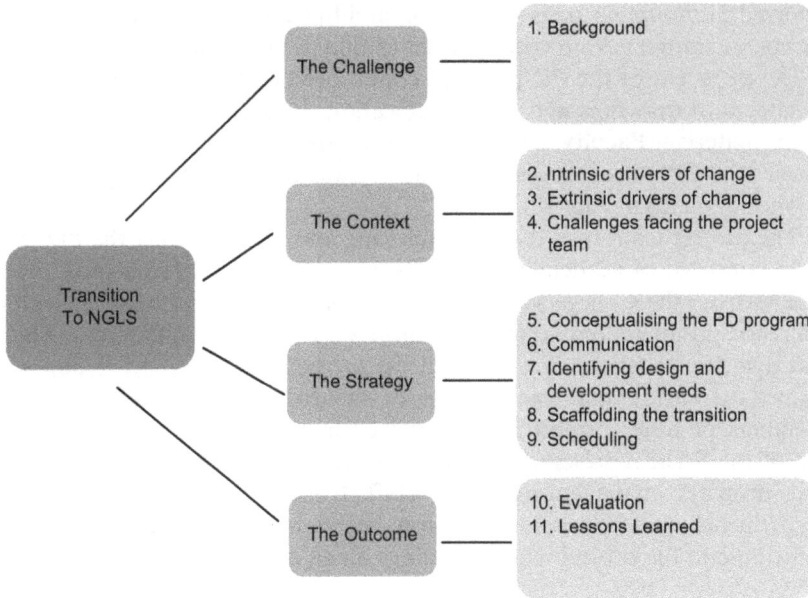

Fig. 1. The Implementation Case Study Approach (CAPAM).

360 students, some with seating designed to provide opportunities for collaboration; lectorial and interactive tutorial spaces of various capacities that facilitate both teacher-led and team work; technology-enhanced project spaces; less formal conversational spaces, and a discursive theater suitable for enriched case-based learning. Learning is not confined to formal spaces, as ubiquitous wireless capability, "follow me printing," breakout areas and student "portals" encourage students to work collaboratively outside formal learning spaces.

Technology in the learning spaces supports collaborative learning, the use of mobile devices and facilitative rather than didactic teaching modes. The layout and seating arrangements in all but the largest theaters are designed to encourage student engagement, interaction, and group-based learning activities.

The PD program was designed to prepare and support faculty to make the best use of the pedagogical and technological potential of the NGLS in the SAB. The program's distinctive characteristics include its scope, scale, complexity, and timelines. In scope and scale, the program addressed the PD needs of over 700 faculty. The complexity of the required change process involved 11 discipline areas in 6 schools and full and part-time faculty teaching courses ranging from vocational education to postgraduate.

Development of the PD program commenced early in 2011, drawing on architectural drawings and ICT specification documents in the absence of other material. Faculty had no access to the building during the early stages of the PD program, as construction was ongoing. The physical transition took place in July 2012.

The project team tasked with developing and implementing the PD program consisted of academic developers, researchers, and media production experts from the College's Academic Development Group, together with a reference group representing the College's various discipline areas. Short and dynamic timelines characterized the project. The reference group was formed to ensure that each aspect of the PD plan met faculty needs. Members of other project teams involved in the construction and fitting out of the SAB, representatives of the university's information technology and property management areas, staff from academic administration departments, and representatives from technology firms, were invited to contribute to the project team's meetings on an ad hoc basis.

THE CONTEXT

Changing Teaching Practice: An Intrinsic Process

There are few universally accepted tenets regarding best practice in supporting faculty to move into new types of teaching spaces. Blackmore, Bateman, Loughlin, O'Mara, and Aranda (2011) note that there has been "... little recognition of the preparation required for faculty and students to effectively transition into using new learning spaces in terms of pedagogies, as well as setting realistic expectations and contingency planning" (p. 15). They highlight the risk of faculty reverting to what Thomson, Jones, and Hall (2009) refer to as "default pedagogies" or "the way we used to do things," rather than to explore different teaching methods and to innovate.

Given that the brief of the project team was to foster a reimagining of teaching practice and innovation, the team explored the various drivers of attitudinal change that would need to be tapped to bring about the required transformation in teaching practice. Effective implementation of change strategies is broadly determined by the alignment between extrinsic drivers and what Trowler (2008) refers to as "existing subjectivities."

These intrinsic forces consist of personal priorities/circumstances and individual belief systems. Trowler notes that consideration should be given to how these forces will be affected by the introduction of an innovation because the proposed change can have both positive and negative effects on individuals or groups of stakeholders. He states that "New practices sometimes involve, or threaten, a change to an individual's persona, to their view of themselves, and to the way they think others see them …," and that this "… may enhance or limit the chances of successful implementation" (p. 136). Elton (2003) summarizes the challenge, stating that "The dissemination of an innovation … is an exercise in change and hence, requires an understanding of change strategies and the management of change" (p. 200). He argues that teaching remains largely a private endeavor.

As a widespread transformation of teaching practice was needed to fulfill the promise of the new learning spaces, the challenge faced by the project team was to use their understanding of faculty concerns noting the existence of "existing subjectivities," to produce an effective PD program.

Extrinsic Drivers of Change: The SAB as a Catalyst

March and Olsen (as cited in Starkey, Tempest, & McKinlay, 2004) differentiate between individual and institutional actions as causal agents of change. They suggest that an institutional response is needed to stimulate a change in individual beliefs because the outcomes of PD will be prioritized and aligned by individuals in favor of their own needs and interests, rather than those of the institution. In this way, the need to prepare faculty for the transition into the new spaces represented such an institutional response and an extrinsic catalyst for change.

Elton (2003) also notes that the most effective change in higher education is both top-down and bottom-up in nature. The application of change strategies that rely on the intrinsic efforts of diverse faculty representing multiple disciplines would not be sufficient to affect the required transformation. The extrinsic driver of the reimagining of teaching practice was the impending physical transition, represented by the PD program. To achieve an effective transformation of teaching practice it was necessary to combine the efforts of the institution and individual academics. A coordinated, systematic, and flexible approach was needed to ensure that the pace, degree and focus of change was maintained in order to achieve institutional outcomes.

Challenges Facing the Project Team

The project team faced the challenge of designing a PD program that addressed the institution's strategic imperatives represented by the design and construction of the new learning spaces (top-down) while concurrently meeting the individual needs of faculty (bottom-up). The literature was only partially helpful in providing useful examples of similar projects.

At a strategic level, the overarching aims of the PD plan were focused on teaching practice in the NGLS that promoted student engagement and maximized pedagogical potential of the spaces. How these outcomes would be manifested would vary because of the distinct cultural, technical, and operational attributes of each academic discipline. Freeman and Johnston (2008) argue that discipline-specific support models, as opposed to those involving central groups, work well in supporting teaching and learning. As Bennett (2001) notes, faculty frequently have knowledge and access to centrally provided PD support, but they often prefer to consult colleagues instead, acting primarily on intrinsic needs.

Trowler (2008) associates teaching and learning regimes with Bourdieu's notion of *habitus*, "… a set of dispositions, perceptions and actions which give people who are immersed in them a 'feel for the game', an intuitive understanding of what is 'right', even in the absence of explicit rules or procedures" (p. 55). For faculty whose professional experience primarily comprised standing at a lectern or sitting or standing behind a classroom desk, the notion of "what is right" would be fundamentally challenged by the absence of a lectern or a desk, or in smaller learning spaces even the sense of a "front." In this respect, additional consideration needed to be given to the psychological change process that affects emotions, perceptions, and motivation.

Blackmore et al. (2011) reviewed the literature to identify the connections between learning spaces and learning outcomes. Their findings run parallel with the authors' view that much of the current literature explores the relationship between the physical learning environment manifested by NGLS and learning outcomes, rather than the psychological relationship between outcomes and how the spaces are used (p. 5). As a result the project team found little in the literature to assist in the design of a PD program that had at its core the need to inform and transform faculty attitudes, values and priorities.

Blackmore et al. (2011) identified gaps relating to the connections between pedagogical design and NGLS and categorized them into four types: design; implementation, and transition; consolidation; and, sustainability/re-evaluation (p. 3). References to these stages appear to be unevenly distributed with most research related to the design phase, some to the transition and consolidation phases, and few addressing evaluation and sustainability issues (p. 5). The gaps in the literature have a common thread, revealing the paucity of research and evidence about the impact on teacher practice of NGLS, and limited references to long-term change.

Apart from limitations in the existing literature base, the complex nature of this project also proved challenging. The College offers programs for the vocational education and training sector, as well as undergraduate and postgraduate coursework and research programs in Accounting, Economics, Entrepreneurship, Finance, Information Systems, International Business, Logistics, Management, and Marketing. Class sizes vary between over 1,000 for first year undergraduate subjects to as few as 15 for specialist postgraduate study. The required scope and scale of faculty support had to address the PD needs of 400 permanent and 300 part-time faculty teaching across several academic disciplines. The scope of the plan was as broad as it was deep. A number of logistical and operational issues also added to the complexity of the project. All support strategies had to be designed and scheduled to be accessible by the largest number of faculty whose physical availability varied widely.

THE STRATEGY

Conceptualizing the Professional Development Program

To meet the complex nature of the project, the project team was informed by Schon's (1971) change management model, and one of innovation diffusion by Rogers (1995). Schon (1971) noted that the "classical," centrally managed process of innovation diffusion which rests on the basic assumptions that "an innovation to be diffused exists fully realized in its essentials, prior to its diffusion," and that "... diffusion is the movement of an innovation from a centre out to its ultimate users" (p. 81). He also states that "... directed diffusion is a centrally managed process of dissemination, training and provision of resources and incentives" (p. 81). This approach clearly emphasizes the central role of the institution.

Conversely, Rogers (1995) describes a decentralized diffusion system in which decision-making is widely shared with innovation adopters who serve as their own change agents. A preference for independent action by faculty responding to a top-down initiative is further highlighted by Bates (2000) who noted that faculty usually operate independently. Interaction with peers, adaptation to change and professional growth is central to the success of strategic educational change and innovation projects. The independent work of professional educators and academics leads them to have significant influence on the successful implementation of an innovation. Faculty need time to interpret, understand, contextualize, and adopt the change. Given these apparently contradictory aspects to the project, a combined approach was adopted in the design and management of the PD program.

Communication

To ensure that their design of learning spaces would meet the needs of faculty and students and accommodate future innovative practice the project's architects engaged with these stakeholders to discuss their vision of an ideal learning environment. Data-gathering sessions were conducted to explore how learning spaces could be designed to enhance the relationships between students and peers, students and faculty, and students and content. The resulting design of the spaces was thereby "grounded" both in the architects' understanding of contemporary learning space design and the pedagogical priorities of faculty.

This enacted a process in which decision-making was widely shared with faculty, establishing a foundation upon which early innovation adopters could choose to serve as change agents for themselves and others within their groups. This early consultative approach was also adopted by the project team in the design of the PD program.

The PD project team represented a central communication conduit for liaising with project managers and other stakeholders. At various times throughout the process, the project team found themselves alternating between conveying a message to college faculty on behalf of a central group and advocating on behalf of the faculty to central groups.

In a 12-month period, the project team undertook an intensive period of consultation with the reference group in which all discipline areas were represented. The role of the meetings was to iteratively "push" and "pull" information between the project team and all faculty in the college. Feedback was elicited through the reference group about preferred teaching approaches, familiarization with educational technology, and perceived skill deficits. This method resulted in a detailed picture of the nature of support required and the locus of greatest need.

Communication strategies targeted the individual needs of different audiences while acknowledging the specific and unique organizational culture they are sited within, and influenced by. The communication plan addressed the needs of the entire College by acknowledging the cultures, relationships and interactions of different groups. The plan included faculty:

- across the full range of innovation adopters;
- from disparate discipline areas; and
- who were teaching at different academic levels and significantly differing class sizes.

Posters and "quick guides" with information about the number of rooms of each type and their location were distributed widely throughout the college. The posters provided a reference for room layouts to inform faculty choice of learning spaces for timetabling purposes. Bookmarks with names of reference group members and the URL of support resources were distributed to all faculty.

To facilitate information two-way flow between those coordinating various projects related to the SAB and faculty, and to prevent the potential for confusion that might disrupt the positive messages being disseminated through the PD program, a blog was created to open an ongoing discussion on all matters related to the impending move to the SAB. A significant number of posts were related to teaching and learning in NGLS. Together with the PD project reference group, the blog became a key conduit for the dissemination of information and clarification of issues, both perceived and real.

Identifying Design and Development Needs

The design of the PD program aimed to improve the student experience by:

- extending the thinking of faculty about the philosophy and practice of student engagement;
- providing opportunities for faculty to extend their skills, relating to the use of both technology and space, within their own disciplines; and
- providing a range of learning experiences and tools for faculty that would be accessible and useful over the long term.

The design of support strategies was informed by the work of Steel and Andrews (2012, pp. 242–265), who identified six key issues that affect the adoption of new approaches to teaching practice

1. Pedagogical and technology-related beliefs – Teachers' underlying belief systems can represent differing and sometimes conflicting interests, beliefs and values. How teachers conceptualize these complex and differing beliefs can dramatically influence teaching practice in new learning spaces.
2. Pedagogical image for use of ICT – Many teachers are unfamiliar with how technology-enriched spaces can be optimally used. Some learners may know more than the teachers about new technology. Thus there is a need for teachers to have time and frameworks to develop an individual pedagogical image relevant to ICT.
3. Technologies and space – Teachers who may not have used or experienced current technologies and/or innovative spaces, may have difficulty identifying the "affordances," that is, positive features of spaces that offer potential for action, and "constraints."
4. Curriculum agendas – Because teachers are inclined to transfer their accustomed methodologies and practices of their respective disciplines to new spaces (Kirkup & Kirkwood, 2005), translating curriculum to blended online models, for instance, can be fundamentally problematic.
5. Student diversity – Preparing inclusive curriculum to address the wide diversity of learner needs and characteristics is a challenge for all teachers. Students' ability to develop digital literacy is a critical aspect of new learning spaces because it is related a variety of modes and flexible approaches to learning and assessment. "Overlooking this can result in poor student learning outcomes in these new spaces" (Kennedy et al., 2009).
6. Pedagogical design and contexts – The pedagogical context incorporates complex variables connected to learning and teaching. While one teacher's learning design may fit their own pedagogical context; it may be unsuitable for another. The challenge for teachers is to use learning designs efficiently and effectively in new spaces.

Scaffolding the Transition: The Components of PD Program

The need to specifically address "existing subjectivities" in a timely manner was a key requirement of the PD program which was structured around four interdependent and interrelated components:

- PD face-to-face sessions to cover topics related to teaching in NGLS;
- print and PD resources to supplement and complement the face-to-face sessions;
- a fully functioning replica of one type of NGLS for faculty training, practice and scheduled teaching; and
- guided familiarization tours for all faculty of each type of new learning spaces, during and after fit out.

The identification of PD topics was informed by a variety of sources. Architectural drawings and specifications provided information about the physical environment and technology. The project team's exploration of relevant literature regarding NGLS provided the theoretical underpinning related to the transition, and the consultative process conducted through the reference group elicited the concerns and PD priorities expressed by faculty.

Anticipating the need for just-in-time pedagogical support, a comprehensive set of resources about learning and teaching in NGLS was made available online through the college's intranet for ease of access and for those who were not available to attend face-to-face sessions.

Care was needed to ensure that the theoretical ideas incorporated did not become a straitjacket that curbed the creativity and innovative thinking of faculty. Table 1 represents some of the strategies employed to address the transition issues identified in Steel and Andrews' (2012) study.

Scheduling

Long (2009) considers that the timing of PD is a key factor in transitioning staff to enhanced learning spaces. He states, "What absolutely cannot happen regarding PD for these spaces is to wait until they are built" (para. 4). Scheduling the PD program was important because it had to be implemented systematically, incorporating medium and short term information needs.

All PD sessions were scheduled well in advance and were promoted across the college through printed posters and brochures, through various university online information channels, and directly through school representation in the reference group. Faculty registration was arranged through an online booking system. Lunchtime and drop-in sessions offered prior to the move were repeated in the first semester of occupancy. In total, 63 face-to face-PD sessions were conducted prior to occupancy, attended by 669

Table 1. Summary of Issues Addressed through the PD Program.

Issues	Strategy
1. Pedagogical and technology-related beliefs	On the basis of findings in the literature and confirmation by the project reference group information and workshops sessions were arranged to introduce some concepts associated with NGLS and to address individual concerns.
	To complement the PD sessions, a variety of supporting resources was sourced and developed and made available online and in hard copy, with the aim of responding to concerns that were expressed "anywhere and anytime."
	To familiarize faculty with the layout and specifications of each of the different types of spaces available in the SAB, posters were produced showing floor plans, layout, furniture allocation and full specifications related to lighting, type of furniture, capacity, educational technology and recommendations for use.
2. Pedagogical image for use of ICT	Training resources such as user guides and tip sheets had to be developed for collaboration technology in some spaces as soon as the testing of the technology was complete. Educational technology "quick guides" were developed for each type of room and made available online and in hard copy. These provided ideas and scenarios of how teaching innovations such as "flipping the classroom" could be supported and enhanced by the specific affordances and technology inherent in the design of each type of space.
	As the building neared completion and educational technology was installed in the spaces, orientation tours were arranged and scheduled to suit construction and fit-out schedules.
3. Technologies and space	Prior to the relocation a replica of the technology-enhanced learning space was used to deliver face-to-face PD sessions, thus facilitating the modeling of teaching practice possible in such spaces. This "practice space" was available as a teaching space outside of PD sessions for all faculty, providing an authentic environment for faculty to experience, before occupancy, teaching in an NGLS that closely replicated spaces in the SAB.
4. Curriculum agendas	Curriculum-related issues and concerns were canvassed in the project reference group. Concerns unrelated to learning and teaching were identified and relayed through this group to project managers.
	School-specific sessions were facilitated to address the needs of individual discipline areas. Topics were identified through discussion and negotiation with project reference group members.

Table 1. *(Continued)*

Issues	Strategy
5. Student diversity	Workshops were scheduled for all college faculty to address specific topics including learning and teaching in NGLS; student interaction in traditional lectures; technology to enhance the classroom experience; assessment tasks for collaborative learning; learning management in NGLS; and technical training for specific mobile and collaborative technologies.
	In addition, 46 drop-in sessions were offered for individuals and small groups. These scheduled sessions addressed individual concerns and PD needs on an ad hoc basis as the date of occupancy drew closer.
6. Pedagogical design and contexts	Most scheduled PD sessions were recorded on video and placed online for access by those who were unable to attend. The conduct of the sessions modeled best practice through interactive delivery, panel discussions and showcasing of peer teaching. In this way, the sessions addressed the "existing subjectivities" of faculty and iteratively commenced the process of change prior to occupancy.
	Faculty who had already adopted innovative teaching approaches were invited to participate in the development of video vignettes showcasing best practice. The videos included interviews and recordings of live teaching events. Students were also invited to contribute their perspective on what constitutes engaging teaching. These video vignettes were placed online for access by all faculty prior to occupancy.

individuals. All faculty had access to the various resources specifically designed to support and foster teaching in the SAB.

Toward the end of the implementation of the PD program and just before occupancy, the new learning environment and its prospective users were brought together through tours of specific types of spaces with academic development, information technology and audio-visual staff present to answer questions from participants. The tours provided an invaluable hands-on orientation and enabled faculty to prepare for teaching with some familiarity of the NGLS and their affordances. Seventeen tours were conducted over a period of four months prior to occupancy and were attended by most faculty.

On occupancy in July 2012, with classes about to commence, the project team was satisfied that every opportunity had been made available for faculty to begin a longer process of transitioning their teaching practice to take advantage of the affordances of the new teaching and learning environment in the SAB.

THE OUTCOMES

Many post-occupancy evaluations of the physical attributes of new spaces focus on design aspects with little or no assessment of faculty and students' experiences of inhabiting and working in them. For this reason, there remains little long-term evidence in the literature about whether new and improved spaces lead to changes in teacher practice or whether learning or teaching experiences are impacted either positively or negatively.

A key aspect of any evaluation is to assess whether any transformative outcomes of the project are sustainable. Lee, Tan, and Dixon (2011) ask, "... long term, after the training has finished, do staff continue to work in ways that are intended by the design of particular spaces, or do they adapt the spaces to their practice" (p. 12)? To answer this question, the evaluation of the PD program has to focus on the behavioral and attitudinal change exhibited by faculty, rather than the physical design of the new spaces. Moreover, Pettigrew, Woodman, and Cameron (2001) state that "Judgments about success are likely to be conditional on who is doing the assessment and when the judgments are made" (p. 701).

Without external benchmarks with which to evaluate the success of the PD program the project team drew on evidence from pre and post-occupancy faculty surveys and structured interviews to assess the alignment of teaching practice to NGLS to meet the university's strategic vision: "... to be a global university of technology and design ...," and having an approach to education that "... will emphasize learning from action and experience" (RMIT University, 2010). Embedded in the plan is the goal to offer students opportunities for collaboration, team work, a sense of belonging, a creative culture, and opportunities to excel. These goals could only be met through a close alignment between the affordances of the NGLS and their use in practice.

The aim of the PD program was to improve the student experience by:

- extending the thinking of faculty about the philosophy and practice of student engagement;
- providing opportunities for faculty to extend their skills, relating to the use of both technology and space, within their own disciplines; and

- providing a range of learning experiences and tools for faculty that would be accessible and useful over the long term.

Three streams of enquiry were used as formative evaluation, undertaken from the start of the project. In the first, an online survey assessed the reaction-level perceptions and views of faculty who participated in the ongoing PD activities. In the second, regular feedback was sought from the reference group to inform the project's progress and assess the appropriateness of the topics chosen, the communication processes used to disseminate information, and to elicit views of the broader college community that were represented in the reference group. In an iterative review process, appropriate changes to the program were made immediately an omission or a need was identified. The third formative measure was the presentation of quarterly progress statements from the project team to the university group responsible for strategic oversight of the building construction and fit out, comprising the university's senior learning and teaching representatives. The progress statements ensured alignment between the PD program and any changes to the physical environment which might impact teaching strategies.

Post-occupancy, the project team sought to assess the impact of the PD program by identifying transformative outcomes that would be sustainable over the long term.

Summative feedback from faculty was sought at three stages after the physical move. The first online survey was administered soon after the move was completed, early into the first semester of teaching in the new building. This initial survey was intended to establish a benchmark to identify future changes to teaching practice, rather than a definitive statement about sustainable transformation. 80% of respondents made positive comments about the opportunities presented by the NGLS in the SAB and some had already incorporated changes to their teaching approach or stated that they were planning to do so. The responses indicate the emergence of key themes including:

- the enthusiastic adoption of new technology;
- the increased use of group-based activities resulting from the configuration of learning spaces;
- an appreciation of the design elements enhancing opportunities to innovate; and
- an increase in "flipped classroom" approaches resulting in more activity-based work in class.

These responses suggest that the new environment was being associated with the sort of good practice teaching models demonstrated in the various PD sessions. When asked to identify the most significant positive aspect of their room, over 60% of respondents identified factors associated with potential improvements in teaching. The PD program appears to have raised awareness of alternatives to traditional teaching practice for many staff, and that the NGLS fosters and supports their adoption. Despite some initial operational challenges the potential of the collaboration software to increase the quality of student engagement and to support group work generated positive comments.

A second summative survey was conducted twelve months after occupation in which faculty expressed their views of the SAB as "a positive and exciting learning environment" which is "brilliant to teach in," having "a fantastic vibe" and which "... engages students with their learning experiences." Respondents indicated that there was an increase in the use of interactive activities in class to generate student engagement and greater adoption of "flipped classroom" teaching approaches compared with before the move to NGLS.

Eighteen months after the occupation of the new building, semi-structured interviews were conducted with program managers representing the Management, Accounting, Business IT, Economics and Finance academic disciplines. The role of program manager was chosen not only because of its association with specific discipline areas, but also because these individuals generally have knowledge of teaching practice within their own disciplines. The interviews explored whether there had been any changes to established pedagogical practice, and respondents' views in general about teaching in the NGLS. Four significant factors emerged which point to transformative outcomes in teaching practice.

1. There is an increase in group work and collaborative learning fostered by the NGLS environment compared with the pre-occupancy learning spaces.
2. The layout of rooms with student "pods" simplifies and reinforces the role of the teacher as a facilitator, and supports teacher-student interaction.
3. In some cases the need to review assessment strategies and learning activities became necessary to take full advantage of NGLS affordances.
4. Respondents in all but one discipline area have explored, and in many cases incorporated "flipped classroom" strategies. This change stands in

sharp contrast to pre-occupancy faculty beliefs that a flipped classroom model was impractical and unworkable.

A number of factors contributed to the generally positive views of the NGLS on occupancy. Given the diverse PD needs addressed by the program and broad participant profile, the project team's showcasing and modeling their teaching approaches in a space that closely replicated the future teaching environment of the SAB proved invaluable in motivating and supporting faculty. In addition, the responsive program design process, the provision of a mix of hard copy and soft copy resources, scheduled PD sessions complemented by just-in-time resources, catering for groups of stakeholders as well as individual faculty, face to face and video presentations, and the oversight of a stakeholder reference group as a communication channel between the project team and faculty, strengthened the impact of the program and ensured the ongoing support of stakeholder groups in the university.

The process undertaken effectively addressed these particular circumstances and was sufficiently flexible in its key elements to be applied in other institutions transitioning to NGLS. Interest has been expressed by other higher education institutions in adopting or adapting individual elements of the process to suit their own needs.

LESSONS LEARNED AND CONCLUSION

Dewey and Dewey's (1915) oft-cited observation, that "... no book or map is a substitute for personal experience; they cannot take the place of the actual journey" (p. 74). represents the truth of any change or PD initiative. This dictum encompassed the twofold nature of the transition for faculty. First, relinquishing the "tyranny of the lectern" in order to confront the changed social hierarchy within the learning spaces presented by the transition from "the sage on the stage" to "the guide on the side" and second, implementing changes to established curriculum in order to maximize the potential of the new spaces. Churchill's (1944) observation that "We shape our dwellings; thereafter they shape us" reveals the challenge. The building that now houses staff and students from RMIT's College of Business reflects the qualities of the people who designed it. Post-occupation, it is anticipated that the people who work in the building will, with appropriate support, absorb some of its innovative qualities and translate them into renewed teaching practices. Just how changes in technology-enriched new learning spaces influence teacher practice remains under-explored; as do the complexities of constraints and challenges that impede change.

The affordances of the new learning spaces facilitate the collaborative learning ethos that underpins the university's student-centered learning model. As different faculty and very different groups of students will use the new spaces, faculty need to identify with, adapt and develop the learning environment to meet their own needs, both discipline-based and cohort-based. This requires them to re-imagine their own teaching practice.

This case study focused primarily on the implementation of a large scale change management strategy, facilitated through consultation and professional development to address issues associated with the adoption of new teaching practices that were identified by Steel and Andrews (2012). Halfway through year two of the post-occupancy period the project team can with some confidence claim to have designed, developed and delivered a PD program that addressed the needs of faculty across discipline groups, levels of experience and the innovation adoption continuum. The key lessons learnt from the process described in this case study support the observations from the literature:

1. The project team acknowledged that individual priorities and belief systems would affect responses to proposed innovations.
2. A coordinated and flexible approach is necessary to maintain the pace, degree, and focus of change.
3. Using both top-down and bottom-up change management approaches proved necessary to acknowledge institutional and individual stakeholder's imperatives.
4. Effective two-way communication with representatives of discipline groups was found to be of critical importance in managing the complexity of the project centralized/diffusion approaches and ensuring the relevance to the PD program.
5. The provision of flexible access to resources is essential to address basic information needs and just-in-time pedagogical support for a diverse faculty profile across several discipline areas.
6. Identifying a range of factors as a framework for the design of such a program is essential. In this project the six factors identified by Steel and Andrews (2012) proved to be relevant and useful: pedagogical and

technology-related beliefs; the use of ICT; the relationship between technologies and space; curriculum agendas; student diversity; and pedagogical design for specific contexts.

7. The need for systematic implementation in clearly defined stages that incorporate medium and short term information needs of all stakeholders is essential for effective project management.

The transition from the old to the new learning environments, toward what Barrett and Zhang (2009, p. 4) describe as a "finished beginning" commenced when the SAB was occupied and teaching commenced. The "finished beginning" signaled the start of the second phase of the change process, which requires more targeted development, designed for and applied to the reality of pedagogical potential. The SAB journey continues.

REFERENCES

Barrett, P., & Zhang, Y. (2009). *Optimal learning spaces design implications for primary schools.* SCRI Research Report Series. University of Salford, Salford, UK.

Bates, A. W. (2000). *Managing technological change: Strategies for college and university leaders* (1st ed.). San Francisco, CA: Jossey-Bass.

Bennett, R. (2001). Lecturers' attitudes to new teaching methods. *International Journal of Management Education, 2*(1), 42–58.

Blackmore, J., Bateman, D., Loughlin, J., O'Mara, J., & Aranda, G. (2011). *Research into the connection between built learning spaces and student outcomes: Literature review.* Retrieved from http://www.eduweb.vic.gov.au/edulibrary/public/publ/research/publ/blackmore_learning_spaces.pdf

Churchill, W. (1944, 28 October). *Speech delivered to the house of commons.* London.

Commonwealth Association for Public Administration and Management. (2010). *Overview of case study models and methodology.* Retrieved from http://www.capam.org/_documents/reportoncasestudymethodologies.pdf

Dewey, J., & Dewey, E. (1915). *Schools of tomorrow.* New York, NY: E. P. Dutton.

Elton, L. (2003). Disseminations of innovations in higher education: A change theory approach. *Tertiary Education and Management, 9,* 199–214.

Freeman, M., & Johnston, C. (2008). Improving teaching and learning through discipline-specific support models. *International Journal of Management Education, 7*(1), 61–71.

Kennedy, G., Dalgarno, B., Bennett, S., Gray, K., Judd, T., Waycott, J., ... Krause, K. (2009). *Educating the net generation: Implications for learning and teaching in Australian universities.* Sydney: Australian Learning and Teaching Council. Retrieved from http://www.netgen.unimelb.edu.au/

Kirkup, G., & Kirkwood, A. (2005). Information and communications technology (ICT) in higher education teaching: A tale of gradualism rather than revolution. *Learning Media and Technology, 30*(2), 185–199.

Lee, N., Tan, S., & Dixon, J. (2011). *A comprehensive learning space evaluation model.* Swinburne University, Melbourne: Australian Learning & Teaching Council. Retrieved from http://www.olt.gov.au/system/files/resources/PP8-920%20Swinburne%20Lee%20 Final%20Report%202011.pdf

Long, G. (2009). *Professional development for 21st century learning and teaching.* Retrieved from http://blog.garethl.com/2009/04/proessional-development-for-21st.html

Pettigrew, A. M., Woodman, R. W., & Cameron, K. S. (2001). Studying organizational change and development: Challenges for future research. *Academy of Management Journal, 44*(4), 697–713.

RMIT University. (2010). *Transforming the future: Strategic plan.* RMIT 2015. Retrieved from http://www.rmit.edu.au/about/strategy

Rogers, E. M. (1995). *Diffusion of innovations* (4th ed.). New York, NY: The Free Press.

Schon, D. A. (1971). *Beyond the stable state.* New York, NY: Random House.

Starkey, K., Tempest, S., & McKinlay, A. (2004). *How organizations learn: Managing the search for knowledge.* London: Thomson.

Steel, C., & Andrews, T. (2012). Re-imagining teaching for technology-enriched learning spaces: An academic development model. In M. Keppell, K. Souter, & M. Riddle (Eds.), *Physical and virtual learning spaces in higher education: Concepts for the modern learning environment* (pp. 242–265). Hershey, PA: IGI Global.

Thomson, P., Jones, K., & Hall, C. (2009). *Creative school change research project.* Final report. Newcastle.

Trowler, P. (2008). *Cultures and change in higher education: Theories and practice.* New York, NY: Palgrave Macmillan.

CHAPTER 11

A NEW APPROACH TO PROFESSIONAL LEARNING FOR ACADEMICS TEACHING IN NEXT GENERATION LEARNING SPACES

Barbara de la Harpe and Thembi Mason

ABSTRACT

The promise of Next Generation Learning Spaces appears to remain unfulfilled. This chapter explores why and how the design of professional learning for academics teaching in such spaces can and should be transformed. It takes a fresh look at why old professional development is failing and proposes a new way to engage academics in their own professional learning. Rather than continuing with traditional professional development that is most often, ad hoc, formal and centrally driven, comprising mandated professional development workshops and a website that may only be visited once, the chapter explores the move from 'old' professional development to 'new' professional learning. It draws on the fields of organisational theory, cognitive theory and behavioural economics.

New professional learning is characterised by a 'pull' rather than a 'push' philosophy. Academic staff themselves drive their own learning, choosing

The Future of Learning and Teaching in Next Generation Learning Spaces
International Perspectives on Higher Education Research, Volume 12, 219–239
ISSN: 1479-3628/doi:10.1108/S1479-362820140000012015

what, when and how they want to learn to become better teachers. Multiple and various learning opportunities embedded in day to day work are just-in-time, self-directed, performance-driven and evaluated within an organisational system. In this way the institutional setting influences behaviour by 'nudging' habits and setting defaults resulting in academics making the 'right' decisions and doing the 'right' thing. By addressing the compelling issue of how to enhance academic staff teaching capability, this chapter can help university leaders to think beyond the professional development approaches of yesterday. Aligning with this new direction will result in enhanced learning and teaching in the future.

Keywords: Professional learning; professional development; staff capability; learning and teaching; change management; transformative learning

CURRENT CONTEXT

The university landscape is shifting (Barber, Donnelly, & Rizvi, 2013; Bok, 2013; Bokor, 2012). The role of the university in society as creators and guardians of knowledge is being challenged. The value add of universities is also coming under question as knowledge becomes more and more ubiquitous and available online. Competition from private providers and global tertiary players is putting pressure on universities in attracting and retaining students. Student expectations are also changing. Digital technologies are transforming the way students engage in their learning and the student learning experience.

Additionally, lectures are slowly disappearing from universities. Teaching spaces are being turned into Next Generation Learning Spaces to encourage a different type of learning and teaching. Spaces are being built or retrofitted to increase active learning and a more student-centred approach to teaching. While Next Generation Learning Spaces vary in their exact characteristics, they typically are:

- carefully planned to facilitate interactions between groups of students;
- designed for large numbers of students and allow for flexible use and arrangement of furniture;
- constructed to enable the academic to both teach and facilitate the class from anywhere in the room; and
- technology-enabled to encourage active learning.

Next Generation Learning Spaces are claimed to be 'disruptive', pressing academics to rethink their teaching approach. According to Oblinger (2005, p. 14), '[a]n active, collaborative teaching and learning philosophy is often manifested in a different design. Space can either enable – or inhibit – different styles of teaching as well as learning'. The new design of Next Generation Learning Spaces requires a re-conceptualization of pedagogy to maximise their effectiveness (Oblinger, 2005). There is no 'front' in a Next Generation Learning Space, with tables arranged so that large numbers of students working in groups can share work using technology. It is more difficult to lecture with students sitting in small groups, with half the class with their backs to the front.

To date, universities around the world have spent millions of dollars transforming teaching spaces into Next Generation Learning Spaces. For example, the United States spent around US$50 billion between 2004 and 2007 on university physical facilities (Oblinger, 2005). In the United Kingdom, £902 million went towards university capital grants in 2008 (HEFCE, 2008) and £562 million was set aside for 2010–2011 initiatives (HEFCE, 2010). In Australia, the Government injection of '… more than $5 billion is transforming Australia's tertiary landscape – with universities, TAFEs and training centres as well as science and research facilities getting a much needed makeover … This investment was long overdue, serving to address decades of neglect and bring campuses across the country into the 21st century' (DIISRT, 2012, pp. 3–4).

Despite this considerable investment in Next Generation Learning Spaces there is evidence that the full potential of these spaces is not yet being fully realised. For some academics, this kind of teaching environment encourages them to (re)think their pedagogy and practice to one that is active, student-centred, technology-rich and authentic. For others, support is needed to help them do so. Next Generation Learning Spaces require universities to rethink how to support staff to make the much needed shift in teaching for enhanced learning. As the EDUCAUSE Learning Initiative Advisory Board (2009, p. 63) point out, '[w]ith all the tools now available to us, a failure to create expansive, inclusive, and active learning environments would dishonor the mission of higher education …'.

PROFESSIONAL DEVELOPMENT NOW

Traditionally, universities have supported academic staff to enhance their teaching practice, including for teaching in Next Generation Learning

Spaces in a number of ways. Typically these include short, intensive in-house training/induction activities; a series of centrally run workshops that are often ad hoc and disjointed; a certified tertiary teaching and learning programme or by supporting attendance at disciplinary-based conferences. In addition, most universities would have a generic website dedicated to teaching and learning. Where online modules are available they are often a component of induction focussing on compliance education, including topics such as ethics, equity, copyright and occupational health and safety, rather than learning and teaching.

Hart (2011, p. 1), points out that for many organisations '... the current state of workplace learning is one where there is a heavy focus on formal, content-rich courses ...'. Such 'just-in-case' professional development may or may not directly deal with academic staff current needs. In addition, traditional professional development approaches often lead to a superficial accumulation of knowledge, layer upon layer, rather than an ongoing re-conceptualisation of educational practice (Boud & Hager, 2012; Cross, 2010; Feixas & Zellweger, 2010; Hart, 2011; Webster-Wright, 2009). Levine (2006, p. 109) likens many contemporary professional development programmes for enhancing teaching to '... the fabled Wild West town ... unruly and disordered'.

Moreover, professional development that comprises workshops as the main strategy for academics to attend at set times, or 'just-in-case', have been found to be insufficient in developing the professional teaching expertise of academics that, in turn, impact on student outcomes (Hattie, 2009; Parsons, Hill, Holland, & Willis, 2012).

As far back as the mid-1980s, questions have been raised around the impact of such traditional professional development approaches. A meta-analysis of 91 studies that explored the effectiveness (or not) of professional development concluded that '... of all the different types of training structures, independent study is the most effective' (Wade, 1985, p. 54). Similarly, the study by Birman, Desimone, Porter, and Garet (2000) found that '[a]n activity is more likely to be effective in improving teachers' knowledge and skills if it forms a coherent part of a wider set of opportunities for teacher learning and development'. Additionally, Timperley, Wilson, Barrar, and Fung (2007) found that professional learning is most effective if it uses active learning strategies and is offered over time.

Academics are often resistant to engaging in professional development activities, citing lack of time or lack of relevance of programme to their context. Low attendance is not uncommon. A significant lack of attendance is often reported by those running professional development activities (workshops/conferences), despite academic staff registering. This rings true for all professional development. A study of continuous professional development (CPD) for dentists (Barnes, Bullock, Bailey, Cowpe, & Karaharju-Suvanto, 2013, p. 5) found that the factors preventing engagement in CPD '... included time since graduation, costs, work and home commitments ... interest and convenience' and barriers to implementing changes to workplace practices were around '... availability of materials, resources and support from colleagues'.

Additionally, the culture of academia is not encouraging of professional development. Most academics are employed by universities based on their expertise in a research field. As Bok (2013, pp. 2−3) points out of universities in America '... high regard in ... [global rankings] ... is largely due to the excellence of their research rather than the quality of education they provide'. Academics are not required to have a teaching qualification despite teaching being a significant part of their role. It is assumed that academics keep up with their teaching knowledge through their research, including through reading, collaboration with colleagues, publishing and attendance at discipline focused conferences. Thus, the teaching aspect of their role is often taken for granted. For many academics, '[s]pending time on training courses is time spent avoiding the main purpose of a lecturer's raison d'etre at a university − research' (Quinn, 2012, p. 73).

Lastly, the beliefs academics hold about teaching also influences whether they will engage with professional development or not (Quinn, 2012). Quinn identified four beliefs that impacted on academic staff engagement with professional development, as follows:

- a belief that the main purpose of their role is to research and that universities reward researching (engaging in professional development for teaching is not important).
- a belief that students are the problem since they are underprepared and not at the standard required (engaging in professional development not required rather students need development).
- a belief that teaching is simple, intuitive focused on skill development and there is nothing to learn about it (engaging in professional development is not needed since teaching is easy).
- a belief that engaging in professional development is to fulfil a policy, or meet a personal strategic intent, such as gaining promotion (engaging in professional development would only be to satisfy an institutional requirement or a compliance need, or for personal gain).

In a university world where there is casualisation of staff, massification of student numbers, globalisation of the student body, growth in the use of technology, a focus on developing learner capabilities and 'agency', and a need to connect what is learned to industry, the simple truism of the intuitive 'academic' teacher is obsolete. No longer can academics ignore engaging in professional development that enhances knowledge of educational theory and contemporary practice.

There is a growing body of literature that professional development needs to become more sophisticated in order to support academics develop the capabilities that teaching of the future requires (Boud & Hager, 2012; Cross, 2010; Hart, 2011; Hattie, 2009; Hunzicker, 2011). Finding new ways for academics to develop the capacity required of a 21st century practitioner and to continually develop their teaching practice is needed as a matter of urgency. New ways must be found, since as reported above, the traditional, 'just-in-case' model is proving to be insufficient and not fit for purpose.

Next we describe a professional learning approach for academics that can be sustainably applied to the whole of a university rather than being simply left up to individual academics. The approach responds to the need for academics to enhance their teaching in Next Generation Learning Spaces. It was developed as part of an Australian Government Office for Learning and Teaching funded project — Not of a Waste of Space: professional development for staff teaching in Next Generation Learning Spaces. The professional learning approach allows for individualised and flexible professional learning that works for both the novice and the more experienced academic (de la Harpe & Mason, with Koethe, Faulkner, & McPherson, 2013).

NEW APPROACH TO PROFESSIONAL LEARNING

Contemporary literature and theory reveals a number of characteristics of professional learning of the future. Professional learning is more effective if it is continuous and situated in work; embedded in a holistic system that is performance-driven and (self)-evaluated (Organisational theory); learner-centred, self-organised and self-managed; and if it provides opportunities to learn from others (Cognitive theory); 'nudges' intentions to engage in professional learning and to make good choices and includes an element of fun (behavioural economic theory) (Adam & de Savigny, 2012; Ajzen,

1985, 1991; Angner & Loewenstein, 2010; Avineri, 2012; Cross, 2010; Dawnay & Shah, 2005; Gee, 2003, 2004, 2005, 2012; Hart, 2011; Hattie, 2009; Senge, 1990; Thaler & Sunstein, 2009; Werbach, 2012).

Based on these characteristics, a new approach to professional learning for teaching in Next Generation Learning Spaces is presented in the sections that follow. The new approach is designed to be holistic, interactive and adaptable, supporting universities in the challenge of maintaining best practice or bringing about a paradigm shift in the way academics teach in Next Generation Learning Spaces. The new approach (see Fig. 1) is

- continuous and situated in work, and comprises
  - a work plan strategy
  - an email strategy
  - online resources
  - local network meetings
  - posters, tear-off guides and bookmarks

In the sections later, each of the aspects and the literature that underpins them is discussed.

Situated in Work

The institutional timetabling system is used to identify academic staff who are timetabled to teach in a Next Generation Learning Space. These staff are then automatically included in the professional learning approach.

Boud and Hager (2012, p. 18) argue that professional learning '... must be located in what professionals do and how they do it'. In their view, academic learning should be seen as,

> ... a normal part of working and indeed most other social activities. It occurs through practice, in work settings from addressing the work challenges and problems that arrives. Most learning takes place not through formalised activities, but through the exigencies of practice with peers and others, drawing on expertise that is accessed in response to need. Problem-solving in which participants tackle challenges which progressively extend their existing capabilities and learn with and from each other appears to be a common and frequent form of naturalist development. (Boud & Hager, 2012, p. 22)

Recent literature suggests that locating professional learning in the practice of work and focusing on enhancing learning rather than knowledge acquisition is most successful. Learning that is continuous and happens in

Continuous and situated in work

Workplan strategy

Workplan objective setting

Mid-year self and manager review

End of year self and manager review

What do I want to achieve? (Outcomes)

What activities will I undertake to achieve this? (Activities)

Choice of activities include
Self-directed study
Peer partnership program
Peer review proce
Grad Certificate module

Online resources

Library guide with articles, videos, case studies, links

Personalised email prompts continue weekly throughout second semester

Code cracked, certificate sent

Badges

Email strategy

Personalised email triggered by timetable introduces the space and technology in the room

Theroy of Planned behaviour emails

Crack the code game to teaching in NGLSs

Personalised email prompts continue weekly throughout the first semester.Prompt academics to engage in professional learning and provide links to resources, including exemplary practice, videos, articles, websites and other existing professional learning resources. Game comprising quests in order to 'Crack the Code' to teaching in NGLS.

Voluntary participation in local **network meetings**
Bookmark with link/QR code to online resources and contact name handed out by local learning advisor

I have been timetabled into a new learning space

What does using the space well look like?

How do I teach in this space so that students are engaged?

How can I use the space with my students?

How do I use the technology in this space?

What resources are available to help me to teach in this space

Posters and tear-off guides of teaching strategies in spaces

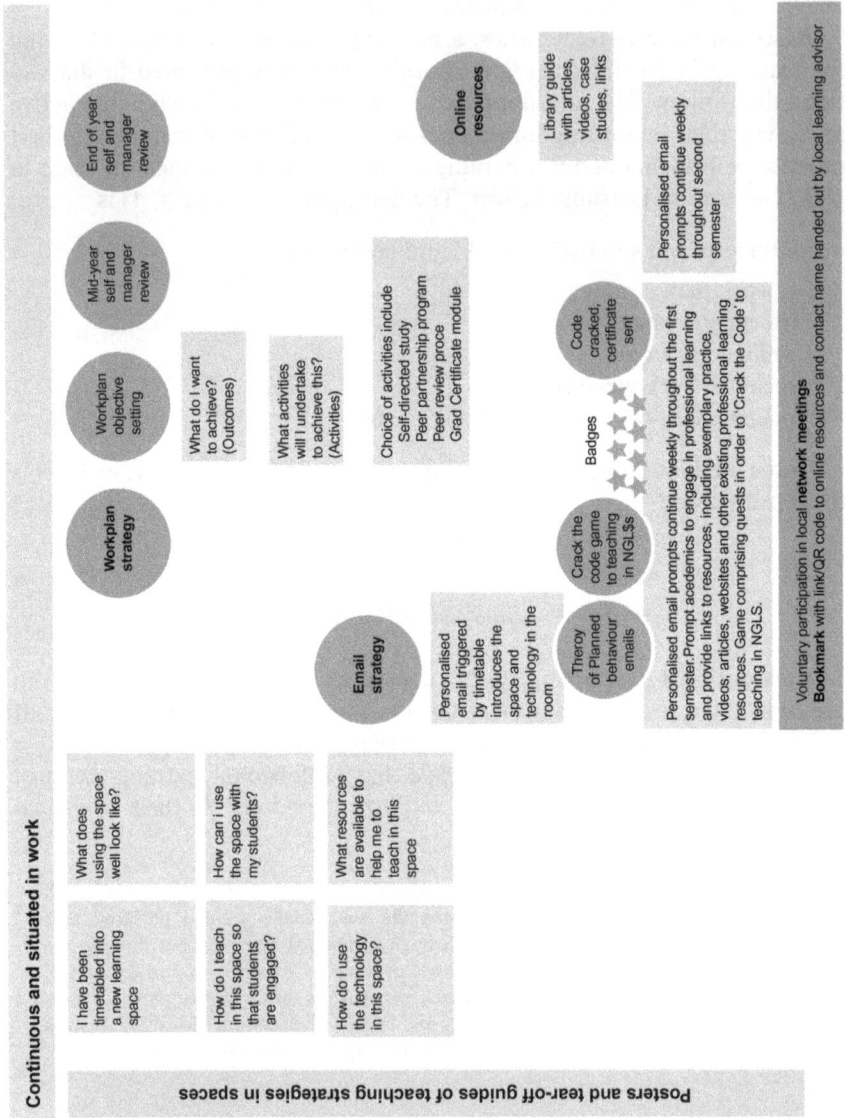

Fig. 1. New Professional Learning Approach for Teaching in Next Generation Learning Spaces and Elements.

the work setting has been found to be essential for workers to remain up to date. Many studies have found that this is a powerful way to learn, with '[s]tudy after study finding that at least 80% of how workers learn to do their jobs ...' this way (Cross, 2010, p. 45). Cross likens formal learning to taking a bus '[e]veryone starts at the same place, goes to the same destination, and arrives at the same time ...' in contrast, learning that is situated in work is more like riding a bicycle where the rider is in control and able to start when they are ready, move at their own pace and change direction as required (Cross, 2010).

Work Plan Strategy

In the new approach, academics are responsible for their own professional learning and are accountable for taking action. This involves them creating/agreeing learning outcomes aimed at enhancing their teaching in Next Generation Learning Spaces in their annual work plan or performance review discussion, determining activities to achieve the outcomes and setting performance indicators to measure success as part of their mid (if applicable) and end of year performance review. Institutional outcomes could be cascaded to pre-populate work plans of those staff teaching in a Next Generation Learning Space where an online system is in place.

Thus, work plans with clearly stated outcomes around professional learning for teaching in Next Generation Learning Spaces are agreed with line-managers and include mid and annual review, and self and manager feedback. They are the vehicle to agree and anchor professional learning in the university system, whilst giving academics choice over their professional learning. This approach allows academics choice in what, when and how they want to learn or engage, but within a system where outcomes are evaluated.

A number of professional learning options can be provided. This gives academics choice and allows them to begin where they are 'at' in terms of enhancing their teaching in Next Generation Learning Spaces. Some options include engaging in a Peer Partnership programme or a Peer Review process, undertaking self-directed learning (including, for example, a scholarship of learning and teaching project) or completing a module from the Graduate Certificate in Tertiary Teaching and Learning. Most of these choices already exist within universities.

The work plan strategy draws on recent literature that suggests having processes that require staff to self-manage their learning needs within a clear accountability framework is most effective (Cross, 2010; Hart, 2011). It is also underpinned by behavioural economic theory, involving choice architecture and 'nudges'. Behavioural economics has shown that people are not always rational decision makers, instead they often make irrational or unpredictable decisions that appear impulsive, habitual or emotional rather than planned and which do not follow the neo-classical economic model of decision-making behaviour (Angner & Loewenstein, 2010).

Behavioural economic theory (Thaler & Sunstein, 2009) argues that rational judgment and decision-making does not always prevail and the way choices are presented influence decision-making. Choice architecture does not mandate or prevent choices but rather aims to influence good choices. By designing the environment using choice architecture, individuals are 'nudged' to make the 'right' decision and are not deprived of their freedom to make decisions and choices. According to Thaler and Sunstein (2009, p. 4), '[g]ood [choice] architects realize that although they can't build the perfect building [professional learning program] they can make some design choices that will have beneficial effects'. In line with this theory, environments are designed or changed so that defaults make it easy for people to do the 'right' or make the 'right' decisions that nudge habits and indirectly influence behaviour. Universities should aim to make engaging in professional development an easy choice for staff and the path of least resistance.

Email Strategy

A series of 14 emails that are personalised and specifically designed for academic staff timetabled to teach in a Next Generation Learning Space are sent over the course of a teaching semester/period (see Fig. 2). Emails either encourage academics to undertake professional development activities and provide resources (Theory of planned behaviour emails in weeks 1, 3, 6, 9 and 11) or invite them to participate in a professional learning game (Quest

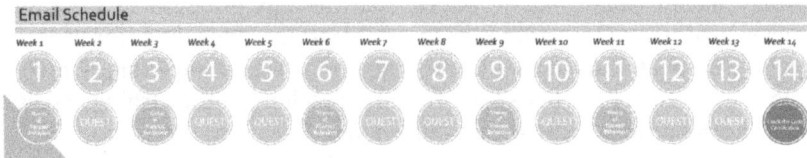

Fig. 2. Email Schedule Showing Theory of Planned Behaviour and Quest Emails.

emails in weeks 2, 4, 5, 7, 8, 10, 12, 13 and 14). Academics can 'opt-out' if they do not want to continue receiving the emails.

The emails (five) that encourage academics to engage in professional learning and provide resources are underpinned by the Theory of Planned Behaviour (Ajzen, 1985). According to the theory, a person is most likely to intend to engage in a behaviour if they evaluate that behaviour positively (attitude toward the behaviour), perceive social pressure to engage in the behaviour (subjective norm) and believe that the behaviour will be easy to perform (perceived behavioural control). Emails are, therefore, designed and presented to influence attitudes, subjective norms and perceived behavioural control, since all three influence intentions to increase engagement with professional learning (see Fig. 3).

The emails (nine) that invite academics to participate in a game exploring the opportunities that Next Generation Learning Spaces offer comprise completing eight quests in order to 'Crack the code' to teaching in Next Generation Learning Spaces (see Fig. 4). At the completion of each Quest the academic receives a redeem code or passcode. They are then asked to submit this code to a website whereupon they receive a badge with a letter – one of the letters towards 'cracking the 8 letter code' to teaching in a Next Generation Learning Space. Once all the letters are received and the 'code is cracked' a certificate of completion from a senior university learning and teaching leader, for example, Pro-Vice Chancellor (Learning and Teaching), Deputy Vice Chancellor (Learning and Teaching) is automatically generated.

On the way to 'cracking the code' extrinsic and intrinsic elements are included. Extrinsic elements involve for example coffee vouchers and a certificate of completion that can be used for promotion or teaching award applications. Intrinsic elements focus on providing activities that result in

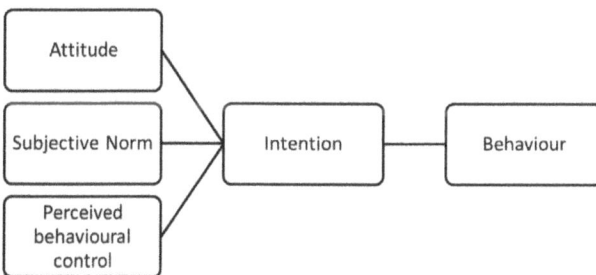

Fig. 3. Elements of the Theory of Planned Behaviour.

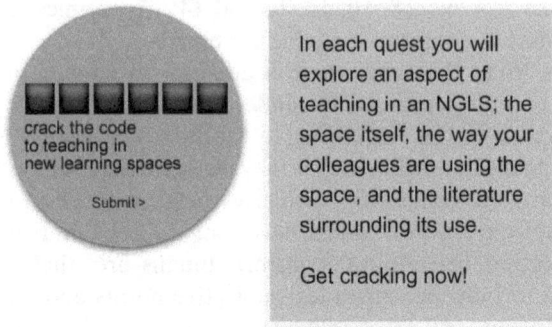

Fig. 4.   Introduction to 'Crack the Code' to Teaching in Next Generation Learning
Spaces Game.

feelings of being supported to teach better, being helped to stay up to date, being on the cutting edge and being able to maintain currency. They also provide a sense of personal satisfaction from completing the quests and cracking the code.

The interactive 'Crack the Code' game is underpinned by gamification theory (Werbach, 2012). Gamification is the application of game elements and techniques to activities in non-game settings, incorporating elements of social learning, competition, cooperation, exploration and storytelling. According to Gee (2012, p. xviii), people can choose to learn things from books, movies and television, but in games learning is core and unavoidable, since it is built into their design.

> Those who engage in playing games do not just do things and make decisions, they learn things and master them. If they do not, they do not leave the first level of a game. Imagine a book that constantly had quizzes and tests at the end of each section (oops, that's a textbook). Few people would consider it fun (few people consider textbooks fun). But games constantly assess players. Every action is a test with feedback, and the boss at the end of a level is a 'final exam' for that level. Games have found that both learning and constant assessments of that learning are a 'turn-on' for people. And players pay lots of money for this turn-on. The textbook makers can only marvel in envy.
>
> Good games work because they know that learning is a deep drive for humans, a drive that school has managed to kill for many. Games are simply spaces for learning and problem-solving with a 'win' condition (beating each level and the game as a whole). But to sell, they have to organise learning in engaging and motivating ways. They have to tap into the innate drive for learning and mastery that is inside all human beings.

A continuous and targeted email strategy keeps staff engaged and provides an element of fun, 'nudging' them to do the 'right' thing.

Online Resources

The very best of the numerous resources already available online are contextualised and (re)packaged in a Library Guide for academic staff teaching in Next Generation Learning Spaces. Creating a library guide about teaching in Next Generation Learning Spaces in collaboration with University Librarians is easy to do and is a sustainable approach (see http://rmit.libguides.com/newlearningspaces). Resources can include articles, videos, case studies, links to other university sites. Useful topics to include: make the space work; make teaching more effective, make technology work, manage learners well and get ideas from colleagues. Since SpringShare software has been adopted by most universities for the creation of library guides in Australia, creating a library guide allows universities across the sector to share resources by easily adopting and adapting each other's guides.

Access to online resources which are relevant, varied, up to date and immediately applicable is underpinned by constructivist learning theory (Jonassen, 1994) and allows staff to build their capabilities, 'just-in-time' and 'just-for-me', supporting learner-centred and self-directed learning (Zimmerman, 1989).

Network Meetings

Academics timetabled to teach in Next Generation Learning Spaces are personally invited to form a local school network. Network meetings allow academic staff teaching in Next Generation Learning Spaces to get together regularly during the teaching period. Ideally meetings are formed and facilitated in-context, by a person responsible for learning and teaching leadership and/or support in the school. A moderate budget for catering and for guest speakers should be provided.

It is important that meetings are contextualised depending on the needs of the academic staff and, thus, can be organised in different ways. For example, external guest speakers can be invited to prompt discussion about teaching in Next Generation Learning Spaces; academics in the school can be invited staff to speak about how they teach in a Next Generation Learning Space; facilitated sessions for staff to bring along their 'problems of practice' in teaching in these spaces for peer feedback and discussion can also be arranged.

Local network meetings are underpinned by social constructivist learning theory. They provide face-to-face, peer supported and social networking opportunities for academic staff to discuss and share their approaches to teaching in Next Generation Learning Spaces for those who want to learn in this way.

Posters, Tear-off Guides and Bookmarks

Posters that focus on the negative impact of a didactic approach to teaching, for example student dis-engagement and non-attendance are designed for display in Next Generation Learning Spaces (see Fig. 5). These posters

Fig. 5. Posters Using Loss Aversion Theory.

prompt academic staff to reflect on their teaching approach and their student responses to their teaching in Next Generation Learning Spaces.

Posters draw on the theory of loss aversion research (a component of behavioural economic theory) which suggests that negative messages about what might be lost are more effective in changing behaviour than positive messages about what can be gained (Fuller, 2009; Kahneman & Tversky, 2000). Loss aversion theory has been successfully employed by the Transport Accident Commission and stop drinking and smoking campaigns.

Tear-off guides placed in Next Generation Learning Spaces describe teaching strategies that encourage more interactive use of the space and provide step by step instructions on how to implement them. Examples of strategies include 'Think-Pair-Share', 'Plus-Minus-Interesting' or 'Role playing' (see Fig. 6). Academics teaching in the spaces can 'tear off' these guides to adapt their teaching.

Bookmarks refer staff to online resources and provide the name of the local learning and teaching leader/support in the school. QR codes are provided so that academic staff can simply go straight to the online resources using a QR reader on their phone or tablet making it easy for them to access information.

The tear-off guide and bookmark strategies are underpinned by behavioural economic theory, specifically choice architecture and 'nudge' theory, since they are designed to provide easy access to information and effective teaching strategies and to 'nudge' academics to try them. They also act as prompts to remind and encourage that is 'nudge' staff to engage in professional learning.

PROFESSIONAL LEARNING OF THE FUTURE

In this chapter a new approach was presented for transforming the professional learning of academics teaching in Next Generation Learning Spaces which can be sustainably applied across a university and not simply left up to individual academics.

The approach is set within a rigorous, organisational accountability framework, as well as being performance-driven and (self-)evaluated, making it a core part of a dynamic and complex whole of organisation system. The work plan strategy anchors professional learning in work ensuring that academics take responsibility for their own professional learning and are held accountable for taking action. It allows academics choice in what, when and how they want to learn or engage, but within a system where outcomes

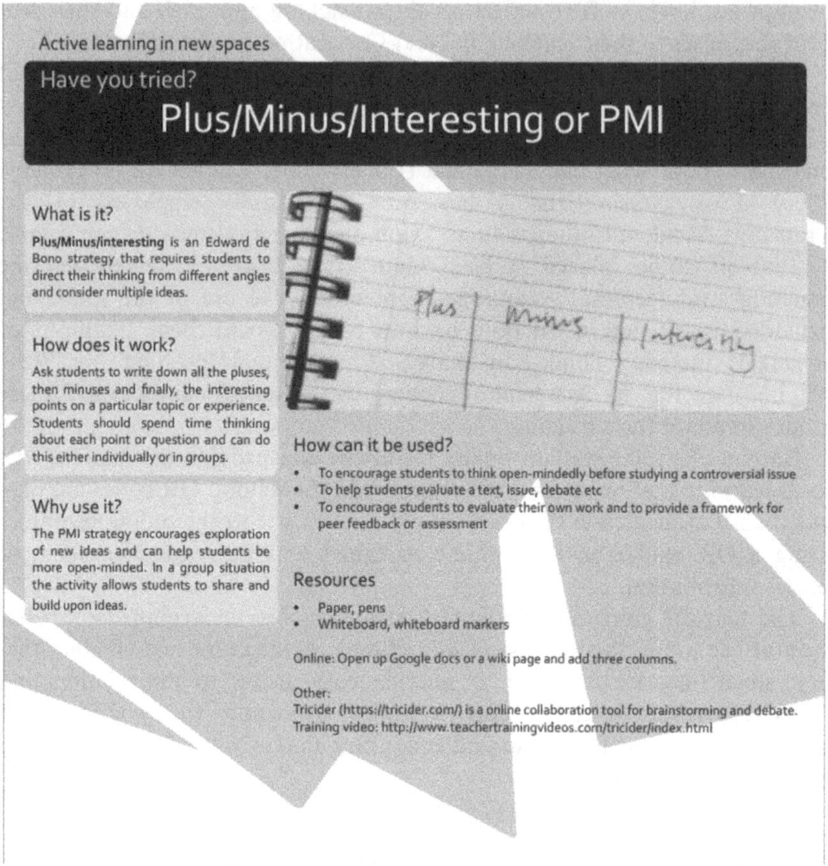

Active learning in new spaces

Have you tried?

Plus/Minus/Interesting or PMI

What is it?

Plus/Minus/interesting is an Edward de Bono strategy that requires students to direct their thinking from different angles and consider multiple ideas.

How does it work?

Ask students to write down all the pluses, then minuses and finally, the interesting points on a particular topic or experience. Students should spend time thinking about each point or question and can do this either individually or in groups.

Why use it?

The PMI strategy encourages exploration of new ideas and can help students be more open-minded. In a group situation the activity allows students to share and build upon ideas.

How can it be used?

- To encourage students to think open-mindedly before studying a controversial issue
- To help students evaluate a text, issue, debate etc
- To encourage students to evaluate their own work and to provide a framework for peer feedback or assessment

Resources

- Paper, pens
- Whiteboard, whiteboard markers

Online: Open up Google docs or a wiki page and add three columns.

Other:
Tricider (https://tricider.com/) is a online collaboration tool for brainstorming and debate.
Training video: http://www.teachertrainingvideos.com/tricider/index.html

Fig. 6. Tear-Off Guide.

are supported and evaluated. This element signals that the organisation supports academic engagement in professional learning and as a result contributes to improving the culture of professional learning in academia. A culture that encourages professional learning has been shown to be one of the most successful ways to impact student outcomes positively (Hattie, 2009).

In the new approach behavioural economic theory, specifically choice architecture, is applied responsibly in a number of ways to 'nudge' staff to make good professional learning choices. Firstly, academic staff, who are teaching in Next Generation Learning Spaces, are identified through the timetabling system and are automatically included in a purposefully designed and contextualised email strategy. Secondly, individualised learning outcomes for enhancing teaching in Next Generation Learning Spaces are negotiated or automatically cascaded into academic staff work plans. Thirdly, in work plans, academic staff are given a choice of professional learning activities from which to choose. Fourthly, resources are made easily available to staff through emails that provide links to online resources and tear-off guides placed in Next Generation Learning Spaces that 'nudge' academics to think about trying something new. Finally, bookmarks are distributed with a link/QR code to online resources and the name of an academic staff developer whom they could contact for support. Thus, the use of choice architecture makes it easier for people to make the 'right' decisions or to do the 'right' thing. This is achieved by making positive and helpful changes to the environment that 'nudge' habits and set defaults.

The professional learning approach outlined above is also based around systems thinking. The use of systems thinking recognises that the professional learning of academics is complex and has many interacting components (Adam & de Savigny, 2012; Senge, 1990). By taking into account aspects of the institutional context, lost opportunities for improving the teaching of academics when ad hoc and 'just-in-case' initiatives are offered can be mitigated (see Fig. 7).

A more contemporary approach to professional learning is embedded in day to day work and is performance-driven and (self)-evaluated. It is underpinned by a 'pull' philosophy and driven by academic staff learning. It is set within a context that encourages self-direction and good decision-making. It includes multiple opportunities that are just-in-time, just-for-me and are fun and engaging. Overall, professional learning of the future:

1. is *continuous* and *situated* in *work*;
2. is embedded in a *holistic* system that is *performance-driven* and *(self)-evaluated*;
3. is *learner-centred, self-organised* and *self-managed*;
4. is enriched by learning *with* and *from one another*;
5. is supportive of making good choices *'nudging' intentions* to engage in professional learning; and
6. is *fun* using elements of gamification.

Next Generation Learning Spaces encourage students to have much greater agency in their learning and encourage a project-based curriculum,

Integrated Organisational, Cognitive and Behavioural Economic Approach to Professional Learning

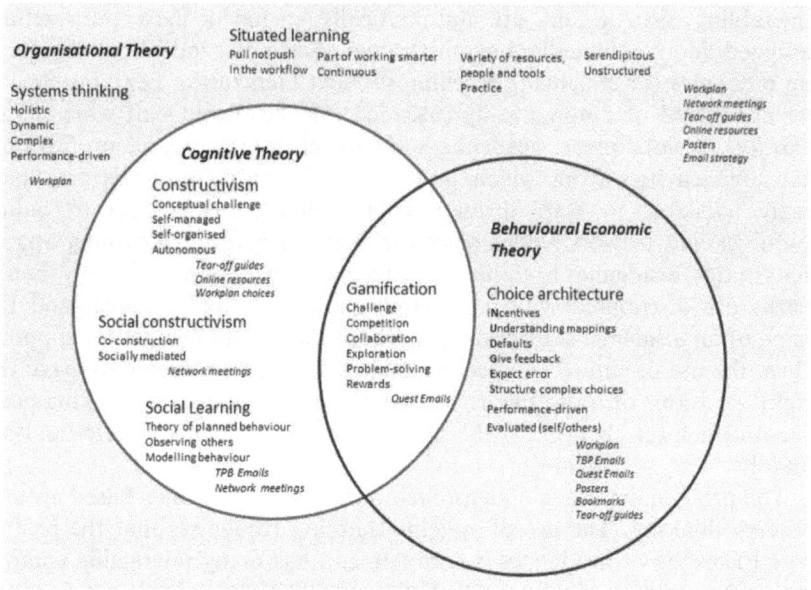

Organisational Theory

Situated learning
Pull not push   Part of working smarter   Variety of resources,   Serendipitous
In the workflow   Continuous   people and tools   Unstructured
                                                   Practice

Systems thinking
Holistic
Dynamic
Complex
Performance-driven

Workplan

Cognitive Theory

Constructivism
Conceptual challenge
Self-managed
Self-organised
Autonomous
Tear-off guides
Online resources
Workplan choices

Social constructivism
Co-construction
Socially mediated
Network meetings

Social Learning
Theory of planned behaviour
Observing others
Modelling behaviour
TPB Emails
Network meetings

Gamification
Challenge
Competition
Collaboration
Exploration
Problem-solving
Rewards
Quest Emails

Behavioural Economic Theory

Choice architecture
iNcentives
Understanding mappings
Defaults
Give feedback
Expect error
Structure complex choices
Performance-driven
Evaluated (self/others)

Workplan
TBP Emails
Quest Emails
Posters
Bookmarks
Tear-off guides

Workplan
Network meetings
Tear-off guides
Online resources
Posters
Email strategy

Fig. 7. Professional Learning Approach for Teaching in Next Generation Learning Spaces Showing Theories.

mirroring industry practice. Students engage within a carefully scaffolded learning environment in both formal and informal ways, working with others and on their own, finding out information, following up on a question through Google, listening to other students or discussing an issue with their teacher.

If universities want students to be active, lifelong learners taking responsibility for their own learning then the system that is set up for academics to learn about good teaching should parallel this approach. In so doing, academics can be supported to understand the ways that teaching and learning pedagogies have changed and start to internalise a new set of pedagogical norms. Knowing 'how to teach' and 'how to use technology' in Next Generation Learning Spaces is essential. Professional learning of the future, like effective student learning, is active and student-centred, with online and face-to-face components as required (de la Harpe et al., 2013).

The promise of Next Generation Learning Spaces cannot remain unfulfilled. By addressing the compelling issue of staff professional learning, this chapter can help senior university leaders to think beyond the professional development approaches of yesterday. It offers an institutional framework that enables a new professional learning approach, resulting in enhanced learning and teaching and an improved culture of teaching for the future. Whilst the design of Next Generation Learning Spaces are meant to 'nudge' academics into new ways of teaching, this chapter has demonstrated that universities also need a 'nudge' to find new ways of supporting the professional learning of academics teaching in these spaces.

ACKNOWLEDGEMENTS

We would like to acknowledge the Australian Government Office for Learning and Teaching who provided the support for the project: Not a Waste of Space: professional development for staff teaching in Next Generation Learning Spaces, although the views expressed in this publication do not necessarily reflect the views of the Australian Government Office for Learning and Teaching. We would also like to thank all those involved in the Not a Waste of Space project: Megan McPherson (Project Manager, RMIT University), Sheona Thomson (Queensland University of Technology), A/Professor Kenn Fisher (University of Melbourne), Dr Wesley Imms (University of Melbourne), A/Professor Kym Fraser (Victoria University) and Diana Taylor (Curtin University). In addition, the project team would especially like to thank Dr Emily Koethe, Lauren Ferro and Nick Faulkner for their contribution.

REFERENCES

Adam, T., & de Savigny, D. (2012). Systems thinking for strengthening health systems in LMICs: Need for a paradigm shift. *Health Policy and Planning*, *27*, iv1—iv3.

Ajzen, I. (1985). From intentions to actions: A theory of planned behavior. In J. Kuhl & J. Beckman (Eds.), *Action-control: From cognition to behaviour* (pp. 11—39). Heidelberg: Springer.

Ajzen, I. (1991). The theory of planned behavior. *Organisational Behavior and Human Decision Processes*, *50*, 179—211.

Angner, E., & Loewenstein, G. (2010). Behavioral economics. In U. Mäki (Ed.), *Handbook of the philosophy of science. Philosophy of economics* (Vol. 13). Amsterdam: Elsevier.

Avineri, E. (2012). On the use and potential of behavioural economics from the perspective of transport and climate change. *Journal of Transport Geography*, *24*, 512—521.

Barber, M., Donnelly, K., & Rizvi, S. (2013). *An avalanche is coming: Higher education and the revolution ahead.* London: Institute for Public Policy Research. Retrieved from http://www.ippr.org/images/media/files/publication/2013/04/avalanche-is-coming_Mar 2013_10432.pdf

Barnes, E., Bullock, A. D., Bailey, S. E. R., Cowpe, J. G., & Karaharju-Suvanto, T. (2013). A review of continuing professional development for dentists in Europe. *European Journal of Dental Education, 17*(1), 23–28.

Birman, B. F., Desimone, L., Porter, A. C., & Garet, M. S. (2000). Designing professional development that works. *Educational Leadership, 57*(8), 28–33. Retrieved from http://cemse.uchicago.edu/computerscience/OS4CS/landscapestudy/resources/Birman-Desimone-Porter-and-Garet-2000.pdf

Bok, D. (2013). *Higher education in America.* Princeton, NJ: Princeton University Press.

Bokor, J. (2012). *University of the future: A thousand year old industry on the cusp of profound change.* Australia: Ernst and Young. Retrieved from http://www.ey.com/Publication/vwLUAssets/University_of_the_future/$FILE/University_of_the_future_2012.pdf

Boud, D., & Hager, P. (2012). Re-thinking continuing professional development through changing metaphors and location in professional practices. *Studies in Continuing Education, 34*(1), 17–30.

Cross, J. (2010). They had people called professors … ! Changing worlds of learning: Strengthening informal learning in formal institutions? In U. Ehlers & D. Schneckenberg (Eds.), *Changing Cultures in Higher Education* (pp. 43–54). Berlin, Springer.

Dawnay, E., & Shah, H. (2005). *Behavioural economics: Seven principles for policy-makers.* London, UK: New Economics Foundation. Retrieved from http://www.neweconomics.org/publications/entry/behavioural-economics

de la Harpe, B., & Mason, T., with Koethe, E., Faulkner, N., & McPherson, M. (2013). *Not a waste of space: Professional development for staff teaching in Next Generation Learning Spaces, ID11–2050.* Final report to the Australian Government Office for Learning and Teaching, Melbourne.

DIISRT. (2012). *Building a smarter future: Australia's cutting-edge tertiary education and research facilities.* Report of the Australian Government Department of Industry, Innovation, Science, Research and Tertiary Education, DIISRTE 12/217. Retrieved from http://www.innovation.gov.au/highereducation/ResourcesAndPublications/HigherEducationPublications/Documents/BuildingASmarterFuture.pdf

EDUCAUSE Learning initiative Advisory Board. (2009). Opening up learning: From spaces to environments. *EDUCAUSE Review, 44*(3), 62–63.

Feixas, M., & Zellweger, F. (2010). Faculty development in context: Changing learning cultures in higher education. In U. Ehlers & D. Schneckenberg (Eds.), *Changing cultures in higher education* (pp. 85–102). Berlin, Springer.

Fuller, J. (2009). *Heads, you die: Bad decisions, choice architecture, and how to mitigate predictable irrationality.* Per Capita Research Paper, Melbourne. Retrieved from http://www.percapita.org.au/01_cms/details.asp?ID=215

Gee, J. P. (2003). *What video games have to teach us about learning and literacy.* New York, NY: Palgrave/Macmillan.

Gee, J. P. (2004). *Situated language and learning: A critique of traditional schooling.* London: Routledge.

Gee, J. P. (2005). *Why video games are good for your soul: Pleasure and learning.* Melbourne: Common Ground.

Gee, J. P. (2012). Forward. In C. Steinkuehler, K. Squire, & S. Barab (Eds.), *Games, learning and society: Learning and meaning in the digital age.* New York, NY: Cambridge University Press.

Hart, J. (2011). *Social learning handbook synopsis.* Centre for Learning & Performance Technologies. Retrieved from http://c4lpt.co.uk/social-learning-handbook/social-learning-handbook-synopsis/

Hattie, J. (2009). *Visible learning: A synthesis of over 800 meta-analyses relating to achievement.* London: Routledge.

HEFCE. (2008). *HEFCE supports higher education in England with increased funding of £7.5 billion.* Retrieved from http://www.hefce.ac.uk/

HEFCE. (2010). *Funding for universities and colleges in 2010−2011.* Retrieved from http://www.hefce.ac.uk/

Hunzicker, J. (2011). Effective professional development for teachers: A checklist. *Professional Development in Education, 27*(2), 177−179.

Jonassen, D. H. (1994). Thinking technology: Toward a constructivist design model. *Educational Technology, 34*(3), 34−37.

Kahneman, D., & Tversky, A. (2000). *Choices, values, and frames.* New York, NY: Cambridge University Press.

Levine, A. (2006). *Educating school teachers.* Retrieved from http://www.edschools.org/pdf/Educating_Teachers_Report.pdf

Oblinger, D. (2005). Leading the transition from classrooms to learning spaces. *EDUCAUSE Quarterly, 1,* 14−18.

Parsons, D., Hill, I., Holland, J., & Willis, D. (2012). *Impact of teaching development programmes in higher education.* London: The Higher Education Academy. Retrieved from http://www.heacademy.ac.uk/assets/documents/research/HEA_Impact_Teaching_development_Prog.pdf

Quinn, L. (2012). Understanding resistance: An analysis of discourses in academic staff development. *Studies in Higher Education, 37*(1), 69−83.

Senge, P. M. (1990). *The fifth discipline.* New York, NY: Double Day/Currency.

Thaler, R., & Sunstein, C. (2009). *Nudge: Improving decisions about health, wealth, and happiness.* London: Penguin Books.

Timperley, H., Wilson, A., Barrar, H., & Fung, I. (2007). *Teacher professional learning and development: Best evidence synthesis iteration [BES].* Wellington: Ministry of Education. Retrieved from http://www.educationcounts.govt.nz/data/assets/pdffile/0017/16901/TPLandDBESentire.pdf

Wade, R. K. (1985). What makes a difference in inservice teacher education? A meta-analysis of research. *Educational Leadership, 42*(4), 48−54.

Webster-Wright, A. (2009). Reframing professional development through understanding authentic professional learning. *Review of Educational Research, 79*(2), 702−739.

Werbach, K. (2012). Gamification. *Coursera.* Retrieved from https://www.coursera.org/course/gamification

Zimmerman, B. J. (1989). Models of self-regulated learning and academic achievement. In J. Zimmermm & D. H. Schunk (Eds.), *Self-regulated learning and academic achievement: Theory, research, and practice* (pp. 1−25). New York, NY: Springer-Verlag.

SECTION IV
THE FUTURE OF DESIGN
IN NEXT GENERATION
LEARNING SPACES

CHAPTER 12

DEVELOPING THE BRIEFING FOR THE DESIGNING OF THE LEARNING LANDSCAPE: REFLECTIONS ON RMIT (ROYAL MELBOURNE INSTITUTE OF TECHNOLOGY) UNIVERSITY OF TECHNOLOGY & DESIGN'S APPROACH TO NEXT GENERATION LEARNING SPACES

Leon van Schaik

ABSTRACT

Designing learning environments is increasingly about mediating between the interactions in real and virtual space of largely self-organising learning communities. Traditional ways of briefing designers are less and less proficient, as the demands made on space become less timetabled, more

The Future of Learning and Teaching in Next Generation Learning Spaces
International Perspectives on Higher Education Research, Volume 12, 243–266
ISSN: 1479-3628/doi:10.1108/S1479-362820140000012017

probabilistic. 'learning landscapes'[1] are proposed in which clusters of activity can be seen to be taking place across a field, that activity can be browsed, audited and fully engaged with. Such organic flows of interest and concentration are hindered by traditional demarcated space models, and attempts to enable the flows through 'flexible' interlinking of rooms fail.

There is evidence[2] that the organic interactions between learners grow exponentially when these learners are connected together as virtual communities in open, robust virtual platforms. But this works best when these interactions are grounded from time to time in real places. How can designers best provide spaces that support learning in real and virtual space? Should design teams be composed of people with skills in devising real and virtual space?

Increasingly the answer is 'yes', and this places strains on procurement processes. Built form can take a long time to deliver. So can virtual platforms take time to devise and make operable. Can these processes be aligned? The concepts for RMIT's Design Hub, a physical design research platform, were developed through research conducted twelve years before the building was completed. Many of the gap years were taken up with establishing the financial basis for constructing the Hub. During this time the concepts were validated by testing with various potential user groups, and a further tranche of international investigations validated the level of innovation being sought. The process for RMIT's Swanston Academic Building (SAB) was smoother and shorter, but it involved a year in which a 'learning landscape' concept was moulded through intensive work with user client focus groups.

Neither of these projects has a virtual doppelganger, though both have sophisticated and evolvable IT systems. The Hub embeds a process of curating research interaction and dissemination that is hampered by this fact. The mediated learning landscape of the SAB falls short of the originating concepts, – because space constraints did not allow for an undivided, flowing landscape. A well designed virtual counterpart could have provided what the insertion of walls has obscured. Should all future innovative learning and researching environments have a virtual counterpart from the outset?

There is an emerging trend for such paired environments in creative city thinking and in museums. Surely briefing and procuring real and virtual environments in tandem will enliven future space use in universities?

Keywords: Designing; real and virtual space; briefing; learning landscapes

INTRODUCTION: THE PURSUIT OF ARCHITECTURALLY INNOVATIVE LEARNING SPACE

Many horizons of understanding have washed forth and often back across the endeavour of briefing and designing spaces for learning during the forty-five years since (in 1966) I designed an A. S. Neil inspired Primary School. Those self-directed learning principles were published in 1921. In the 1960s Leslie Ginsberg,[3] the English Planner, would give a lecture at the Architectural Association in London in which he demonstrated that planning solutions to generally recognised problems took thirty years to implement, by which time the problem had changed.[4] Howard Gardner (1999), arguing that whereas it used to take ten years to master a disciplinary practice, it now takes seven, is amongst those who think that human processes have speeded up since the advent of the Internet (1982). Despite this, in the designing and commissioning of university learning spaces, significant alternating lags and exploratory spurts persist.

For two decades, adopting an unusual and pioneering procurement approach, RMIT has pursued innovative architectural approaches to the provision of learning spaces (Schaik, London, & George, 2010). The two most recently completed projects (RMIT Design Hub, and Swanston Academic Building), and a major project currently in progress (New Academic Street) form the immediate context for this chapter.

LAGS AND SPURTS IN BRIEFING PRACTICE

It is crucial to understanding what we ask our consultants to do for us that we are aware of the patterns of lags and spurts in briefing practice and the strangely frequent recursions to past thinking that characterise the formulation of briefs. What are the major features of the intellectual frame-works that shape briefing? We who commission learning facilities segue from visionary advances to quantitative obsession, and back again. This oscillation has a deep history. In the reconstruction period in Europe after the Second World War, after so much basic infrastructure had been lost, the predominant focus was on housing normative existing models of learn-ing practice. The issue was access to space, as traditionally understood, and innovation was concentrated on provision through systems building. In the United Kingdom, for instance, schools and new universities were built using CLASP (Consortium of Local Authorities Special Programme), a prefabrication system devised in the 1950s. Except at institutions where space use involved the infiltration of pre-existing structures such as country mansions, normative models of lecture rooms, tutorial rooms, studios, workshops and laboratories were taken as givens. Issues of square metres per student, ratios of students to book holdings in libraries, timetabling and occupancy levels dominated discussion. Spatial models were relatively unquestioned.

Computers, which were a new factor in university thinking, were large machines requiring special housing. (The first Internet message sent was from one such computer to another.) In industry, a typical creative indus-tries office located its large computers in a glass room near reception, where clients could watch them whiz and whirr, and see them being attended to by white-coated programmers. The future seemed to consist of larger and larger machines. Then in the 1980s the Apple desk computer began to chal-lenge this vision and opened up the first glimpses of a distributed learning system not dependent of pre-scripted space types. And A. S. Neil concepts of self-paced, self-organised learning flooded back into currency.

SPATIAL FORM THAT SUPPORTS SELF-DIRECTED LEARNING

Let me return to my 1960s primary school design. This school was a reac-tion against the uniform standardised models of the post-war reconstruc-tion period. It provided on two levels, undivided and contoured platforms supported by half enclosed semi-circular 'home base' cells. The platforms were fringed with hollows cupped just enough by a perimeter curtain wall to suggest and promote informal gathering. Supporting this 'learning landscape' (as we might call it today, but did not then) was that creature of the pre-information age era, a Resource Centre: one of the few daring initiatives of the period, these gathered together physical material, bringing the audio, the visual, and textural mediums together in localised, quasi-libraries.

Pupils and staff were free to roam, collecting learning materials and topics, and setting up camp as and when they needed to. This design approach, predicated as I understood it, on a 'provide the context and leave the learning to pupil dynamics' is a wave that flows forward and back more than any other. Those arguing for universal or minimum standards of learning and for the maximum spatial envelope that can be afforded do not appreciate learning landscapes, but those who argue for individual pathways to self-actualisation promote them. This is a classic dispute between the high and the low levels in Maslow's hierarchy. Although entertainingly a recent posting on social media scrawls at the base of Maslow's pyramid, below the 'survival' base, the word INTERNET, the self-actualisation position receives its current energy from the impact of the Internet on learning modes. As recently as a decade ago a bitter battle between the two camps erupted over the design of RMIT's new campus in Vietnam, one party trying to make the plan fit a traditional classroom approach, the other seeking to insert more functionally undetermined space.

These observations stem from the writer's long history in designing for self-structured learning. In the late 1970s, working for The Urban Foundation in Soweto, I designed the 'Funda Centre' (literally 'knowledge centre'). This was my first Higher Education project. The design concept stemmed from my first major project after graduation, The Colindale Public Health Laboratory in North London, where I devised a graphic system for documenting the needs of disparate research methodologies and proposed a sinuous flowing floor plan that allowed different laboratories to grow and shrink over time.[5] At the Funda Centre the design linked a number of learning centres along a colonnaded verandah that dropped down a long slope to an area of flat ground that it then curled around and cupped into a quadrangle with an open side. Here were housed – in separate buildings – a number of community organised learning clubs, each with its own constitution and legal persona: a Mathematics society, a Science club, a cluster of English Language and Performing Arts groups and a Music society. Each with its own collegial, self-initiated, learning practices. Each entity determined its needs and was provided with spatial shells that could be (and in some cases have been) extended at right angles away from the link verandah as their programmes grew or changed. The community learning groups, who raised much of the funding themselves, fitted out the shells. Here as in the primary school that I had designed fifteen years earlier, what the architect provided was a 'learning landscape' with an indicative 'regime of care' designed into it through the architecture of the link verandah and the portals to each learning society's space. The form, as time has proved, encourages loitering at the portals of each learning society building and that gives itself to the creation of events joining all the societies. Although a dim resonance with the collegial structure of ancient universities with each college differently endowed and governed is evident the design was based on indigenous settlement form precedents from the region, chiefly in nearby, democratic and independent Botswana. These forms defied the orthogonal, cadastral rectangularity of classical campus design. Also in mind was an axiom of Alvar Aalto, that master of organic planning, who said when talking of campus planning, words to the effect: 'always leave spaces for the next generation to work in ...' And another generation of architects has indeed added to the campus (Jamieson, Fisher, Gilding, Taylor, & Trevitt, 2000).

DRIVING INNOVATIVE ARCHITECTURE TO REFLECT AN INSTITUTIONAL MISSION

My next period of involvement in learning space design commenced rather more than twenty years ago, when I began to think about and influence the way in which RMIT briefs and designs its spaces, its buildings and the urban landscape that they form and that holds them. The initial aim was to make the institution reflect its ambition to be in the forefront of technical education and research. The investment impulse was the need to address the absence of any capital investment over a twenty-year period. Student numbers stagnated after the Colombo Plan terminated, but in the late 1980s overseas students began to be enrolled on a fee-paying basis, and on an ethical charter that required the institution to maintain the provision of space for students, whatever their origin, at normative standards. Benchmarks were set against the other Universities of Technology (Adelaide, Brisbane, Perth and Sydney). A major capital programme commenced. RMIT built eight major buildings and several urban spaces between 1992 and 2013 (Schaik et al., 2010, p. 118).

As I stated earlier, at RMIT this was more than a quantitative approach. The institution's centenary commission had made much of the need to relate dynamically to the city, and I argued that this could be achieved by signalling the experimental mission through architecture, and this was accepted (Schaik, 2013a), but the underlying driver was quantitative. For instance, Building 220 at RMIT's Bundoora Campus was conceived with a flexible open plan, re-configurable as learning practices changed, but when the user client – an Education Faculty with conservative space models in mind – reviewed the design, it was undermined and the plan was subdivided into normative cells of offices and classrooms. The basic need for quantities of space blind-sided the administration to this subversion of a higher academic mission.

TECHNOLOGY CHANGE AS A DRIVER OF SPATIAL INNOVATION

Another dynamic in brief design emerged between March 1989 and December 1990, when we began to wonder what impact the World Wide Web would have on our facilities. As Dean I diverted the entire capital budget of my faculty to providing computers for staff and commencing the establishment of computer labs for students. The university established a vast 'computer barn'. As the term 'barn' suggests the emphasis was on basic access in an undifferentiated shell, not on the spatial requirements of new learning practices.

As RMIT scrambled to surf the wave, building a local area network, the Chancellery wondered whether in time, excepting laboratories with specific technical functions, it would be able to sell off some of its buildings. A future of dwindling need for access to physical space seemed to lie ahead.

This thinking was, as I found on a contemporaneous study tour[6] procuring elsewhere. The architecture school in ETH Zurich then had an information technology budget equal to RMIT's total spend on IT. In the school at ETH, lecture theatre use collapsed, a ceremonial theatre being retained for lectures by visiting stars.[7] Lecture rooms became workshops for prototyping designs developed digitally. Some of these where archaeological reconstructions, some modelled the performance of glass architecture in the Alps: studying the past or projecting the future, all seemed digital. Student work, including design work, was submitted and assessed on line. At first it seemed that the need for face to face meeting was being reduced to a pattern of initiating projects at the start of semesters, publicly reviewing them at mid semester, and exhibiting them at the end of semester. But the demand for personal interaction was intense and felt by staff and students alike. Before the advent of the smartphone, staff met students by email arrangement, and not in classrooms, but in the school café. Students met each other there to work on assignments. The Dean's biggest facilities headache was providing enough café space on a campus on the urban fringe. A decade later the entire campus was laced through with cafes.

GETTING AHEAD OF THE WAVE OF TECHNOLOGICAL CHANGE

Working on RMIT's School of Architecture and Design (Bird, 1997) 'Visualising the Virtual Concourse', a recurring Architecture Elective, RMIT Master of Architecture Professional Degree 2002–2006, staff, students and programmers modelled self-generating learning communities formed by students browsing in a virtual concourse where they would choose between offerings (and modes of learning) presented by staff. We used a new interactive platform (now reaching the general market) that enabled the exchange of large data files, the mutual modelling of the quality of learning interactions, and the possibility of constant feedback during learning. Our research led us to in depth consultations with Mediserve, where it was evident that the virtual did not work without a real counterpart. Our emphasis had been on how to increase the information that a virtual environment carries, so that it provided more of the clues that a physical environment provides. It shifted to the notion of the companion space (see Schaik & Watson, in press). In this space real time information could be exchanged, events arranged. It is hard now, in the era of smartphones, to recall how difficult and labyrinthine the learning environment was, particularly for students of the broad inter-disciplinary programmes of business, most of which courses were offered part time, and many after normal working hours. Interactions between cohorts had to be arranged to fixed timetables. Rather like trying to meet friends in Venice before the mobile phone, assignations had to be pre-planned, and if something went wrong, there was no way of retrieving the situation. All too often students would arrive for a timetabled class to find a scribbled note advising them that the lecturer was ill, and the class cancelled. Naturally this demotivated students and eroded their perception of the university as a competent provider. A way out of this dilemma emerged as the university began to understand the potentials of the internet environment.

THE PARADOX THAT EMERGES AHEAD OF THE WAVE OF CHANGE

Contemporaneously early adopters at RMIT and allied universities dreamed of capturing courseware and selling it online. Then MIT made its courseware freely available online.[8] Later Stanford and Oxbridge followed suite.[9] There was consternation. What was the message? The IT 'dawn chorus' of 'content is king' started to seem questionable. If the courseware of the world's top universities was freely available, the point of difference offered by universities changed. The open access universities were being trumped by the most exclusive universities, confident that this free offer would in no way undercut their operations because the physical experience that they provided enabled students to interact with each other on beautiful campuses that carefully celebrated their institutional histories,[10] the colleges[11] – 'each tub on its own bottom' – charged with bringing students into contact with great thinkers treated 'like princes'. Rather than being a revenue stream, the free offer of courseware opened up new pathways into these institutions and gave them a tool to counter the charge that they were elitist.

The emphasis in universities everywhere swung back to providing the kinds of places and the kinds of people that attracted students. Briefing models shifted towards challenging architects to devise new spatial ways of offering students comfortable proximity to their peers and to the ritual events of the disciplines they were pursuing. Staff too had to be cossetted. This is no easy venture, and the challenges of designing for quality peer-to-peer learning and new forms of interaction with content developers are massive. Lags and spurts lead to both advances and disappointments.

RMIT's manifesting of its mission had measurable results in the swags of awards its buildings won, and in the upward spiralling of student satisfaction in student surveys. The university was not alone in this. From direct experience I know that amongst many others, the University of Cincinnati (Schaik et al., 2010, pp. 101–108) instituted a programme of commissioning good architecture and better campus planning in a process that transformed the university's ability to attract and hold good staff, and attract students from interstate. A decade of investment in great design, innovatively pursued, with an unparalleled ability to co-commission good architects and make them work in consort on projects created one of the most remarkable campuses in the United States. This was a programme so successful that the succeeding university President could concentrate on enhancing the quality of the staffing (Schaik et al., 2010, pp. 101–107).

CASE STUDY 1: VERTICALLY INTEGRATED
SCHOLARSHIP AS A BRIEFING MODEL
(DESIGN HUB)

RMIT's next phase of development commenced with the adoption of the integrated scholarship model promoted by Ernest Boyer and his colleagues (Boyer, 1990; Glassick, Huber, & Maeroff, 1997). The university adopted (for a while) their concept of four strands of interwoven scholarship: Discovery, Integration, Application and Dissemination. This model, derived from the most comprehensive study of what the staff in universities actually do, dismissed the administrative fiction that divides activity between learning and research. Incidentally the field research found that only in schools of architecture was this integration actively pursued, albeit unknowingly (Boyer & Mitgang, 1996). Out of this concept was born the idea of a university building not tailored to learning practices or to research practices, but to a vertical integration between learning, research and professional or industrial working life. In pursuit of this ideal, I made study tours to Finland, to the University of Art and Design then occupying the old factory buildings of the Finnish fabric and glassware enterprises on the fringes of Helsinki. The ideal was a cohabitation of apprenticeship, research and practice in warehouse space that could be revamped as practices evolved. Here studio teaching and research ateliers existed side by side in what had been warehouses. These were occupied in the manner of creative industry practices: open plan, minimally subdivided, punctuated with project bases, resource banks and meeting areas – learning, researching and practicing cohabiting the same internal landscape. As in design practice, in which teaching, learning and research cohabit, it was hard to tell the work of undergraduates and researchers apart.[12]

At RMIT, an iconic site on the civic spine of Melbourne was earmarked, and a brief evolved. Ten years later, under another Vice Chancellor, the building – its concept laboriously verified by internal user focus groups and external profiling through the international consultancy DEGW[13] – came into being designed to its original, ten-year old brief. The building, designed by architect Sean Godsell, has an external skin of circular discs (see Illustration 1) and stacks several clear span floors in a parallel configuration of wide warehouse spaces and a long room – see typical plan (Illustration 2) above a number of ritual spaces: a lecture theatre, a multipurpose room, a workshop, an audio laboratory, a design archive, a cafe and a large design gallery.

Illustration 1. External view. The circular discs of the façade act as a shade screen, tracking the passage of the sun. They are designed to be replaced by solar cells. *Source*: © Earl Carter, reproduced with permission.

Illustration 2. This is a typical floor plan showing the wider Warehouse space (61) and the Long Gallery (60) divided by a long core of circulation and services (16 and 17 are toilets, 20 is a store, 30 is a utility space). There is a coffee station at the one end of the service core (49). *Source*: © Sean Godsell Architects, reproduced with permission.

These are furnished from a kit of parts tested with the focus groups and including tables, shelving, credenzas, screens and chairs. The logic of the brief is being validated as the building is being occupied by research teams focused on projects and with the masters programmes in design that form an essential part of an integrated scholarship of design. Illustrated here are a warehouse space and a long room in exhibition mode (Illustrations 3 and 4).

What lagged? The IT infrastructure has evolved since occupation, responding to the needs of the users. Though these needs were profiled a decade ago, prior to occupation the swift pace of technological change means that normatively IT managers only plan only two or three years ahead, and a change of guard in the minding of RMIT's IT processes hampered the development of a comprehensive IT system suitable to un-programmed activity. Contrastingly, on the environmental engineering side, architect and engineers work from the outset on an integrated concept. The building's internal, well-tempered environment was however fully developed in the design process and has exceeded user expectations. The building has built in potential for upgrading its energy performance, notably in the design of the external screen, designed to accept solar cells when they become affordable in large numbers. The Design Hub is set to

Illustration 3. A Warehouse space in exhibition mode. More usually it is occupied with work stations arranged in the space by the occupying project teams. *Source:* © Photographer Kevin Francké, reproduced with permission.

Illustration 4. A Long Gallery in exhibition mode. These spaces have a high turnover of use, switching from interim review seminars to overflow work space to formal exhibition use. *Source:* © Photographer Ramesh Ayyar, reproduced with permission.

deliver — as has some features of the pioneering Council House 2 design (Tan, 2007) — significant gains through increased user well-being and reduced rates of sickness for users.

CASE STUDY 2: USING SPATIAL DESIGN TO DRIVE CHANGE IN LEARNING PRACTICES (SAB)

The Design Research Hub joins a series of Australian Institute of Architecture award winning RMIT buildings, collecting Victorian Chapter awards including the named award for a new institutional building and the overarching Victorian Architecture Award. The Swanston Academic Building, completed at the same time, also won an award in the institutional category.

The Swanston Academic Building, designed by Lyons Architects, shown in a street view foregrounding a 'student portal' in Illustration 5, took seven years to deliver, from conception to occupation. It started with the idea of a 'learning landscape': a term conveying the ambition to array a

Illustration 5. Exterior, Building 80, Swanston Academic Building, showing one of the 'student portals'. *Source:* © Lyons Architecture/John Gollings, reproduced with permission.

wide variety of learning opportunities in hollows across an undulating surface broadly visible to potential learners who browse the options from the ridges between. Housing largely business programmes, the largest suite of programmes in the university, the Vice Chancellor saw this building as the change agent that would 'future proof' this aspect of the university's learning offerings. No space that was not capable of transformation into an interactive, peer-to-peer learning environment was acceptable, except for one large, forward facing, tiered lecture theatre shown from inside in Illustration 6. This embodies everything we have learned[14] about such spaces (Seakins, 2013). It has open views to the street. At its lowest level, speaker and escort can enter and establish their presence. At an upper level, browsers can overlook from acoustically separated spaces, enter and stand, filter in and sit. Those needing to leave can exit graciously at the upper rear. All those in the auditorium can hear each other without the need for roving microphones. Interaction between speaker and audience and

Illustration 6. Lecture Theatre, Building 80, Swanston Academic Building [not the view to the street]. *Source*: © Dianna Snape, reproduced with permission.

audience and audience is effortlessly natural. All other tiered learning spaces are re-configurable to suit group learning. A complete range of spaces in a wide variety of sizes and configuration was devised, filling the lower floors of the building. Axonometric views of two of these floors are shown in Illustrations 7 and 8. These learning spaces were work-shopped with staff in a large scale learning practices change initiative, a major undertaking for the university academic professional development team and the design team. Trial timetabling was used to test the layouts as the design proceeded.

Floor Plans and Illustrations

The plans and illustrations here indicate the large array of learning spaces offered. The upper floors house staff in small collegial campus layouts.

The experiment has been very successful. Housing five thousand students at peak times, the occupancy rate of 30% in the former academic building with its standard lecture rooms and seminar rooms, is − in this building − consistently around 80%. More significantly, the investment in un-programmed student portals, spaces that extend on all levels from the

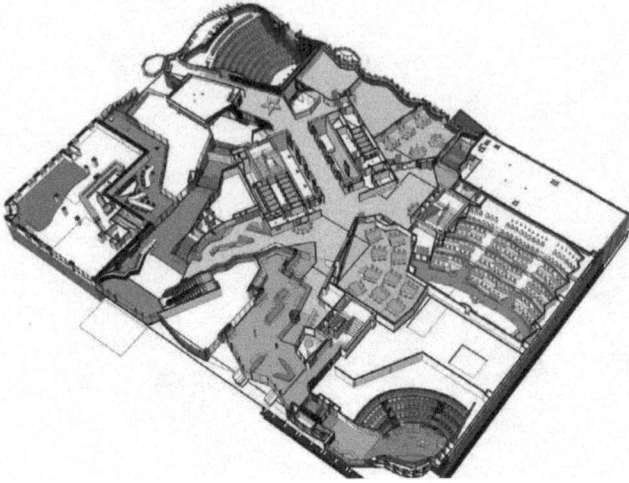

Illustration 7. Level 2, Swanston Street Entry, Building 80, Swanston Academic Building. Swanston Street, the Civic Spine of the city, is lower left. The lecture theatre is in the bottom corner. *Source*: © Lyons Architecture, reproduced with permission.

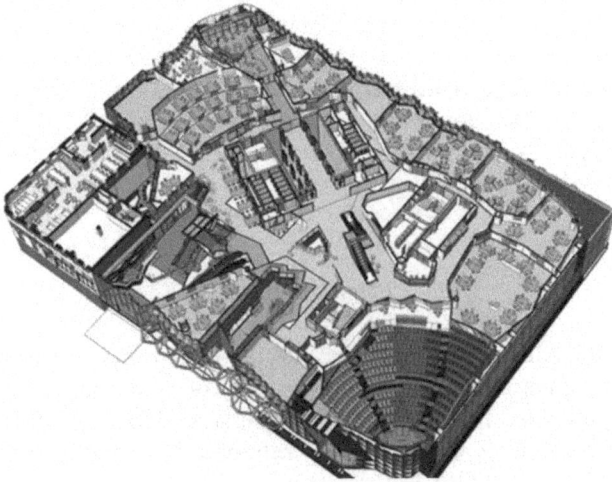

Illustration 8. Level 3, Building 80, Swanston Academic Building. The lecture theatre is lower left. *Source*: © Lyons Architecture, reproduced with permission.

circulation core to external areas at the perimeter, each serviced by an independent coffee cart or café retailer, has resulted in a building that is always occupied, with students appropriating every available space for individual and group work. Even on public holidays students are drawn to the building, filling the portals (Illustrations 9 and 10) and invading empty teaching spaces, utilising a backbone of high-speed Wi-Fi access and owning, as their tweets prove, this series of vibrant spaces. As yet unpublished post occupancy evaluation surveys also show that they regard the building as their own, a tangible benefit of enrolling at RMIT.

In the design process for the Swanston Academic Building the new IT management group developed their brief alongside the architects and in consort with the learning practices change programme. The wireless design is tailored to the key concepts of self-directed, peer-to-peer learning and tutorial guidance rather than 'chalk and talk'.

Is this notion of interactive learning practice new? Certainly not. Much of the modern world's financial system and its media processes originated in the coffee houses of the age of enlightenment. Overlaid on this creative ferment was a regimentation and formalisation impelled by the factory organisation systems of the industrial revolution. Reactions against this over ordering arose again and again. Even in the days of fascist Spain, an explosion in educational opportunity occurred when in a pop-up list, anti-middle class move the system was thrown open – in one year – to all school leavers with university entrance scores. Of thousands, only hundreds could get into lectures. As they left the theatres the others besieged them. What did they say? How could they have said that? Are you sure? This is what the texts state! Learning is a peer-to-peer process that those of us who devise learning environments – the scholarship of dissemination – should not forget.

WHEN SPACE SUPPORTING SELF-DIRECTED LEARNING HAS BECOME THE NORM, WHAT NEXT?

Which brings us to the next stage in our quest for innovative design of learning environments: this latest generation of university buildings has been procured under the leadership of a Vice Chancellor who insists on a vision that encompasses evolving learning practices, and who has a history of understanding the importance of great spatial quality to the student and staff community of the present, but even more so, to that of the future. RMIT's latest project, the 'New Academic Street', is emerging from what we have learned

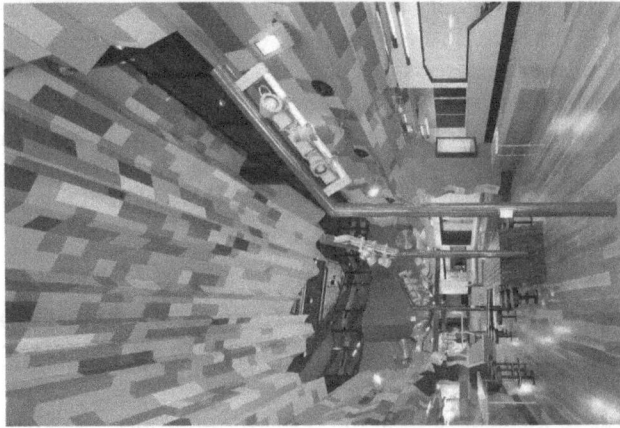

Illustrations 9 and 10. 'Student Portal', Building 80, Swanston Academic Building, one of several. *Source:* © Lyons Architecture/John Gollings, reproduced with permission.

from our completed projects. As Vice Chancellor Gardner has argued in creating this project, every university now faces the issue of what to do with aged infrastructure built around the notion of fixed timetables and set teaching patterns. Vast hulks of buildings sit on campuses all over the world, unappealing utilitarian objects hated by staff and students alike.[15] The New Academic Street drives public spaces through RMIT's 1960s and 1970s Buildings 10, 12 and 14, grey 12-story blocks of laboratories, classrooms and departmental offices, designed in the then prevailing Polytechnic manner. A constellation of architectural firms, one large and four small, is delivering this revolutionary cracking open of RMIT's hulks. The design opens the buildings up and links them into the laneways and streets of the city. It drives pathways into the heart of the library, it drives new access ways up through the disciplinary departments and it breaks down divisions between knowledge services and pastoral care services. It creates integrated 'regimes of care' for students. It permeates the ground plane with retail services of every kind, with space for pop-up shops and pop-up events and exhibitions showcasing student work, making sure that the inner city campus is itself a piece of the rich city environment that research (Florida, 2002; Saunders, 2010) suggest is vital to the generation of cultural capital.

In this it follows RMIT's approach to opening up its urban landscape. In 2000 I convened an urban design symposium to determine the guidelines for developing the urban spaces of RMIT's city campus, and this formed the basis of a series of briefs to Peter Elliott who began a process – still in progress – of reconnecting the external spaces of the campus to the laneways and streets of the city, most of which were closed off during the 1970s. This process transformed the ground surface of the campus from a tarmac surfaced car park into a succession of pedestrian pathways and courtyards. Every transformation has won accolades from students in the student satisfaction surveys, and has repeatedly won awards for Urban Design. This has become quite literally a learning landscape, hosting events large and small, and becoming a home away from home where before there was no place for students to be, other than in a timetabled classroom.

COMMISSIONING CONSULTANTS FOR THE NEW UNIVERSITY

Our commissioned architects, selected on criteria that emphasise the need for creative thinking (Schaik et al., 2010, pp. 14–35), grasp fully the

concept of the campus in the city, the city in the campus that is the leitmo-
tif of our vision of the future campus. This is no accident. Commencing
twenty years ago, we have deployed a criterion based selection process
(Schaik et al., 2010, pp. 14–15), constantly monitored and improved. This
places great emphasis on the ability of consultants to think laterally, bringing new ideas to bear on our briefs. Most recently, to support the pace of
change in our facilities, we have established lists of architects capable of
meeting our criteria, so that timely appointments can be made for smaller
projects in two cost ranges: below five million dollars, and below twenty
million dollars. Larger projects continue to follow our process of an open
call for expressions of interest on the basis of our long-standing criteria.
The most significant difference between these criteria and those of many
who have adopted a criterion based process since we pioneered this
approach is that we don't seek prior experience of a building type
(Table 1).

RESISTANCE AND INERTIA

Introducing criterion based selection for architects has transformed the
way we use architects. We are now trying to extend this approach to
other key areas of design but it is proving difficult to involve environmental engineers and IT designers at the same concept breaking level.
For very similar reasons: both disciplines are wedded to the supply chains
that dominate their industries and they seek to default to industry norms.
The Design Hub has proved to us that a good environment must have
good air, good lighting, access to the outside and it must respond to
weather cycles, not attempt to override them. We know that we cannot
live isolated without damaging the overall environment; we know that
when we do our health suffers. But an entire industry is in chains to a

Table 1. A Set of Criteria Designed to Engage the Energies of Ambitious
and Emerging Practices, Adopted by Campus Planning Committee and
Ratified by the RMIT Council.

1	Demonstrated capability and ambition for creative and innovative design
2	Demonstrated ability to think laterally
3	Demonstrated capacity to relate to and service a complex client
4	Demonstrated capability to deliver on time and to budget
5	Due diligence requirements regarding financial standing and indemnity insurance

method of producing air-conditioning through ducting and compressing air. And it is very reluctant to move away from the dominant paradigm of current air-conditioning practice. Meanwhile the university is in the process of upgrading its entire services infrastructure to meet 25% reduction in greenhouse gases, a minimum four star Green rating for all major building refurbishments and a minimum five star Green rating for all new building developments. RMIT is participating in the Greener Government Buildings (GGB) programme, a broad State Government initiative aimed at reducing greenhouse gas emissions and water consumption.

There can be a similar lag in the IT context, where we are offered the latest that is being produced, rather than what our students are already anticipating. 'Look beyond the screens!' is the cry of our facilities brief makers! Neil Sigamoney, Deputy Director of Strategic Sourcing and Procurement, has been refreshing our procedures. He argues: 'The opportunity is for institutions like RMIT to lead change by engaging more strategically with a core group of technology experts and technology change leaders. Our strategic position as a University of Technology and Design coupled with our innovative thinking in future learning space design should enable us to convince some of these large global organisations to collaborate on future IT technology and design solutions'.[16]

Ideogram (Illustration 11)

This ideogram (Schaik, 2010, 2013b) symbolises the conflicting mental spaces that play through the minds of brief makers. We stand on a pillar of precedents – descriptions and visions of past, current and future practices. Our mental processes are framed by differing intellectual influences – A. S. Neil, accounts of the Spanish shift to democracy, Ernst Boyer's integrated scholarship, the successes of Finnish design education and industry, the history of rates of adoption of new practices. One eye is on the immediate demands of the present; the other is searching for a definable future target worth aiming for. This search is impelled through three horizons, each promising results, being overtaken by events and ricocheting onto the next horizon, trailing old habits. This forward-looking gaze passes through a forest of the developing cores of serving disciplines: Architecture, Environmental and Information Technology Engineering. This forest is fringed with the visionary leaps of other institutions.

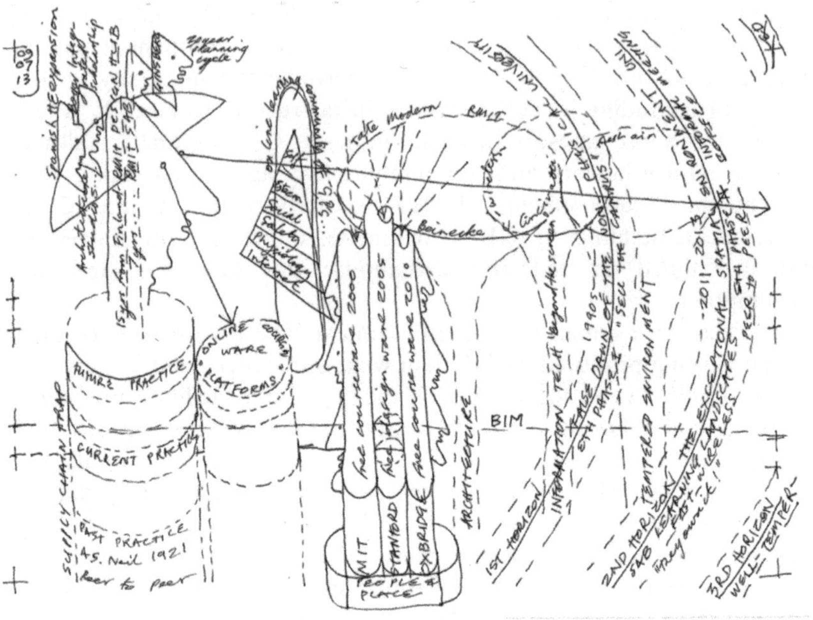

Illustration 11.   Ideogram. *Source*: Leon van Schaik.

CONCLUSION

Lurking behind this account is the fact that students are creating environments for themselves, whatever we design. These environments combine real and virtual space in ways somewhat known to us, largely understood by surmise and largely outside the capability of our formal briefing processes. Visionary facilities managers and academic development and student services professionals like the current generation at RMIT are very conscious of this. Our latest completed projects work well with this unpredictable real and virtual space usage. The briefing for our consultants on our next project, the New Academic Street, requires them to create an environment that is as much about the virtual as it is about the real, and demands that the design provides the richness of a creative city. Here all information, library and pastoral care services will be integrated with informal study areas. Without this the project will fail to be the real counterpart to our students' virtual worlds. It will fail to be the tool that enables academics to apply the practices that they are developing for next generation learning spaces.

NOTES

1. This term became current at RMIT during the briefing phase (mid-2000s) on the Swanston Academic Building. It conveys the ambition to array a wide variety of learning opportunities in hollows across an undulating surface, real and/or virtual, broadly visible to potential learners who browse the options from the ridges between. The walls around the rooms shown in the illustrations are the result of spatial compression. The concept relied on the unpublished PhD of Nicholas Murray (2007–2010) Sound and Space: An Architect's Investigation, supervised by the writer. This proposed arrays of acoustic shells that would make a browse-able landscape feasible.

2. In developing RMIT's Virtual Concourse 'learning landscape', the writer consulted Dr Lynn Robertson of Medeserve, whose research on the learning behaviour of Medical Practitioners prompted this assertion. This was supported at the eLearning and eTraining Roundtable at Griffith University, 7–9 August 2002.

3. Then Director of the Graduate School of Planning at the Architectural Association.

4. In his book, McLouglin (1992) makes a similar case, using Melbourne as his case study.

5. As project architect at RMJM from 1969 to 1971 I conducted the briefing, including an early virology laboratory, and produced the preliminary design, realized a decade later by others.

6. April–May 2000.

7. On a later visit I discovered that not enough lecture theatres had been retained, and visiting star Zaha Hadid was mildly ironic about giving her lecture in a neighbouring Chemistry lecture theatre complete with basins and taps.

8. The OpenCourseWare (OCW) project has made course materials for MIT classes available online free of charge since 2002.

9. Massive Open Online Courses (MOOC's) exploded into the academic consciousness in summer of 2011 (Waldrop, 2013).

10. I document the approach of the Ivy League in the book Schaik et al. (2010, pp. 108–113).

11. These quotations come from discussions with the Dean of the Graduate School of Design during my semester there as a visiting professor in 1994.

12. A similar approach, but much later in briefing, and not a new-build but the conversion of a warehouse, can be retrieved from http://www.utas.edu.au/architecture-design/about/our-facilities

13. DEGW was a briefing consultancy founded by Francis Duffy, Peter Ely, John Worthington and Luigi Giffioni. See reference list, now Space Agency in AECOM.

14. The same principles informed the lecture theatre in the design hub and in a large ritual lecture theatre designed by Allan Powell on RMIT's Bundoora campus.

15. Tuomey O'Donnell is engaged in a similar design at the University of Budapest, commissioned by the Soros Foundation.

16. Emailed comment in response to draft of this chapter, 29 August 2013.

REFERENCES

Bird, D. (1997). *Constructing a learning environment: An interview with Leon van Schaik.* Melbourne: UltiBASE. Retrieved from http://ultibase.rmit.edu.au/Articles/june97/schaik.htm

Boyer, E. L. (1990). *Scholarship reconsidered: Priorities of the professoriate.* Princeton, NJ: The Carnegie Foundation for the Advancement of Teaching, Princeton University Press.

Boyer, E. L., & Mitgang, L. D. (1996). *Building community: A new future for architecture education and practice.* Princeton, NJ: The Carnegie Foundation for the Advancement of Teaching, Princeton University Press.

Florida, R. (2002). *The rise of the creative class. and how it is transforming work, leisure, community and everyday life.* New York, NY: Basic Books.

Gardner, H. (1999). *The disciplined mind: What all students should understand.* New York, NY: Simon & Schuster.

Glassick, C. E., Huber, M. T., & Maeroff, G. I. (1997). *Scholarship assessed: Evaluation of the professoriate.* San Francisco, CA: The Carnegie Foundation for the Advancement of Teaching, Jossey-Bass.

Jamieson, P., Fisher, K., Gilding, T., Taylor, P. G., & Trevitt, A. C. F. (2000). Place & space in the design of new learning environments. *HERDSA (Higher Education Research and Development Society of Australasia Journal)*, *19*(2), 231–237

McLouglin, B. J. (1992). *Shaping Melbourne's future?* Melbourne: Cambridge University Press.

Saunders, D. (2010). *Arrival city: How the largest migration in history is reshaping our world.* Sydney: Allen and Unwin.

Schaik, L. V. (2010). The poetics of the ideogram. In M. Garcia (Ed.), *The diagrams of architecture* (pp. 104–111). Chichester: Wiley.

Schaik, L. V. (2013a). *Cities of hope: Corrigan building 8* (pp. 22–26). Melbourne: RMIT Gallery.

Schaik, L. V. (2013b). *Ideograms* (pp. 8–12). Melbourne: Lyon Housemuseum.

Schaik, L. V., & London, G., with George, B. (2010). *Procuring innovative architecture.* London: Routledge.

Schaik, L. V., & Watson, F. (in press). *Pavilions, pop-ups and parasols: The impact of social media on physical space.* Architectural Design.

Seakins, B. (2013). RMIT Bundoora west lecture theatre. *Architecture Australia*, *102*(1), 30–36.

Tan, S. F. (2007). Design objectives & strategies. *Architecture Australia*, *96*(1), 101–104.

Waldrop, M. M. (2013). *Massive open online courses.* Scientific American, Retrieved from http://www.scientificamerican.com/article.cfm?id=massive-open-online-courses-transform-higher-education-and-science

CHAPTER 13

LEARNING SPACE EVALUATIONS – TIMING, TEAM, TECHNIQUES

Lisa Germany

ABSTRACT

Many universities are currently investing significant sums of money into refurbishing existing learning spaces and/or building further infrastructure (including Next Generation Learning Spaces (NGLS)) to support learning and teaching in the face-to-face context. While this is usually welcome by staff and students, there is often a concern that designs are not informed by input from appropriate stakeholders.

This chapter brings together information from a range of sources to provide practical ideas and advice on designing robust, whole-of-lifecycle evaluations for learning space projects. By incorporating pre- and post-occupancy stages, involving a wide array of stakeholders and looking beyond surveys and focus groups as evaluation techniques, universities can ensure that future designs take into consideration the experiences and context of staff and students at the institution as well as lessons learned from previous projects.

Keywords: Learning spaces; evaluation; evaluation cycle; evaluation techniques; design; assessment

The Future of Learning and Teaching in Next Generation Learning Spaces
International Perspectives on Higher Education Research, Volume 12, 267–288
Copyright © 2014 by Emerald Group Publishing Limited
All rights of reproduction in any form reserved
ISSN: 1479-3628/doi:10.1108/S1479-362820140000012018

INTRODUCTION

In 2008, researchers from three Australian universities came together to investigate the state of play of learning spaces evaluation (Lee & Tan, 2011). They felt that while there had been '... much attention to the design of learning spaces ... evaluations of learning spaces have been limited in depth, rigour and theoretical grounding, and were heavily reliant on informal or anecdotal evidence' (p. 3). What they found verified their suspicions, but that is not to say that individual ideas and techniques that could be brought together to form a comprehensive learning spaces evaluation approach did not exist.

This chapter is designed to bring together key information about evaluating learning spaces from multiple sources and provide practical advice on how to design a robust evaluation for a learning space project, including the timing, team and techniques that could be used. We have started to use this framework to ensure designs for new refurbishments, Next Generation Learning Spaces (NGLS) and informal spaces at Victoria University are informed by previous user experience and align to University strategic priorities.

TIMING

Typically, if a learning space is evaluated at all, the evaluation occurs once teachers and students have started using the space. This is known as a post-occupancy evaluation and is often used to elicit feedback on what staff and students like and don't like about a particular space. While this is useful information to feed-forward into the next learning space project, it occurs far too late to ensure the space under investigation will meet the expectations of the users and the institution.

For this reason, several authors have argued that pre-occupancy evaluations (evaluations undertaken before the space is ready for use) are also critical in any learning space project. Lee and Tan (2011) proposed a model for the development of learning spaces in which evaluation at the key stages of design, construction and occupation elicits concerns and ideas from staff and students and foregrounds them to be addressed or incorporated before the next stage is undertaken. The Pedagogy-Space-Technology (PST) Design and Evaluation Framework (Radcliffe, 2008) also takes this approach but recommends that evaluations begin even earlier, at the concept stage, aligning with the advice of Lippincott (2007) and the practice of Lee (2008). The following sections draw upon the ideas of these and other authors to outline the types of evaluation that should be incorporated into the various stages of a learning space project.

Concept Stage (Pre-Occupancy)

Evaluation at the concept stage of a learning spaces project should be undertaken at several levels to arrive at a complete and common understanding of the intended outcomes and possible impacts across all stakeholder groups. It can be argued that without understanding the institutional motivations for the project, the post-occupancy evaluation will be unable to measure the degree to which the original goals of the project have been met (Powell, 2008).

At the highest level, evaluation at the concept stage is about clarifying the purpose of the project and the desired outcomes for the institution (Lippincott, 2007). This includes a robust discussion of plans for the future of learning and teaching at the institution, and what additional initiatives (e.g. curriculum redesign, professional development) may be required to support staff and students in transitioning their practice to align with this ideal (Radcliffe, 2008).

These discussions should be informed by an evaluation at the user level that elicits information from staff and students about what they perceive as working well and what they perceive as lacking in the institution's current suite of learning spaces. They should also take into account 'lessons learned' from previous learning spaces initiatives, particularly around stakeholder engagement and issues with implementation (Radcliffe, 2008).

Design Stage (Pre-Occupancy)

With the high-level outcomes for the learning spaces project determined during the concept stage, the design stage evaluation should be focused around gathering and analysing:

- student and staff feedback from post-occupancy evaluations of previous learning spaces initiatives;
- student and staff design ideas for the proposed space (e.g. Gibbons & Foster, 2007);

- feedback from IT/AV and facilities departments around maintenance and technical support, based on previous learning spaces initiatives;
- feedback from academic support around usability and training, based on previous learning spaces initiatives; and
- ideas and best practice from projects that achieved similar outcomes at other institutions (Lee & Tan, 2011; Radcliffe, 2008).

This information should then be synthesised and used to further inform initial design concepts.

Although all stakeholder groups should be represented in the design team itself, the broader user community should also have the chance to provide feedback on iterations of design concepts. Lee (2008) created a reference group consisting of students, academics, management, and services departments for this purpose, and at Victoria University we are holding open forums where all users at the relevant campus are invited to participate and provide feedback. We have adopted several design-changing ideas articulated through these forums and intend that this opportunity for staff and students to provide feedback on design concepts will encourage personal engagement with the spaces (perhaps as a champion or at least an advocate) once they are complete.

Construction Stage (Pre-Occupancy)

The main type of evaluation that takes place during construction is carried out internally within the project team and is primarily related to project management — is the project on time, on budget and within scope with little risk. It is during this stage that those departments that work closely with contractors should evaluate the working relationship, an assessment that may potentially influence future engagement with the company.

However, it is also the time to ensure that stakeholders are kept up to date with progress (Lee & Tan, 2011), and while this is not strictly an evaluation, it can again influence engagement and evaluation feedback down the track. Examples of communications may include:

- updates on construction progress and any special considerations that have been taken into account in the scheduling. For example, letting everyone know when demolition will start and the fact that the project attempted to schedule this noisy work for during the semester break and outside of core teaching hours;

- promotion of the types of spaces that are being constructed, including the rationale behind the design and computer generated imagery of what the spaces will look like once completed;
- information about the types of technology that will be available in the spaces; and
- practical advice about how the spaces might be used pedagogically for a variety of disciplines.

By maintaining regular communications about the spaces under construction, it is possible to build excitement and encourage staff to start thinking about how they might utilise these new opportunities. It also ensures that staff and students are aware that although they may be inconvenienced during the construction phase, the project has tried to minimise these disruptions.

Occupation Stage (Post-Occupancy)

The occupation stage is a critical time for evaluation, providing an opportunity to explore whether the space has achieved its intended purpose as specified during the concept stage. To date, the majority of learning space evaluations have focused on gathering information once staff and students have occupied the space and, in summary, were designed to elicit information that demonstrates value or effectiveness, measures satisfaction, reveals unintended use cases and identifies needed changes (Lippincott, 2007).

Often, however, these evaluations are only carried out once, relatively soon after the space has opened. Unfortunately, it is unlikely that a single evaluation will provide sufficient information to assess the success of the space and inform future learning spaces projects, as some of the desired effects of a project (for example, a change in teaching practice or assessment practice) may take some time to manifest. To this end, a more extensive timeline for post-occupancy evaluation might include:

1. 1 month after occupancy – to gather data on users' first impressions and perceptions of how the spaces will work (Dowling & Lee, private communication).
2. 6 months to 1 year after occupancy – to measure the differences between first impressions of a space and actual experiences over time (Dowling & Lee, private communication).
3. longitudinal – to determine whether the space has a long-term impact on teaching practice and student learning and whether the design was

future-proof (including from a maintenance perspective). In particular, it would be useful to explore whether teachers have incorporated new assessment techniques that make full use of opportunities that may be provided in the NGLS (Crisp, 2014).

At each of these timings, there are a large number of elements to potentially be evaluated, all of which feed into how staff and students use and experience the space. The Technology, Architecture and Furniture model (Education Queensland, 2013, 'About TAF') suggests a division of these elements into four main categories: environmental, functional, emotional and pedagogical (Table 1), in which each of the main groups of stakeholders should have various levels of interest. For example, one might expect teachers and students to have a keen interest in all four categories as they all impact the user experience in the space. On the other hand, although IT/AV staff may primarily be interested in the functional category (to determine how well the technology has worked and what maintenance issues have arisen), they could also be looking at elements in the environmental category (to determine how the acoustics, lighting and temperature have affected the performance of AV equipment) and the pedagogical category (for feedback on how cables and wiring are potentially impacting pedagogy in the space) for a full understanding of what has worked and what hasn't with respect to the IT/AV fit-out of the space.

While few would disagree that 'Learning, rather than heating systems, lighting controls, or computer projectors, should be at the center of learning space design' (Oblinger, 2004, p. 1), it does assume that the environmental and functional elements of a learning space are the best

Table 1. One Possible Categorisation of the Different Elements of a Learning Space That Should Be Evaluated.

Environmental	Functional	Emotional	Pedagogical
Indoor air quality	Furniture (chairs, tables)	Colour	Flexibility
Acoustics (internal, external distractions)	Fixtures (whiteboards, pinboards, power)	Vistas	Configuration
Lighting (daylight, artificial light)	Technology (Wi-Fi, projection options, computing options)	Security	Student outcomes
Temperature (heating, cooling)	Adequate space for number of students	Ownership	Teacher outcomes
	Accessibility		
	Floor coverings		
	Utilisation		

they can be to support learning. However, we know from experience that this is often not the case, and several papers have linked poor environmental elements with reduced student engagement (Hunley & Schaller, 2006) and impacted student achievement (Higgins, Hall, Wall, Woolner, & McCaughey, 2005).

In a recent series of focus groups conducted at Victoria University, the primary concerns of teaching staff were around these environmental elements. It quickly became clear that teaching staff did not have the headspace to discuss the functional or pedagogical elements of the spaces, as questioning along these lines was almost immediately turned around to environmental issues once more. In a way, this aligns with the fundamental premise of Maslow's Hierarchy of Needs (Maslow, 1943), the idea that our most basic needs must be satisfied before we are ready to consider more advanced needs. In the learning spaces context, if there are issues with the heating, cooling or air quality, we are not going to be thinking about different technologies and pedagogies to support learning.

This demonstrates that while it might be tempting to leap right to the heart of the matter evaluate whether the space has achieved the high-level goals as defined in the concept stage, investigating the environmental and functional basics to understand how they feature in the feedback from staff and students is an important part of post-occupancy evaluation. It is critical for understanding what has worked, what hasn't and what should be altered for next time.

That's not to say that the high-level goals should be ignored. In their investigation into the state of play of evaluating learning spaces in the university sector, Lee and Tan (2011) did find a tendency for evaluations to gather feedback predominantly around the functional aspects of the design and staff and student satisfaction with the space. This is possibly because robustly examining how a space impacts student achievement or teaching practice is very difficult, and convincing techniques and evidence to support these notions has only emerged recently.

In particular, the learning spaces research team at the University of Minnesota has had the unusual opportunity to apply a quasi-experimental approach to investigating their new Active Learning Classrooms (ALC). They have partnered with instructors who teach identical sections of their courses in two very different learning environments – a traditional classroom with student tables facing the front of the room, and a technology-enhanced active learning space equipped with collaborative tables and multiple LCD screens. Brooks (2011) showed that students taught in the ALC outperformed their peers who were taking the same course in the traditional classroom, and Brooks (2012) showed a causal relationship between the physical space and the behaviour of teachers and students.

These are two of the first studies to robustly explore the pedagogical elements of learning spaces and strongly suggest the worth of one design over the other. It demonstrates that this ultimate aim for our evaluations, although difficult to achieve, is possible.

TEAM

Several authors have provided recommendations for who should be involved in the design phase of learning spaces projects. Oblinger (2004) suggested that administration, teaching staff, students (undergraduate, graduate), facilities, planning, information technology, library and teaching and learning support should all be at the table during this phase of a project. The Next Generation Learning Spaces Project at University of Queensland (Radcliffe, 2008) added design and technology professionals from the University and nationally to the list, while Lee (2008) kept the design group small but formed a reference group (students, teachers, management and services departments) and a management group to contribute to the Project Hub at Swinburne University of Technology.

These recommendations align with Jamieson's (2007) observation that different areas (facilities, timetabling, IT/AV, teachers, academic developers, architects, students) have potentially conflicting ways of 'seeing' classrooms within universities, dependent on their involvement in and responsibility for them. As a slightly simplistic example, a facilities department might see spaces as projects and assets that need to be managed, space management and timetabling may see a complex jigsaw puzzle that needs to be arranged in such a way that utilisation is maximised, AV/IT see spaces in terms of what technology could be installed, teachers see spaces for engaging with students, and students see spaces to engage with their teachers and learn. A concrete example comes from Dane (2008) who wrote of a Space Allocation Manager who raised the issue that the 'utilisation rates' for a NGLS were below expectations. This was in contrast to the views of the teachers involved in the pilot who were unanimous in their support for the space and the collaborative learning it encouraged.

While the literature offers up some advice about who should be involved in the design of learning spaces, far less has been written around who should be involved in the development of evaluation protocols and instruments. In particular, one might conclude from the discussion of timing in the previous section, that different stakeholders might take the lead on the evaluation in different stages of the project. For example, executives within the organisation with responsibility for learning and teaching should perhaps drive evaluation in the concept phase, the design team (including architects) should drive evaluation in the design phase, and facilities managers should drive evaluation during the construction phase of a project.

For post-occupancy evaluations, it makes sense that at least some members of the design team (those familiar with social research methods) should be involved in the development of evaluation instruments to ensure that the evaluation aligns with the principles and proposed outcomes for the space. However, this could also be used as an opportunity to invite other stakeholders with an interest in learning spaces and the scholarship of learning and teaching to bring in other perspectives.

Taking it one step further, inviting students into the evaluation team provides insight into what normally happens day-to-day in the type of space under evaluation and may reveal alternate lines of questioning that would otherwise not have been considered. This has been used to great effect by the learning spaces evaluation team at the University of Minnesota who have established a Learning Environments Research Partnership Model that includes undergraduate students, faculty members teaching in the space and a research expert (Walker, Brooks, & Baepler, 2011). In particular, the undergraduate researchers '… worked with the other team members to establish the project's research design, create the research instruments, and collect and analyse data'. They also '… underwent training on the protection of human subjects and research methodology' (http://www.educause.edu/ero/article/pedagogy-and-space-empirical-research-new-learning-environments), setting them up for the future if they decide to pursue social research avenues.

TECHNIQUES

Social science literature advocates for studies that utilise several different evaluation methods so that key themes and issues can be triangulated across multiple techniques. If the same findings can be concluded from more than one set of data, we can be more confident about the validity of our results.

There are many different traditional and innovative evaluation methods that could be used at any stage of the concept-design-construction-occupation cycle for a learning space. The following examples showcase several ideas that have come specifically from the evaluation of learning spaces. Where possible, references have been provided for more detailed information and examples.

Surveys

Surveys are one of the most commonly used tools for learning space evaluations as they are easy to administer, can potentially reach a large user base and are not time-intensive for researchers. While they can be effective in ascertaining the level of satisfaction of users with the space and the various elements contained therein, the data they elicit tends to be broad rather than deep and they are rarely able to reveal why users feel the way they do. To this end, they offer little guidance for the design of future building projects (Powell, 2008) and are often followed up with focus groups to probe more deeply around the ideas uncovered by the survey.

Individual Reflective Techniques

In these techniques, students are essentially recruited as co-researchers and asked to record their own actions or reflect on a question in order to contribute to the data gathered for evaluation. These techniques often reveal detail in the thoughts and the day-to-day life of a student that conventional interviews alone could not achieve.

Design Charrettes

A charrette is an intensive process through which draft solutions to a design problem are created. Gibbons and Foster (2007) used this technique in their Undergraduate Research Project, providing the following scenario to participating students: 'Imagine that the library has a big, new, empty space … and they ask YOU to design it. You can put up walls or not have walls. You can buy furniture, hire staff, have the amenities and comforts that you want … It is exactly the way you wanted it to be and you love it and want to go there a lot. Show us what it looks like' (p. 22). Nineteen students took part, and although individual designs had some unique 'quirky' elements, five common elements also emerged from this process giving them a good baseline from which to work.

When it came time to look at the fittings and furnishings of the space, Gibbons and Foster (2007) ran a second series of design charrettes with students. In this iteration, they gave students '... a plan of the space and a wide selection of furniture cutouts made to scale, along with markers, sticky notes, scissors, and glue. ... [and asked them] to design and furnish the space to meet their needs' (p. 26). Again, there were remarkable similarities between the twenty-one finished designs, and disturbingly, these designs did not in any way reflect the designs created by the library renovation team on how they thought students would like the space arranged.

Photo Surveys
In this technique, participants are given a list of things to photograph over a period of time. Once they have obtained their images, they are interviewed to elicit further information about the images taken and how they relate to the items on the list.

Briden (2007) used this technique to see from the student perspective, specific items of interest to their study of undergraduate student life at the University of Rochester. Having students contribute imagery on, for example, their favourite place to study, and then following up with individual interviews to reveal why, '... provided answers to specific questions we were asking, ... gave us hints that were confirmed through other investigations, and other [findings that] were completely unexpected' (p. 45).

A similar approach was used by Nixon, Tompkins, and Lackie (2008), in which students were asked to take no less than five images corresponding to how they went about completing a particular assignment, and five images on how they use and feel about the campus in general. Prompts for each were provided to assist the students in formulating the types of photos that might be relevant. The photographs were used in follow-up interviews where students were asked to elaborate upon their decisions to take the photos, and the images themselves.

Keppell and Riddle (2012) also incorporated this technique into their exploration of technology use. Students were texted at irregular intervals over a 24-hour period and encouraged to take photographs of where they were, what they were doing, who they were with and how they were feeling. These photographs of their 'day' were then discussed in a focus group scenario.

Visual Mapping
The essence of the visual mapping technique is that participants are provided with a map of the area under evaluation and asked to draw in where

they go during a typical visit. For example, Jordan and Ziebell (2008) asked students to mark the sequence of their activities on a floor plan and include comments about what activities they did and how long they spent on each activity.

Clark (2007) '... gave students a map of the campus and key surrounding areas and asked them to mark their movements [over the course of one day] on this map, indicating when they arrived at each place and when they left it' (p. 48). Students were interviewed about their day when they returned their map. In fact, follow-up interviews with participants are common in this technique, in order to better understand the information in the map. The technique has also been modified for use in focus groups for this reason.

Nixon et al. (2008) modified the technique of Clark (2007) to track movement over a longer period of time and to be able to clearly indicate multiple visits to a single location. It was also modified to be able to elicit information about specific locations within the individual buildings on campus. This mapping exercise (along with the photo surveys described above) provided the basis for the follow-up interview with researchers about how students utilise the campus.

Reflective Diaries

In this approach, participants describe, or better still, reflect on their activities over a period of time in a diary. This appeared to work well for Anders, Calder, Elder, and Logan (2008) who had focus group participants document their use of different spaces in order to further validate focus group information; however, Gallagher, Pearce, and McCormack (2008) point out some limitations to the method. They found that despite providing students with careful training in the use of the diary, the entries tended to be descriptive rather than true reflections. While this may be sufficient to gauge student satisfaction with learning spaces, it falls short of revealing what impact the space has had on student learning, the purpose of their evaluation.

Other Techniques

Although the study of Keppell and Riddle (2012) was specifically mentioned in relation to photo surveys, they actually mixed several of the above techniques and offered students the opportunity to use a camera, a diary or a voice recorder to record their moment in time. By offering students a wide variety of tools to capture their reflections, they '... encouraged the participants to provide as rich and detailed an account as possible of their experiences' (p. 13).

Gallagher et al. (2008) drew upon the unique opportunity presented by the Victoria University Rovers – students who occupy a support role within the Learning Commons spaces under evaluation at the University. In particular, they tapped into the end-of-shift reports submitted by each Rover, transcripts of Rover debriefing sessions and reflections on the Rover blog to augment data collected through student reflective diaries and surveys. However, they acknowledge that '... more effective methods need to be developed to triangulate the perceptions of the Rovers themselves with those of student users of the [space]' (p. 104).

Facilitated Group Discussions

Facilitated group discussions (usually in the form of focus groups) are another mainstay of learning spaces evaluations and are typically used to follow up on ideas that have emerged through a survey. The most common format for these discussions is a semi-structured interview that prompts the participants for further information that may help to interpret the survey results.

While focus groups provide a quick method for gaining multiple perspectives, they do have limitations. In particular, and in the context of learning spaces evaluations, Lee and Tan (2013) identified that the interview-based formats '... yielded little useful data for a deeper understanding of design requirements [and had] ... a tendency for "group-think" or dominant members to overwhelm the data' (https://libjournal.uncg.edu/index.php/jls/article/view/503). Several techniques have emerged to try and overcome these barriers.

'Movers and Shapers' Focus Group

The 'Movers and Shapers' focus group method used in the Learning Landscape Project at Cambridge University (Howell, 2008) endeavoured to break down the stranglehold of dominant participants and 'group-think' common in traditional facilitated group discussions. In this approach, participants are divided into groups for a series of 15 minute 'mini-discussions' around a table with a facilitator. At the end of the 15 minute time interval, participants at each table randomly select a card that identifies them as either a 'mover' or a 'shaper'. The 'movers' change tables and enter their new mini-discussion to challenge what has gone before. The 'shapers' remain at their table and attempt to convince the 'movers' of what was previously discussed. This is repeated until the end of the session, which lasts for at least an hour. These focus groups produced a wealth of qualitative data and were found to be stimulating and engaging for participants.

Diamond Ranking within a Focus Group

Participants are divided into groups and given nine images to consider. Each group is required to rank the images in terms of preference and form them into a diamond shape with the most preferred image at the top of the diamond and the least preferred image at the bottom (Woolner et al., 2010). Participants are then encouraged to annotate the diamond to further explain their rankings.

Lee and Tan (2013) applied this technique to the evaluation of an informal learning space at Swinburne University of Technology, giving students nine images of different areas within the learning environment to rank according to preference. Rather than using annotations, they had each group of students discuss and provide the rationale for their preferences, explaining how they decided upon their arrangement. Further discussion was used to explore consensus or disagreement within the groups.

Both sets of researchers found that this technique was very good for invoking self-generated discussion within the group, as it required participants to 'make the case' for their preferences in order to achieve group consensus on the ranking.

Visual Mapping within a Focus Group

Woolner et al. (2010) also utilised two versions of the visual mapping technique described in the 'Reflective Techniques' section. In one version, they had students and school staff indicate on their maps the places they liked and places they didn't like with different coloured stickers. In the other, they had participants indicate 'places that work' and 'places that don't work' on their maps. Researchers then initiated discussions within the focus group context to elicit explanations, opinions and ideas from the participants.

Lee and Tan (2013) modified this technique further by asking participants to draw their typical route on a transparency overlaid on a map of the space under evaluation. Maps from all participants were then overlaid on top of each other and the resulting discussion explored the similarities and differences for individual routes.

Evaluation by Design within a Focus Group
Jordan and Ziebell (2008) extended the design charrette technique discussed previously to the focus group scenario. They undertook design workshops with groups of students, asking them to sketch their ideal spaces that would best support three different types of learning activity: group work, individual assignment work and preparing for exams.

Lee and Tan (2013) expanded upon this idea by giving their groups of participants a selection of abstract objects (pins, string, beads, ice cream sticks, etc.) to design their ultimate space, rather than having them sketch it. The idea is that these 'play' objects would provide '… sufficient and flexible items that would facilitate creative solutions, promote positive play and not confuse or overwhelm participants' (https://libjournal.uncg.edu/index.php/jls/article/view/503). To guide the process, they specifically asked participants to first think about the space itself and consider what type of equipment they would have and where they would place it. They were then asked to specifically consider the use of technology in the space. A whole-of-group discussion within the focus group setting then elicited further information on choices made and drew out rationales for the similarities and differences in the designs.

Fig. 1 shows an example output from this type of activity run during the evaluation of a NGLS at Victoria University. The NGLS was a very flexible space with large areas of writable surface, flip-top tables on castors, LCD screens for students to plug into and a variety of hard and soft furniture. Each group of participants (three in each group) was given a large sheet of paper that approximated the shape of the space under evaluation and play objects to represent different elements in their redesign of the space. Boxes 1–5 in Fig. 1 indicate elements that already exist in the space and box 6 shows a completely new addition proposed by the group. In looking at the design, and in the discussion that ensued, the following information was revealed:

> Box 1: In this area there is a writable surface and an LCD screen that a student group can plug their laptop into for better visibility of the screen. The group has made a note 'magic button that you press and this screen always works', indicating that there were issues with the technology during the semester. Staff verified in the discussion of their design that there had been several issues where students were not able to connect their laptops successfully to the screens around the room.

> Box 2: This existing area has a curtain that can be pulled around into a circle to isolate a group of students in a private space. Even despite the

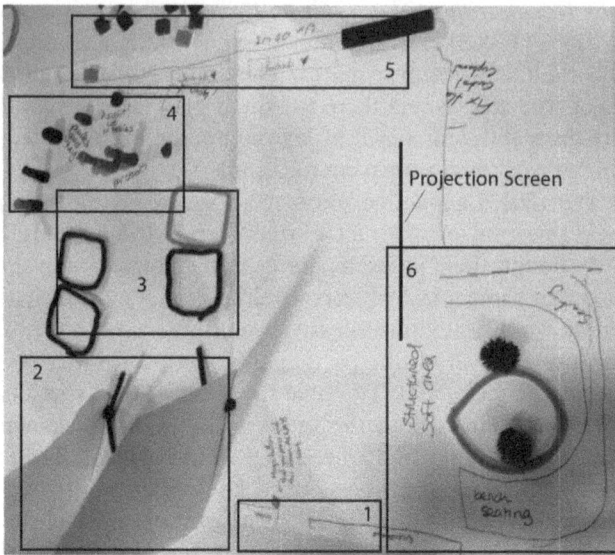

Fig. 1. Example Output from an 'Evaluation by Design' Activity within a Focus Group.

issue during the semester of the curtain falling off the rail (hidden behind the upright paper is a note to 'please fix the curtain'), the fact that it appears in the redesign suggests it was seen as a valuable design element in the space and a couple of members of this group revealed in their commentary that they used this to isolate a specific activity that students would rotate through.

Box 3: These pipe-cleaner rectangles represent the easily moveable flip-top tables available in the space. Staff commented on how easy they were to operate and move around the room to enable different styles of group work and appreciated the opportunity to fold them all up on occasion and push them completely out of the way.

Box 4: The space has a number of upholstered low stools for students to sit on. This group suggested that the space should have additional work-spaces at different heights to encourage different types of interaction and have added round tables at standing height (similar to tables often found at cocktail receptions) and bar stools in their design.

Box 5: This side of the room is a wall of windows under which there is bench seating. The bench seats were clearly a favourite in the room as indicated by the love-hearts.

Box 6: This area is 'hidden' or sectioned off when the main projection screen is activated and extends from the ceiling. The group felt that it was a bit of a 'dead' space that could be better utilised as a structured soft area with further bench seating, low tables and beanbags. They felt that because it was isolated behind the projection screen, this could be a 'quiet area' to escape the hustle and bustle of the rest of the activity going on in the space. Informal observations of how students use the space outside of class time revealed that this area was usually where students could be found lying on beanbags working quietly — anecdotally validating that it is seen as a bit more of a quiet, secluded area.

Observations

Passive observations are not as prevalent in the literature around learning spaces evaluation, possibly because they are best performed by trained observers and can require a significant investment of time. However, they do offer particular advantages in that they provide rich information of how a space is *actually* used and an important validation of self-reported behaviours of students and teachers (Hook & Rosenshine, 1979). The ways in which observations have been used in learning spaces research ranges from informal, ad-hoc observations through to carefully tested, rigorous observations, and everything in between.

In the evaluation of the Science Learning Centre (Matthews, Andrews, & Adams, 2011), researchers recorded general observations about the space for 15 minutes and then observed a specific group of students or an individual for another 10 minutes. Information such as activity, location, interactions, mood, reactions to the environment and 'interesting events' were collected before the individual or group was approached to participate in a 10—15 minute informal interview. Comments made by the students in these informal interviews were later verified with their observed behaviour.

Perhaps the most rigorous use of observation has come from the team at the University of Minnesota who developed and made extensive use of an explicit observation protocol in the evaluation of their new ALC (Brooks, 2012; Walker et al., 2011; Whiteside, Brooks, & Walker, 2010).

This protocol has been tested for reliability and validity and requires the observer to document specific activities (identified in the observation form) occurring in the classroom at intervals of 5 minutes. These observations were a critical component in the quasi-experimental approach that allowed the researchers to demonstrate the causal relationship between the physical space and the behaviour of teachers and students (Brooks, 2012).

The above examples require a researcher to be present in the space in order to carry out the observations. However, several contributors to Radcliffe, Wilson, Powell, and Tibbetts (2008) have suggested making use of remote video recording to do the same. Mitchell, Winslett, and Howell (2008) in particular suggested making use of '... time-lapse recording of the way in which the space is configured and reconfigured by students ... [in order to] provide an understanding of how the use of space changes across the academic semester' (p. 92).

These same researchers also reported a more radical take on traditional observation methods where, rather than observing students directly, they undertook an informal analysis of the level of activity undertaken in group collaboration sessions by investigating the student content left on the whiteboards at the end of each day. This revealed that mobile collaboration opportunities were used twice as much as the same opportunity if it was fixed to a wall.

Another alternative method to traditional observation has been utilised by Hunley and Schaller (2006) who made use of photographic techniques to enable their observations. Specifically, in the initial evaluation, photographers followed a designated path through the buildings under evaluation to take photographs from designated locations each hour, at roughly a quarter past the hour, for a week. The intent is now to build up a longitudinal study of how the spaces are used over a two-year period.

Institutional Data

A final way to evaluate learning spaces is through the use of 'institutional data'. This is a bit of a catch-all that includes data that is automatically logged by some means. In the case studies presented in Radcliffe et al. (2008), several examples of institutional data are mentioned including computer login data, wireless usage data, room booking data, door counts and helpdesk enquiries. Other possibilities include information from remote management tools (e.g. from room AV control systems), Radio Frequency Identification (RFID) tracking and incidents reported through facilities and IT service desks. Opportunities for gathering institutional data to assist in the evaluation of learning spaces are limited only by what data is automatically collected by your institution, their policies and your imagination.

TAKE HOMES

This chapter has drawn upon the literature to suggest a robust approach to the evaluation of learning spaces. The focus on timing, team and techniques highlights that running an online satisfaction survey once teachers and students have started using the space is not sufficient, and suggests the following take home messages:

- the evaluation strategy should be one of the first considerations when planning a learning spaces project;
- evaluation should be embedded at all stages of the learning spaces project and beyond;
- the evaluation should be aligned with and assess the institutional goals for the learning space project;
- the evaluation should aim to collect information across the complete range of elements of a learning space — from environmental through to pedagogical — to fully understand the successes and issues with the space;
- the evaluation should involve a variety of stakeholders that can bring different perspectives to the development of evaluation instruments; and
- the evaluation should use a variety of techniques that allows for a complete exploration of how the space impacts learning and teaching.

REFERENCES

Anders, D., Calder, A., Elder, K., & Logan, A. (2008). Investigating the dynamics of an integrated learning space at James Cook University. In D. Radcliffe, H. Wilson, D. Powell, & B. Tibbetts (Eds.), *Learning spaces in higher education: Positive outcomes by design*. St. Lucia: The University of Queensland. Retrieved from http://www.uq.edu.au/nextgenerationlearningspace/proceedings. Accessed on December 2, 2013.

Briden, J. (2007). Photo surveys: Eliciting more than you knew to ask for. In N. F. Foster & S. Gibbons (Eds.), *Studying students: The undergraduate research project at the university of Rochester*. Chicago, IL: Association of College and Research Libraries. Retrieved from http://www.ala.org/acrl/sites/ala.org.acrl/files/content/publications/booksanddigitalresources/digital/Foster-Gibbons_cmpd.pdf. Accessed on December 2, 2013.

Brooks, D. C. (2011). Space matters: The impact of formal learning environments on student learning. *British Journal of Educational Technology*, *42*(5), 719–726. doi:10.1111/j.1467-8535.2010.01098.x

Brooks, D. C. (2012). Space and consequences: The impact of different formal learning spaces on instructor and student behavior. *Journal of Learning Spaces*, *1*(2), 1–16.

Clark, K. (2007). Mapping diaries, or where do they go all day? In N. F. Foster & S. Gibbons (Eds.), *Studying students: The undergraduate research project at the university of Rochester*. Chicago, IL: Association of College and Research Libraries. Retrieved from http://www.ala.org/acrl/sites/ala.org.acrl/files/content/publications/booksanddigital resources/digital/Foster-Gibbons_cmpd.pdf. Accessed on December 2, 2013.

Crisp, G. (2014). Assessment in next generation learning spaces. In K. Fraser (Ed.), *The future of learning and teaching in next generation learning spaces*. (Vol. 12). International Perspectives on Higher Education Research. Bingley, UK: Emerald Group Publishing Limited.

Dane, J. (2008). Deakin University immersive learning environment (DILE): An evaluation. In D. Radcliffe, H. Wilson, D. Powell, & B. Tibbetts (Eds.), *Learning spaces in higher education: Positive outcomes by design*. St. Lucia: The University of Queensland. Retrieved from http://www.uq.edu.au/nextgenerationlearningspace/proceedings. Accessed on December 2, 2013.

Education Queensland. (2013). *Technology, architecture and furniture*. Retrieved from http://www.learningplace.com.au/deliver/content.asp?pid=49664. Accessed on December 2.

Gallagher, A., Pearce, A., & McCormack, R. (2008). Learning in the learning commons: The learning commons at City Flinders and St Albans campuses. In D. Radcliffe, H. Wilson, D. Powell, & B. Tibbetts (Eds.), *Learning spaces in higher education: Positive outcomes by design*. St. Lucia: The University of Queensland. Retrieved from http://www.uq.edu.au/nextgenerationlearningspace/proceedings. Accessed on December 2, 2013.

Gibbons, S., & Foster, N. F. (2007). Library design and ethnography. In N. F. Foster & S. Gibbons (Eds.), *Studying students: The undergraduate research project at the university of Rochester*. Chicago, IL: Association of College and Research Libraries. Retrieved from http://www.ala.org/acrl/sites/ala.org.acrl/files/content/publications/booksanddigi-talresources/digital/Foster-Gibbons_cmpd.pdf. Accessed on December 2, 2013.

Higgins, S., Hall, E., Wall, K., Woolner, P., & McCaughey, C. (2005). *The impact of school environments: A literature review*. Retrieved from http://www.ncl.ac.uk/cflat/news/DCReport.pdf. Accessed on December 2, 2013.

Hook, C. M., & Rosenshine, B. V. (1979). Accuracy of teacher reports of their classroom behavior. *Review of Educational Research*, *49*(1), 1–12.

Howell, C. (2008). *Movers and shapers*. Research Methods Paper. Retrieved from http://www.caret.cam.ac.uk/blogs/llp/wp-content/uploads/llp_research20methods_moversshapers_v03.pdf. Accessed on December 2, 2013.

Hunley, S., & Schaller, M. (2006). Assessing learning spaces. In D. G. Oblinger (Ed.), *Learning spaces*. EDUCAUSE. Retrieved from https://net.educause.edu/ir/library/pdf/PUB7102.pdf. Accessed on December 2, 2013.

Jamieson, P. (2007). Rethinking the University classroom: Designing 'places' for learning. Paper presented at the Inaugural Next Generation Learning Spaces Colloquium. Retrieved from http://www.uq.edu.au/nextgenerationlearningspace/Jamieson.pdf, University of Queensland

Jordan, E., & Ziebell, T. (2008). Learning in the spaces: A comparative study of the use of traditional and 'new generation' library learning spaces by various disciplinary cohorts. In D. Radcliffe, H. Wilson, D. Powell, & B. Tibbetts (Eds.), *Learning spaces in higher education: Positive outcomes by design*. St. Lucia: The University of Queensland. Retrieved from http://www.uq.edu.au/nextgenerationlearningspace/proceedings. Accessed on December 2, 2013.

Keppell, M., & Riddle, M. (2012). Distributed learning spaces: Physical, blended and virtual learning spaces in higher education. In M. Keppell, K. Souter, & M. Riddle (Eds.), *Physical and virtual learning spaces in higher education: Concepts for the modern learning environment*. Hershey, PA: IGI Global.

Lee, N. (2008). The Hawthorn project hub at Swinburne University of Technology. In D. Radcliffe, H. Wilson, D. Powell, & B. Tibbetts (Eds.), *Learning spaces in higher education: Positive outcomes by design*. St. Lucia: The University of Queensland. Retrieved from http://www.uq.edu.au/nextgenerationlearningspace/proceedings. Accessed on December 2, 2013.

Lee, N., & Tan, S. (2011). *Final report 2011: A comprehensive learning space evaluation model*. Retrieved from http://www.olt.gov.au/project-comprehensive-learning-space-swinburne-2008. Accessed on December 2, 2013.

Lee, N., & Tan, S. (2013). Traversing the design-language divide in the design and evaluation of physical learning environments: A trial of visual methods in focus groups. *Journal of Learning Spaces, 2*(2).

Lippincott, J. (2007). Assessing Learning Spaces. Paper presented at the Library Assessment conference, Charlottesville, VA.

Maslow, A. H. (1943). A theory of human motivation. *Psychological Review, 50*(4), 370–396.

Matthews, K. E., Andrews, V., & Adams, P. (2011). Social learning spaces and student engagement. *Higher Education Research & Development, 30*(2), 105–120.

Mitchell, G., Winslett, G., & Howell, G. (2008). Lab 2.0. In D. Radcliffe, H. Wilson, D. Powell, & B. Tibbetts (Eds.), *Learning spaces in higher education: Positive outcomes by design*. St. Lucia: The University of Queensland. Retrieved from http://www.uq.edu.au/nextgenerationlearningspace/proceedings. Accessed on December 2, 2013.

Nixon, A., Tompkins, H., & Lackie, P. (2008). *Curricular uses of visual materials: A mixed-method institutional study*. Northfield, MN: Carleton College, Dean of the College Office. Retrieved from http://apps.carleton.edu/curricular/support/assets/CUVMFinal. PDF. Accessed on December 2, 2013.

Oblinger, D. G. (2004). *Leading the transition from classrooms to learning spaces*. Retrieved from https://net.educause.edu/ir/library/pdf/NLI0447.pdf. Accessed on December 2, 2013.

Powell, N. (2008). Evaluation and the pedagogy-space-technology framework. In D. Radcliffe, H. Wilson, D. Powell, & B. Tibbetts (Eds.), *Learning spaces in higher education: Positive outcomes by design*. St. Lucia: The University of Queensland. Retrieved from http://www.uq.edu.au/nextgenerationlearningspace/proceedings. Accessed on December 2, 2013.

Radcliffe, D. (2008). A pedagogy-space-technology (PST) framework for designing and evaluating learning places. In D. Radcliffe, H. Wilson, D. Powell, & B. Tibbetts (Eds.), *Learning spaces in higher education: Positive outcomes by design*. St. Lucia: The University of Queensland. Retrieved from http://www.uq.edu.au/nextgenerationlearningspace/proceedings. Accessed on December 2, 2013.

Radcliffe, D., Wilson, H., Powell, D., & Tibbetts, B. (2008). *Learning spaces in higher education: Positive outcomes by design.* St. Lucia: The University of Queensland. Retrieved from http://www.uq.edu.au/nextgenerationlearningspace/proceedings. Accessed on December 2, 2013.

Walker, J. D., Brooks, D. C., & Baepler, P. (2011). Pedagogy and space: Empirical research on new learning environments. *EDUCAUSE Quarterly, 34*(4). Retrieved from http://www.educause.edu/ero/article/pedagogy-and-space-empirical-research-new-learning-environments. Accessed on December 2.

Whiteside, A. L., Brooks, D. C., & Walker, J. D. (2010). Making the case for space: three years of empirical research on learning environments. *EDUCAUSE Review Online.* Retrieved from http://www.educause.edu/ero/article/making-case-space-three-years-empirical-research-learning-environments. Accessed on December 2.

Woolner, P., Clark, J., Hall, E., Tiplady, L., Thomas, U., & Wall, K. (2010). Pictures are necessary but not sufficient: Using a range of visual methods to engage users about school design. *Learning Environments Research, 13*(1), 1−22. doi:10.1007/s10984-009-9067-6

CHAPTER 14

MOVING FROM CAMPUS TO COMMUNITY

Amanda Achterberg

ABSTRACT

Victoria University is one of the few Australian dual-sector institutions that offers vocational, further, and higher education programs. The University offers short courses, apprenticeships, certificates, diplomas, degrees, and postgraduate studies to 40,000 students. The campuses are primarily located in the western region of Melbourne (Australia) but include Sydney and international sites. The predominant student cohorts come from low socio-economic backgrounds and are the first in family to attend a university.

This chapter reports on the joint partnership between local councils and Victoria University in the development of collaborative learning hubs that anticipate broader access to learning for community members whilst providing links back to larger campus locations. The intended aim of these partnerships is to increase tertiary participation and completions, whilst engaging/reengaging local community members in the art of learning.

The University has embarked on a project to design and implement collaborative learning hubs that provide tertiary courses in a number of local councils.[1] The project builds on the strategic directions of both the

The Future of Learning and Teaching in Next Generation Learning Spaces
International Perspectives on Higher Education Research, Volume 12, 289–298
Copyright © 2014 by Emerald Group Publishing Limited
ISSN: 1479-3628/doi:10.1108/S1479-362820140000012019

councils and the University, which sees itself as the University of Opportunity for people who would traditionally struggle to be successful in tertiary education. The two councils that Victoria University is part-nering with are Hume City Council and Hobsons Bay City Council.

Keywords: Collaborative learning hubs; councils; partnerships; flipped learning

INTRODUCTION

According to Ernst and Young (2012), the current Australian university model of a broad-based teaching and research institution, with a large campus infrastructure – will prove unviable in all but a few cases over the next 10–15 years. There are many factors that have provoked this need for change and they include the democratization of knowledge and access (where, when, and what people learn), contestable student markets, global mobility, industry integration, and the emergence of digital technologies (Ernst & Young, 2012). This shift in educational paradigms has provided the motivation for universities to become both entrepreneurial and responsive in the ways in which they provide tertiary education.

Tertiary education can no longer rely on traditional teacher-led delivery approaches. On the contrary, there is an overwhelming imperative for universities to develop 21st century pedagogies that engage students in applied and situated learning as the forefront of adult learning practices (Hamden, McKnight, McKnight, & Arfstrom, 2013). The process of learning is particularly successful when it is context driven and supports opportunities for students to build independent learning skills, become self-directed, goal orientated, and practical learners (Fidishun, 2000).

Successful learning occurs when there is the right mix of space, technology, and appropriate activities to engage students, improve participation, and create positive experiences that enhance learning. This success can be evidenced when the right balance of integrated technology, tailored learning, and facilitated delivery methods are employed in a blended learning approach.

Blended learning is the purposeful integration of classroom face-to-face learning experiences with online learning experiences. The concept of integrating the strengths of synchronous (face-to-face) and asynchronous (online) learning activities is appealing to students as the learning is facilitated through multiple delivery modes, thus catering for the varying learning styles and time commitments of each cohort of students (Garrison & Kanuka, 2004).

Universities are not alone in their need to engage, retain, and successfully transition students through tertiary education into the growing and adapting world of work. Often, local government agencies and councils are compelled to do the same thinking, planning, and engagement work with their community members. Local councils are now committing and developing long-term educational plans that embed a culture that strengthens learning and employment pathways for their community members. A measure of success for these council led plans is the ongoing engagement and involvement of universities in the provision of collaborative tertiary education, through the move from campus to community collaborative learning hubs.

THE TRADITIONAL UNIVERSITY

Many universities have campuses, largely with buildings that cater for large cohorts of students tailored around learning that occurs in a lecture theatre surrounded by four walls and tiered seating. The traditional university model is that of broad-based teaching and research activities, where administration underpins the work of the university and policies and procedures are the drivers of the organization (Ernst & Young, 2012). The traditional model has become somewhat archaic in the new world where information can be accessed anywhere and anytime, eliciting the need for universities to shift their thinking to develop learning and teaching models that embrace the modern knowledge economy, accept diversity in how and where people learn and provide adaptability for the future.

The Ernst and Young (2012) paper articulates clearly the driving forces behind the need for universities to be better equipped to adapt to the changing world. In this technology rich environment, students are able to construct knowledge anywhere, anytime and that construction can be transferred and shared instantly. This sharing and transferability also means that access to content is open for all and not restricted to the elite or the academically gifted. With the uncapping of student numbers per university in 2012, Australian universities have seen unprecedented competition for students. As noted in the Ling and Fraser chapter in this volume (2014), some universities have been motivated to develop learning and teaching models and spaces that foster student engagement and interactivity and promote the application of knowledge and skills in real world contexts. The continuing changes in digital technology has also aided in the shift in educational paradigms by allowing students access anywhere, anytime, and in (almost) any learning environment.

However the motivation to change for universities is not only fostered through the development of modern online learning management systems, but the development of engaging and interactive in-class approaches. These aim to enhance the student experience through the use of purposeful blending of course content and the application of knowledge. This leads to the need for universities to invest in the building of capability for traditional academics to become facilitators of learning rather than directors of learning (Prensky, 2001).

MERGING LOCAL COUNCIL AND UNIVERSITY STRATEGIC OBJECTIVES

The goal to increase tertiary participation through to completion is no longer a driver that sits purely on the pages of university strategic plans. These goals have now become reality for local councils to increase productivity for the community and provide education and training in areas of need, whilst promoting prosperity and growth for the municipality. This is evident in two key changes to both Hume City Council and Hobsons Bay City Council views; one on education (where and when learning occurs) and two in the progressive development of integrated learning centers.

Victoria University is committed to its mission to support Melbourne's West through the provision of tertiary education engagement opportunities; this has been through strong collaborations with the local councils in which the university maintains campuses. Overtime, campus-based delivery has decreased and the need for multiple campus locations has been reduced, resulting in the rationalization and consolidation of campus locations. Throughout this process, it has been the intention of the local councils and the university to maintain a tertiary education presence in the community, occurring through the provision of collaborative learning hubs, situated in the local councils integrated learning centers.

In order to determine community member needs, the councils have invested significant resources into researching the demographics and needs of their community members. The councils are utilizing both Australian Bureau of Statistics (ABS) data and specific demographic research data that provide detailed profiles of the current education levels of community members, cultural and financial backgrounds and working history, to provide evidence to build needed educational platforms that both engage and reengage community members as learners. These reports provide the foundation for long-term educational plans that councils are developing, to explore and begin to address the ongoing educational needs of their communities. Each council has also provided new innovative buildings that foster a culture of collaborative learning and build on individual experiences. These council learning centers have been developed to aid in the provision of adult education, where learning occurs through social interaction (Merriam & Brockett, 2011).

The education objectives of the councils involve full course delivery in areas that are identified as in short supply. The key outcomes arising from the collaboration between Victoria University and each of the local councils has been the development of course profiles for each learning hub. These profiles have been developed in response to the detailed demographic research conducted in the councils and the identified needs in each community. Each course profile aims to engage varying cohorts across the community; disengaged youth, mothers returning to work, career changers, and skills deepening for existing workers. The key profiles involve the popular disciplines of education, business, community services, and information technology.

This course development and provision is only possible through connections and established partnerships with tertiary education providers, that lead educational programs to build community members capacity while studying where they live. This partnership allows for the University to align its innovative learning and teaching directions to facilitate learning more broadly, with less reliance on the sizeable costs of servicing full campuses. The exciting approach between the University and the community is the development of council integrated learning centers designed to unite library resources, learning support, technology access, and community development activities under one roof. These precincts not only mimic campus life, they also provide modern collaborative learning environments that are colorful, comfortable, and targeted at small group sizes, which are much less daunting for underprepared students.

FACILITATING LEARNING IN A NEW AGE

Victoria University is broadening its traditional campus based delivery by embarking on the design and development of collaborative learning hubs, in the local community, for the community members. The pedagogical approach to learning in these hubs is focused on active and collaborative

AMANDA ACHTERBERG

learning that is student-centered and facilitated by the teacher/lecturer. The design of the hubs facilitates this student-centered teaching approach allowing for multiple modes of instruction and learning (Chism & Bickford, 2002; Oblinger, 2005).

The "Flipped Learning" model, where the traditional teaching, lectures, and content are placed in an online learning management system for students to engage with prior to the face-to-face class time, is an example of the type of student-centered approach used in the hubs (Bergmann & Sams, 2012). Class time is then spent in collaboration where teachers can facilitate the learning with their students, whilst developing skills in problem solving and critical reflection (King, 1993). The other advantage of this approach is that students have greater time to interact with their peers and learn through social interaction whilst applying the discipline content to real life contexts.

The Flipped Learning model provides that bridge to a learner-centered classroom environment, thereby enabling deeper learning (Bergmann & Sams, 2012). Engagement with online components of learning is generally focussed on to the revised Blooms Taxonomy (Anderson & Krathwohl, 2001) intellectual behavior levels where students are recalling, understanding, explaining, and identifying key concepts/theories. Whereas the face-to-face components of learning are based on activities in the classroom that are action based, authentic, connected and collaborative, innovative, high level, engaging, experience based, project based, inquiry based, and self-actualizing. This approach supports students to apply and analyze the theories/content previously learned in real life work scenarios, consistent with the high order learning at the top of Blooms taxonomy scale (Anderson & Krathwohl, 2001). By flipping the learning, students become more independent in their learning and teachers become facilitators. Facilitating learning allows teachers to enrich the student experience, by applying adult learning principles (Fidishun, 2000). The interaction between the learning spaces and the learning approaches promotes and fosters lifelong learning in the community (Hillier, 2008).

The discipline areas that are a natural fit for delivery in the collaborative learning hubs include business, education, community services, social sciences, arts, and information technology. The flexibility of the spaces allows for varying program types ranging from vocational skills development, tertiary preparation, pathways to degree, workforce development, and postgraduate research programs. The aim of the hubs is, where possible, to have full program delivery and assessment. Some programs can be taught entirely in the hubs. Some programs which include units that use facilities such as labs, are be taught in the hub and on campus. However, there are some discipline areas that can't be taught in the hubs. Discipline areas such as applied, physical, natural and health sciences, engineering and building and construction require specific laboratories and physical equipment throughout the program. There are limits to the education profile that can be provided through the hubs.

COLLABORATIVE LEARNING SPACE DESIGN

A learning space should be able to motivate learners and promote learning as an activity, support collaborative as well as formal practice, provide a personalised and inclusive environment, and be flexible in the face of changing needs. (Joint Information Systems Committee, 2006, p. 3)

The learning hubs in each council's learning center have been designed to focus on the learning and teaching activities that promote collaboration. The spaces have been designed on the following principles:

- Flexible furniture to promote various learning and teaching approaches and to provide adaptability over time.
- Informal breakout areas to promote human collaboration inside and outside of the learning space.
- Writable surfaces to promote creative thinking and problem solving.
- Technology enriched to broaden the scope of activities in both the physical and virtual learning environments.

These contemporary learning spaces contain flexible furniture configurations for both formal and informal learning approaches, rich technology to promote connections to mainstream campus locations, and interactivity to foster human engagement and applied learning (Dawes, Hargreaves, James, & Rasmussen, 2012). The learning and teaching activities in the hub can range from briefing sessions, individual problem solving, group work, presentations, debates, role plays, case scenarios, interviews, promoting the need for the face-to-face classes to be active and interactive. The high definition video conferencing installed in each space allows for the teacher and the students to be a part of a broader learning community, where students can converse across campuses on key topics and guest lecturers/industry experts can become part of the learning activities. Though the learning spaces cannot be future-proofed they can be adapted to accommodate change over time (see Fig. 1).

Fig. 1. Collaborative Learning Hub, Hume Global Learning Centre –
Broadmeadows. Photo taken by Emina Mesinovic (2013).

In 2014, there will be a coordinated review of the university's next generation learning spaces. This evaluation will include the community-based
collaborative learning hubs and focus on the teacher and student perspectives of the learning experience. The process for evaluating the learning
spaces will be developed in line with Germany's chapter in this book.

CONCLUSION

The development of local council based collaborative learning hubs aim to
align the learning needs of the various councils with the strategic directions
of the University. As these spaces contain flexible furniture configurations
and rich technology they aid in the facilitation of learning by fostering
human engagement and applied learning. Though multiple discipline areas
can use the spaces, there are some disciplines that are a natural fit including
business, education, community services, social sciences, arts, and information technology.

The learning and teaching approaches in each of the hubs can vary
according to the needs of the community members, allowing for teachers
and students to be a part of a broader learning environment, where students

can converse across campuses on key topics and guest lecturers/industry experts can become part of the learning environment.

NOTE

1. Local councils form a further layer of government below federal and state governments and are established to provide services across each municipality (waste collection, town planning, and community engagement activities).

REFERENCES

Anderson, L. W., & Krathwohl, D. R. (Eds.). (2001). *A taxonomy for learning, teaching and assessing: A revision of Bloom's Taxonomy of educational objectives: Complete edition.* New York, NY: Longman.

Bergmann, J., & Sams, A. (2012). *Flip your classroom: Reach every student in every class every day.* Moorabbin: Hawker Brownlow.

Chism, N. V. N., & Bickford, D. J. (2002). Improving the environment for learning: An expanded agenda. In N. V. N. Chism & D. J. Bickford (Eds.), *The importance of physical space in creating supportive learning environments: New directions in teaching and learning* (No. 92). San Francisco, CA: Jossey-Bass.

Dawes, L., Hargreaves, D., James, J., & Rasmussen, G. (2012). *From tiers to tables — Enhancing student experience through collaborative learning spaces.* Queensland University of Technology. Retrieved from http://www.aaee.com.au/conferences/2012/documents/abstracts/aaee2012-submission-151.pdf

Ernst & Young. (2012). *University of the future.* Australia: Ernst & Young.

Fidishun, D. (2000). *Andragogy and technology: Integrating adult learning theory as we teach with technology.* Proceedings of the 2000 Mid-South Instructional Technology Conference. Murfreesboro, TN: Middle Tennessee State University.

Garrison, R., & Kanuka, H. (2004). Blended Learning: Uncovering its transformative potential in higher education. *Internet and Higher Education, 7*(2004), 95−105.

Germany, L. (2014). Learning space evaluations — Timing, team, techniques. In K. Fraser (Ed.), *The future of learning and teaching in next generation learning spaces* (Vol. 12). International Perspectives on Higher Education Research. Bingley, UK: Emerald Group Publishing Limited.

Hamden, N., McKnight, P., McKnight, K., & Arfstrom, K. (2013). *A review of flipped learning report.* Washington, DC: Flipped Learning Network and George Mason University. Retrieved from http://www.flippedlearning.org

Hillier, Y. (2008). *Reflective teaching in further and adult education.* London: Continuum.

Joint Information Systems Committee. (2006). *Designing space for effective learning: A guide to 21st century learning space design.* Retrieved from www.jisc.ac.uk. Accessed on August 12, 2012.

King, A. (1993). From sage on the stage to guide on the side. *College Teaching, 41*(1), 30−35. Retrieved from http://www. edweek.org/ew/articles/2012/10/03/06khan_ep. h32.html

Ling, P., & Fraser, K. (2014). Pedagogies for next generation learning spaces: Theory, context, action. In K. Fraser (Ed.), *The future of learning and teaching in next generation learning spaces* (Vol. 12). International Perspectives on Higher Education Research. Bingley, UK: Emerald Group Publishing Limited.

Merriam, S., & Brockett, R. G. (2011). The professional and practice of adult education: An introduction. San Francisco, CA: Jossey-Bass.

Oblinger, D. (2005). Leading the transition from classrooms to learning spaces. *EDUCAUSE Quarterly*, *1*, 14—18.

Prensky, M. (2001). *Digital natives, digital immigrant* (Vol. 9, No. 5). MCB University Press. Retrieved from http://www.marcprensky.com/writing/Prensky%20-%20Digital%20 Natives,%20Digital%20Immigrants%20-%20Part1.pdf

CHAPTER 15

TRANSFORMING THE STUDENT EXPERIENCE THROUGH LEARNING SPACE DESIGN

Jennifer Sparrow and Susan Whitmer

ABSTRACT

This chapter focuses on the challenges and the possibilities that exist for College and University leadership, academic planners, instructional technologists, campus planners, architects, and others involved in building the transformative student experience that has been the underpinning of education since the Raphael's School of Athens. Students need to engaged in the learning and have meaningful interactions with the faculty and classmates.

Economic and societal influences during the first decade of the 21st century have illuminated the demand for access to education through emerging technologies in both physical and virtual spaces. These new opportunities have not developed without painstaking disruptions to conventional models for academic and campus planning. The disruptions have led to opportunities to pilot new modalities for curriculum development that blend both online and on ground learning. Parallel opportunities exist for piloting learning spaces that support blended learning.

The Future of Learning and Teaching in Next Generation Learning Spaces
International Perspectives on Higher Education Research, Volume 12, 299–315
ISSN: 1479-3628/doi:10.1108/S1479-362820140000012020

Academics and campus planners alike have realized that there is no one-size-fits-all solution to planning effective formal and informal learning spaces. What is clear is moving the student experience from one that is transactional to transformational requires adhering to grounded best practices in teaching, learning, and campus planning, establishing a team of informed and engaged stakeholders, and developing empathy and authenticity in the planning process for both the spaces and the pedagogies.

Keywords: Learning theory; learning spaces; pedagogy

LEARNING IN THE 21ST CENTURY

The New Science of Learning: Learning Theory for the 21st Century

A shift from an industrial economy to a knowledge economy in the United States during the second half of the 20th century illuminated the fact that the traditional model of instructionism (Papert, 1993) in higher education was not sufficient to educate students in a highly complex and competitive global society. At the same time, researchers in the neuroscience, psychology, sociology, and computer science disciplines began to collaborate on improving the learning experience by collectively gaining a better understanding of how the mind works, how people learn, and how they use knowledge in their everyday lives (Sawyer, 2006).

Grounded in the foundational research of theorists Dewey, Lewin, Vygotsky, and others, a convergence of research on learning has led to new opportunities for understanding the connection between what we know about how people learn and the environments that support the activities of learning experiences. Dewey (1980) championed active learning that included interactions between the student and the environment. A consensus of findings regarding how people learn published by the National Research Council (NRC) (Bransford, Brown, & Cocking, 2000) includes:

- Learning with understanding is important – acknowledging that learning facts are important for thinking and problem solving, but learning facts and procedures alone do not prepare a student for understanding complex concepts and applications.
- People construct new knowledge and understandings based on what they already know and believe (e.g., Cobb, 1994; Piaget, 1952, 1973a, 1973b, 1977; Vygotsky, 1962, 1978).

• Helping students take control of their own learning is important. If understanding is important, students must learn how to recognize through reflection when they understand and when they need more information.

The findings from the NRC have informed a new understanding of the role of the physical environment in enhancing the learning experience (Sawyer, 2006). These findings are supported by learning theory focused on active learning, social constructivism, connectivism and metacognition and problem solving. Bonwell and Eison (1991) described active learning as opportunities for students to do more than just listen. Students "must read, write, discuss or be engaged in problem solving" (Bonwell & Eison, 1991, p. iii). Active learning is supported by learning spaces that allow for students to be engaged with the content in a variety of ways. Bandura (1986) developed his social learning theory with the perspective that students learn within a social context. His theory included not only attention and retention of material but also reproduction and motivation. Learners without motivation will not be active and engaged in their learning, hindering attainment of higher-order thinking skills. Learning spaces should be flexible and allow students to interact with each other and the professor and they should be welcoming and comfortable spaces. Siemens (2004) defined connectivism as a process of learning that connects nodes and information sources. While focused on the ways that technology can enable some of these connections, connectivism can guide planning for learning spaces to include opportunities for students to interact and engage with fellow learners. Gagne (1985) outlined the importance of metacognition, the ability to understand one's own learning and how that learning occurred, as an important phase of the learning process. Metacognition is a critical for both the acquisition and transfer of learning.

Modes of Learning

Current research for planning learning spaces reveals that there is a strong connection between student mindsets, work modes, activities within learning spaces, and the planning of the learning spaces. Thornburg (2013) describes three types of spaces that accommodate various modes. Within formal and informal learning spaces, the various modes might take the form of campfires where people gather around to learn from experts. The expert may be in person or may communicate through various technologies.

A second mode reflects the need for peers to share information in an informal setting. While students have opportunities to share information through their personal devices, there still seems to be a desire for in person sharing of ideas. This type of setting is referred to as the watering hole. The third space described by Thornburg is the cave. Time for reflection is a critical element of the learning process. In the more recent past, many of our formal and informal learning spaces have been planned without spaces that provide an opportunity to reflect on prior learning in order to develop new learning. The cave provides a quiet, individual space for the student to take what they have learned, carefully reflect and internalize the learning.

As we continue to learn more about the connection between learning modes, use modes, activities and learning spaces, it becomes more important for us to consider how to design spaces that meet a variety of needs of the students throughout their academic career.

Getting Students to Think Differently about Their Learning

As with any changes made to a process or an environment, the stakeholders need to figure out how the fit within those changes. This is especially true for today's learners. An unfortunate outcome of far too few schools embracing active and engaged learning is that many learners today are unable to imagine learning spaces that are anything other than stand-and-deliver lectures that require students to simply regurgitate facts on an exam. Students should be given a framework for these collaborative and interactive learning spaces. Early on in their college careers, they should be encouraged to take ownership over their learning, become engaged learners, collaborate with their peers, and become critical thinkers and problem-solvers. These active learning activities are known to increase knowledge retention (Bonwell & Eison, 1991) and increase student retention within courses (Tinto, 1993).

In addition to getting students to think differently about their learning, it is critical to empower students to think differently about learning spaces. A majority of students have come from high schools with chairs and desks in rows. The very nature of these new flexible learning spaces, possibly disorganized, sometimes without a traditional front of the classroom, and maybe arranged differently each time the students enter the room, can cause trepidation. Faculty can take time to frame the active and engaged learning that will be happening in the classroom to allay fears and provide students with the background knowledge necessary to leverage the learning spaces effectively. By empowering students to take ownership over their learning and the spaces, faculty give them an opportunity to utilize the space to best meet their learning needs. Ownership might include the ability to move furniture to meet the needs of the learners, the ability to bring any computer/tablet into the learning space and be functional, or the ability to interact with other learners.

Faculty Development Around Learning Spaces and Pedagogy

The idea of "if you build it, they will come," is partially true when discussing new learning spaces. What institutions want to avoid is creating these transformational learning spaces that are simply utilized for lecture-style teaching. These new learning spaces encourage a pedagogical shift, in which colleges and universities have to make a concerted and strategic effort to promote faculty development within this new paradigm. Vygotsky (1978) defined a zone of proximal development for learners that stated learners learn their best when they work within a range of skills and knowledge. Learners that are presented with material that is too simple, do not increase their understanding of the subject matter. Learners that are working with material where they do not have the appropriate background knowledge or vocabulary become functionally illiterate and are unable to grow in their understanding of new material.

Similar to Vygotsky's (1978) theory, an instructor can have a zone of space and pedagogical development. If a space is too traditional, there will be little opportunity for faculty to think differently about their teaching. If the only learning spaces a professor is exposed to is a lecture hall with stationary seats with side tables, there is not much room for thinking beyond a stand-and-deliver style of teaching. If however, a faculty member is given a 21st century flexible learning space with flexible seating and immersive technologies, they can begin to think about collaborative learning, social constructivism, active learning, and metacognition and reflection in new and interesting ways. However, it should be cautioned that faculty dropped into completely different learning environment may not understand how they fit in the learning process. It is critical that faculty are provided extensive opportunities, both formal and informal, to think about their role in these new learning spaces and their teaching styles. This should be done in conjunction with concrete examples of learning theory and its instructional implications.

The Connection Between Learning Theory and Learning Space Design

Learning spaces can be leveraged the advance learning theories. Active learning requires spaces that allow students to be engaged with the course materials beyond simply listening to a lecture. Bandura's social learning theory requires students to interact with each other as they develop an understanding and categorization of new knowledge. Traditional lecture halls provided little opportunity for social interaction in meaningful ways. Kolb and Kolb (2005) defined experiential learning theory as a process of knowledge creation "through the transformation of experience" (p. 194). They defined the learning cycle as: experiencing, reflecting, thinking, and acting.

Learning spaces at colleges and universities are being rethought to enhance student engagement and interaction. However, older spaces on campus "embody the pedagogical philosophies of their designers" (Monahan, 2002, p. 4). A lecture hall with tables and chairs bolted to the floor embodies the pedagogy of stand and deliver, or sage on the stage. Conversely, a flexible learning space with moveable furniture and collaborative technologies embraces pedagogy of active and social learning (Rook, 2013). Architects and learning space designers should have an intimate understanding of learning theories and be able to define those theories as functional requirements when envisioning and building learning spaces.

Brown (2005) matched learning theory principles with learning space application and then matched the learning theory to traits of the net generation. Ideal learning spaces would be flexible enough to be leveraged for a variety of learning theories. While one space may not support all learning theories, it is important for space planners to be cognizant of both the characteristics and learning needs of students. Brown demonstrated that collaborative and cooperative learning requires small-group workspaces. Active learning, encouraging discovery, and multiple learning resources require space for a variety of tools and technologies. Flexible spaces can meet a variety of these requirements and allow students and faculty to think about learning as an active activity, not simply just passive listening.

BEST PRACTICES IN LEARNING SPACE PLANNING

There has never been a more exciting and challenging time to be involved in learning space design. The introduction of social scientists (anthropologists, sociologists, and psychologists) into the field of design has opened new opportunities for empathetic research into the daily lives and academic experiences of students and faculty. The convergence of research on how people learn along with technological and political influences has led to a fragmented collection of conversations, research studies, and prototyped spaces with little thought to the planning process. Establishing a set of best practices for the learning spaces planning process provides a framework for increased stakeholder engagement, improved communication, a better understanding of the importance of connecting learning spaces to the academic and institutional plans, and a better understanding of the student and faculty experiences on campus. Examples of best practices might include the following.

Make Sure the Right People Are at the Planning Table

No matter the level of planning, (master plan, project specific, space specific), it is important that the right stakeholders are at the table. A stakeholder is defined as, "one that has a stake in an enterprise" (merriam-webster.com, 2013). In the planning process, it is important that this group be multidisciplinary and diverse. Depending on the purpose of the planning team, there might be an opportunity to create a small team of advisors who would form a "learning spaces" team. This team could be a subset of the broader planning team specifically focusing on the tasks of space inventory, space effectiveness, and other metrics related to campus learning spaces. Monahan (2002) suggests that learning space projects should have heterogeneous architects that design hybrid spaces that include collaborative and flexible spaces. The teams should have the stakeholders for higher education including experts in learning theory, learning technologies, teaching faculty from diverse disciplines and with a variety of teaching experiences, and representation from the registrar's office that can fully understand the implications of the newly designed spaces on course scheduling and planning. An ideal team would include visionary thinkers who are willing to think differently about learning spaces, faculty that are willing to rethink their teaching in these new spaces, and administrators who will value the risk and iteration process necessary as faculty refine their teaching methodologies to meet the needs of their students and to leverage the affordances of the learning spaces. Students should also be brought to the table to have input into the learning spaces. Learners should be encouraged to think about new learning spaces outside of the paradigm of traditional lecture halls. They should be shown model learning spaces, be encouraged to think creatively about how they learn, and be exposed to modern learning theory to ensure creative thinking about and ownership of these learning spaces.

Educate the Stakeholders

Expertise in learning theory, instructional design, technology, or architecture is not required to participate in learning space planning. However, to advance the dialogue on creating exemplary and transformational learning opportunities for student and faculty within the physical and virtual campus, we must step outside of our comfort zone and be willing to learn from each other. For planners, this means educating ourselves on the student learning experience and the language of teaching and learning. For faculty, it means understanding the planning process so that you can engage in dialogue with planners leading to your desired outcomes and the functional requirements of the space. For the technology team it means rebranding your team so that you are recognized as campus leaders and leveraging your expertise in educating others. The technology team should be partners in learning with technology as a set of tools that can help facilitate the learning outcomes. For administrators, being educated in the process of teaching, learning, and planning means being better prepared to create the vision that aligns institutional, campus, and learning space planning. For architects, it means designing with pedagogy in mind and actively listening to the vision of faculty, the learning technology team, and administrators. All stakeholders on the learning space planning team should be listening to and researching the needs of current and future students. All members of the team should spend time talking to students, understanding how the space and technologies can interact to increase active and engaged learning.

Design with Empathy

As spaces are in the design and development phase, the design team should get as close as possible to the user experience, which needs to include both students and faculty. Understanding the student and faculty experiences in a holistic framework creates an opportunity to plan both formal and informal learning spaces that fully immerse the students in their learning experiences. Designing with empathy encompasses much more than traditional programming. This work involves an understanding of the student and faculty workday, the campus journey for students and faculty alike, and student behaviors and social norms in a variety of learning environments. Designing with empathy is an excellent opportunity for disciplines to work together, leveraging the expertise of social scientist and campus planners.

Design for the Unknown

As technologies rapidly change, there is a need to design with the future in mind. This is a challenge in any arena, but particularly as technologies have become such a critical tool in learning and the pace of technological innovation outpaces the rate as which institutions can adapt. The rapid pace of change related to the economic, social, political, and technological drivers within the higher education ecosystem requires planners to design for the unknown and unexpected. All spaces on campus, both the formal and informal must be designed to meet the current needs of students and faculty but remain nimble enough to adapt to changes in technological and pedagogical advancements.

Create a Continuous Improvement Loop for Planning Learning Spaces

A critical dimension to learning space development is putting into place an iterative approach to planning spaces. This is very difficult to accomplish in difficult economic times, but if well planned this approach might offer both operational and financial benefits. The punch-list of a project should not be the final destination. It is important to understand how you will know what's working and not working in the space as it relates to an enhanced learning experience. It is also critical to assess learning spaces for utility and effectiveness. The data collection should include feedback from both faculty and students in what is working and what is not. Some changes may be linked to the physical space, others may be directly tied to faculty development or framing the use of the space for students. A more in-depth examination of the evaluation of learning spaces can be found in Germany's Learning Space Evaluations chapter in this book. Germany suggests that there are several milestones in the development of learning spaces that should be evaluated. These evaluations should include the goals of each stage of the learning space development and include diverse stakeholders.

Connect Learning Spaces to the Mission and Academic Plan

For many campus planners, the most challenging aspect of planning learning spaces that transform the student experience is connecting planning to the institution's mission and academic plan. While this objective is rarely found in traditional campus planning models, its significance in the planning process cannot be overstated. Narum (2012) refers to this concept as "planning with the end in mind" (p. 1). She further suggests:

> Such discussions help avoid ad hoc decisions about spaces, they help establish some institutional benchmarks for determining how renewing of programs and space (which go hand in hand) fits into your mission and shapes your planning. (p. 1)

How does a planning team go about connecting planning to the institutional mission? The first step is to understand the current state of the institutional mission. Most colleges and universities have two missions. The first is the espoused mission. This is what the institution says that it does. The espoused mission can be found on most college and university Web sites as their mission statement. The enacted mission is what the institution actually does (Kuh, Kinzie, Schuh, & Whitt, 2005). The best case scenario is that the gap between the espoused mission and the enacted mission is small. If the gap is large, it is the responsibility of the planning team to ask the questions necessary to understand how best to address the disparity within the framework of learning spaces. Questions might include (Narum, 2012):

- When was the last time we revised or reaffirmed our mission?
- What are our institutional priorities? How have they been determined?
- How does our current academic plan connect to our mission? Is it compatible with our understanding of the future in which our students will live and work?
- Do the changes we envision for our spaces for learning [exist] within our mission and academic plan? Do they reflect broader institutional visions for learning? Do they reflect our vision for the future?
- Does our thinking about spaces for learning represent several independent visions or a coordinate, institution-wide vision? Do current budgets and master plans for campus spaces reflect a broader institutional vision? (p. 1)

Taking time to re-examine and align the learning spaces plan will improve the chances that all learning spaces on campus will enhance the student and faculty experience.

A framework for a series of case studies and essays funded by the National Science Foundation for the Learning Spaces Collaboratory (2013) asked similar questions that should be asked prior to the start of the campus planning process:

- What do we want our learners to become?
- What activities make that becoming happen?
- What spaces enable those experiences?
- How do we know?

Uncovering the answers to these questions requires a commitment from all of the stakeholders involved in the academic and campus planning process. Understanding the answers to these questions helps to build a consensus about the importance of the role of place and connects the dots between how students learn, what they learn, and where they learn.

SPACES TO SUPPORT LEARNING

There are many types of model learning spaces that can be utilized as models when planning for space transformation (Fig. 1). The models should be a guide for what is possible, but design teams should be encouraged to think about their specific learners and faculty. Each institution has unique characteristics that may guide the design thought process. The model learning spaces are outlined later.

Learning Studio

The Learning Studio model is a research-based approach to learning spaces developed for maximum opportunities for peer-to-peer and student-faculty engagement. In the Learning Studio, lectures and active-group-based problem solving activities take place in the same space. The faculty might start a class in a typical lecture style and then switch to group work. As the pedagogical style changes, so does the tools of the space. The Learning Studio is highly nimble with flexible furniture (tables and chairs on casters); the appropriate combination of low-tech (marker boards) and high-tech devices.

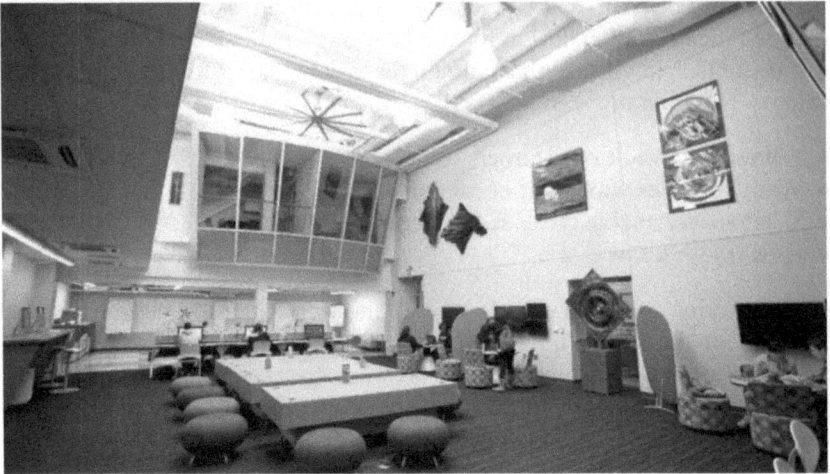

Fig. 1. Learning Spaces that Nurture Discovery and Co-Creation are Vital to the Development of Critical Thinking and Communication Skills. *Source*: Photo courtesy of Chris Radcliffe, Noel Studio for Academic Creativity, Eastern Kentucky University.

Flipped Classroom

The Flipped Classroom model has emerged from the convergence of the popularity of online video lectures and the increased pressure from educational governing bodies to improve the higher-order skill levels of college and university graduates. Studies show that online video lectures slightly outperform lectures given by faculty in person. There are even better results from online video lectures that are interactive (Cohen, Ebling, & Kulik, 1981; McNeil, 1989; Zhang, Zhou, Briggs, & Nunamaker, 2006). Bishop and Verleger (2013) define the flipped classroom as "an educational technique that consists of two parts: interactive group learning activities inside the classroom, and direct computer-based individual instruction outside the classroom" (p. 5). The activities that take place within the context of the flipped classroom vary depending on the discipline. Because the primary activities inside the spaces are active and problem-based, the space should be designed to support group work as opposed to a lecture-style layout. The furniture in the flipped classroom should provide some level of flexibility as the size and types of groups involved in the activities may vary.

This pedagogical model requires the both analog (marker boards) and digital technologies be supported.

Active Learning Classrooms

Active Learning Classrooms (ALC) are technology enhanced flexible learning spaces designed to accommodate large scale classes. Supported by a high level of technology, the ALCs are designed to facilitate problem-based learning with an emphasis on group activities, peer-to-peer and faculty-student engagement. These spaces have evolved from pioneering work on student-centered learning spaces at the Massachusetts Institute of Technology (MIT) and North Carolina State University. The University of Minnesota has in most recent years become a reference point for a model of the Active Learning Classrooms. The ALCs at the University of Minnesota represent a typical layout planned with large, round tables that seat nine students. Each group of nine can be divided into teams of three for group-based work. Each table is equipped with laptop plug-ins allowing student work to be shared on a dedicated wall-mounted flat-screen monitor or projection screen. The instructor controls the laptops from a centralized unit facilitating the sharing of content from any of the student groups. A team of researchers from the University of Minnesota have been responsible for the most comprehensive research involving experimental controls to evaluate the extent to which these types of formal learning environments affect teaching and learning (Brooks, 2012). The conclusions of their studies have shown a causal relationship between learning spaces; instructor behavior; and student on-task behavior.

Lecture Halls

There has been considerable debate in the past five years around the value of the lecture hall. While there is little doubt that the lecture hall is here to stay, the shift from passive learning to active learning has challenged planners to re-imagine these large-scaled spaces with designs that support the active learning model. New technologies are helping to bridge the gap between the traditional model of the lecture hall and the current expectations to engage the student during that fifty-minute time period. Instructors are incorporating immediate response devices (clickers) into their lectures.

Others are leveraging a multi-media approach to engaging the student. New construction of lecture halls permits the introduction of tiers that are deep enough to accommodate two rows of tables on the same level. This allows the instructor to move seamlessly from lecture to short group assignments with very little disruption. One example of a lecture hall designed for active learning is located in Jordan Hall at the University of Notre Dame (2013) in Southbend, IN. This space consists of two 250 seat auditoriums that each has five seating levels. These technology enhanced spaces include three large 21-by-12-foot screens in the front of each of the rooms and robust wireless capacity allowing the students to actively respond to questions posed by the instructor in real time. Research related to this new typography for lecture halls and its effect on improved learning outcomes is quite limited.

Writing Centers

Writing Centers are spaces that provide resources to students in developing and practicing critical thinking skills, high level communication skills, and information literacy. These informal spaces are typically situated within or near the campus library and serve all disciplines and student cohorts. The Noel Studio for Academic Creativity located at Eastern Kentucky University is an exemplar model for writing centers. This space is located in the Crabbe Library in the center of the campus. The Noel Studio is equipped with a variety of flexible furniture, writing surfaces, and technologies that support students as they:

- Practice and review oral and nonverbal communication using private rooms equipped with recording capabilities.
- Interact with composition and research using touch-screen monitors.
- Brainstorm and map ideas on wall-to-wall and mobile whiteboards.
- Collaborate with peers in both open and private settings.

Researchers at Eastern Kentucky University have noted that there have been improvements in critical thinking skill performance represented in written communication projects. Anecdotally, students have shown an increase in confidence in "identifying the thesis and purpose of their assignment, considering their topic from multiple viewpoints, using the information for their consultation, and employing creativity as a result of the consultation" (Learning Spaces Collaboratory, 2013).

Learning Commons

Learning Commons have most recently been associated with the library. These have evolved in the past ten years from a destination that met the needs for social learning to a multi-faceted hub that meets the just-in-time needs of the student throughout their academic workday. Well planned learning commons provide informal student-owned spaces where students can study or do project work in groups or study alone surrounded by the ambient traffic and noise of fellow students. Located within the Learning Commons, student academic support spaces such as a Center for Academic Success and/or Tutoring services provide students with just-in-time support which is conveniently located and meets the students where they are. Research on the effectiveness of the Learning Commons as it relates to student outcomes has been very difficult to capture. Developing a controlled study in such an informal space is not within the realm of possibilities for most campuses. There is evidence that well planned learning commons do increase the number of visits to the library, increase visits to tutoring sessions and academic support, and increase the level of peer-to-peer academic engagement.

Maker, Hacker, Innovation (MHI) Spaces

MHIs are spaces that are supporting learning in new ways, providing an opportunity for students to learn by working on projects that they are interested in. MHIs are a result of the convergence of the Maker movement, new advances in technologies (students design and develop their own projects), and an interest in developing a culture of innovation across campus. These spaces are student-owned and student managed. Many of the MHIs started in the Engineering discipline but have open access for any student on campus. Opening access to these spaces has created an interest in developing MHIs in more centrally located areas of campus providing greater access and more approachable environments for all students. Reimagining the Library has provided the perfect opportunity for piloting the MHIs. Research on the impact of learning in MHI spaces is in early stages.

CONCLUSION

Learning theories should inform the practice of teaching. The underlying concepts of learning theories, such as connectivism, social constructivism, and active learning all include the interaction of students with the material, the instructor, and other learners. Learning spaces can be leveraged in a variety of ways to support learning. The most ideal learning spaces would be flexible enough to meet a range of desired activities within the space. An ideally designed learning space could be a learning studio in the morning, a lecture space in the afternoon, and a maker space in the evening. There critical factors in ensuring the success of these spaces:

- bring together informed stakeholders, including faculty, students, and administration in the planning and implementation of the space;
- educate faculty and students on the potential uses of the spaces and empower all users to leverage the space and associated technologies;
- create a cycle of assessment and continuous improvement that can be shared with the larger community; and
- connect the learning spaces' functionality to the university's mission and vision.

By combining good pedagogy, flexible and purposeful learning spaces, and the broader mission and goals of the university, we can transform student experiences.

REFERENCES

Bandura, A. (1986). *Social foundations of thought and action: A social-cognitive theory.* Upper Saddle River, NJ: Prentice Hall.

Bishop, J., & Verleger, M. (2013). The flipped classroom: A survey of the research. *Proceedings from the ASEE annual conference & exposition.* ASEE, Atlanta.

Bonwell, C., & Eison, J. (1991). *Active learning: Creating excitement in the classroom.* ASHE-ERIC Higher Education Report. Washington, DC: The George Washington University.

Bransford, J., Brown, A., & Cocking, R. (2000). *How people learn.* Washington, DC: National Academy Press.

Brooks, D. (2012). Space and consequences: The impact of different formal learning spaces on instructor and student behavior. *Journal of Learning Spaces, 1*(2). Retrieved from https://libjournal.uncg.edu/index.php/jls/article/view/285/282

Brown, M. (2005). Learning spaces. In D. Oblinger (Ed.), *Educating the net generation.* Boulder, CO: EDUCAUSE.

Cobb, P. (1994). Theories of mathematical learning and constructivism: A personal view. *Symposium on trends and perspectives in mathematics education.* Klagenfurt: Institute of Mathematics.

Cohen, P., Ebling, B. J., & Kulik, J. (1981). A meta-analysis of outcome studies of visual-based instruction. *Educational Technology Research and Development, 29*(1), 26–36.

Dewey, J., (1980). *Art as experience.* New York, NY: Perigee Books.

Gagne, R. (1985). *The condition of learning*. New York, NY: Holt, Rinehart & Winston.

Kolb, A., & Kolb, D. (2005). Learning styles and learning spaces: Enhancing experiential learning in higher education. *Academy of management learning & education, 4*(2), 193–212.

Kuh, G. D., Kinzie, J., Schuh, J. H., & Whitt, E. J. (2005). *Student success in college: Creating conditions that matter*. San Francisco, CA: Jossey-Bass.

Learning Spaces Collaboratory. (2013). *The LSC guide: Planning for assessing learning spaces*. Washington, DC. Retrieved from http://www.pkallsc.org/assets/files/LSCGuide-Planning forAssessing(1).pdf

McNeil, B. J. (1989). *A meta-analysis of interactive video instruction: A 10 year review of achievement effects*. Moscow, ID: University of Idaho.

Merriam-Webster online. (2013). *Stakeholder*. Merriam-Webster online. Retrieved from http://merriam-webster.com. Accessed on August 20.

Monahan, T. (2002). Flexible space & built pedagogy: Emergent IT embodiments. *Inventio, 4*(1), 1–19.

Narum, J. (2012). *Focusing on the relationship between mission and planning learning spaces*. Retrieved from http://pkallsc.org

Papert, S. (1993). *The children's machine: Rethinking school in the age of the computer*. New York, NY: BasicBooks.

Piaget, J. (1952). In M. Cook (Trans.), *The origins of intelligence in children*. New York, NY: International Universities Press.

Piaget, J. (1973a). *The child and reality: Problems of genetic psychology*. New York, NY: Grossman.

Piaget, J. (1973b). *The Language and thought of a child*. London: Routledge and Kegan Paul.

Piaget, J. (1977). *The grasp of consciousness*. London: Routledge and Kegan Paul.

Rook, M. (2013, April 25). *How learning theory contributes to the design of a learning space*. Innovation Studio. Retrieved from http://innovation.ed.pus.edu/2013/04/how-learning-theory-contributes-to-the-design-of-a-learning-space. Accessed on September 1.

Sawyer, R. K. (Ed.). (2006). *The Cambridge handbook of the learning sciences*. New York, NY: Cambridge University Press.

Siemens, G. (2004). *Connectivism: A learning theory for the digital age*. Retrieved from http://www.elearnspace.org/Articles/connectivism.htm. Accessed on September 25, 2013.

Thornburg, D. (2013). *From the campfire to the holodeck: Creating engaging and powerful 21st century learning environments*. San Francisco, CA: Wiley.

Tinto, V. (1993). *Leaving college: Rethinking the causes and curse of student attrition* (2nd ed.). Chicago, IL: The University of Chicago Press.

University of Notre Dame. (2013). *Twin lecture halls*. University of Notre Dame College of Science. Retrieved from http://science.nd.edu/about/facilities/jordan/twin-lecture-halls/. Accessed on August 22.

Vygotsky, L. (1962). *Thought and language*. Cambridge, MA: MIT Press.

Vygotsky, L. (1978). *Mind in society: The development of the higher psychological processes*. Cambridge, MA: The Harvard University Press (Originally published 1930, New York, NY: Oxford University Press).

Zhang, D., Zhou, L., Briggs, R. O., & Nunamaker, J. F. (2006). Instructional video e-learning: Assessing the impact of interactive video on learning effectiveness. *Information and Management, 43*(1), 15–27.

SECTION V
THE FUTURE OF RESEARCH
IN NEXT GENERATION
LEARNING SPACES

CHAPTER 16

THE FUTURE OF RESEARCH IN NEXT GENERATION LEARNING SPACES

Kym Fraser

ABSTRACT

This chapter looks to the future of research in next generation learning spaces. It begins with a review of the literature and concludes with the implications for future research. The review demonstrates that most 'next generation learning space' research has focused on the design and evaluation of spaces. We know that students like the spaces, but we don't know if the spaces alone are effective in improving student learning or if the spaces in combination with changed pedagogic practices and/or curriculum design improve learning. There are many opportunities for researchers to provide much needed evidence to institutions on the interrelationships between next generation learning spaces design, teaching practices, curriculum design and learning outcomes.

Keywords: Assessment; institutional support; next generation learning space design; pedagogy; research; student outcomes

The Future of Learning and Teaching in Next Generation Learning Spaces
International Perspectives on Higher Education Research, Volume 12, 319–339
Copyright © 2014 by Emerald Group Publishing Limited
All rights of reproduction in any form reserved
ISSN: 1479-3628/doi:10.1108/S1479-362820140000012022

INTRODUCTION

As described in earlier chapters in this volume (Carr & Fraser, 2014; de la Harpe & Mason, 2014; Ling and Fraser, 2014), considerable expenditure has occurred worldwide in the development of next generation learning spaces. Given this investment, it is imperative to explore how these spaces can be designed, used and evaluated to capitalise on pedagogical understandings, digital technologies, student outcomes and sustainable learning designs. In this chapter I review the literature to determine current research about next generation learning spaces.

As the term 'next generation learning space' didn't appear until the latter part of the first decade of this century, and as the terms 'learning spaces' and 'new learning spaces' precede the term, the literature search focused on all three terms. The literature for this review was sourced from the ERIC, Education Research Complete and A + Education (Australian) databases; the Office of Learning and Teaching project report website; a Google search of websites and follow up on references in relevant articles. Over 100 articles, reports and websites were reviewed. The review is structured in terms of three key areas in the next generation learning space literature: the design of learning spaces; the evaluation of learning spaces and pedagogic research in learning spaces. The chapter finishes with a section on the implications of the literature review for future research in next generation learning spaces.

DESIGN OF LEARNING SPACES

Arguably the learning space literature first appeared at the turn of the century and since that time, the vast majority of that literature has been devoted to the design and evaluation of spaces. In the main, this literature identifies strategies, models, approaches, rules, steps, frameworks and principles to underpin the design of spaces. There is much debate in the learning space design literature as to which design principles best underpin the development of new learning spaces, and that debate depends in part on what the spaces are designed to achieve (Brown & Lippincott, 2003; JISC Report, 2006; Johnson & Lomas, 2005; Long & Ehrmann, 2005; Milne, 2006; Oblinger, 2005). Radcliffe, Wilson, Powell, and Tibbetts (2008) are perhaps the most inclusive when suggesting that the factors that underpin experimentation in the design of learning spaces include a shift to more learner centred pedagogy, new technologies, generational change and changes in social patterns and finances.

Very few researchers in this area use a framework to develop their lists/ guiding principles and very little of the research shows explicitly how the principles identified relate to the pedagogic principles and activities that the authors are trying to achieve. Arguably the work is, at best, not constructively aligned (Biggs, 1996) and at worst, atheoretical. Broadly the literature (refer to the Appendix) suggests that when designing a learning space, universities need to:

1. follow a set of *rules* (Johnson & Lomas, 2005; Souter, Riddle, Sellers, & Keppell, 2011) and
2. underpin the development with design *principles* (Johnson & Lomas, 2005; Mitchell et al., 2010; Oblinger, 2006).

Rules

The following rules or steps that institutions need to take when designing next generation learning spaces are drawn from the literature.

1. Identify the institutional context (Johnson & Lomas, 2005).
2. Specify learning principles meaningful to that context (Johnson & Lomas, 2005; Radcliffe et al., 2008).
3. Define the learning activities that support these principles (Johnson & Lomas, 2005; Radcliffe et al., 2008).
4. Develop clearly articulated design principles (Johnson & Lomas, 2005; Mitchell et al., 2010; Radcliffe et al., 2008).
5. Create a set of requirements (Johnson & Lomas, 2005).
6. Determine a methodology for evaluating the space from pre-design through to post occupation (Lee & Tan, 2011).
7. Identify reliable data about how the space will be used (McFarlane & Bailey, 2006).
8. Consult with a wide range of stakeholders including administrative staff, academics, students (undergraduate and postgraduate), and staff in facilities, planning, information technology, library and teaching and learning support (Lee & Tan, 2011; Oblinger, 2005; Radcliffe et al., 2008; Souter et al., 2011).
9. Determine what tensions arise from the differing needs of those who will use the space (Lee & Tan, 2011).

10. Consult with external colleagues who have developed and evaluated spaces (Souter et al., 2011).
11. Withhold 15% of building budget to modify and adjust spaces after construction (Souter et al., 2011).
12. Foster the crucial elements of informal learning such as: comfortable seating; protection from weather; access to power; Wi-Fi; extended hours of access; access to food; lockers and reconfigurable spaces, including lighting and furnishings (Souter et al., 2011).
13. Support students' own technologies and technological preferences (Souter et al., 2011).
14. Develop 'sandpit' or experimental spaces to develop and test proto-types (Souter et al., 2011).

Design Principles

Step 4 in the 'Rules' above requires the development of a clearly articulated set of design principles to guide the project. Many of the authors cited in the 'Rules' section articulate a set of design principles, while not necessarily referring to them by that name. In this chapter I have chosen to report the design principles articulated in the Australian Learning and Teaching Council funded project 'Retrofitting University Spaces' (Mitchell et al., 2010) as this was the most rigorous of the research reviewed in this area. This project team developed their principles based on the work of earlier authors. They also articulated a clear framework for developing the princi-ples, and, uniquely, that framework included not only a pedagogic basis but also a product design basis. This work added a rigour and internal con-sistency to their design principles that was lacking in the design principles espoused by previous research. The Mitchell et al. (2010) design principles also appeared to incorporate virtually all of the principles articulated by previous research.

Mitchell et al. (2010) underpinned their design principles framework with the question-driven Pedagogy-Space-Technology (PST) framework illustrated in Table 1 (Radcliffe et al., 2008). Mitchell et al. (2010) used the PST framework to develop their guidelines for retrofitting learning spaces from each of the three PST perspectives. The authors then collated the guidelines, removing duplication between the three PST perspectives and identified 25 design guidelines for learning spaces. The authors further ana-lysed the guidelines from the perspective of key stakeholders (students,

Table 1. Question[a] Driven Pedagogy-Space-Technology Framework for Developing Learning Spaces.

Focus	Life Cycle Stage	
	Conception and design	Implementation and operation
Overall Pedagogy	What is the motivation for the initiative? What type(s) of learning and teaching are we trying to foster and why?	What does success look like? What type(s) of learning and teaching are observed taking place? What is the evidence?
Space	What aspects of the design of the space and provisioning of furniture and fittings will foster these models of learning and (teaching)?	Which aspects of the space design and equipment worked and which did not? Why?
Technology	How will technology be deployed to complement the space design in fostering the desired learning and teaching patterns?	What technologies were most effective at enhancing learning and teaching? Why?

[a]*Source:* Radcliffe et al. (2008, p. 3). The project report provides an expanded set of detailed questions that can be asked.

teachers and support staff) and overlayed the PST framework with a modified LUCID framework (Kreitzberg, 2008) that comes from the field of product design. The LUCID framework includes engagement, empowerment, ease of use and trust as the key elements in the design of interactive products. This analysis of the 25 guidelines from the perspectives of the two frameworks led to the collapsing of the 25 guidelines to produce eight principles to guide the design of spaces. Next to each principle in Table 2, I have indicated other authors whose work supports the essence of the principle.

The design literature focuses on the rules and principles of designing next generation learning spaces as summarised earlier. The other well developed area in the learning spaces literature is evaluation.

THE EVALUATION OF LEARNING SPACES

As indicated in the introduction, most of the learning space literature focuses on the design and evaluation of spaces. In 2009 the Australian Learning and Teaching Council funded the project 'Evaluating Learning Spaces' which reviewed the evaluation of spaces. This section relies primarily on the findings of that project.

Table 2.   Design Principles That Underpin the Design of Learning Spaces.

	Principles
Engagement	Principle 1: Spaces should support a range of learners and learning activities (Oblinger, 2005; Punie, 2007; Radcliffe et al., 2008; Souter et al., 2011).
	Principle 2: Spaces should provide a quality experience for users (Souter et al., 2011).
Empowerment	Principle 3: Spaces should help foster a sense of emotional and cultural safety (Punie, 2007; Souter et al., 2011).
	Principle 4: Spaces should enable easy access by everyone (Souter et al., 2011).
Ease of use	Principle 5: Spaces should emphasise simplicity of design (Radcliffe et al., 2008).
	Principle 6: Spaces should integrate seamlessly with other physical and virtual spaces (Skill & Young, 2002; Souter et al., 2011).
Confidence	Principle 7: Space should be fit-for-purpose, now and into the future (Punie, 2007).
	Principle 8: Spaces should embed a range of appropriate, reliable and effective technologies (Punie, 2007; Radcliffe et al., 2008).

Source: Adapted from Mitchell et al. (2010, p. 1).
References at the end of each principle have been added to indicate other authors who have discussed these principles.

Lee, Tan, and Tout (2011) identified approximately 100 articles, reports, presentations and books that focussed on the design and evaluation of learning spaces, making the following comments:

- 'In general, these articles appeared to stress the need for more flexible, technology embedded, student-centred spaces' (Lee et al., 2011, p. 3).
- There is '… little empirical evidence on the evaluation of learning spaces' (Lee et al., 2011, p. 3).
- Some researchers such as Milne (2006) and Weaver (2006), '… claim that having student-centred learning spaces will improve student learning outcomes. However, these articles reflected little empirical evidence to support their claims' (Lee et al., 2011, p. 3) (Woolner, Hall, Higgins, McCaughey, & Wall, 2007a; Woolner, Hall, Wall, & Dennison, 2007b).
- It is important to conduct pre-design evaluations as well as post-occupancy evaluations to guide learning space design, encourage '… accountability among stakeholders, encourage end-user input to lessen the risks of unwanted problems, and provide feedback for future developments and improvements' (Lee et al., 2011, p. 3) (Brown & Lippincott, 2003; Harper, Hedberg, Wills, Agostinho, & Oliver, 2002; Leonard, 2007; Radcliffe et al., 2008).

- It is important to involve a range of stakeholders in space design evaluation in order to incorporate pedagogic needs into the design (Dittoe, 2007; Lee, 2007; Lee et al., 2011; Oertel, 2005; Woolner et al., 2007a, 2007b).
- It is important to realise that different stakeholders may hold conflicting interests. (Lee et al., 2011)
- Institutions typically do not fund evaluations as part of their funding for the design of spaces (Lee & Tan, 2011).
- The acoustics of learning spaces is an ongoing problem in spaces where collaborative learning is fostered, in particular with large groups (Lee & Tan, 2011).
- There is a '... lack of longitudinal and comparative research regarding the impact of campus design on learning and teaching practice' (Lee & Tan, 2011, p. 2).
- The sector needs to find proxies for student learning outcomes in order to evaluate the impact of the design of spaces on student outcomes (Lee & Tan, 2011).

The basic message that we can distil from this list of concerns is that when designing spaces, we need to intentionally fund a range of evaluative strategies that involve stakeholders. We also need to use purposeful evaluation to underpin any claims that we wish to make about the *impact* of the spaces on student outcomes and teaching practices.

Lee and Tan (2011) identified the need for, and developed (Fig. 1), a 'baseline development model' to underpin evaluation approaches for the

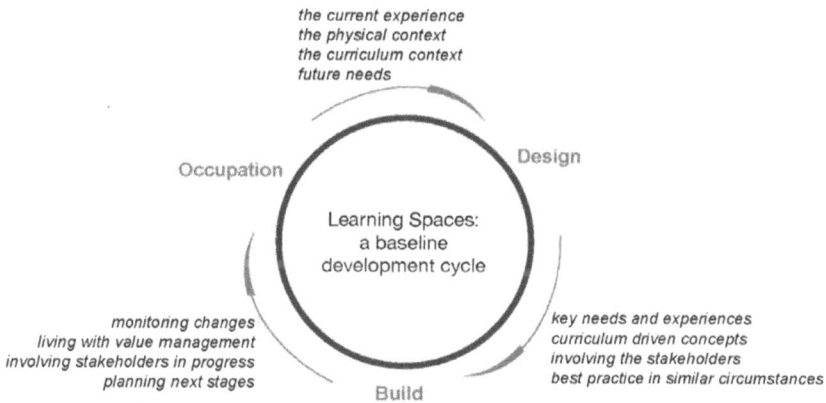

Fig. 1. The 'Evaluating Learning Spaces' Baseline Development Model (Lee & Tan, 2011, p. 5).

design of learning spaces. They used this framework to underpin several quite different space design evaluations in their project. The model allowed for different evaluation approaches to be used to cater for different contexts.

In the baseline development model, Lee and Tan (2011) identified

> three interconnected stages of design, build and occupy, during which particular concerns were likely to be addressed by evaluation. This cycle presupposes a process of evaluation that is similar to that of the action- research cycle. Specifically, that each round of evaluation should inform subsequent stages, and subsequent projects, while taking into account diverse questions and contextual factors. Alongside this cycle, dimensions of stakeholders and needs were to be investigated. (*ibid.*, pp. 4–5)

The Evaluating Learning Spaces project also produced a web based 'toolbox' of evaluation strategies that have been used at universities in Australia and overseas. While many of the evaluation strategies used are relatively traditional (frequency of use, student and teacher satisfaction surveys, focus groups, interviews), non-traditional approaches are also captured, for example 'Milne (2006) suggests using photo surveys with journal entries and surrogate student profiles to elicit brainstorming among stakeholders during workshop sessions' (Lee et al., 2011, p. 3).

Lee and Tan (2011) concluded that there is not an effective 'one size fits all' approach to learning space design; there is '… significant value in providing spaces that are dedicated to particular cohorts' (*ibid.*, p. 13); there is a need for support in order for lecturers to change their teaching practices; and the design of courses needs to take into account that students come to the spaces with different expectations and skill sets.

In light of these comments, I turn now to the literature on pedagogy and facilitating learning in next generation learning spaces.

PEDAGOGY AND FACILITATING LEARNING

Since the development of their '7 Principles of good practice in undergraduate education' (Chickering & Gamson) in 1987, researchers have developed lists of principles for effective teaching/effective learning in higher education (A. Radloff, private communication, 2012; Ramsden, 2003; Van Note Chism, 2002). Principles such as learning being active, connected, interactive/social, reflective and applied (A. Radloff, private communication, 2012), have implications for the design of next generation learning spaces in areas such as the type and arrangement of furniture, the acoustics of the space, the technology used and its accessibility, as well as the type of spaces developed (Radcliffe et al., 2008).

As noted in the introduction Van Note Chism (2002) was one of the first researchers to link learning principles with learning space design arguing that to facilitate connected, active learning in a social context, we need to develop a range of spaces for different activities and cohorts (Van Note Chism, 2002).

Tom, Voss, and Scheetz (2008) argue that the design of learning spaces has been inspired by student-centred learning approaches. Other authors argue that changed spaces change teaching practice (JISC Report, 2006). However Lee and Tan (2011), in their review of the literature, note that there is little evidence that changes in spaces effect long-term change in practice saying that in the literature to date, '... there are no details regarding the interaction of space and teaching practice, curriculum and students' (*ibid.*, p. 12). They go on to argue that the tertiary sector needs to engage in long-term evaluations to determine if a changed space changes teaching practices, perspectives and activities.

In line with Lee and Tan's comments, a search of relevant databases found very little research about pedagogy in new learning spaces in tertiary settings. The dominant tertiary literature is about the design and the evaluation of spaces. Having said that, there is, some literature on changing teaching practices.

Oblinger (2005) was one of the first researchers to connect the design of teaching spaces with pedagogic practice. Her basic argument was that new learning spaces should foster high levels of student-to-student and student-to-staff contact to create opportunities for active and collaborative learning (George, Erwin, & Barnes, 2009). Further research out of the United States in the science disciplines focused on using next generation learning spaces to both change teaching practices and improve student learning outcomes (Beichner et al., 2007; Dori et al., 2003).

The most well-known pedagogic research in tertiary next generation learning spaces comes out of the SCALE-UP project from North Carolina State University (Beichner et al., 2007) and the TEAL project from Massachusetts Institute of Technology (Dori et al., 2003). Both SCALE-UP and TEAL are Physics-based projects which incorporated both space redesign and course redesign, to change classes from teacher dominated lectures to problem solving focused classes where students would be more active and collaborative. These projects demonstrated increased class

attendance, reduced failure rates and improved student conceptual understanding. Walker, Brooks, and Baepler (2011) from the University of
Minnesota, also found that student learning improved when tertiary teachers incorporated more active, student-centred pedagogical approaches
when they moved to new learning spaces. Whiteside, Brooks, and Walker
(2010), also from the University of Minnesota, found that even when
teachers try to be consistent when teaching the same course to students in
traditional and new learning spaces, different learning environments affect
teaching and learning activities.

The TEAL and SCALE-UP projects have been criticised for not excluding confounding factors from their research design (Brooks, 2011). For
example different staff taught students in different ways (traditional vs.
more collaborative) and in different spaces (traditional and new). Brooks
(2011), from the University of Minnesota, in an effort to overcome the confounding factors of the TEAL and SCALE-UP research, conducted a
quasi-experimental study in which the same instructor taught the same curriculum in two different spaces (traditional and new) to two sections of first
year Biology students. He also had each section taught at the same time of
day, but on different days of the week. His research found that the student
group in the new learning space, while as a group having a significantly
lower average American College Testing (ACT) score than the group in the
traditional space, performed at the same level as the group in the traditional space. In effect they outperformed the traditional group (ACT scores
are USA national test results and students take the test before going to
University). In a follow up article Brooks (2012) demonstrates through a
small study of a single course that the type of learning space shapes teacher
and student behaviours.

The extent to which new spaces are an incentive for teachers to change
their practice (to use the technology, to better engage students) is still an
unknown in the tertiary sector. There is little information about how academics use the next generation learning spaces, whether when moving into
these spaces we change our teaching and assessment practices, or whether
we persist with our teaching practices 'in spite of the new spaces'.

School-based research in the United States has shown that school teachers made few changes to their teaching practice when moving into new
spaces (Cuban, 2001). In Australia, in a review of new learning spaces literature in the School sector, Blackmore, Bateman, O'Mara, and Loughlin
(2011) concluded that "...a participatory or "generative design" process
will improve teacher practices which in turn will benefit students' learning
experiences' (p. 8). In effect they argue that significant *professional*

development needs to be provided to school teachers when they were asked to teach in new learning spaces and that the curriculum need to change along with the spaces.

Aligned with the pedagogic research, the only literature that I found that spoke directly to the professional development of tertiary teachers teaching in next generation learning spaces was the 2012 Steel and Andrews chapter. The authors note in the chapter that professional development for teaching in technology rich spaces has received little attention. They propose a model to support professional development in this area. Section III in this book contributes to the literature on the ways in which institutions may support teaching professional learning to effectively teach in next generation learning spaces.

LITERATURE REVIEW IMPLICATIONS FOR FUTURE RESEARCH

The design and the evaluation literature suggest several opportunities for further research in both of these areas. Lee and Tan (2011) in their analysis of the learning space evaluation literature argue for the need for longitudinal and comparative research and for research that provides a richer evaluation by including, if relevant, less traditional evaluation strategies, such as narrative and ethnographic inquiry, and observational studies using video, movement tracking and group activities. They also noted that there is a need to conduct pre-design evaluations and that there is little evidence that learning spaces improve student outcomes. There are considerable opportunities for researchers to trial their 'baseline model' to underpin the design of the evaluation of next generation learning spaces. The PST framework developed by Radcliffe et al. (2008) provides opportunities for research that uses the framework to underpin the design of spaces.

The review of the literature in this chapter has identified many other research gaps to which I will now turn.

Institutional Support

An overarching research question that chapter authors in this book have begun to answer is 'What are effective ways that institutions can support teaching staff to use next generation learning spaces most effectively and with the best student outcomes?' There are many areas of research that fall within that overarching research question, including:

- curriculum design in next generation learning spaces;
- the impact of next generation learning spaces on teacher practice;
- the impact of next generation learning spaces on student learning outcomes;
- the impact of the external, organisational and personal domains on pedagogic practice;
- the effective professional learning support for teaching in next generation learning spaces;
- assessment;
- work integrated learning (WIL);
- internationalisation of the curriculum;
- mobile technology; and
- acoustics.

Each of these areas is discussed below. Two of the discussion points, curriculum and teaching practice, have been combined in the discussion.

The Impact of the External, Organisational and Personal Domains on Pedagogic Practice

Carr and Fraser (2014) identify factors categorised in three domains that influence pedagogic practices in next generation learning spaces. As tertiary schools/departments/institutions work to facilitate changed teaching practices to facilitate improved student outcomes, there is a wealth of opportunity to identify which factors in which domains afford the most effective changes in teaching practice and student outcomes.

Curriculum Design and Teaching Practices

Very few articles discuss in detail changing the curriculum to support the more student-centred learning practices which next generation learning spaces are designed to foster. Exceptions are Beichner et al. (2007), Deslauriers, Schelew and Wieman (2011), Dori et al. (2003), and Walker et al. (2011). There are at least two different types of research projects that would usefully help to fill some of the gaps in this area. One project type would involve documenting a change in curriculum and comparing student outcomes pre and post the use of the next generation learning spaces. The second project type would determine if academics change their practices and curriculum when they move to teach in these spaces.

Another gap in the curriculum literature relates to the development of employability skills in new learning spaces. Next generation learning spaces are designed to foster collaborative learning and as such the opportunities for conducting research on teaching and assessing skills such as team work and communication are manifest.

Student Outcomes

While some articles claim that next generation learning spaces would improve student learning (Oblinger, 2005), most of the research in this area focused on staff and student perceptions and satisfaction with the space, not on student learning outcomes per se. Very little research demonstrated a change in student outcomes with the introduction of the new spaces, with the exception being the study by Brooks (2011). Several studies demonstrated that new learning spaces in combination with a changed curriculum improved Physics student learning outcomes (Beichner et al., 2007; Dori et al., 2003).

There is ample scope for research in different disciplines to compare student outcomes between the same course taught in a next generation learning space and taught in a traditional space, while holding all other variables constant (Brooks, 2011), as best as one can in higher education settings.

Effective Professional Learning Support for Teaching in Next Generation Learning Spaces

The chapters in this book by Hall and Palaskas (2014) and de la Harpe and Mason (2014) have begun to address the dearth of literature in this area. There is still a lot of scope for further research, even in applying the programmes and approaches used in those two chapters to different discipline areas. There is also a desperate need for research which shows a clear link between professional learning, changes in teaching practice and improved student outcomes.

Assessment

While there appears to be very little research to show that next generation learning spaces prompt a change in teaching practice, there appears to be no research that has studied whether academics change their assessment practices when moving to teach in next generation learning spaces. Arguably, while academics may change their curriculum to encourage student collaboration and the use of technology, anecdotally students are then assessed by very traditional means that may not necessarily assess the skills and knowledge that the curriculum fosters. A study comparing assessment practices pre and post next generation learning space occupation would advance the literature in this area.

Another piece of research that would be useful for the sector would be the identification of assessment practices that assessed the types of student-centred learning that next generation learning spaces are designed to foster: active, collaborative and peer-based approaches to learning that use the technology available in these spaces.

WIL

WIL experiences cover a large range of educational opportunities, from class based case studies and simulations to work place and community based learning opportunities. Next generation learning spaces expand the possibilities for class-based WIL. For example, students can access remotely located databases and industry specialists as they work on complex and authentic cases and problems, or be involved in crowd sourced science experiments.

The development of WIL experiences in next generation learning spaces provides an opportunity of teaching staff to conduct research into the impact that different types of WIL experiences have on things like student perceptions of their employability, industry and community engagement and student outcomes.

Internationalisation of the Curriculum

There appears to be no literature on internationalising the curriculum through the use of new learning spaces. Research in this domain could involve colleagues from the one university who teach on national and overseas campuses, or cross institutional research between academics in different countries who teach the same courses. Pedagogic research that could be carried out includes:

- comparative studies of the same course taught in next generation learning spaces at Australian and overseas campuses;
- studying the impact on student outcomes by incorporating opportunities for students to work with overseas students through next generation learning spaces; and
- projects that incorporate into courses literature from non-Western countries.

Mobile Technology
Technology is always in transition and as such, the key lesson learnt from the literature is the importance of future proofing spaces in terms of the technology used in the space. In part, recent approaches to do this have focused on using technology that students bring to the spaces (laptops, phone, tablets). There is therefore, some scope to conduct research into the use of mobile technology in next generation learning spaces to facilitate student learning outcomes. As such it may be useful for teaching staff to work with IT staff to research the impact of using mobile technologies on student outcomes.

Acoustics
There is also an opportunity for academics to work with industry to improve the acoustics in large spaces in which many students work collaboratively. There may also be an opportunity to work further with other industries in the design of furniture, technology and buildings. There is, therefore, potential for academics to work with architects, furniture providers, acoustics providers and property developers along with property services groups, to research the design of learning spaces.

CONCLUSION

In light of the considerable expenditure worldwide in the development of next generation learning spaces, it is imperative that we determine the effectiveness of these spaces to support excellent teaching practices and successful student outcomes. It speaks poorly for the sector that a decade plus after the appearance of quite different learning spaces, we can say in very few cases and discipline areas that they afford improved learning outcomes for students. We know that students like the spaces, but we don't know if the spaces alone are effective in improving student learning or if the spaces in combination with changed pedagogic practices and/or curriculum design improve learning. There are many opportunities for researchers to provide much needed evidence to institutions on the interrelationships between next generation learning spaces design, teaching practices, curriculum design and learning outcomes.

REFERENCES

American Association for Higher Education, American College Personnel Association, and National Association of Student Personnel Administrators. (1998). Learning principles and collaborative action. In S. Engelkemeyer & S. Brown (Eds.), *Powerful partnerships: A shared responsibility for learning* (Vol. 51, pp. 10–12). Washington, DC: AAHE Bulletin.

Beichner, R., Saul, J., Abbott, D., Morse, J., Deardorff, D., & Allain, R. (2007). Student-centred activities for large enrollment undergraduate programs (SCALE-UP) project. In E. Redish & P. Cooney (Eds.), *Research-based reform of university physics* (pp. 1−42). College Park, MD: American Association of Physics Teachers.

Biggs, J. (1996). Teaching through constructive alignment. *Higher Education, 32*(3), 347−364.

Blackmore, J., Bateman, D., O'Mara, J., & Loughlin, J. (2011). *Research into the connection between built learning spaces and student outcomes.* Literature Review. Retrieved from http://www.deakin.edu.au/arts-ed/efi/pubs/deecd-reports-blackmore-learning-spaces.pdf

Brooks, D. (2011). Space matters: The impact of formal learning environments on student learning. *British Journal of Educational Technology, 42*(5), 719−726.

Brooks, D. (2012). Space and consequences: The impact of different formal learning spaces on instructor and student behavior. *Journal of Learning Spaces, 1*(2). Retrieved from http://libjournal.uncg.edu/ojs/index.php/jls/article/view/285/282

Brown, M., & Lippincott, J. (2003). Learning spaces: More than meets the eye. *EDUCAUSE Quarterly, 26*(1), 3.

Carr, N., & Fraser, K. (2014). Factors that shape pedagogical practices in next generation learning spaces. In K. Fraser (Ed.), *The future of learning and teaching in next generation learning spaces* (Vol. 12). International Perspectives on Higher Education Research. Bingley, UK: Emerald.

Chickering, A., & Gamson, Z. (1987). Seven principles for good practice in undergraduate education. *American Association of Higher Education Bulletin, 39*(7), 3−7.

Cuban, L. (2001). *Oversold and underused: Computers in the classroom.* Cambridge, MA: Harvard University Press.

de la Harpe, B., & Mason, T. (2014). A new approach to professional learning for academics teaching in next generation learning spaces. In K. Fraser (Ed.), *The future of learning and teaching in next generation learning spaces* (Vol. 12). International Perspectives on Higher Education Research. Bingley, UK: Emerald.

Deslauriers, L., Schelew, E., & Wieman, C. (2011). Improved learning in a large-enrollment physics class. *Science, 332,* 862−864.

Dittoe, W. (2007). Learning spaces and student success. Retrieved from http://www.canfieldco.com/uploads/Learning_Spaces_and_Student_Success.pdf

Dori, Y., Belcher, J., Besette, M., Danziger, M., McKinney, A., & Hult, E. (2003). Technology for active learning. *Materials Today, 6,* 44−49.

George, G., Erwin, T., & Barnes, B. (2009). Learning spaces as a strategic priority. *EDUCAUSE Quarterly, 32,* 1.

Hall, C., & Palaskas, T. (2014). Transition to next generation learning spaces. In K. Fraser (Ed.), *The future of learning and teaching in next generation learning spaces.* International Perspectives on Higher Education Research (Vol. 12). Bingley, UK: Emerald Group Publishing Limited.

Harper, B., Hedberg, J., Wills, S., Agostinho, S., & Oliver, R. (2002). Formalising the description of learning designs. *Proceedings of the 2002 annual international conference of the Higher Education Research and Development Society of Australasia* (pp. 496−504). HERDSA ACT, Australia.

JISC Report. (2006). *Designing spaces for effective learning.* London: JISC. Retrieved from http://www.jisc.ac.uk/publications/programmerelated/2006/pub_spaces.aspx

Johnson, C., & Lomas, C. (2005). Design of the learning space: Learning and design principles. *EDUCAUSE Review. 40*(4), 16−28.

Kreitzberg, C. (2008). *The LUCID framework: An introduction.* Princeton Junction, NJ: Cognetics Corporation.

Lee, N. (2007). You want me to do what? Implementing professionally-focused, project-based learning across disciplines. Paper presented at the Higher Education Academy annual conference. Harrogate.

Lee, N., & Tan, S. (2011). *A comprehensive learning space evaluation model.* Final report. Australian Learning and Teaching Council Ltd., Sydney. Retrieved from http://www.swinburne.edu.au/spl/learningspacesproject/

Lee, N., Tan, S., & Tout, D. (2011). Evaluating learning spaces literature review. Sydney: Australian Learning and Teaching Council Ltd. Retrieved from http://www.swinburne.edu.au/spl/learningspacesproject/

Leonard, R. (2007). Spaces for learning, *Architecture Australia.* Retrieved from http://architectureau.com/articles/spaces-for-learning/. Accessed on April 16, 2013.

Ling, P., & Fraser, K. (2014). Pedagogies for next generation learning spaces: Theory, context, action. In K. Fraser (Ed.), *The future of learning and teaching in next generation learning spaces* (Vol. 12). International Perspectives on Higher Education Research. Bingley, UK: Emerald.

Long, P., & Ehrmann, S. (2005). Future of the learning space: Breaking out of the box. *EDUCAUSE Review, 40*(4), 43–58.

McFarlane, A., & Bailey, J. (2006). NUCLEUS project, teaching and learning space group final report. Bristol University.

Milne, A. (2006). Designing blended learning space to the student experience. In D. Oblinger (Ed.), *Learning Spaces.* Washington, DC: EDUCAUSE.

Mitchell, G., White, B., Pospisil, R., Kiley, S., Liu, C., & Matthews, G. (2010). *Retrofitting University learning spaces.* Final report. Support for the original work was provided by the Australian Learning and Teaching Council Ltd. An initiative of the Australian Government. Retrieved from http://learnline.cdu.edu.au/retrofittingunispaces/index.html

Oblinger, D. (2005). Leading the transition from classrooms to learning spaces. *EDUCAUSE Quarterly, 1,* 14–18.

Oblinger, D. (2006). Space as change agent. In D. Oblinger (Ed.), *Learning spaces.* Washington, DC: EDUCAUSE. Retrieved from www.educause.edu/learningspaces

Oertel, L. (2005). Quality framework for school evaluation and consequences for school design and assessment. Evaluating quality in education facilities (pp. 60–67). Retrieved from http://www.oecd.org/education/country-studies/37905267.pdf

Punie, Y. (2007). Learning spaces: An ICT-enabled model of future learning in the knowledge-based society. *European Journal of Education, 42*(2), 14.

Radcliffe, D., Wilson, H., Powell, D., & Tibbetts, B. (2008). *Designing next generation places of learning: Collaboration at the pedagogy-space-technology nexus.* Sydney: The Australian Learning and Teaching Council Ltd. Retrieved from http://www.olt.gov.au/resource-designing-next-generation-places-of-learning-uq-2008

Ramsden, P. (2003). *Learning to teach in higher education.* London: Routledge Falmer.

Skill, T., & Young, B. (2002). Embracing the hybrid model: Working at the intersections of virtual and physical learning spaces. *New Directions for Teaching and Learning, 92,* 23–32.

Souter, K., Riddle, M., Sellers, W., & Keppell, M. (2011). *The spaces for knowledge generation.* Final report. The Australian Learning and Teaching Council Ltd. An initiative of the Australian Government. Retrieved from http://www.olt.gov.au/search/apachesolr_search/the%20spaces%20for%20knowledge%20generation

Steel, C., & Andrews, T. (2012). Re-imagining teaching for technology-enriched learning spaces: An academic development model. In M. Keppell, K. Souter, & M. Riddle (Eds.), *Physical and virtual learning spaces in higher education.* Herschey, PA: Information Science Reference.

The Evaluating Learning Spaces Toolbox of Evaluation Strategies. Retrieved from http://www.swinburne.edu.au/spl/learningspacesproject/database/index.html

Tom, J., Voss, K., & Scheetz, C. (2008). The space is the message: First assessment of a learning studio. *EDUCAUSE Quarterly, 31*(2), 14.

Van Note Chism, N. (2002). A tale of two classrooms. *New Directions for Teaching and Learning, 92,* 5−12.

Walker, J., Brooks, D., & Baepler, P. (2011). Pedagogy and space: Empirical research on new learning environments. *EDUCAUSE Quarterly, 34*(4). Retrieved from http://www.educause.edu/ero/article/pedagogy-and-space-empirical-research-new-learning-environments

Weaver, M. (2006). Exploring conceptions of learning and teaching through the creation of flexible learning spaces: The learning gateway − A case study. *New Review of Academic Librarianship, 12*(2), 14.

Whiteside, A., Brooks, D., & Walker, J. (2010). Making the case for space: Three years of empirical research on learning environments. *EDUCAUSE Quarterly, 33*(3), 1−8.

Woolner, P., Hall, E., Higgins, S., McCaughey, C., & Wall, K. (2007a). A sound foundation? What we know about the impact of environments on learning and the implications for building schools for the future. *Oxford Review of Education, 33*(1), 47−70.

Woolner, P., Hall, E., Wall, K., & Dennison, D. (2007b). Getting together to improve the school environment: User consultation, participatory design and student voice. *Improving Schools, 10*(3), 233−248.

APPENDIX: RULES AND PRINCIPLES OF LEARNING SPACE DESIGN IDENTIFIED IN KEY LEARNING SPACE LITERATURE BETWEEN 2005 AND 2011.

Johnson and Lomas (2005)	Oblinger (2005)	Oblinger (2006)	Long and Ehrmann (2005)	JISC Report (2006)	Punie (2007)
Steps to design a space:	Spaces need to be:	Factors to consider for space design:	Spaces should be:	Spaces should be:	Learning spaces are:
(1) Identify the institutional context	Designed around people	Analysis and data gathering of existing space to curricular reform. Disciplinary needs differ from each other	Designed for people not ephemeral technologies	Flexible	Connecting social spaces
(2) Specify learning principles meaningful to that context	Support multiple types of learning activities	External benchmarking	Optimised for certain learning activities, not just stuffed with technology	Future proofed	Personal digital spaces
(3) Define the learning activities that support these principle	Enable connections internally and externally	Learning modes: such as purpose of learning. Existing space use: understand how current spaces are being used	Emphasise soft spaces	Bold	Trusted spaces
(4) Develop clearly articulated design principles	Accommodate information technology	Gap analysis: current versus emerging pedagogy practices	Useful 24 hours a day	Creative	Pleasant and emotional spaces
(5) Create a set of requirements	Designed for comfort	Curricular reform	Zoned for sound and activity	Supportive	Blur boundaries between function specific rooms
(6) Determine a methodology for assessing success.	Reflect institutional values	The team: various stakeholders	Enable technologies brought into the space not technologies built into the space	Enterprising	Creative, flexible spaces
			Allow invisible technology and flexible use		Open and reflexive spaces
					Knowledge management systems

Appendix. (*Continued*)

George et al. (2009)	Radcliffe et al. (2008)	Mitchell et al. (2010)	Souter et al. (2011)	Souter et al. (2011)
Preliminary survey to inform the design of learning spaces should measure:		Spaces should:	Design rules	Design principles
Basic human needs (comfort, convenience, support for the learner).	Pedagogies	Engagement principles Principle 1: Spaces should support a range of learners and learning activities. Principle 2: Spaces should provide a quality experience for users.	Withhold 15% of building budget to modify and adjust spaces after construction	*Comfort*: a space which creates a physical and mental sense of ease and well-being
Teaching (method, technology and tools, flexibility, effectiveness).	Space	Empowerment principles Principle 3: Spaces should help foster a sense of emotional and cultural safety. Principle 4: Spaces should enable easy access by everyone.	Learning space designs must be context-specific	*Aesthetics*: pleasure which includes the recognition of symmetry, harmony, simplicity and fitness for purpose
Learning (style, technology and tools, flexibility, effectiveness).	Technology	Ease of use principles Principle 5: Spaces should emphasise simplicity of design. Principle 6: Spaces should integrate seamlessly with other physical and virtual spaces.	Spaces should be 'future proofed' and non-deterministic: that is should incorporate maximum adaptability and not be unduly dependent on current technology	*Flow*: the state of mind felt by the learner when totally involved in the learning experience
Engagement (communication, collaboration, interaction, sense of community).		Confidence principles Principle 7: Space should be fit-for-purpose, now and into the future. Principle 8: Spaces should embed a range of appropriate, reliable and effective technologies.	Students' own technologies and technological preferences should be supported	*Equity*: consideration of the needs of cultural and physical differences

The importance of student-driven design: generally speaking this is not done well, and we should be seeking student input	*Blending*: a mixture of technological and face-to-face pedagogical resources
The crucial elements of informal learning: comfortable seating; protection from weather; access to power; Wi-Fi; extended hours of access; access to food; lockers; and reconfigurable spaces, including lighting and furnishings	*Affordances*: the 'action possibilities' the learning environment provides users, including such things as kitchens, natural light, Wi-Fi, private spaces, writing surfaces, sofas
The need for a systematic way to design informal learning	*Repurposing*: the 'potential for multiple usage of a space' (*ibid.*, p. 22)
'Sandpit' or experimental spaces should be used to develop and test prototype designs. This also supports the professional development of teaching staff	
Desperate need for a range of spaces to support (formal) active learning (*ibid.*, p. 20)	

ABOUT THE AUTHORS

Amanda Achterberg (Bachelor of Applied Science (Physical Education) Graduate Certificate in Vocational Education and Training; Master of Education) started her educational career in a private secondary college in the west of Melbourne as a physical education teacher. She then extended her educational expertise into the Vocational Education and Training Sector working as an Education Manager in a private registered training organisation. Amanda's journey continued into the tertiary sector at Victoria University as a Course Coordinator, she then progressed to the Manager of Quality. In 2011, she returned to a Faculty role leading and developing teachers as the Associate Dean of Teaching and Learning. In this role she developed the Teaching Staff Capability Framework, introduced the Faculty to the 'Flipped Learning' blended delivery model and worked to design and develop new collaborative learning spaces for staff to utilise. In the role as the Senior Advisor (Educational Innovation), her key responsibilities were to drive innovation in learning and teaching, establish external partnerships and build staff capability across the University. She has recently taken on the challenging role of Director, Vocational Education (Quality) at Victoria University.

Nicola Carr (PhD, M Ed, Grad Cert Tertiary Teaching & Learning, Post Grad Dip Ed Studies, B. Comm (Hons)) has been involved in research about the integration of digital technologies into learning and teaching in the school and higher education sectors for over a decade. Her recent work has focused on the development of transformative pedagogies that integrate digital technologies and the factors that influence these practices. Nicola is a teacher and researcher at RMIT University's School of Education who prefers to teach in next generation learning spaces where she can explore her own transformative pedagogical practices.

Geoffrey T. Crisp is Dean, Learning and Teaching at RMIT University. Prior to taking up this appointment, Geoff was Director of the Centre for Learning and Professional Development at The University of Adelaide. Geoff completed BSc (Hons) at the University of Queensland in 1977 and PhD in chemistry from the Australian National University in 1981. Geoff lectured in chemistry at the University of Melbourne and the University of Adelaide for 18 years, then moved into online education and academic development. Geoff received the University of Adelaide Stephen Cole the Elder Award for Excellence in Teaching (1999), the RACI South Australian Branch Stranks Medal for Outstanding Achievement in the field of Chemical Education (2003), a Carrick Associate Fellowship (2006) and an ALTC National Fellowship (2009) and is a HERDSA and ASCILITE Fellow. His areas of expertise are leadership in learning and teaching, enhancing academic practice and e-assessment.

Jo Dane (BA [Interior Design], Graduate Certificate of Higher Education, PhD Candidate) is a designer, educator and researcher with a passion for educational transformation enabled through research-based design practice. She has been researching education theory and learning environments for over 12 years, with a particular interest in developing new space typologies for effective learning in higher education. As an academic and designer, Jo demonstrates an understanding of teaching and learning behaviours that integrally informs the design process.

Jo works as an educational planner with global architectural firm, Woods Bagot, focusing exclusively on education projects. Consulting activities include masterplanning, education accommodation scheduling, designing new generation learning spaces, libraries and student hubs, post occupancy evaluations, and academic workshops. Jo also follows educational trends forecast for the future and considers how their implementation will impact on the design of physical and digital campus environments.

Barbara de la Harpe has been involved in the education sector for over 20 years holding a number of senior leadership positions. Her most recent role is Executive Dean of the Faculty of Business, Education, Law and Arts at The University of Southern Queensland. Prior to this role, Barbara has been Acting Pro Vice Chancellor and Vice President at RMIT's College of Design and Social Context. With an extensive teaching, research and publication record and the winner of numerous national funding grants, Barbara has been acknowledged by the Higher Education Research and Development Society of Australasia (HERDSA) as a leader in the field of Higher Education curriculum and pedagogy. Barbara's contribution has been recognised also through numerous awards including the Walter D Neal Medal for Excellence in Research, an Australian College of Education Prize for Excellence in Teaching and a Citation for Outstanding Contribution to Student Learning.

Marcia Devlin is the Deputy Vice Chancellor (Learning and Quality) at Federation University, Australia. Professor Devlin is a nationally and internationally recognised expert in tertiary education. Areas of particular expertise and interest include quality, equity, leadership, teaching and learning, student engagement and digital education. Her research incorporates both theoretical and practical investigations into contemporary tertiary education, policy, e-pedagogy and curriculum. She holds an Australian Research Council grant on international student policy and recently led to completion an Office of Learning and Teaching-funded national research project on effective teaching and support of students from low socioeconomic status backgrounds. Professor Devlin is the member of numerous Editorial and Advisory Boards and is frequently invited to deliver national and international keynote addresses, workshops and seminars. As the author and co-author of hundreds of reports, articles and papers, Professor Devlin writes frequently on higher education issues for the print and online media.

Rebecca England is an Information Technology Lecturer in the School of Engineering & Information Technology at Charles Darwin University (CDU) where she has been a faculty member since 2008. Her areas of specialisation are software development and web development. She has a Computer Science degree from CDU and a Masters in Information Technology from Queensland University of Technology.

Research interests include mobile application development and the integration of mobile devices into learning environments. Closely associated with these is the investigation into successful assimilations of technology and learning generally, and especially that of mobile technologies in New Generation Learning Spaces. Rebecca is currently involved in a faculty program that is investigating 'flipping' the classroom and has included an early level programming class in the project.

Kym Fraser (B Ed (Honours), MSc, PhD), is the Associate Director of the Continuing Education Development team in the Centre for Collaborative Learning and Teaching at Victoria University. She has worked for over 20 years in the tertiary education sector in Australia, the United Kingdom, Hong Kong, and the United States of America. She edited the book "Education Development and Leadership in Higher Education," has been a past editor of the HERDSA Green and Gold Guide Series and is the author of "Studying for Continuing Professional Development in Health" and "Student Centred Teaching." Kym is currently leading the OLT funded project "A Creativity Skills MOOC for Australian Coursework Masters

Students." Her research interests include: changing pedagogies in next generation learning spaces; the impact of graduate certificates in tertiary education and tertiary teaching induction programs on student learning; and developing academic development research cultures.

Lisa Germany (BSc (Hons), GradDipSciComm, PhD) is the Associate Director of Blended Learning in the Centre for Collaborative Learning and Teaching at Victoria University. She works extensively with the ITS and Facilities departments at the University and is responsible for the day-to-day business ownership of educational technologies and learning spaces – ensuring they are fit-for-purpose and approached from an education perspective. She is currently involved in the design of learning spaces for three new building projects and is rolling out a full-life-cycle evaluation methodology for learning spaces across Victoria University.

Roger Hadgraft (BE (Hons), MEngSc, DipComSc, PhD, FIEAust), is a civil engineer with more than 20 years involvement in leading program renewal in engineering education, with a particular focus on problem/project-based learning (PBL) supported by educational technology, at RMIT, Monash and Melbourne Universities. He is an Australian Learning and Teaching Council Discipline Scholar in Engineering and ICT, having co-developed the draft national academic standards for the discipline (the Threshold Learning Outcomes). He recently led a new Bachelor of Sustainable Systems Engineering at RMIT and was the Foundation Director for the Science, Health and Engineering Education Research (SHEER) Centre at RMIT. He is currently Deputy Dean, Learning and Teaching in the School of Engineering and Technology at CQ University.

Cathy Hall-van den Elsen (BA (hons), MA, PhD, Grad Dip Tertiary Teaching and Learning) is the Senior Manager of the Academic Development Group at RMIT University's College of Business. Dr Hall has taught in the field of international higher education programs for 10 years and has worked in academic development for tertiary educators for 5 years. She has led project teams to design and implement innovations in teaching and learning, including the development of guides and handbooks for academic staff in multiple locations and learning environments. In 2012 Dr Hall designed and coordinated a project to support a transition in the teaching and learning approaches of more than 600 faculty and 6000 students when they moved from a traditional building to RMIT's state of the art Swanston Academic Building, characterised by Next Generation Learning Spaces.

Mike Keppell (PhD (Calgary); M Ed (Calgary), B Ed(PG) (Qld), BHMS (Ed) (Qld)), is Executive Director and Professor, Australian Digital Futures Institute http://www.usq.edu.au/adfi/ at University of Southern Queensland and Director of the Digital Futures Collaborative Research Network http://www.usq.edu.au/digital-crn (DF-CRN) a research partnership with Australian National University (ANU) and University of South Australia (UniSA). The DF-CRN involves over 90 academic researchers. Mike is also Project Director, Regional Universities Network (RUN) Maths and Science Digital Classroom project and Project Director, Aged Care Community, Education, Research and Training Program (ACCERT) as well as Project Director of the HEPPP project: Making the connection: Improving access to higher education for low socio-economic status students with ICT limitations. He is also co-leader of the Network of Australasian Tertiary Associations (NATA) which has a vision to facilitate a sustainable collaborative network between established higher education associations (ACODE, ascilite, CADAD, HERDSA, ODLAA). Mike has a long professional history in higher education in Australia, Canada and Hong Kong and has worked at five universities. His research focuses on digital futures, learning spaces, blended learning, learning-oriented assessment, authentic learning and transformative learning using design-based research. See http://nataonthenet.blogspot.com.au/ Mike currently leads and manages projects worth over 12 million dollars.

Helen Larkin (M App Sc (Research), B App Sc (OT), Grad Dip Health Admin, Grad Cert Higher Ed) is a Senior Lecturer and Teaching and Learning Coordinator in the School of Health and Social Development at Deakin University and brings over 30 years of clinical, management and research experience to her teaching. Helen's specific research interests are based around the scholarship of teaching and learning; specifically curriculum development and review, reflective practice, work integrated learning and inter-professional education, particularly in the area of universal design practice. Helen has received recognition for her teaching through a number of awards at both University level and nationally including a 2011 Australian Learning and Teaching Council Citation for Outstanding Contribution to Student Learning and in 2013 she received an Award for Teaching Excellence from the Office for Learning and Teaching.

Peter Ling is Adjunct Associate Professor at Swinburne University, Melbourne, Australia. Peter has headed academic development units at RMIT University and Swinburne University. Peter was principal researcher in several national projects including: The development of academics and higher education futures, Australian Learning and Teaching Council, 2012, and project officer for Learning Without Borders, Enhancing Leadership in Transnational Education, Office for Learning and Teaching, 2013. Peter has acted as evaluator for several national projects including Evaluation of Learning Spaces, 2010, an Australian Learning and Teaching Council project. Peter authored "From a community of scholars to a company" in K. Fraser (Ed.), Education development and leadership in higher education, 2004; and co-authored Delivering digitally: Managing the transition to knowledge media, 2002. Peter has been co-editor of issues of Higher Education Research and Development and Innovative Higher Education. Peter holds a B Com, B Ed, M Ed, and PhD from the University of Melbourne.

Thembi Mason is a Senior Advisor, Learning and Teaching in the Design and Social Context College at RMIT, currently working closely with the School of Education. Thembi's background and experience is in the area of learning and teaching with a specialisation in using educational technologies and blended learning. Thembi has worked across all educational sectors, including secondary school education, adult education, VET, and Higher Education. She has worked in Education and Multimedia since 2001. Thembi has also worked on a number of learning and teaching projects including an Australian Government Office for Learning and Teaching funded project which investigated professional development approaches for New Generation Learning Spaces. Thembi is undertaking her PhD in the area of learning and teaching leadership.

Anastasia Morrone is the Associate Vice President for learning technologies and provides leadership in several important campus and university-wide initiatives that are designed to create a rich learning environment that will help promote the transformation of teaching and learning through the innovative use of technology. As Dean of IT (IUPUI), Morrone works closely with the chancellor's office, the executive vice chancellor, faculty council representatives, and other deans, providing leadership and direction on campus IT issues. As an Associate Professor of Educational Psychology, her research interests center around innovative learning environments that enable new ways of teaching. In addition, she remains deeply committed to new models for professional development that are designed to meet the needs of today's faculty, staff and students. Morrone has a PhD degree in Educational Psychology from the University of Texas at Austin and a Bachelor of Science degree in Technical Communication from the University of Minnesota.

Claire Nihill (B Arts (Hons), M Arts (Literary Studies)) has been in the equity and diversity space within Higher Education in Australia for the past 10 years. She has been working as an equity practitioner, supporting students with disability, and students with a refugee and/or asylum seeker background with direct support, to feel included and part of university life. Her current research interests include inclusive practice and accessibility for students within the curriculum. She has recently been the senior project officer on a Higher Education Participation and Partnership project (HEPPP) around inclusive practice and learning at Deakin University, Victoria. With a background in education, she is currently completing her PhD in creative arts and is interested in embedding inclusive practice within curriculum, professional development and learning.

Tom Palaskas is a Senior Advisor, Academic Development at RMIT University's College of Business. His career focus has been on the design of learning events that foster and support student engagement in blended and fully online modes, the application of educational technology and the exploration of teaching in Next Generation Learning Space (NGLS) contexts. He has applied his extensive experience in these areas working in higher education and training settings in Libya, Papua New Guinea, Indonesia, Thailand, the United Arab Emirates and Australia.

Leon van Schaik (AO, B Arch Studies (Ncle), AADip (SADG), M Arch (UCT), PhD (CNAA), RIBA, LFAIA, LFAA), is Professor of Architecture with an Innovation Chair in Design Practice Research at RMIT University. A writer and academic with research interests focusing on spatial thinking, the poetics of architecture, urban design and the processes involved in procuring innovative architecture, Professor van Schaik has been responsible for promoting a dynamic culture of architectural innovation through practice-based research. He supports local and international architectural culture through design practice research and significantly his leadership in the procurement of exemplary architecture through his role at RMIT, resulting in some of Melbourne's most distinguished contemporary buildings which have had a profound impact on architectural discourse and practice in the city over the past two decades.

Rhona Sharpe is Head of the Oxford Centre for Staff and Learning Development. Her degree and PhD in psychology originally led her to lecturing position at the University of Plymouth. However, since then she has worked as an educational developer in higher education for 20 years. She now leads a team at Oxford Brookes University, who run workshops, online courses, and offer consultancy for higher education institutions across the United Kingdom and internationally. She is also Associate Lecturer for the Institute of Educational Technology at the UK Open University at the weekends. Rhona's interest in the role of technology in learning led her to direct a number of high profile and nationally regarded learner experience projects, which culminated in the creation of the ELESIG community. She is a Senior Fellow of the Staff and Educational Development Association, a Fellow of the Higher Education Academy and a National Teaching Fellow.

Jennifer Sparrow is currently the Senior Director of Networked Ventures and Emerging Technologies at Virginia Tech. For more than 15 years, she has championed the use of technology to engage students in the learning process. She has a passion for working with faculty to explore new technologies and their potential implementations in teaching and learning. Her current projects involve the convergence of technologies and learning spaces to create interactive and engaged learning opportunities. Jennifer's conversations around technology focus on increasing digital fluency for students, faculty, and life-long learners.

Jennifer received her bachelor's degree from Smith College, her master's degree from Florida Gulf Coast University, and doctorate from the University of Central Florida. She is the winner of the 2013 EDUCAUSE Rising Star Award. She is a part-time blogger, an infrequent tweeter, technology explorer, and struggling photographer with a biting sense of humor and not enough hours in her day.

Barbara White is currently Senior Lecturer in Information Technology at Charles Darwin University specialising in human computer interaction and learning. She is also Associate Dean Learning and Teaching in the Faculty of Engineering, Health, Science and the Environment. Her recent PhD research investigates how the materiality of Next Generation Learning spaces shapes the educational practices of students and lecturers. With a long term interest in how technology can enable rich interactive learning, Barbara has been awarded a number of university teaching awards locally and nationally and has been the recipient of three ASCILITE awards for educational software (multimedia and web). Her interest in learning space research began in 2003 with a Hewlett Packard University grant of first generation tablet PC computers when current university spaces did not readily facilitate embedding these technologies. She recently completed an ALTC learning space project with partners at Queensland University of Technology and Edith Cowan University.

Susan Whitmer Herman Miller's Lead Researcher – Education, has spent more than 25 years with Herman Miller immersed in research. Whitmer is currently tasked with studying the trends, challenges, and opportunities that will impact the future of the learning experience. She conducts field research and gathers data from students, teachers, and administrators— information Herman Miller uses to inform thought leadership and the development of new education solutions.

Whitmer earned a degree in design from Ringling College of Art and Design. She has a Master of Business Administration from Brenau University and a Master of Science in Accessibility and Inclusive Design from the University of Salford in the United Kingdom. Whitmer has written numerous white papers and co-authored several articles on learning spaces, including peer-reviewed papers for Open House International and the National Collegiate Inventors and Innovators Alliance 2011 conference and the Society of College and University Planners.

Greg Williams is a Senior Lecturer and Associate Head of School of the School of Indigenous Knowledges and Public Policy in the new Australian Centre for Indigenous Knowledges and Education at Charles Darwin University. He has worked as a lecturer affiliated with Charles Darwin University (CDU) for over 20 years both in Vocational Education and Training and Higher Education. With a background in science education, his interests lie in exploring appropriate pedagogies in inter-cultural contexts, particularly for Indigenous people learning in the field of natural and cultural resource management, and issues related to knowledge-making in inter-cultural contexts. Involvement with the ALTC learning spaces project has been an important opportunity to investigate the way in which appropriate Indigenous pedagogies and knowledge-making intersects with our understanding of 21st Century learning spaces and digital technologies.

Sue B. Workman, Associate Vice President for client services and support at Indiana University, provides university-wide leadership for the development and management of resources to enhance the use of information technology in teaching and learning and for the support of technology used by all members of the Indiana University community. Workman sets the vision for the client virtualization model for the university and for the development and adaptation of IT services to meet the changing needs of faculty, students, and staff. She establishes external vendor relationships and negotiates contracts for enterprise license agreements. Workman is a member of the AT&T Higher Education Advisory Council; the Dell End

User Computing Customer Advisory Council; the Adobe Education Advisory Board; the EDUCAUSE IT Issues Panel; the EDUCAUSE Core Data Survey Planning Committee; the EDUCAUSE 2012 Program Committee; and an author and presenter for EDUCAUSE and ACUTA. Workman has a BS in Mathematics from the University of Indianapolis.

INDEX

Academic Commons, 54
Academic standards, 72, 75, 110, 156
Accessibility, 102, 151, 157, 163–164, 272, 327
Active Learning Classrooms, 50, 273, 311
Active surface, 106
Adaptable, 123, 135, 139–140, 143, 225
Affordances, xix, xx, 4–7, 12, 17–18, 31–32, 35–36, 40–43, 65, 85, 87, 90, 97, 133, 135, 141, 181, 189–192, 194, 199, 208, 210–212, 214, 216, 305
Agency, 26, 30, 34–35, 125, 140, 191, 224, 235, 265
Agility, 24, 132–133, 135, 138
Assessment, xix, 3, 6–7, 14–15, 18, 60, 77, 85–98, 103–104, 109, 116–117, 124, 151, 153–154, 157–158, 161–162, 184, 208, 211–212, 214, 267, 270–272, 294, 314, 319, 328, 330–332
  2.0, 86–87, 90–91
  diagnostic, 88–89, 91, 93, 97
  formative, xix, 89, 91, 93, 94, 95, 96, 97, 161
  learning oriented, 3, 7, 14–15, 18
  stealth, 96, 97
  summative, xix, 86, 89, 96, 97, 161
  tasks, 14, 15, 77, 85, 87–90, 93, 95, 96–97, 151, 157, 161
Augmented reality, 93–94
Australian Qualifications Framework, 75–76
Authentic environments, 210

Behavioural economic theory, 224, 228, 233–234
Bradley review, 148
Briefing practice, 245
BYOT (Bring Your Own Technology), 47, 55, 57

Change, xviii, 10, 14–15, 31, 34–37, 48, 51, 54, 68, 70, 72–73, 90, 98, 101, 103–107, 109–110, 118, 151–152, 155, 157, 175–176, 179–181, 184–186, 189, 191–192, 194, 199–206, 211–212, 214–217, 220, 227, 249–251, 254–257, 259, 262–263, 271, 279, 290, 292, 295, 307, 321, 326–331
  agent, 203, 206, 256
  management, xx, 205, 216
  strategies, 202, 203
Choice architecture, 228, 234–235
Cloud software, 56–57
Cognitive theory, xxi, 219, 224
Collaborative Learning Studio, 50–51

Communication, 9, 13, 28–30, 37,
74, 76–78, 80, 110–113, 124,
133, 136, 142, 159, 187, 201,
206–207, 213, 215–216, 271,
305, 310, 312, 326, 331
conduit, 159, 206
dissemination of information,
207
online information channels, 209
plan, 207
strategies, 207
two-way flow, 207, 216
Complexity theory, 66–67, 69–71,
79
Commissioning of university
learning spaces, 245
Computer classrooms and labs,
55, 61
Concourse, 250, 265
Confidence, 24, 38–42, 76,
116–117, 125–126,
131–133, 135, 138–139, 152,
191, 216, 312, 324
Connected, xvi, 4–6, 8, 12, 18,
55–56, 79, 101, 104,
114–115, 118, 123, 135, 137,
143, 181, 193, 208, 244, 294,
326–327
Connectivism, 7–8, 66–68, 79, 301,
313
Connectivity, 12, 71, 93, 163
Constructive alignment, 77, 157
Constructivism, 7, 66–69, 74, 79,
124, 176, 301, 303, 313
cognitive constructivism, 67
social constructivism, 67–69,
74, 176, 301, 303, 313
Convergent response, 89
Creative appropriation, 125
Criterion based selection, 262

Critical reflection, 68, 167, 188, 294

Design, xv, xvii, xx, 3–6, 14–18,
28, 38–41, 47–51, 53–54,
65–67, 71–73, 75, 77–82,
85–88, 92–93, 96–97,
101–102, 104–105, 110,
113–115, 117, 123–124, 126,
128, 130–131, 143, 147–151,
153, 155–164, 167, 175,
185–186, 199, 201, 204–208,
210–213, 215–217, 219, 221,
228, 230, 237, 243–252,
254–255, 257, 259, 261–265,
267–277, 279, 281–282, 289,
293–295, 299, 301–307, 309,
311, 313, 319–330, 333
evidence centered, 96, 97
innovative, 259
learning space, xvi, xviii, xix,
xxi, xxii, 3, 17, 18, 26, 47, 65,
206, 248, 263, 272, 293,
299–313, 337
principles, xix, 16, 17, 18, 38, 47,
96, 147, 320, 321, 322–323,
324
Desire paths, 4, 7, 15–16, 18
Digital citizenship, 3–4, 7–9, 18
Digital footprint, 9
Digital literacies (refer to Literacies)
Disability Discrimination Act,
163–164
Disability Standards for Education,
164
Disruption(s), xxii, 28, 30, 114, 271,
299, 312
Divergent response, 89–90

Ease of use, 24, 38–40, 42,
323–324

Empowerment, 38–40, 323–324
Engagement, 3–4, 6–8, 11, 13–14,
  17–18, 30, 35, 38–40, 52, 69,
  71, 74–75, 79, 86–89,
  96–97, 103, 107, 117, 133,
  135, 137, 140, 150, 156–160,
  163, 166, 201, 204, 207, 212,
  214, 223, 229, 232, 234,
  269–270, 273, 291–292,
  294–297, 304–305, 309, 311,
  313, 323–324, 332
Environments, 5–7, 9–10, 12, 16,
  25, 33, 47–48, 58, 70–72,
  78–80, 85, 88, 105, 115–116,
  118, 123–124, 128, 131–137,
  142, 147–148, 150, 155–156,
  163–165, 184, 199, 217, 221,
  228, 243–245, 259, 264, 273,
  275, 293, 295, 300, 307, 311,
  313, 328
  built, xx, 150, 156, 183–185, 199
  flexible learning, 52, 302, 303,
    304, 311
  learning, xxi, 5, 7, 10, 14, 16, 17,
    18, 25, 33, 37, 40, 47, 48, 49,
    52, 67, 70, 72, 78, 79, 80, 88,
    115, 118, 136, 140, 142, 184,
    200, 204, 206, 212, 214, 216,
    217, 221, 250, 256, 273, 275,
    280, 291–292, 295, 303, 307,
    311, 328
  physical, 147, 150, 155, 209, 213,
    250, 301
  virtual, xix, 60, 61, 82, 147,
    163–165, 250
Evaluation, xxi, 15, 18, 75, 128,
  134, 162, 183, 201, 205,
  212–213, 259, 267–271,
  273–285, 296, 307, 319–320,
  323–327, 329
  formative, 213
  impact, 278, 285
  interviews (*refer to* Interviews)
  summative, 89, 96, 97, 161, 213,
    214
  survey (*refer to* Surveys)
  techniques, 267, 275–285

Flexible open plan, 249
Flipped classroom, 49, 90,
  108–109, 177, 213–215
Flipped university, xviii, 310
Future proof, 34–35, 42, 47, 52,
  256, 333

Gamification, 85–86, 96, 117, 230,
  235
Greener Government Buildings
  program (GGB), 263

Hidden work, 23–25, 27, 29–31,
  33, 35–43
Higher Education, 3–5, 7, 9, 11,
  13–15, 17, 23, 47, 61, 65–66,
  68, 71, 74–78, 85–86, 88, 90,
  101–105, 107–110, 118, 123,
  128, 131–132, 147–150,
  152–154, 161, 163, 165, 167,
  175–176, 178–183, 187, 190,
  192–193, 199, 203, 215, 219,
  221, 243, 247, 267, 289,
  299–300, 305, 307, 319, 326,
  331
  massified, 149
Hunt Library, 53–54

Indiana University, 47, 50–51, 54
Integrated scholarship, 252, 254,
  263
Intentionality, 133, 140

Interviews, 128−132, 137, 211−212,
    214, 276−278, 283, 295, 326
IUanyWare, 56, 58

JISC (design) principles, 47, 49

Knowledge, 3−8, 16−18, 23−31,
    33−39, 41, 43, 54, 65, 67, 69,
    71−72, 75−76, 78, 80,
    85−89, 92−95, 98, 103−104,
    106, 110−114, 118, 124, 137,
    142, 152−155, 157, 159−162,
    178, 181−182, 184−185, 187,
    189−193, 200, 204, 214, 220,
    222−225, 247, 261, 290−292,
    300, 302−304, 332
  functional, 88
  procedural, 88, 92, 93
  work, 23, 24, 25, 26, 27, 29, 31,
    33, 36, 37, 39, 41, 43
Knowledge Commons, 54

Learning, 3−18, 23−43, 47−55,
    57−59, 61, 65−82, 85−98,
    101−118, 123−143,
    147−168, 175−194,
    199−217, 219−237,
    243−252, 255−257, 259, 261,
    263−265, 267−281,
    283−285, 289−297,
    299−314, 319−333
  active, xvi, 15, 28, 30, 34, 35, 36,
    41, 49, 50, 51, 52, 74, 78, 79,
    80, 220, 221, 222, 259, 273,
    300, 301, 302, 303, 304, 311,
    327
  activities, xix, 37, 40, 66, 68, 73,
    75, 77, 78, 81, 86, 89, 91, 95,
    96, 102, 107, 114, 118, 123,
    124, 137, 143, 151, 157,
    159−161, 190, 201, 214, 235,
    290, 295, 302, 310, 328
  collaborative, xvi, xix, 13, 14,
    50, 51, 63, 68, 72, 73,
    101−118, 150, 154, 163, 184,
    189, 194, 201, 211, 214, 216,
    274, 291, 292, 293, 294,
    295−296, 303, 325, 327, 331
  effective, 66, 67, 72, 81,
    128−129, 134, 142, 157, 326
  environment, xxi, 5, 7, 10, 14,
    17, 18, 25, 33, 37, 40, 47, 48,
    49, 52, 67, 68, 70, 71, 72, 78,
    79, 80, 88, 115, 118, 136, 137,
    140, 142, 165, 168, 184, 204,
    206, 211, 214, 216, 217, 236,
    250, 256, 259, 273, 275, 280,
    293, 295, 296, 303, 307, 328
  experiential, 73, 304
  facilitated, 35
  graduate, 76−77, 153, 157, 158,
    162
  hubs, xxii, 72, 289, 291, 292,
    293, 294, 295, 296
  online, 5, 52, 69, 72, 73, 92, 108,
    118, 124, 140, 290, 292, 294
  outcomes, xv, xix, 9, 14−15, 48,
    66, 68, 69, 71, 75, 76, 77, 78,
    79, 93, 96, 97, 110, 111, 112,
    147, 153, 157, 158, 159, 161,
    162, 194, 204, 227, 235, 306,
    312, 324, 325, 330, 331, 333
  mobile, 33, 35
  modes, 72−83, 103, 107, 114,
    180, 187, 247, 250, 301−302
  personalised, xv, xviii, 3−18,
    185
  pictures of, xv, xviii, 23−43
  professional, xx, 185, 190,
    219−237, 330, 331

repertoires of, 26, 42
seamless, 3, 4, 7, 10, 11, 12, 13, 18, 20, 115
self-directed, 227, 231, 245, 246–248, 259–261, 290
situated, 6, 66, 67, 69–71, 74, 78, 79, 124, 290
studio-based, 114
transformative, 49, 134, 184, 186, 187, 190, 192, 193, 212, 213, 214
workplace, 155, 166–167, 222
Learning hubs (*refer to* Learning)
Learning landscapes (*refer to* Learning)
Learning Spaces Collaboratory, 48, 53, 309, 312
Learning space design (*refer to* Design)
Learning space literacies (*refer to* Literacies)
Learning studios (*refer to* Learning)
Libraries, 5, 54–55, 125, 163, 246–247
Literacies, 4, 7–10, 16–18, 162
digital, 8, 9–10, 12, 124, 125, 126, 142, 208
learning space, xviii, 4, 16–18, 320, 323, 337

Massive Open Online Courses (MOOC), xix, 72–73, 85–86, 90–91, 102, 107–109, 118, 181, 265
cMOOC, 91
xMOOC, 91
Materialities, 28
Meta-analysis, xix, 123–124, 127, 142

MIT, 51–52, 118, 251, 265, 311
Mobile technologies (*refer to* Technology)

New spatial way, 251
North Carolina State University, 49–50, 53, 156, 311, 327

Participation in tertiary education, xxii, 7, 13, 24, 26, 42, 290–291, 293
Partnerships, xxii, 74, 289–290, 293
Pedagogy, 38, 42, 66, 78, 90, 101–102, 106–108, 154, 157–158, 176, 181, 185, 188–189, 192, 221, 268, 272, 275, 300, 303–304, 306, 314, 319, 321–323, 326–327
default, 202
framework, xv, xix, 30, 67, 79
practice, 176, 185
upside-down, 49
Penn State University, 54
Pictures of learning (*refer to* Learning)
Principles of Universal Design, 147, 150, 155–158, 160–161, 164, 167
Principles of Universal Design for Learning, 147, 150, 155–158, 160–161, 167
Problem-based learning, 95, 101, 116, 311
Procurement, 105–106, 244–245, 263
Professional development, xx, 59, 81, 193, 199–200, 205, 216, 219–224, 228, 237, 257, 269, 329
components of, 208–209

design, 257
implementation, 200
issues addressed, 215–216
program, 200, 201, 205–206,
    216
scheduling, 209–212
student experience, 308
support strategies, 205, 208
Project team, xx, 199, 201–206,
    209, 211–213, 215–216, 237,
    254, 270, 322
consultation with, 206
decision-making, 96, 190, 206,
    228

Repertoires of learning (*refer to*
    Learning)
Research, 3, 11, 16, 23, 31, 33–34,
    39, 47, 50, 53–54, 57, 65–66,
    76, 80, 85, 90, 101, 103, 105,
    107, 112, 118, 123–124,
    126–128, 130, 133, 136, 142,
    147–148, 164, 175–176, 182,
    193, 199, 205, 219, 221, 223,
    233, 243–244, 247–248, 250,
    252, 254–255, 261, 265, 267,
    273, 275–276, 283, 289–294,
    299–301, 305, 309, 311–313,
    319–323, 325–333
Richness of a creative city, 264

SCALE-UP (Student-Centered
    Active Learning
    Environment with Upside-
    down Pedagogies), 49–52,
    327–328
Self-awareness, 142, 152
Semantic web, xix, 85–86, 91–92
Situated learning, 6, 66–67, 69–71,
    74, 78–79, 124, 290

Sociofugal, 27
Sociopetal, 27
Software, 8–9, 28–29, 33–37,
    41–42, 47–48, 54–61, 93,
    95, 180, 214, 231
on-demand, 55–57
virtualized software, xviii, 48,
    54, 56
Spaces
collaborative, 48, 98, 149
informal, xvii, 5, 6, 53, 149, 268,
    312, 313
literature, 283, 323, 328, 337
net generation, xv, 304
new generation learning, xv, 191
next generation learning, xv,
    xviii, xix, xx, xxi, xxii, 3–8,
    10, 12–18, 23–28, 31,
    33–36, 38, 40–43, 47–49,
    51–55, 57–59, 61, 65–82,
    85–87, 89–91, 93, 95,
    97–98, 101–103, 105–107,
    109, 111, 113–115, 117–118,
    123–125, 127, 129–131, 133,
    135, 137, 139, 141–143,
    147–156, 160, 163–164,
    167–168, 175–194,
    199–216, 219–222,
    224–227, 229–237,
    243–245, 248, 252, 255–257,
    259, 261, 263–264, 267–271,
    273–276, 278–279, 281,
    283–285, 289, 291, 294–296,
    299–314, 319–333
real, xxi, 244, 264
re-configurable, 249, 257
scheduling, 209–212, 305
timetabling, 246, 257, 274
types of, 301, 309
virtual, 5, 6, 12, 13, 87, 90, 264

Staff capability, 220
Stakeholders, xxi, 199, 203, 206,
    215, 217, 267, 270, 272, 275,
    285, 300, 302, 305–307, 309,
    314, 321–322, 324–326
St. Louis University, 52
Strategic Planning, 56, 292
Students, xv, xviii, xix, xxii, 7, 14,
    26, 28–39, 41, 47–58,
    60–61, 65–75, 77–82,
    85–91, 93–98, 101–110,
    114–118, 124–125,
    129–132, 134, 136–141, 143,
    147–157, 159–167, 177, 180,
    182, 184–185, 187, 189–194,
    201–202, 206, 208, 211–212,
    214–216, 220–221, 223, 226,
    235–236, 246, 248–251, 257,
    259, 261, 263–264, 267–285,
    289–291, 293–296,
    299–309, 311–314, 319,
    321–322, 326–328,
    331–333
    attributes, xi, 27, 123–126,
        128–132, 134, 136, 140,
        142–143, 162
    with disabilities, 149, 163–164
    diversity, 149, 151–152, 160,
        165, 166, 208, 211
    engagement, 14, 52, 97, 150,
        163, 201, 214, 291, 304
    experience, xxii, 60, 87, 157, 182,
        190, 194, 199, 207, 212, 272,
        292, 294, 299–314
    international, 153, 182
    low socio-economic status, 148,
        289
Surveys, xxi, 58, 131, 212, 251, 259,
    261, 267, 276–279, 326
Systems thinking, 235

TEAL (Technology Enabled Active
    Learning), 51–52, 327–328
Teaching practice, xviii, xx, 52, 65,
    67, 73, 81, 106–108, 167,
    176–177, 179–180,
    183–185, 187–189, 191,
    193–194, 199–200,
    202–204, 208, 210–214, 216,
    221, 224, 271, 273, 319,
    325–328, 330–331, 333
    adoption of new approaches,
        208
    default pedagogies, 202
    extrinsic drivers, 201–203
    extrinsic subjectivities, 202
    inclusive, 149, 157, 167
    intrinsic process, 202–203
    student engagement, 14, 52, 97,
        150, 163, 201, 204, 207, 212,
        214, 273, 291, 304, 311
Technology, xvi, xvii, xviii, 4, 7–9,
    13, 23–26, 28–43, 47–60,
    66, 70, 73, 79, 81, 86, 91, 104,
    106–107, 109, 114–118,
    123–135, 138–143,
    149–150, 154, 156–157, 160,
    164, 176–185, 189–193,
    201–202, 206–213,
    216–217, 220–221, 224, 226,
    231, 236–237, 243, 248–249,
    263, 268, 271–272, 274, 277,
    280–281, 290–291,
    293–296, 301, 306, 311–312,
    321–324, 327–333
    digital, 9, 23, 24, 25, 26, 28–31,
        32, 34, 35, 36, 37, 38, 40, 41,
        42, 43, 150, 157, 160, 220,
        290, 291
    mobile, 4, 31–36, 37, 41–42,
        104, 140, 333

Tertiary education, 7, 13, 24, 26,
   42, 103, 106, 290–293
Theory of planned behaviour, 228,
   229
TILE (Transform, Interact, Learn,
   Engage), 50, 52

United Nations Convention on the
   Rights of Persons with
   Disabilities, 163
United States, 47–48, 53, 76, 221,
   251, 300, 327–328
University of Denver, 54
University of Iowa, 47, 50, 52, 60

University of Minnesota, 50, 273,
   275, 283, 311, 328
University of South Florida, 47,
   60
Un-programmed student portals,
   257

Vertical integration, 252
Virtual world, 94–95, 264

Work integrated learning, 150, 155,
   165–167, 330
Workplace learning (*refer to*
   Learning)